MW00345457

PSI TREK

Books by Laile E. Bartlett

BRIGHT GALAXY
MOMENT OF TRUTH (with J. R. Bartlett)
THE VANISHING PARSON
NEW WORK/NEW LIFE

PSI TREK

A world-wide investigation
into the lives of psychic people
and the researchers
who test such phenomena as:
healing, prophecy, dowsing,
ghosts, and life after death

LAILE E. BARTLETT

MCGRAW-HILL BOOK COMPANY
New York   St. Louis   San Francisco
Toronto   Hamburg   Mexico
London   Sydney

The author is grateful for permission to quote from previously copyrighted materials:

Mind-Reach: Scientists Look at Psychic Ability by Russell Targ and Harold Puthoff, copyright © 1977 by Russell Targ and Harold Puthoff, reprinted by permission of Delacorte Press/Eleanor Friede.

Psychic Archaeology by Jeffrey Goodman, copyright © 1977 by Jeffrey Goodman, reprinted by permission of Berkley Publishing Co.

Psychic Healers: True Stories of America's Most Unusual Healers, copyright © 1974, 1976 by David St. Clair, reprinted by permission of Doubleday & Company, Inc.

Adventure Unlimited: A Diviner Travels the World by Evelyn Penrose, copyright © 1958, reprinted by permission of Neville Spearman Ltd.

Dowsing: The PSI Connection by Francis Hitching, copyright © 1977 by Francis Hitching, reprinted by permission of Doubleday & Company, Inc.

My Passport Says Clairvoyant by M. B. Dykshoorn and Russell H. Felton, copyright © 1974 by M. B. Dykshoorn and Russell H. Felton, reprinted by permission of the authors' agent, Jay Garon-Brooke Associates, Inc.

Thoughts through Space by Harold Sherman and Sir Hubert Wilkins, by permission of the publisher, Fawcett Books Group, The Consumer Publishing Division of CBS Inc. Copyright © 1951 by Sir Hubert Wilkins and Harold Sherman.

How to Make ESP Work for You by Harold Sherman, by permission of the publisher, Fawcett Books Group, The Consumer Publishing Division of CBS Inc. Copyright © 1964 by Harold Sherman.

"A Few Magic Passes" by Mark Jonathan Harris, reprinted with permission from the February 13, 1978, issue of *New West*, copyright © 1978 by *New West*.

1 2 3 4 5 6 7 8 9 D O D O 8 7 6 5 4 3 2 1

LIBRARY OF CONGRESS CATALOGING IN PUBLICATION DATA

Bartlett, Laile E
Psi trek.
Bibliography: p.
Includes index.
1. Psychical research.   I. Title.
BF1031.B312   133.8   80–22178
ISBN 0–07–003915–1

Book design by Stanley Drate.

for
Elizabeth

WHO HAS FOLLOWED EACH TWIST OF MY JOURNEY
WITH CHUCKLES AND LOVE

and
J. B. E.

WHO (WHEREVER SHE IS) WILL BE
DELIGHTED

Preface

The world of psychic phenomena is wildly controversial, and sometimes frightening. It is beyond existing knowledge; it defies all explanations, and challenges scientific principles and laws. Controversial? Even the experts in the field don't agree.

Thus I thought it time for someone with academic sympathies and training, but outside the field—no grants to seek, no ax to grind—to take a fresh look. That's what I set out to do.

How did I, a university sociologist, get into such a role? It began when I was reporting on a conference on the subject for an international magazine. The whole thing intrigued me: Here were psychiatrists and educators, researchers and psychics, probing the intricacies and mysteries of Psi. The piece I wrote started the ball rolling, for then letters started to pour in—psychic incidents and adventures, questions and problems—from every part of the country. Later they came in in Japanese, Spanish, German, Portuguese, from every part of the world.

At this point, my Ph.D./researcher background got the best of me. I had to find out what was going on. What do we know about Psi, and what can we believe?

For more than two years, I have pored over the literature, visited parapsychology centers and laboratories in Scotland, England, Holland, Germany, Canada, the United States, and Japan. I monitored researchers at their professional gatherings—in San Francisco, St. Louis, Edinburgh—heard their papers, their problems, their debates. I followed up with conversations, correspondence, and interviews, most of which I tape recorded. I tracked down dowsers, healers, sensitives, and psychic practitioners at their conferences, or in their workshops, and in their homes. Again, I enlisted them in discussion, correspondence, sometimes a whole weekend of taped interviews. My file cases are overflowing with dozens of transcripts.

I see myself, not as an apologist for Psi or against it, but as an opener of doors. For example, what's it like to be a sensitive? What kind of people are psychics? What light can they shed on the larger mystery of Psi?

Another door to be opened is that of the therapist. What input can the psychiatrist and counselor bring? What of the healer? The mystic? What insights from other places and times? The wisdom of the ancients? The working knowledge of the primitive, the shaman, the medicine-man?

What of the patient and dedicated Psi scientists—with little funding and less support, struggling against the odds in a misunderstood context, usually swimming against the tide?

The hardest part of my assignment was a self-imposed ground rule: To hold on to a cautious skepticism, while retaining an open mind. Slowly I learned that my research gave me a point of view. In its barest, boiled-down essence, it is this:

1. There *is* something to Psi. We don't know what it is, how it works, why it works, but we know that Psi exists.

2. Psi is already being used. While we endlessly debate "Is Psi so?" others, the world around, are busy applying it.

3. But beware! To admit the "Psi possibility" is to make oneself vulnerable to its dangers and deceptions. Like fire, electricity, and atomic energy, the powers of Psi can be used for devastating ill, or for great good.

4. We need more money and support for conscientious, responsible Psi research.

5. The implications of Psi are breathtaking and profound, for the human condition and for our place in the cosmos.

Acknowledgments

Many dozens of people have had a hand in the making of this book. They have opened doors, shared experiences, sent material, answered unending questions, and offered the gracious hospitality of offices, laboratories, and homes.

More than academic footnotes, their contributions remain in my memory: the historic English cottage with dowsing lore overflowing, the PK-testing machine provided in Holland though others were waiting to use it, the group in Missouri hastily assembled for my benefit, the pancakes rassled up by my German host as we talked into the night. . . .

How can I convey my appreciation? Just naming names won't do it. (A great many of those who helped me don't even appear in these pages.)

Every one of you is special, and every one of you is different. I give you all my heartfelt thanks, once again.

LAILE E. BARTLETT
Berkeley, California

Contents

1

COME WITH ME!

Nancy Turley was driving home from grocery shopping along a familiar street in Charleston, West Virginia, that quiet afternoon in July, 1973. Suddenly and without warning, she heard a deep male voice bellow "Stop!" She jammed on the brakes just as a car screamed through a red light at the intersection, cutting straight across her path. "If I hadn't stopped," she exclaims, "that car would have rammed right into me!"

It was cold for April, in Bath, Maine, where Baptist minister Bob Ater was listening to the six o'clock news. It was even colder in New Hampshire, where a blizzard was raging, and two students who had set out to climb Mt. Washington were reported missing. Searchers had uncovered no clues.

It suddenly hit Bob: What if those were *my* kids! The ages of the missing University of Maine students were nineteen and twenty-one, exactly the same as Bob's older boys.

Riffling through a stack of U.S. maps, he found a Texaco road guide that showed the Presidential Range in some detail. Spreading it on the kitchen table, he placed his ballpoint pen on Crawford Notch, where the climbers' car had been found. Intently focusing all his attention, he asked, "Where is the trail the hikers took?"

His excitement surged when the pen moved "as though in a

1

track," northeast on the green-colored mountain section of the map. As if guided by a hand, it continued to glide steadily toward Pinkham Notch. "In that instant, I *knew* that *Pinkham Notch,* not Crawford Notch as reported on TV, had been the hikers' real starting place," Bob recalls. The pen then slid along a route different from that announced in the news: around Mt. Clay, the foothills of Mt. Washington, toward Mt. Adams; at a point between Adams and Jefferson, it abruptly came to rest. He *knew* they were there, sheltered and safe.

Having neither a telephone nor a car at that time, Bob walked— or more exactly, ran—to a pay phone about three blocks from his home. Somewhat breathlessly, he told Jonathan Lingell, the weather observer atop Mt. Washington, that he had "located" the two. On hearing where, Lingell acknowledged that that was the one area the search team had not explored. After eight days, a rescue party found the students, Jane Gilotti and David Cornue, in a shelter at Edmand's Col, midway between Mt. Jefferson and Mt. Adams. Weather conditions were still so bad it took another day to get them out.

As the pair explained, they had changed their route at the last minute, and did start from Pinkham Notch.

A nineteen-year-old California girl agreed to represent her family at a funeral. Elaine had barely known old Mrs. Black, but was the only one of the family who could get away at that time. When the time came for the funeral, however, Elaine had an unexplainable and overpowering urge to visit her mother. Abruptly changing her plans, she boarded a bus bound in the opposite direction, and nervously counted the minutes before reaching her parents' furniture store.

On arriving, she felt foolish to find them taking a rest break in chairs at the front window. She "knew" she must get them out of there. "I'm hungry!" she exclaimed. "Let's get something to eat." No sooner had she rushed them to the back room than a crash rocked the building. A large black sedan had plowed through the front window at full speed, shattering the glass and destroying the chairs in which they had been sitting.

One night, as he was launching a lecture in downtown Manhattan, the speaker was shaken to see a man in the audience rise to his feet abruptly, and charge noisily out. The man looked distressed, his footsteps determined.

The incident haunted the memory of lecturer Pir Vilayat Inayat Khan. One day, three years later, the man came to another gathering of Pir Vilayat's Sufi Order and asked, "Do you remember when I rushed out of your lecture so suddenly? You probably don't, it was so long ago. While you were talking, it suddenly hit me: 'My wife's committing suicide!' I got home just in time. She had already turned on the gas."

Voices? Uncanny knowledge? Premonitions? Incidents such as these, unexpected and spontaneous, are reported in this country every day, by average, run-of-the-mill citizens. Other kinds of occurrences are reported as well, not all of them spontaneous. Some are invited, in fact: wished-for, worked-for, even planned.

At the U.S. National Earthquake Information Service in Denver, John Derr carefully logged an incoming prediction in the Service's computer. The date: May 31, 1976. The sender: Clarisa Bernhardt. The forecast: an earthquake in the Western Pacific area on June 26, which would register 7.0 on the Richter Scale. On June 26, at 4 A.M., the earthquake occurred. It was on the island of New Guinea, and registered 7.1.

"Such accuracy is remarkable," Dr. Derr declares, "far beyond the possibility of chance." Arizona scientist Jeffrey Goodman concurs. "Mrs. Bernhardt has accurately predicted the magnitude, location and time of several major earthquakes, months in advance. At the moment, her record stands at seven out of seven!"

Fourteen-year-old Susan Jacobson went to look for a summer job on May 15, 1976, but failed to return home for dinner. After the police had searched her Staten Island, New York, area for three weeks to no avail, her distraught parents turned to Dorothy Allison, a Nutley, New Jersey, housewife, who had a reputation for finding lost people.

"Susan's body is on the island," she told them. "Do the letters M, A, R mean anything to you? She is near those letters. From that marshy place you can see two sets of twin church steeples, two bridges, and a burned-out car."

After a search, her father found the site, a boulder with large

letters M, A, and R painted on it, and to his astonishment, two
bridges, a burned-out car, and, across the bay in New Jersey, two
sets of double church spires. Family and friends combed the aban-
doned shipyard at the location, Mariner's Point. Since the place
was too waterlogged to make any headway, they urged the police
to help them by bringing in bloodhounds. "We deal with facts,
not with psychics" was their response.

Twenty-two months after Susan's disappearance, two boys found
the body in the exact spot Allison had cited, a shaft from which
the water had been drained. "I was within four feet of her and
never knew it!" the anguished father lamented.

"It is one of the most tragic cases I have ever worked on,"
said Mrs. Allison. "This family could have been spared that long,
unhappy ordeal."

The same sort of unexplained, and unexplainable, psychic happenings are sometimes evoked on scientific expeditions, and even
in the lab.

At Maimonides Dream Laboratory in Brooklyn, a "sender" attempted to transmit a picture, which he had taken from a sealed
envelope, to a subject sleeping in another room. The picture, randomly selected for the experiment, was Orozco's action-filled *Zapa-
tistas,* depicting a scene from the 1910 Mexican Revolution, in which
a number of insurgents rage against a background of massive mountains and clouds.

When awakened in another room of the lab, the receiver, William
Erwin, reported dreaming of a thundercloud, mountains, Mexico,
war, and the "Mayan-Aztec type of civilization."

Hearing a man say he could heal animals just by "laying on
of hands," Canadian biochemist Bernard Grad challenged him.
"How can *touching* do that?" Grad asked. "Besides, if healing is
a matter of *faith,* somehow 'all in the head,' how can an *animal*
expect to be healed?"

To test the claim, Grad lightly wounded 48 mice by removing
a piece of skin from the back of each. Dividing the mice into three
groups, he gave the first group to the healer to hold, warmed the
second group to the temperature of the healer's hands (lest the

warmth itself produce the healing), and gave the third, a control group, no treatment at all.

The results? The rate of healing in the group touched by the healer was significantly greater than that in the other two groups. The results were the same each time the experiment was repeated.

South of the border, a National Geographic–Smithsonian Institution archaeological expedition witnessed an adventure more tantalizing than the artifacts they ultimately found. The setting was the small village of Tres Zapotes, fifty miles from the Mexican city of Vera Cruz, where the expedition's leaders believed prehistoric cultures had probably met, mixed and left remains. After weeks of careful digging, however, nothing turned up.

With the short season rushing by, the staff and workers were all discouraged. One evening, a Mexican workman almost eighty years old, Emelio Tegoma, sought out C. W. Weiant, the assistant director. "Come where I show you," he urged Weiant, "you find what you look for. I 'see things'—'hidden things,' far away."

It was a tough decision: with time pressing, should they move an entire crew and all their equipment, to a new site, on the whim of an illiterate peasant? Nothing in the new area, two thirds of a mile away, looked any more promising than the old one. But they took the plunge and moved.

Within twenty minutes of the first shovelful they knew the choice was right. The dig was rich with archeological treasure, beyond their most hopeful anticipation. Stone yokes and sculptures; two layers of human remains; a series of telescoped sections of clay tubing, believed religious in nature, to aid the escape of the soul. "In every way," one historian of the expedition, Stephan Schwartz, says in his account, "the old man fulfilled his promise and more so, by means of his remarkable psychic vision."

Events such as these are not confined to North America. They happen on every continent, around the world.

ENGLAND: At a concert in the town hall of Birmingham, a woman was suddenly seized with an icy chill. Her uncle, who lived in Australia, suddenly appeared between herself and the orchestra. "Not transparent or filmy," she declared, "but entirely solid—lying in bed, with an appealing look on his face." She hadn't seen him for a long time, and didn't know he was ill, so couldn't fathom the clarity and emotional impact of the experience. A few days later, the word came: her uncle had died, at the very moment she had seen him.

JAPAN: A man focused his thoughts on a woman in another room of a Tokyo lab. Each was hitched to a battery of instruments and closely monitored by the staff. The minute he concentrated on her, her breathing and involuntary functions speeded up, while his slowed down. The moment he released his concentration, her respiration and nerve lines flattened out, and his immediately climbed to normal.

BRAZIL: In the town of Congonhas do Campo, a humble laborer named Arigó did pinpoint diagnosis, psychic healing and psychic surgery for twenty years, with no more formidable equipment than a rusty knife.

He said it was "nothing," that a German medical student, called "Dr. Fritz," whispered play-by-play information and instruction in his ear. Arigó removed a tumor from the elbow of a flabbergasted American doctor/researcher who went there to check him out. With no preparation or anesthetic, Arigó made two knife strokes, then squeezed the area, and the tumor popped out. The wound healed cleanly, without a drop of pus, and in a fraction of the normal time.

The doctor confessed his astonishment, since it had happened to him personally. He wryly added that he had been short-changed: Who ever heard of an operation that took only five seconds to perform—no fuss, no muss, no pain? As a matter of fact, he added, he hadn't felt a thing.

SWITZERLAND: A priest once startled the world by locating water for a monastery across the ocean, 6,000 miles away. Holding a pendulum (a small weight on a string) over a sketch of the monastery's grounds, while seated in his own chair in his study in St. Prex, Switzerland, the Abbé Mermet pinpointed the exact location of a supply of water at the Monastery of San Camilo in Popayan, Colombia: 88 feet, 2 inches deep, with a flow rate of 500 liters a minute. When the well was drilled, he was proved right on all counts.

WALES: In 1966, in the mining town of Aberfan, a child told her mother, "I am not afraid to die. I will be with Peter and June." A few days later she added, "I dreamed that I went to school, and there was no school there. Something black had come down all over it." The next day Eryl Mai Jones, her school, her teachers, and all of her schoolmates, 116 children and 28 adults, were buried in the worst landslide the country had ever known.

Eryl Mai was not the only one to foresee the disaster. Many people in many places had premonitions of the tragedy, which they reported to others, *before* the disaster occurred! In dreams and nightmares, they saw screaming children, a school, and a "black, billowing mass." One man in northwestern England even "saw" the word "Aberfan."

Just *look* at the cases spread before us! They are not mere effusions from Southern California, or lore from the backwoods. They are serious reports from all sections of the country, and from many parts of the world; from all kinds of people—male, female, young, old, from housewife, cleric, scientist, peasant, scholar. Some are spontaneous and unexpected; some, cautious and meticulously laboratory controlled.

Every one of these happenings is an unexplained mystery. Still, the fact that it is a mystery does not necessarily mean it is psychic. There's a lot that passes for psychic that isn't. The first thing that Robert Morris does in his introductory parapsychology* classes is to have each student write a description of the most impressive "psychic experience" he or she has ever had (most people have had one). He then has them list every possible *non*-psychic explanation of the incident they can think of. It's amazing, he tells me, how quickly and how often the normal moves in and Psi falls away— a healthy approach to the psychic realm!

How can you begin to absorb it all? And if you do, can you accept it? I'm something of a skeptic. I grew up in an inquiring and academic atmosphere: my own discipline and training for a Ph.D. in Sociology was exacting. So caution is a part of my makeup, and gullibility to be avoided at all costs.

What do you do if that is your background? You go slowly and very carefully, that's what, looking for booby–traps and land

---

* "Parapsychology" is the scientific study of psychic phenomena. "Psi" (pronounced "sigh"), the first letter of the Greek word "psyche," is shorthand for psychic phenomena.

mines. But, you're also intrigued! It comes down to this: you've
got to know!

This book is the story of my efforts to find out: where I went,
what I asked, whom I asked, what I found. I began with two questions: "What's going on here?" and "Is Psi so?"

The first thing I learned as a serious inquirer: Psi is wildly controversial. You can't just "look it up" in an encyclopedia, source-
book, or even a professional journal, because scientists don't agree.
Some of them will tell you "It's a return to the Dark Ages" and
mutter about "a reversion to superstition, old wives' tales" and
worse. Others, hard-nosed physicists among them, take the opposite
stand: Psi is the "new frontier" and "a key to understanding the
universe," no less. To add to the confusion, each side has its Big
Guns: B. F. Skinner and Carl Sagan, for example, reject the psychic
altogether, while Nobel Laureate Glenn Seaborg and the late Margaret Mead implore us, "At least, take a look—there is more to the
cosmos than meets the eye!"

People have wrestled with this tantalizing question since people
began. Do psychic phenomena really exist? If they do, are they
"merely" an extension of human abilities? Or are they, rather, a
manifestation of supernatural powers? Because of its ephemeral nature—fleeting, unfamiliar, even spooky at times—Psi is hard to get
hold of, and even harder to prove.

But why is Psi so controversial? If serious investigators are researching the matter, why the disagreement? Isn't truth *truth?* And
science *science?* And shouldn't bona fide laboratory experiments
come out pretty much the same?

Under the circumstances, no.

Which brings me to my second major lesson as an investigator:
Psi is all-fired difficult to research.

Psychic experiences are overwhelmingly spontaneous, but experiments must be planned in advance. Who knows how and when a
psychic experience will strike? In a taxi? At the opera? In the
shower? What will it be like? How long will it last? You have a
dream, "see" a face, "hear" a voice, "feel" a touch. All at once
you *know* something that was, is, or will be. How can you prepare
and plan for such an event, much less test it? How find witnesses?
If you had them, how could they possibly pick up on your inner
voice or dream?

Again, one of the tenets of science is repeating an experiment under identical conditions, to see if you get identical results. But how can you repeat the precognitive knowledge of a tragic landslide, or your wife's impulsive suicide attempt?

For all the difficulties, parapsychologists are a determined and ingenious lot, and have come up with some effective designs. However, they are up against some inherent problems. Being hooked up to an EEG machine may be all that is needed to turn off the psychic juice. Eliminating "irrelevant variables" may also eliminate authenticity for the sensitive. No matter how theoretically stimulating a test may be for the experimenter, it is often a bust for the person being tested. Psychic Ron Warmoth probably speaks for many when he says, "I only work well when there's a real need." In short, the contrived laboratory situation is hardly as compelling as the spontaneous experience of "seeing" your sweetheart lying in a pool of blood.

If you don't turn off, sooner or later you'll run down. Scientists call this the "decline effect," something almost inevitable in research requiring hundreds of "runs" by subjects trying, say, to sense which of five test cards will turn up next, or to influence the fall of dice by concentration. By the 537th run of a dice-calling session, boredom or exhaustion or both set in. As much-tested Ingo Swann once observed, the mind-numbing, dull, multi-thousand repetitions only succeed in "grinding the diamond into a dust-pile while trying to capture the sparkle."

Let's face it—even the greatest of psychics under the best of conditions can't deliver all the time. Radio and TV personality David Hoy, who makes his living telling people where to look for lost passports and earrings, tells me he figures his "hits" at about 80 percent. Furthermore, he's unable to locate his own cufflinks more often than not! And on my first encounter with clairvoyant Alex Tanous, he fingered a face-down picture from my wallet while we talked, then gave me a summary of what he had "picked up." Embarrassing for us both: not one "fact" was correct! He had the grace and sophistication not to make excuses, but simply shrugged: "So, sometimes it doesn't work!"

If such hurdles in field and lab aren't enough, there is also the ever-present problem of fraud. The best-selling book about a haunted house on Long Island, for example, *The Amityville Horror: A True Story,* has been declared by two investigators to be a hoax. The present occupants of the house have since declared, on public television, that they concur in this opinion. "It's not my fault," the narrator lamely explained. "I only wrote what I was told."

For decades mediums promoted chicanery. There was a veritable epidemic of trance-struck specialists who "communed with the dead." For every bona fide medium, such as the carefully tested Leonore Piper, there were a host of others who were outright charlatans. The unmasking of these dark-room fakes was a blow from which the field has never completely recovered. Even the university laboratory itself has, on occasion, inherited the same sort of problems. More recently, the renowned parapsychology pioneer, J. B. Rhine, had to fire a trusted colleague at Duke University, who tampered with experimental results.

With the present surge of interest in the psychic, fanned by the media, the number of impostors and consequent dangers rise proportionately. The worst of the phonies are the "people helping" type, who prey on the insatiable fascination and credulity of the public, posing not merely as entertainers, but as teachers, readers, counselors and gurus. They take not only your dollars, but sometimes, it turns out, a piece of your mind. It has gone so far that some psychiatrists now offer "psychic salvage jobs" for such victims.

With all this, you may be asking, "Is Psi worth it?" Let me assure you enthusiastically that it is. It adds up to the discovery of new perspectives, the opening of new doors, and even some handles on the age-old questions, such as "Is there life after death?"

In the expanded perspective of Psi, as we shall see, we are offered an escape from the limitations of the purely materialistic and mechanistic framework our culture has imposed on us; a broader and richer milieu within which our thinking can move. It frees us from the bondage of body and brain to which, in the current context, the mind is now tied. It erases the boundaries of the senses as we know them: seeing and hearing, for example, may extend far beyond our normal experience. There may be other senses we have not dreamed of. To work with Psi is to glean a new understanding that erases the arbitrary and linear constrictions of time we now know as Past, Present and Future.

Psi presents us with a new view of human nature. In this new context, a fresh kind of reality opens up: consciousness that moves in and of itself, heavily conditioned by body and brain, but independent of their workings. Here also are powers of knowing and sensing that transcend the limits of time and hurdle the barriers of space. It's a new dimension, within us and "out there," which has never been tapped.

To discover these neglected depths of our non-physical nature—some would say, our most important dimension—is to restore our full and essential humanness, which was taken away when "science" reduced human nature to a material arrangement of chemicals and circuitry, and made the "self" a result, not a cause.

Finally, such exploration seems to present us with new insights into the nature of the universe. It may ultimately lead us to an understanding of the basic energy or life-force that flows through the cosmos in its many forms and holds it together. Hints of some sort of universal unity keep coming through. Individual consciousness, it would appear, is more than individual; it is, rather, part of a consciousness we all share. Each of us is not only tied to, but part of, everyone and everything in the universe. Quantum physicists have begun to catch this vision. As Max Planck explained, "Each individual particle, in a certain sense, at any one time, exists simultaneously in every part of the space." As mystic poet Francis Thompson put it: "Thou canst not stir a flower without troubling of a star."

Thus, there's a Before and After to my story. In the course of my investigations, my questions have shifted from "Is Psi so?" to "How can we *use* it?" and "What does it *mean?*"

PART
I

THE USES

2

BUSINESS:
Beyond the Computer

In the world of business, where facts are facts and reality is dollars, you can't fool around. Yet, the largest fee ever paid to a psychic occurred in that hard-as-rocks business world. The year was 1976; the psychic was Beverly Jaegers, who was nominated for the *Guinness Book of World Records* on that count.

The story is more than clippings and headlines, though it made *Barron's*. I know, because I followed it up: I've seen a copy of the check, and stayed in the split-level ranch house in a St. Louis suburb it paid for.

As Bevy told me, the first time I visited her:

It all started December 30, 1974, when Pete Dixon, a commodities broker, came to see me.

The first thing: he handed me a sealed envelope. "Please tell me what you see." I had no idea what the envelope contained, but ran my fingers over it carefully, all around the edges, and tried to concentrate hard. Suddenly, I *did* start to see things, right behind my eyes. There was a tree, covered with reddish-colored berries. I didn't know what they were, but some kind of natives were picking them—dark people in big hats. Oh yes, and it was raining, not just a drizzle, but hard. They had large baskets, which seemed to me should have been full, but there was only a sprinkling of berries on the bottom, and some of those were shriveled and wizened.

15

"What a crazy thing!" I thought to myself, and asked him, "Does this mean anything to you?"

"I'll say it does!" he shouted, in a funny kind of voice. "In that envelope is my personal hunch that the price of coffee will go up. Now, you confirm it! What you've told me, loud and clear, is that the supply will go down." With that, he dashed off to invest every penny he could scrape together, twenty-four thousand dollars in all, in coffee futures.

The rest is history, as they say. Everything happened to the coffee market after that, and all of it was bad. There was a sudden freeze in Brazil; in Angola political unrest, even Cuban agents and fighting. The price of coffee started to skyrocket, and Pete Dixon is now a millionaire.

It took some time for it to develop. He was very discouraged there for a while, but when it did happen, it happened big. Paul Sarnoff, Vice President of Herzog Commodities, toted up Dixon's account with them on March 30, 1976, and the bottom line read $1,013,745.00. Ten days later, the account was worth over $2 million, and the next Friday had climbed to $2,813,803.27!

"How did he find you?" I wondered. "You can't just advertise 'I'll make you a millionaire!' "

She recalled,

First he had a dream. He was sitting in the broker's office, and saw come through "London price; 2900 pounds sterling." That was crazy—coffee had never gone above 600.

Then, after he saw me being interviewed on TV for tracking down clues in a murder case, he rang me up. "Do you ever do anything except crime?" he asked. I said "No, but I'm willing to try a business experiment. Just seal your question up in an envelope and bring it over." That's what he did. I have the original letter. No company letterhead, no clues, signed "Pete Dixon"—his real name is John Peter Dixon. I couldn't have researched him in advance.

One day, some months later, Pete phoned me again. "I want you to take another look at the coffee market." "Not today, sweetie," I told him. "I'm in a jam. Don't know what we're going to do. We may lose our home." "Don't worry," he said. "I'll buy you a house—start shopping!"

He had paid me for the hours I had put in, so I didn't expect anything more, but I did want a house with room for my office, so I took him up on it. The first place I looked at was here in Creve Coeur—this one. It was just what I wanted. I phoned him, and he came over the next morning to see it. That was before today's prices, of course. He wrote out a check then and there: $2,500 in earnest money, $57,500 two weeks later to close the deal.

Since then, the drawers of her desk have been jammed with envelopes sent by brokers, investors and others for Bevy to "feel."

In the envelope will be a piece of paper with something written on it, folded up as many times as they want. What's written is the name of a stock or a commodity—whatever. I hold it. Never open it. I don't want to know what's in it. I get an answer and write it down on the envelope. See, here is one ready to go to a client in Canada. My comments: "Unusual potential. November interference. Dividend interests which swing. December rewards returns. January returns powerful. February, a hang-up. March difficult but future returns and results turn on the positive." Then, some numbers I put down just as I saw them, then "Great returns later. Stockpile."

Whatever it is, it gives a six-month forecast. The client will know what they want to do with it. I never know what's in the envelope. Sometimes, I'll write a client because I get so powerful an impression, and ask "What was in envelope number four?"

"Oh—here's a letter from one of my clients," she added, rummaging around:

Dear Bevy:

In April, I sent five sealed envelopes to you requesting your impressions of the stocks in each envelope. I was very pleased with the response you wrote on the front of each.

Two of them contained stocks I owned, X and Y. The utility stock does pay good dividends, and the long-term growth of the company appears really good, just as you stated. I purchased Z at 31⅞ in March. By May 28 it was up to 53 and split two for one.

Of the remaining envelopes, your responses were of caution. My questions were answered on the fourth one. ABC Foods was the one you gave a strong warning about. Last week, DEF Foods was considering taking over ABC, so it is in bad trouble. Thanks for the warning.

"That's an example," Bevy shrugged. "I have a drawer full."

Psychic Advisers

The idea that an executive would turn to a psychic for *business* information somehow harks back to the long-buried past, when tribal chieftains called on shamans, and medieval kings, on court soothsayers. But as we shall see, Jaegers is far from being the only psychic in business counseling. Clairvoyant Ron Warmoth is a business specialist, and *Newsweek* did a piece on him, February 15, 1979, in its "Business" section.

"I'm a psychic trouble shooter," he explains. "When firms are in trouble, they come to me: a hitch in a deal, a snafu with real estate, a problem with investments—I'll help them fix it up. I'm not always right," he added carefully, "but I try to be practical. I'm always constructive, and my success rate is about 90 percent."

Though he's based in Los Angeles, Ron's clientele is not. Maria Rolfe in New York (freighters, cruise ships, Bank of Crete, real estate and such) has relied on his services "for twelve to fifteen years."

"He's given me good advice on economic affairs," she told me, "and is very good at spotting trends. He is really fantastic in what he comes up with. No one is infallible, but he is helpful and wise, and does strike it extremely well. When he has no insight on a question, he's not afraid to admit 'I don't know.' But he'll keep trying, if I want him to, and sometimes will deliver on a second try. Some people with psychic ability are afraid of their power. He's not. It's high time we recognized such things."

Another Warmoth client, Houston house designer and real estate developer Roger Rasbach, agrees: "He has amazing insight." In Alaska, Helen Bailey, whose husband was the president of the Bank of Fairbanks, counts on Ron's psychic direction in her business affairs.

Sylvia Smallwood of El Paso, Texas, is another psychic, who puts her talents to business use. She has served a coast-to-coast moving company; a Huntington Beach, California, decorator; and a health clinic in Tijuana, Mexico, among others. "Some people don't want it known that they use psychic help, but others don't mind talking about it, and come back for more."

The astute Kentucky Fried Chicken tycoon Colonel Sanders once invited a psychic to address his shareholders' business meeting.

On Wall Street, clairvoyant Alex Tanous is on retainer as consultant to a brokerage firm president, who confides "I attribute the successful moves I have made to Alex' insight."

"It took me four years to agree to the Wall Street contract," says the conscientious Tanous, who trained for the Jesuit priesthood. "For me, the situation had to be just right. I won't work where the object is mere greed."

A *New York* magazine cover story on January 15, 1979 revealed that "Stockbrokers, diplomats, even psychiatrists are going to psychics." One of those featured was an exotic Italian woman named Chiara, who does pendulum readings for Wall Street brokers, inquiring into the futures of stocks and bonds. As Psi experts don't register at a central bureau, or advertise in the Yellow Pages, the magazine pulled together what it called "the New York Psychic Directory," its own register of the better-known local clairvoyants, with their specialties and fees. Among them was Bill Burns, who trains sensitives at his Center for Psychic Development in Spring Valley, and focuses on "psychic business counseling." One of his clients, cited by the magazine, swears that Burns saved his life and his business, when both were foundering: Burns had sniffed out the fact that his client's partner was embezzling from the company.

Dough in Them Thar Hills

Some psychic counselors specialize even further: locating valuable minerals including gold, silver, and ores; prospecting for oil or advising on land and mineral rights. At this point psychic counseling and dowsing merge.

Paul Clement Brown's specialty is oil. He's a "doodlebugger" as dowsers in the petroleum industry are called. He can, in some uncanny way, tell where, how deep, and how much oil there is in a given area. He has dowsed successful wells for Robert Minkler, president of the Mobil Oil Corporation, and brought in the ten producing wells north of Long Beach, California, that gave the Occidental Petroleum Company its start.

Brown once spotted a well for a "wildcatter," J. K. Wadley, just between two dust-dry holes, one a Richfield Oil Corporation test hole, the other a well drilled by the Seaboard Oil Company. It looked crazy, all right, but on the strength of his record, Wadley took Brown on as his consultant. Less than two weeks later, oil was struck at 2,700 feet, and three others at the site began producing

150 barrels apiece per day. "We have a tremendous supply of oil in this country," Brown explains. "The oil companies just don't know where to look for it." Brown works from the ground, from automobiles, from airplanes, and from a distance with maps.

The ability to find treasure is another string to Ron Warmoth's bow. "I can usually tell from the map whether there is actually oil," he says, "and whether it is worth going in on. I do it just by sight—just look at a map and I know. It comes into my subconscious. I go out and I drive a stake and I say 'Here is where it is.' "

Miner and rancher Bill Wheeler, in Missoula, Montana, says "I have been on quite a few properties with Warmoth, and I know he can tell where a gold or silver vein is, just by walking over it." Once Wheeler showed Warmoth a lean vein of silver; the psychic responded immediately, "I know where there is a better one—over there." Wheeler dug at the spot to which Warmoth pointed, and, sure enough a bigger vein was underneath.

Oil tycoon J. Paul Getty is reputed to have discovered many wells through a dowser, and there are rumored to be handsomely paid dowsers on the staffs of the largest oil prospecting companies.

The late oil billionaire H. L. Hunt enthusiastically declared that he followed psychic hunches in deals involving many millions.

About five years ago, the oil tycoon was in an offshore oil deal involving some five thousand acres. There were several lots available for bids. His geologist reported that four of them were worthwhile, but he consulted a psychic nevertheless. "Which of these lots will be most profitable?" he asked. "Bid on Lot Number 207," he was told, "and be sure you bid high enough to get it." Hunt took the advice, made a substantial bid—$11 million above the nearest competitor—and got Lot #207. "That piece turned out to be the best in the entire area," he testified. "It was fantastically profitable." Within four years the land had more than paid for itself.

On another occasion, Hunt was considering bidding with a combine of other investors in a deal to pipe oil across Canada. His psychic felt there would be endless complications. Her advice was "Don't bid." Hunt refrained, and the advice paid off: endless difficulties did develop in the Canadian pipeline, and Hunt was safely out of them.

The business of "doodlebugging" is not as simple and straightforward as these accounts might suggest. There are powerful conflicts involved. On the one hand, says Paul Brown, there is the skepticism of leaseholders and financiers. On the other is the opposition of geologists and geophysicists in the major oil companies. "All their professionalism and book learning is threatened by my approach. I can beat them every time by a large margin, when it comes to finding oil and gas."

It is impossible to know how many corporations use doodlebuggers surreptitiously today. According to one account, Stanley Vestal, an Oklahoman, asked a scientist why he did not expose the "doodlebug men." The geologist surprised him by saying that to do so would ruin his profession: "More oil has been found by doodlebugs than by regular geologists."

Psychic Executives

It may surprise some to learn that a growing number of company heads use Psi—not just in dealing with specific business matters— but as a comprehensive method of managing all corporate affairs. Some admit it openly, some confidentially, while others explain "Let's just say I'm lucky with hunches."

For years, Sidney S. Baron has accepted paranormal occurrences as an everyday aspect of life. In school, he completed examinations "by instinct." At twenty, he went to work for syndicated columnist Drew Pearson, on radio broadcasts and a series called "Predictions of Things to Come." Many of the forecasts he contributed came true. Today, among friends and family, he correctly predicts illness, marriages and other events. He paints pictures, though he's color-blind. A believer in healing, he can cure his own headaches if he stops for the two or three minutes it takes. At the office, when the telephone rings, he often calls the person by name before he speaks. When chatting with a prospective client, from the "vibes" in the first sixty seconds, he knows whether he is going to be retained.

On a visit to Japan, Baron told his client's board of directors that he foresaw a second revaluation of the yen, and that the dollar would soon be devalued. The directors were incredulous. Less than five months later, the dollar was devalued.

The batting average of his judgments is so impressive that his clients stick with his firm an average of fifteen years. The norm, in his type of business, is less than fifteen months. Baron's sudden and inexplicable decisions, he feels, cannot be understood in conventional terms. He estimates that 10 percent of his counsel is based on logic, 10 percent on experience, and 80 percent on his nonrational intuition.

There is nothing unusual about all this, he holds: Most people are afraid to acknowledge such abilities, and some may be unaware of them; but all the successful people he associates with make decisions in much the same way.

Consider William W. Keeler, former Board Chairman of the National Association of Manufacturers, and recently retired Board Chairman of Phillips 66 Petroleum. Keeler thinks he gets his ESP ability from his mother's side of the family, since both his mother and grandmother, a Cherokee Indian, had frequent psychic experiences. He attributes much of his own business success to unexplained intuitive sensations, which he has been aware of for thirty years. He calls them "gut feelings" and, pointing to his solar plexus, says "I get to feeling it right here, and pretty strong; sometimes so strong that I think of *it* as a fact.

"I've had too many incidents that couldn't be explained as merely coincidences," the Oklahoman observes. "I've had experiences in uncharted areas. My strong feelings toward things have been accurate, when I let myself go." At a Phillips Company board meeting, for example, Keeler was once asked by Mr. Phillips to evaluate a process the company had developed, which might relieve the acute shortage of aviation fuel and crude rubber. He knew that the new refinery process had yet to be tested, and that to instrument it might take three to four years. Despite the obvious problems, Keeler nevertheless found himself announcing that he could get it operational immediately.

"Because of a strong gut feeling, I was satisfied beyond a shadow of a doubt that it would work," he recalls, "though after I made the statement to Mr. Phillips, and had time to think, I began wondering why I had said it, and began worrying like hell." Keeler and his staff were given prime responsibility to process-design the unit. When the plant construction work finished, they were on stream within a week.

The late aeronautics executive, Ambrose Worrall, was associated with the Martin-Marietta Corporation in various managerial and consultative positions for more than forty years. On one occasion, the company won a contract for twenty-eight planes, involving a certain type of ailerons each of which required five hundred very special ball bearings. Unlike others, these bearings would not permit distortion: if they did, the planes would crash.

As the twenty-eight airplanes rolled off the assembly line, a mechanic suddenly noticed that some of the special ball bearings were left over. One plane, at the very least, had been put together with defective ailerons, but which one? Should the entire output be dismantled to find the flawed plane? The cost would be considerable.

Worrall headed out to the assembly line, walked slowly up and down, then abruptly ordered: "Dismantle this one." The mechanics went to work. Within a short time they reported back. *Every one* of the left-over bearings belonged to that aircraft.

Many executives accept this kind of psychic help as it comes. John E. Fetzer, engineer and owner of the Detroit Tigers baseball team and of the Fetzer Broadcasting Company, goes further. Engineers have an interest in psychic phenomena, he theorizes, because "they are accustomed to thinking in terms of frequencies and channels. I think we are dealing with something here that is in the field of radiation; the transmission of energy-forces. So, it's easy for an engineer to see the parallels." Because of his interest in parapsychology, the Michigan executive has created the John E. Fetzer Foundation to aid in scientific Psi research.

A former member of the Federal Reserve Board, Al Pollard, says "I believe in ESP enough to conduct my own business by it. I pay attention to my own intuitive hunches, and act on them, because I have learned to respect them. I have dreamed things that have come to pass. Anytime I get a strong hunch I act on it, although if I'm not careful, my conscious, logical mind will argue me out of it."

Pollard put his philosophy to work years ago, in his own advertising agency, and more recently, in his management firm. His "think tank" seminars for executives attract leaders from all over to his tower suite in Little Rock, Arkansas, where Pollard pushes the constructive uses of ESP in business. "In my dealings," he pointed out to me, "it's the top managers who are willing to talk about intuitive feelings as a part of their decision-making. It doesn't seem to bother them. Rather, it's the middle managers who won't admit, or who hesitate to admit, they're not making 'factual' decisions.

"Long ago, I learned that when you stand up to be counted

among the believers, it attracts an awful lot of people, especially those who have been hiding their feelings and experiences."

The late president of the Princess Coal Company in Huntington, West Virginia, Patrick Price, had psychic abilities tested and confirmed by physicists at Stanford Research Institute (now S.R.I. International).* He found he could obtain by psychic means, at his desk, information about his distant coal fields. Price felt that most people refuse to confront this aspect of themselves, which is why they are unaware of it, don't make proper use of it, or choose to call it "sixth sense" or "gut feeling" or "intuition."

"Out of the Closet"

Of course there must be, also, a great many times when executives guess *wrong*. They tend not to tell about those. However, we do have a ten-year, systematic study that confirms that, for many, Psi is an essential tool in the top executive's kit. For example, the 1974 report, *Executive ESP,* found that 48 out of 64 company presidents in one group firmly believed in ESP. Here were persons, many with engineering degrees, making decisions involving millions of dollars and thousands of shares, who asserted, "I believe in ESP for one reason—*because I use it.*"

This executive/Psi study was conducted by a Professor of Industrial Engineering at the Institute of Industrial Technology in New Jersey, John Mihalasky, who was its director, and a British electrochemist and parapsychologist, E. Douglas Dean, who handled the mechanical aspects of ESP measurement.

Executives, the researchers also found, were beginning to come out of the closet and admit their reliance on Psi. "In the past I would not admit to anyone, especially business people, why my decisions were sometimes so contrary to any logical judgment," electronics executive and founder of the Ampex Corporation, Alexander M. Poniatoff, reveals. Now that he is aware that others also jump over facts, logic, and advice from experts to follow their own inexplicable leadings, he doesn't mind talking about it.

Poniatoff developed his magnetic tape recorder on just such an offbeat hunch. His silent partner was unwilling to put up the money for it until top experts were consulted as to its commercial potential. Five consultants all told him the same thing: "Magnetic

---

* Since most of the Institute research, as cited in these pages, pre-dates its name-change, we shall continue to refer to it as Stanford Research Institute, throughout.

recording has no future." Poniatoff nevertheless knew, deep inside, that the concept was important, and its future was big. "It almost seems," he said later, "that the plans were already in existence, but unknown to me."

It's hard to go against advice and logic and facts, Poniatoff concedes, "but when the unconscious mind knows the answer, it tries to influence or interfere with the conscious mind's 'logical' conclusions."

Before they were done, the researchers came up with some provocative results. They discovered a positive correlation between personality and psychic ability: the strong, dynamic get-things-done type of executive registered higher in Psi talent than did the more placid, easy-going type.

Those who made the greatest profits for their companies scored higher in Psi ability than those who merely held their own. In one test, the "profit doublers" showed 41 percent more Psi talent than those showing less profit.

The researchers were looking especially for powers of prediction: precognition. The higher up the ladder the executive progresses, the more his or her decisions will deal with the future, the unknown. The ability to sense what lies ahead is thus crucial to business effectiveness. From the parapsychologist's viewpoint, there is no way to fake it. One calls a shot; then it is or isn't there.

Not only did the project test for precognition; it developed a computerized test with which to measure it. Since the probability of hiring a superior profit-maker for your company is much increased if you choose a person who scores well in precognition, Mihalasky and Dean advised that, after a firm's selection committee has put potential candidates through the usual tests and interviews, it should subject them to the ESP test.

Another of the project's findings was that when certain relationships within the experimental group changed, the Psi scores changed also. Both men and women lost intuitive prowess in situations which were dominated by the opposite sex. Thus, in contexts where women work under men, or men work under women—what the researchers called "dominance"—even the dynamo-type executive scored lower on psychic performance. In an open group, where there was working equality, and neither sex controlled the operation—a "no dominance" situation—dynamic executives of both sexes outscored the passive types, as before.

Five years after their research report appeared, I asked John

Mihalasky where things stood now: what had happened to the project, were the facts still the same?

"The testing was extended to Canada and Mexico," he told me. "As for the relationship between precognitive ability and profit-making, the earlier findings still hold: higher profit-makers still test higher in Psi ability.

"We have new data, though, on 'dominance.' It still goes both ways for men and women alike; but what we were catching was not a sex factor. It's something much larger. *Any* working context in which one category of person dominates another tends to lower the performance of the dominated group. We found it in ethnic situations also.

"We've *even* found this with relatives. The *Wall Street Journal* picked up on this fact, just after we'd started working on it. They called it the 'S.O.B. factor'—S.O.B. for 'sons of bosses.' Younger men just don't do as well when the Old Man's around."

Captured by Psi

On one of my trips to the Midwest, I became acquainted with an executive who makes home video systems, and compatible films and supplies. His experience is worth recounting because it typifies how Psi can enter the picture unexpectedly and even come to dominate one's life.

He was confronted by a psychic incident in the summer of 1973, and looking back on it now, is frank to admit that that episode, and others following it, changed his life and career. I'll call him Ben Burton.

It started with an apparition, which didn't have any particular form, but I knew it was a mass of some kind of energy. It just sort of floated on past me. Not human in form, but I knew it was intelligence. It terrified me. I had to find out what was going on, and after some asking around in a subtle sort of way, I learned of a psychic in St. Louis named Galena, who had heard of this sort of apparition. I didn't know her before, but she came down to see me, and to see if she could make some kind of contact with what she thought was The Beyond. I didn't agree or disagree with her, but in the process she discovered I had "talents" I hadn't recognized.

She had an assistant, Yvonne, put me into a trance, and after several tries, I 'led' her to a person's home, under hypnosis. I'd never been there, but I described the address and everything. She said, "OK—

if you can do that well, let's 'go' to St. Louis and visit the home of Galena"—go "astrally," I suppose. I did. I found her in bed, ill. Yvonne said, "Examine her body." I didn't know what she was talking about, but all of a sudden, her body opened up and I could see inside. "The only problem I see," I said, "is that she has a terrible upset stomach. There is really nothing serious with the body." She told me to look around the room and say what I saw. I did, and described it, especially a beautiful mirror, reaching almost to the ceiling. Yvonne brought me out of the trance, and said I had described it all exactly, except "Galena does not have a dresser in her room." She telephoned her at that point, and Galena confirmed the stomach upset, and said, "You've got to see my new dresser!"

Now, whether this was something telepathic I was picking up, I don't know, but after that, when I was in bed, pictures would start rolling through my mind, so sharp it was like I was watching TV. I had never read a book on psychic phenomena, and I was concerned. I didn't want anyone to know about it, but I really wanted help. A girl I was acquainted with said, "I know a doctor who is into hypnosis, in fact, I date her son. Would you like to see this lady?"

I went to see this doctor, a practicing physician who also uses hypnosis, Dr. Roberta Holland. She brought in a psychologist from a rehab center who gave me a test, which said there was nothing wrong with me. I was very relieved.

Dr. Holland was treating a little girl who was losing her peripheral vision. Specialists couldn't figure it out; maybe I could help. She asked if I could "see" the girl and the problem. "It is a little Indian girl," I said. "I can see an area on the right temple, I believe—a dark area in back of the eye. It has formed a poison from an abscessed tooth." She sent the girl to a dentist, who said, "The X ray shows a normal tooth, but there is a shadow on the X ray. I don't know what to think." The doctor said, "Pull the tooth." (I had told her they should pull it.) That took care of it.

So, from this remarkable experience, the doctor called me in for other things. It began to move rapidly—clairvoyance, clairaudience. (I would hear someone talking to me—noises.) Finally I had to take Valium to slow my mind down, because I would see faces, thousands of faces—they would flash at me.

Then the doctor started regressing me. She wanted to look into reincarnation, but I kept saying "That's too damned far-fetched!" But I seem to have lived several past lives, and the one that most excited her was my very last lifetime, when I was a physician, in England, and she took me through a complete caesarean childbirth, step by step. I used the eighteen-sixties technique, which is different from today's. She was really astonished.

These lifetimes were done over six months to a year. They're all recorded on tape. I went clear through to my death—the tombstone, the whole thing. She's been trying to get me to verify the English doctor one; it's in Brighton, England. The strangest thing about it was, that from when I was two until the age of twelve, I had the strongest desire to be a doctor. I was torn between movies and medicine. In that lifetime, I was killed: strangled by a belt and thrown into a ditch. In this present lifetime I can remember being terrified by my mother putting a turtleneck sweater on me, when I was six. This reinforces the idea of reincarnation, though I really don't believe it.

Then I started getting messages. I wouldn't accept them for quite a while. I would lie there in a trance, and the words would float by. Finally, I started speaking them. Putting the words together, they made sense. I have now a great deal of material that seems to originate from some alien consciousness.

"Does it put a heavy burden on you?" I asked Ben.

No, but I feel my life is being controlled—no doubt about it! I had one very dramatic emotional experience, which made me feel very close to something. I took it as a religious experience, but I don't think it was, looking back; rather, an experience to get me to pay attention and to open up. I was definitely in contact with some great energy or emotional force. It created an emotional experience in front of witnesses. My family knew something about it, but I was very cautious. (If my banker knew about all this, he'd think I've gone around the bend!) As the years have passed, the religious aspect has faded, but something greater has moved in to take its place.

This strange experience was about five o'clock one evening. I got a message which said "Get your affairs in order. You will be out of your environment for about fourteen days. You are in no danger, but will be gone." A week later, it repeated the message: "Three weeks until the time comes." I assumed I was going to have a meeting with some kind of cosmic force. Whether these things are part of your consciousness, a kind of anticipation, I think it gets all mixed up, and out of it come some things you accept and some you don't. Anyway, it kept saying "Get your business in order."

The day comes. I start getting chest pains. They rush me to the hospital. It looked like some kind of heart attack, but it wasn't. The next day the doctor said, "You've had a little warning. We'll keep you here." The exact number of days I was told I'd be gone was the number of days I was in the hospital, where they did all kinds of tests!

"Was it precognition?" I asked him.

"It was definitely a form of ESP," Ben explained, "whether it was coming from outside or within."

The week after, I went ahead with a trance, and "they" said "There is no damage. You won't have this problem again." Those were the very words the doctor had used in the hospital.

While I was lying there in bed, the nurses had tried to teach me certain exercises. I thought, "How much easier, if this were shown me on TV." The doc came in and I said, "I'm embarrassed, having these nurses try to show me these exercises. Three times, and I still don't understand it! I think I could show you how to make it easier for the patient to understand."

So, while I was rehabilitating, I bought a color camera, got my staff artist, and we put together a couple of five-minute shows. The doc thought it was wonderful. *Going to the hospital launched me on a totally new career—videotape!* Previously, I was a distributor of films only. Because of that hospital experience, I started a whole new company, which absorbed the old one. I have produced ten of the most magnificent films having to do with the heart that have ever been made.

I know I still have something to do. This isn't it, yet. Meantime, it has changed my outlook, my personality, my direction. And, get this—in changing my direction, it took me out of a very limited distribution into a potential for contact with every person on this earth! From forty or fifty thousand potential customers, to millions!

"Are you prepared to be a millionaire?" I asked.

"I've been there once, but now I am starting all over again. But the point is . . ."

"You're being groomed for something?"

"That's *exactly* what Dr. Holland tells me: 'At some point, you will have some great thing to do!' "

"So what you're telling me, Ben, is that all this is integral to your whole life's development and is continuous?"

"Absolutely. I can't escape it."

Mind Over Matter

One of the oldest, most successful tactics in business is a well-known and extraordinarily simple psychic technique. In essence,

it is "mind over matter," an application of psychokinesis, popularly
known as PK.

The principle is that thinking hard about something will make
it so. Think sad thoughts, and you become, and look, sad. Set your
mind on happy things, your face takes on a glow. It works also
with goals. Believe you'll succeed, and, in a self-fulfilling prophecy,
you probably will; assume you're a loser, and that's what you'll be.

How many have latched on to this principle, and in how many
ways? At the end of the last century, French psychotherapist Emile
Coué prescribed the autosuggestive principle, not only for illness,
but in personal life: "In the morning, when you get up, say to
yourself, 'Every day, in every way, I'm getting better and better!' "
In a slightly different form, my mother used it for me: "Be careful
what you wish for—you're going to get it!" When *that* amazing
thought had sunk in, she'd always add, with a twinkle, "And when
you get it, you may not want it!"

The same maxim, which launched *The Power of Positive Thinking*
into an all-time best seller, has for a lifetime been the undergirding
message of its author, Norman Vincent Peale. The Dale Carnegies
and other success-builders seized on the notion too, as did Napoleon
(Think and Grow Rich) Hill, W. Clement ("Positive Mental Atti-
tude!") Stone and other how-to financial wizards. As Stone exhorts
his insurance salespeople, "I feel happy. I feel healthy. I feel terrific!"
Think yourself happy, well, thin, rich—it's psychokinesis, mind over
matter.

Any number of psychics use this device regularly, in their lectures and teaching. In 1978, author Harold Sherman called a national conference (which I attended) based on the unlimited
possibilities of the mind: Your mind has the power to heal, repel,
sense at a distance, know the future, and so on. He preaches it
regularly in his books, the latest of which is *The Power of Visualization.* "Visualization," of course, is to picture what you want.

John Robinson, President of Harper Group, an international
air and ocean freight transportation company, is an avid follower
of this psychic technique. "All that happens to me, I have asked
for," he declared at Sherman's Visualization meeting.

Robinson explained:

> What I picture, happens.
> In my mind, I take off my head . . . Picture it, literally. Get

out all the garbage, fears, doubts, and negatives. Then put it back on again. I use a blackboard to write down what I want to have happen and what I want to do. Once a day, I do "picturing." I've "pictured" friends' ills away, evaporated my wife's glaucoma. I often do "quickies"—"see" a happy time at a party before I get there, or an empty parking place when I need it. On my way home, I see myself happy.

I do "imaging" too. I picture my company as I want it to be. I "saw" us signing the Arabian contract. I "visualized" the business going public.

Harper has a hundred and nine branches, does millions everywhere in transportation. But profit is only a by-product. Making work fun is my goal.

I've a list of words that are positively off limits: "but," "ought to," "hard," "doubt," "categories," "evaluations," "judging." I'm responsible for what I see. I decide on the goals. All that happens to me, I have asked for. I ask for, and get, miracles!

3

DOWSING:
The Ancient Art

I was watching the news in my California living room one evening in 1977, when it turned to the drastic drought situation. It was getting worse. This time, however, the news had a twist: it seemed that a resident in parched Marin County had paid a dowser two hundred dollars to locate a well!

"Do you *really* believe in such things?" an incredulous TV newsman asked.

"All I can say is, if I'm paying two thousand dollars for a well, why not pay a bit more for a likely place to dig it? I'll bet you a hundred dollars the dowser's right on the mark."

By broadcast time, the newsman announced that the network had to pay up: the well came in, not only at the spot where the "divining rod" pointed, but at the exact depth predicted, 26 feet!

Can there be anything to this hoary rite? Surely the labels it goes by, "witching" and "divining," are less than reassuring. The barest glance at the subject, moreover, reveals how it gathers to itself, like a magnet, all manner of tall tales and impossible feats.

Having heard how Bob Ater had found two missing hikers in the White Mountains of New Hampshire, using only a ball point pen and a map, two writers, Emily and Per Ola d'Aulaire, challenged him to dowse their own plot of ground in another state, using only a rough sketch of their property.

"What about the old foundation, here?" Bob immediately asked, pointing to a spot they had neglected to mark, an overgrown concrete slab. Then, studying the sketch intently, pencil poised, he drew a small circle at a spot on the map and a long wiggly line from the front of the house to a terrace in the rear.

The couple stared in disbelief. He had pinpointed exactly the site of the well, and also—where they had hastily left it—the path of their garden hose!

What was going on here? Some form of ESP? Had Bob "seen" their property clairvoyantly? Had he—telepathically perhaps— picked up his information from their thoughts?

"The Ancient Art"

Dowsers are the *doers* of the psychic realm. Pragmatists par excellence, they live on results. Their historic target is water, which they manage to locate not only in likely spots, but on crags and in deserts, or improbably buried under drought-parched earth. Their broader aim, however, is to locate, not just water, but *anything,* lost, hidden, or buried.

What *is* dowsing, really? A form of perception, it taps information the senses aren't privy to. Some hold that it is "extra-sensory," or outside the senses. Some are convinced that it is not extra-sensory at all, but an extension of the senses as we know them, i.e. "extended sensory perception." Still others see dowsing as a kind of "sixth sense," not yet identified scientifically. Is it physical, psychic, or both?

Traditionally, the dowser holds a tool—a forked hazel twig, for example, or maybe a willow wand. She or he walks slowly over the ground in a state of active concentration, "asking" the rod one simple question at a time: "Is there good water here?" The stick will dip, or the wand will bob, at a place where good water can be found. An involuntary pull gives the answer. Sometimes it will wrench so violently as to peel the bark off the stick, or the skin off the hands.

The practice of dowsing is so old we cannot trace its beginnings. To some scholars, rock paintings from eight or nine thousand years ago, in caves near Tassili, Algeria, suggest that humans used the dowsing rod before they learned to read or write. These depict a herder with his cattle, a forked stick in his hand, the rod pointing upward.

A statue of the Chinese Emperor Hwang-Yu, made in 2200 B.C., shows him with a dowsing stick in his hands. Confucius referred to the practice. In 2000 B.C. the Egyptians revealed their knowledge of the art, in a sculpture of a priest with a Y-shaped rod. Pre-Christian rock carvings show that the practice of dowsing was also widespread in Peru.

The Kabbalists, who enshrined word-of-mouth Hebrew tradition, passed on instructions for "Solomon's Rod" in about 1275 A.D.:

> Look for a peach tree, or olive tree, which has not been planted by the hand of man.
>
> The tree must be so young as never to have borne fruit.
>
> In the morning of the day, just before the sun peeps over the horizon, cut a forked branch, not less than fifteen nor more than twenty inches long.
>
> While cutting the branch, repeat these words: "I cut thee in the name of Eloina, Miraton, Aldonay, and Semiplaras, whom I plead to bestow on thee the magic qualities possessed by the rods of Jacob and of Moses and of Aaron, and to impart unto thee the gift and the power to reveal that which is hidden."

Those who eschew the use of dowsing on religious grounds may be astonished to find apparent reference to it in the Bible. "And Moses smote the rock with his rod and water came forth abundantly." (Numbers xx:11)

So potent has been the divining rod throughout history that certain scholars think its secret art was reserved for priests and royalty, who took it as their symbol, in the form of the sceptre.

The first book on the subject, however, deals not with water but with metals. It is credited to a German, Georgius Agricola. His *De Re Metallica,* written in 1556, describes the use of dowsing by miners. One commentator observes,

> In the thousands of treatises that have been published since Agricola's time, it is remarkable how the questions he posed have remained practically the same: Is there some unknown magical force involved? Does the rod move of its own accord, or is it the operator who makes it move? Does it matter what the rod is made of? Above all, does it really work?

Surprisingly sophisticated experiments were conducted over two hundred years ago, to test the dowsing talents of a cattle-herder, Barthélemy Bleton, in southern France. He was the first to undergo a long and successful series of tests. As one reporter relates:

> Over a stone bridge of one arch pass four small wooden aqueducts, carrying water to Nancy. Only the engineer, who had never seen Bleton, knew the exact position of these four rows of pipes, their exact distance apart, and depth below ground, the whole being well covered by earth and vegetation.
>
> He gave Thouvenal [Pierre Thouvenal, appointed by Louis XVI as Inspector of France's mineral waters], secretly, information on this, of which Bleton was entirely ignorant. The latter was then taken across the bridge as though to return to the town, after various experiments had been made in the neighborhood, and without being told that fresh experiments were to be made.
>
> Just before reaching the bridge, he asserted that water was flowing beneath him, and the sensation continued, with slight gaps, while crossing and in front of the bridge, to a distance of five or six feet. He retraced his steps several times, before finding, distinctly, the four channels, and was much astonished to find them so near. He was then told that they were simply four hollow tree trunks, made to serve as aqueducts.

In this example, it is possible that Bleton was picking up his information telepathically from Thouvenal. However, there were other, "double blind," tests such as would be required today, that is, tests in which neither Bleton nor the experimenter knew the location of the target. Bleton dowsed for more than forty years. Records of his feats still startle even the believer.

Though the forked stick and the straight rod are still used by some, other techniques have evolved. Angle or "L rods," usually made of metal—a handle and a straight stick shaped like an L—are common today. So also is the "pendulum," a simple weight on a string, which some use to supplement the rod, or use in its place as the standard dowsing tool. It gyrates, or swings as do rods, in one direction to answer a question yes, and in the other direction, for no.

If contemporary urban types are somewhat unfamiliar with this centuries-old lore, passed down in many societies, their rural counterparts are well aware of it. People always need water. Many a

crossroads community still has its own forked-stick artist, who
stands ready to answer local needs.

Thomas Sherman, who arrived in the foothills of the Ozarks
forty years ago, is just such a natural-born dowser. He doesn't
charge for his services, or even make a point of them, but is glad
to help a neighbor. "There's not much to tell about it," he'll shrug.
"Guess I've dowsed about a hundred wells, and never failed to
find water. I don't know how I do it. Everybody does it differently.
Some people use L rods, peach forks, whale bones, even coat
hangers."

"What do you use?" I asked him, on his Mountain View, Arkansas, road.

"Some funny things, I guess. One day I was out hunting for
squirrels. Had my rifle on my shoulder. All of a sudden, it tips
over and points to the ground. 'How could I have jolted that loose?'
I asked myself. When I was coming back, at the same spot, the
rifle did the same thing again. I says, 'Good land! That *rifle*'s
dowsing!' "

"I've heard some people can dowse with their hands, without
using any instrument at all," I told him. "What do you think about
that?"

"Well, one time I was visiting on a friend's property. We were
standing on a cliff, just talking and looking at the view. All at
once he says, 'It's pretty, all right, but I sure wish I knew where
some water was on this place.' Without thinking about it I said,
'Why, it's right here. We're *standing* on it!'

" 'On the *cliff*?'

"He drilled a well, and sure enough, there it was. I don't know
how I knew it. I just knew."

Finding water on cliffs, mountains, and rocky promontories
blows the minds of us innocents, but it doesn't faze experienced
dowsers. It was par for the course for them in Marin County, where
water turned up almost anywhere but where people expected it.
Dowsers work on a theory quite different from the standard "water
table" approach, which says that most sources depend on the rain.
In brief, hydrologists—geological water specialists—hold that most
available water rises as vapor from lakes and oceans to form clouds,
which are recycled as rain, hail, or snow. Some of the moisture
trickles into the earth to form a "water table"; some of it runs off
into brooks, streams or rivers; the rest is used by plants. In any

case, it is released as vapor to rise again and start a new cycle.

Professional dowsers seek "primary" water, the permanent supply, which flows in underground veins regardless of rain. "Sure, lots of people find water," dowser Jack Livingston explains. "But sometimes it's just a seepage—surface water or a trickle. When the trickle gives out, the well goes dry. I go for *primary* water, *live* water, that won't give out. I look for domes, where several veins meet. I call them 'mothers.'

"No one is perfect," he admits. "You've got to stub your toe sometimes, or be impossible to live with. But a good dowser should have 95 percent success. Drought or no drought, in my thirty years or so in this business, none of the thousand-plus wells I've dowsed has ever gone dry."

Leonardo da Vinci understood the dowser's theory of water veins, which "flow in the earth as does the blood in the human body." His notebooks describe in detail how water surges up to the summits of mountains, "where the waters from below are poured out."

The Modern Schism

If dowsing has so rich a history, what has separated us from it, and it from us? Quite simply, our Western scientific stance. Within this context, dowsing, which does not register with the senses and cannot be measured, is not "real."

The most articulate opponents of dowsing are the technicians whom it challenges: engineers, well-drillers, geologists and government experts. In his *Geology for Engineers,* Joseph M. Trefethen notes: "Superstitions about ground water are still in the minds of many people. One of the better known of these fanciful delusions is the action of a forked stick in the hands of a 'diviner.' "

In 1976, the Executive Director of the National Water Well Association, J. H. Lehr, wrote, "I think it terribly important that the public recognize that ground-water development is a science, not an art based on a cult's mysterious phenomena, which we know in this case do not exist."

The pronouncement that most angered dowsers was "Water Supply Paper #416," an official government bulletin circulated for years by the U.S. Geological Survey, declaring that "Water witching has been thoroughly discredited. To all inquiries, therefore, the Survey gives the advice, not to spend any money for the services of a 'water witch' for locating underground water." The Survey has now toned down its position to the statement that "Knowledge about geology does not equip us to pass judgment on dowsing. Our position is now neutral."

Some dowsers avoid the label: "I just say I'm a 'water finder.' People are glad to have water, no matter how you find it."

Some drillers now have dowsers on their payrolls, or have taken up the art themselves. Wayne Thompson, co-owner of one of the biggest water-drilling operations in Northern California, attributes his company's dramatic recent growth to its knowledge and use of dowsing.

Ed Bailey, another partner in a water-drilling firm, observes that "Drillers can tell a lot about where to drill from geological signs: rock formations, outcroppings at the surface of the earth, the lay of the land. But they're apt to miss water by a few feet. That's where dowsing comes in. That's why I use it.

"A lot of clients don't want to hear about 'witching.' But I go out on the job with my dowsing rod stuck down the back of my pants. I size up my client. If it feels right, I'll absolutely depend on the rod."

Legends in Our Time

So remarkable are the accomplishments of an occasional dowser as to lift him or her above the level of debate. Such a one was Henry Gross, the game warden of Biddeford, Maine. He performed the "impossible," turned skeptics into believers, and hit the jackpot when other authorities failed. He delivered 175 gallons of water a minute to Bristol-Myers, a company of chemists and engineers, at a spot where all local geologists had agreed no such water existed.

So taken with his talents was his neighbor, historical novelist Kenneth Roberts, that he wrote three books touting Gross's feats, and devoted the final years of his own life trying to put dowsing on the map.

Another master, not of the rod, but of the pendulum, was the Abbé Mermet, of St. Prex, Switzerland, whom we have already met. Holding a pendulum over a map, Mermet once startled Swiss authorities with the word that a missing six-year-old boy had been carried off by an eagle. The story was preposterous, but following his directions, searchers found the body in a spot where the boy could not have climbed, high on a mountain in an eagle's nest. On his death, the priest was honored with an obituary by the British scientific journal *Nature.*

Yet another living legend was Evelyn Penrose, who broke credibility barriers on every continent. Not the least of her accomplishments was her appointment, during a severe Canadian drought, as official "Water Diviner" to the Province of British Columbia, which covers an expanse of some 366,000 square miles, four times the size of Great Britain. She wrote:

> One of the first orchardists whom I visited was a young man with one of the best in the Okanagan Valley. His house was charming, and his whole place had an air of affluence and well-being. It was a shock, then, to walk with him down a lane, and see his whole orchard, covering the side of a large hill, wilting and dying; and to have him say, quite simply, that he was facing disaster. We stopped and looked up the hill, and as he was telling me something, suddenly I was nearly thrown off my feet.
>
> I grasped his arm to steady myself. "Water," I gasped. "Lots of water!" I could never stand over underground water without being swung about, the greater the amount of water, the greater the reaction.
>
> He looked at me in amazement, obviously thinking it impossible that there could be water in a spot he knew so well, and over which he walked every day of his life. I followed this underground stream with my rod, to a little wood by the side of the lane. Here I found the intersection of two underground streams, which made the reaction stronger than ever. Later, when he started to dig, at six feet it was necessary to pump water out, and at twelve feet, he had to get the largest pump obtainable. He wrote to me later, saying "I have the best orchard in the Valley, thanks to the Wonder Well. I get 108,000 gallons per day, but I am sure I could get two or three times as much with a larger pump."

Her sensational success earned Penrose the name "The Divine Lady."

We report these successes because it's important to know the potential of dowsing. At the same time it's important to register a caution. Even the "greats" have their failures. Any account of "divining" that would create an impression of smooth effectiveness and infallibility would do a great disservice.

All-Purpose Wonder

So far, we have spoken only of water. Yet there is a world more to dowsing than water, as I very soon learned. The Divine Lady, for example, dowsed for gold in Australia, Roman statuary in England, oil in California, and diamonds in Africa. In early childhood, she had learned from her father, a dowser, that the tin mines of her native Cornwall had been located with the rod.

The wonder of dowsing is, in essence, that it can be used to find anything. It is called on regularly to locate minerals, ores, and veins of any description, to say nothing of oil; cables, wires, and pipes; blockages and leaks; buried treasure, sunken ships, and downed planes; lost objects, money, jewelry, contact lenses, and valuable papers; even people—lost or kidnapped children, hikers and explorers, the bodies of victims who have met with foul play.

Albert Einstein once astonished his hosts on a visit to their country home, by dowsing the location of a troublesome leak in an underground flow of water draining their pond. Distinguished British dowser Major General J. Scott Elliot pinpointed the blockage in a chimney in Dumfriesshire, with a pendulum. Instructing a local builder to remove a particular stone, he reached into the flue at that point to extract a very dead owl.

With rods made from coat hangers, land surveyor and dowser Louis J. Matacia astonished officers at the Marines' Development and Education Center at Quantico, Virginia, in November 1966, by demonstrating how dowsing could be used in the Vietnam war. Going over a mock-up of a typical Southeast Asian village for tactical training of Marines on their way to Vietnam, he located underground tunnels, a cave used as a secret room, a false wall behind which several guerillas could hide, underground communication wires, and pipes. When he and the officers then checked the underground plan on the map, not one of his calls was wrong. In less than half an hour's perusal with his pair of "wire rudders," most of the hidden system had been revealed.

On March 13, 1967, a U.S. Forces newspaper, *The Observer*, dateline Da Nang, announced:

> An old-fashioned method of locating water in arid areas, the divining-rod, has been updated and put to military use in Vietnam.
> A method for locating underground structures and other objects

by use of wires, "Matacia's wire rudders," was used by Marines during the final three days of Operation Independence, three miles west of An Hoa.

Introduced to Marines of the Second Battalion, Fifth Marine Regiment, the divining rods were greeted with skepticism, but did locate a few Viet Cong tunnels.

Private First Class Don R. Steiner, Shadyside, Ohio, a battalion scout with the Second Battalion, First Marine Regiment, tried the rods for the first time on a recent patrol. The rods spread apart as Steiner passed a Vietnam hut.

Upon checking inside the building, Marines discovered a tunnel that led to a family bunker, underneath the trail, right where the rods had reacted.

Other Marines were reported as having found caves, buried objects, caches of food and ammunition, and secret messages in bamboo tubes. By some accounts, they saved many lives.

Despite the variety of uses, most dowsers tend to specialize. Some of the most productive oil wells in the country have been dowsed. This is one specialization about which you'll hear little. Oil dowsers keep a deliberately low profile, for reasons you can probably guess.

Since the range of dowsing uses is so wide, we have space for only a few. One is physical diagnosis, in which Evelyn Penrose sometimes engaged. As she explained in her journal,

I use my pendulum in much the same way as I do in finding water. The point of the left hand is held a few inches away from the patient, who is never touched during the whole proceeding. I begin by pointing at the patient's forehead, then mouth, throat, chest, and so on down to the toes. When the finger points at a trouble spot, the gentle oscillation of the pendulum in my right hand turns into a gyration. If the trouble is serious, it jumps about and whirls madly.

With one of my patients, I began by pointing to his forehead, and the pendulum went wild. "You must have terrible headaches," I said, "probably terrible migraines." I could find nothing wrong with his face or his throat, but when I came to his left side, the pendulum whirled around and I felt as though I were being suffocated (I get the reaction myself for everything that I find, which is one reason I don't like diagnosing diseases).

I told him there was something wrong with his left side, so I went on to the right. The pendulum jumped around madly, so I told him that his right side was covered with scars. Why I told him that, I don't know, for I had never seen the pendulum act quite like that before, and the patient was fully dressed.

He gave no indication whether I was right or wrong. "What about my leg?" he asked. One of them was all right, but the other affected the pendulum violently and gave me a violent pain as well.

The next day, the patient's doctor told Ms. Penrose that the patient suffered severe headaches. He had been gassed in the First World War, which accounted for the feeling of suffocation. His right side had been badly cut up with shrapnel wounds, and one of his legs had been smashed.

After the diagnosis, the doctor asked another young man, who had not spoken, to drive Ms. Penrose home.

Almost the moment after we started, I clapped my hands to my throat and cried, "Oh, I am in agony! What could have happened to my throat? It's so odd—the man I just diagnosed had nothing wrong with his throat." The driver then said, in an angry voice, "I suppose you have got my throat." "Young man," I replied, "I have never seen you before, but I know that if you don't stop smoking you will die, and I am not speaking figuratively, but literally."

What I told him in the car was precisely what his doctor had told him that morning. He had cancer of the throat from excessive smoking.

One of the most far-fetched findings of dowsing, if one can be thought of as more improbable than another, is the recent discovery of "harmful emanations" from veins, faults, or radioactive fissures. Some dowsers are now convinced that many ailments, including arthritis and dangerous heart conditions, even cancer, can be caused by sleeping or sitting for long periods of time over "noxious veins."

The late Joseph Kopp, a Swiss geobiologist, spent his latter years studying the effects of "irritation zones" on humans and animals. He wrote almost fifty papers on geomedicine and geopathology, reporting on the radiation from ground water flows as causes of cancer and other ailments.

Hospital beds located directly over springs and water-flow crossings can pose a serious problem. Kopp tells of a woman totally bedridden for six years with neuralgia and gall bladder problems.

Following a gall bladder operation, which was unsuccessful, her bed was moved. Nine days later, the woman was found by her physician doing the laundry. After several months, the pain completely disappeared, and she was restored to good health.

Four thousand years ago, the dowsing-conscious Chinese Emperor Yu is said to have decreed that investigation be made of building lots, to prevent sickness. Veteran dowser and chemical engineer the late Gordon MacLean pointed out that, although in China for centuries, and in Europe for decades, it has been recognized that health troubles can be brought about by sleeping over veins of flowing water, or noxious rays from radioactive emissions, in this country we are realizing only now that dowsing can help avoid these problems.

A Maryland dowser reported that he had located all the geological clefts in the county in which he lived. Hypothesizing that all the households located above these "GZ zones" would reflect higher incidence of cancer, he enlisted a county health official to determine if this were true. Together, they examined the records at the county court house. The result was that nearly every household in the "GZ zones" had had one or more deaths attributed to cancer.

As with Kopp, prevention became a primary interest for MacLean. "Dowsing," he said, "can determine the most healthful plot for a building site, the proper position for a new building on the site, the best old house to buy, the most healthful rooms in which to sleep if you are already settled in your home."

"Anyone who can use L-rods," MacLean noted, "can be consulted for advice about the proper placing of beds as an aid to health."

When I interviewed the 89-year-old MacLean, he was instructing his students in how to deflect such harmful rays. Said he: "If you find you have been sleeping over bad spots, your first reward after deflection and the resulting attenuation will be completely undisturbed slumber. Children who waken as often as six times in a night sleep soundly after their bed sites have been cleared of harmful rays."

Another dowsing application concerns highway accidents. Some spots on roadways have a disproportionate number of accidents, which cannot be explained in the usual ways. The stretch is straight and smooth; vision is unimpaired; yet at a particular point, accidents keep occurring.

On such apparently safe stretches of highway, drivers tend to switch their attention into neutral, a more relaxed state of mind, letting automatic (subconscious) patterns take over. This is precisely the state of consciousness that is most receptive to outside influences. The impact of even very subtle forces on the steering hands of a relaxed, unsuspecting driver may be momentous. People with slightly epileptic tendencies seem especially susceptible to these forces.

Intrigued by the problem, Bob Ater began dowsing Maine road maps and highways. There are natural causes, he concluded, like faults or veins underneath, as well as man-made: power from electrical substations, high tension lines, radio station antennas, for example. Such power can travel over natural conduits, such as water or mineral veins, or on man-made tracks and highways.

On one map he picked up a bad accident site and "found" a transformer substation nearby. Checking it out on location, he found he was right: there was the accident spot and the substation too. Dowsing the station, he got a powerful reaction with his rod and also spotted several active "leaks." Returning in a few weeks to check the area again, he found police just arriving in response to an accident.

When Ohio dowser James Perkins, a highway department safety engineer, later heard of Ater's work, he asked that Bob dowse maps of his area. Following up on the information and clues he received— one site with many crashes, forty injuries, and two deaths—he was able, at each location, to identify the possible cause. Together he and Bob have sought funding with which to explore the problem in depth. The reactions to their queries have, to date, been uniformly negative. "Fund a dowser for a scientific experiment? No way!"

As word of the wide usefulness of dowsing spreads, hundreds of people have begun to carry rod or pendulum with them to find where to plant a wheat crop or vegetable garden, to identify "safe" food in a supermarket, to clear prescriptions and health products in a pharmacy, and so on. "Has this food been sprayed with dangerous chemicals?" "Is this medicine good for me?" In Japan, we are told, dowsers work all day, with near 100 percent accuracy, determining the sex of baby chicks as they pass by on a conveyor belt.

"*Anyone* can dowse *anything,*" dowser LeRoy Osborne insisted to me, "from your own blood pressure, to the honesty of political candidates."

The Psi Connection

If all this is true, how does dowsing differ from what we call "Psi?" The answer is that it doesn't. There is no clear line separating the two. Both deal with information not generally available. Both do so outside the usual sensory channels. Both work with or without instruments, as the occasion calls for—or as the sensibilities of the seeker require.

We may not understand how either of them works, but from all we can learn, it would seem that the mechanisms for Psi search and dowsing are one and the same. You walk over the ground with a stick to learn where water is, or simply walk or stand, to pick up the same information. In one case, the stick is the instrument for sensing what you seek; in the other, the body. It is a vexed question among dowsers whether the rod, the body, or the mind, picks up the message. In psychometry, a common psychic practice, one holds an object belonging to someone else to get information about that person. In dowsing, to get the same results, one often "imprints" a rod or a pendulum by rubbing it with a possession of the person being sought.

"Getting the Message"

There are a number of theories as to how dowsing works, falling roughly into three categories:

1. PHYSICAL explanations are based on the premise that there is a force of some kind that emanates from the object being sought. The "force" is variously conceived as emissions, vibrations, energy waves, electromagnetic forces, radiation, and so on. These are picked up by some sort of receiving instrument, e.g. willow wand, pendulum, radionic box, or magnetometer, which registers the incoming energy. In Europe the word for dowsing is rooted in this theory: "radiesthésie" in French, or "radiesthesia" in English, means literally "the perception of radiations." The theory is strong in the eastern European bloc, especially in the U.S.S.R., where all "psychic" manifestations are explained in physical terms, consistent with philosophic materialism. Thus dowsing, which reflects the "biophysical effect" (BPE) is known as the "bio-physical method."

Since the aim of the dowser is to get maximum reception of the force from the substance being sought, a few of them are always seeking to develop the "most sensitive instrument possible," experimenting with equipment using magnets, springs, electronic devices, and lights, for example.

No matter how sophisticated the device, however, Zaboj V. Harvalik, scientific adviser to the U.S. Army's Advanced Material Concepts Agency, asserts that the human being is "still more sensitive than any instrument made by our electronic wizards." The human body *is* a form of divining rod, he declares, a "highly developed electronic system." The sensitivity of the body to magnetic anomalies, he goes on, is utterly amazing. "Magnetometric measurements indicate that a dowser reacts to magnetic gradient changes as weak as one milli-micro-gauss, or expressed in another way, 10^{-9} or 0.00000001 gauss."

Human instruments vary enormously as to their degree of sensitivity. Evelyn Penrose, for example, was so delicately attuned to incoming forces as to be swept off her feet, or afflicted with pain.

Though she is an extreme example, Penrose is instructive in exhibiting the toll of psychic "work" on the human body. ". . . the actual finding of water is exhausting," she observed. "It is as if some power or virtue goes out of oneself; and when I finally did five or six homesteads a day (on the British Columbia project), the need was so urgent, I was often so completely exhausted, that I would sleep like a log for nine or ten hours at a stretch.

"Sometimes, when finding large quantities of water, and more especially, when finding oil or minerals, I have been seized with violent physical illness, which I have finally had to call in a doctor to stop." Her first big oil find reduced her to a state of collapse. She testified that if a mineral deposit were strong, she could begin to pick it up 30 or 35 miles away.

Though more research is needed to establish the parameters of human sensibility, Yves Rocard of the Academy of Sciences in Paris has established that 70 percent of the population are able to detect small magnetic stimuli, and Harvalik estimates that nearly 90 percent of us have this ability.

Bob Ater's experience convinces him that different substances have different kinds of emissions, i.e. different strengths and patterns. He can apparently identify, without seeing it, something such as wood or iron by holding his hand directly over it. "In pursuit of the dowsing phenomena, I became aware of the presence and activities of certain electro-emissions, which seem to act and interact upon each other. These seem to be present and active in the substance and aura of my own body, and in the substance and aura of all other materials, whether organic or inorganic.

"After long and exciting experimentation, I observed that I could detect these electro-emissions with my bare hands, follow their pattern repeatedly, and record them on paper. I believe anyone who has the ability to dowse can learn to feel these emissions, and study them as I have."

Harvalik has sought to find exactly where in the body the "sensors" are located. His research suggests the areas of the adrenal glands, at the top of the kidneys, and a spot between the eyes, in front of the pituitary or pineal gland. If physicist Harvalik's findings are refined and confirmed, he may ultimately be credited with having discovered a sixth bodily sense.

2. PSYCHIC. A second, contrasting explanation of how dowsing works is non-physical or psychic: the dowser gets his stimulation not from an external emanation or ray, but by means of some as-yet-unexplained faculty of consciousness itself.

Logical though the physical stimulus-response explanation above may be, the fact remains that people can and do dowse successfully from a distance, on occasion hundreds or thousands of miles away, with no possibility of receiving radiations or emanations physically. On all counts, map-dowsing defies the physical laws of time and space. The reaction is just as strong at a distant point as at a close one, and fails to get stronger as one approaches the point being sought. A dowsing reaction is just as strong over a map, as over the actual site!

We'll deal with the non-physical approaches more fully later on, but in brief, one psychic theory holds that individual consciousness is part of a larger Total Consciousness, which encompasses us all. At some level information in the "pool of consciousness" is instantly and automatically available to any who tune into it. *All* knowledge resides in this reservoir: the depth of a silver vein, the amount of underground water, or the whereabouts of a lost person or treasure. When one asks "Is good water here?" or "Is Mary Jones now alive?" one opens his or her individual consciousness to the universal font. When the answer registers in one's consciousness it also registers in subtle and involuntary muscle activity, resulting in a "dip" of the rod or a twirl of the pendulum.

"No one ever explains *how* the information moves from the Universal Source to the individual consciousness!" I once complained to a psychic. "Just how does the information in Collective Pool 'A' *get* to the individual consciousness, 'B'?"

"It doesn't 'move' from one place to another *at all,*" she replied. "When you open yourself to the fund of information, it's *already there!*"

3. PHYSICAL AND PSYCHIC. A third explanation of the dowsing process combines Hypotheses One and Two. Its proponents argue that dowsing uses both physical and psychic processes: in highway accident experiments, for example, physical emanations may be picked up from under roadways or nearby. In dowsing from a distance, however, or in work with a map, the process is psychic.

Should the first type of theory prove correct, then dowsing is not paranormal at all, but merely an extension of physical forces and sensory perception as ordinarily understood, albeit more delicate and refined. Certainly a great many dowsers take this position. One of them emphatically told me, "Dowsing is dowsing. It should never be mixed up with all that hocus-pocus psychic stuff!" Historically associated with a forked stick and water, it has been set apart in such minds as a unique and separate phenomenon, and does not at all belong in a book on Psi. Many works on dowsing do not discuss or even mention the psychic.

Even the second, more psychic, hypothesis, may turn out to be an extension of, and thus a manifestation of, natural laws. Perhaps, as researcher Francis Hitching suggests, we should not call dowsing "paranormal," but rather, a precious half-forgotten and under-used ability, which needs to be rediscovered and better understood. However, for a number of theorists, it is obvious that dowsing is essentially psychic, and belongs in any consideration thereof.

Whether the energy is generated from outside, inside, or both, the dowser is clearly an essential part of the process, attuned to the target in some super-sensitive way.

Pitfalls

Dowsing, like any other psychic activity, is most frequently triggered by genuine need. "There must be a 'need' to know," dowsing specialist General Scott Elliot avers. This may be why many a dowser can deliver for a genuine client, but not for a skeptic. "With a need to know the answer, the Mind does seem to work with more precision," says Elliot. "I think the reason why dowsers so often fail in tests set to them to demonstrate that dowsing works, is this element of the Need to Know. Under such test conditions, there is seldom a need to know the answer; only a need to show that dowsing works—thus the mind machinery seems to get confused."

Here are some of the more common pitfalls, Elliot advises:

a) OVERCONFIDENCE. Early successes may be so astonishing and so heady that the novice feels invincible. One must have confidence to make it work, but cockiness, which leads to carelessness, is something else. It takes a great deal of practice to read the signs correctly.

b) WISHFUL THINKING. The biggest problem in dowsing, Gen. Elliot believes, is preconceived ideas, wishful thinking about what you'll find. *Dowsing isn't thinking;* it's an unconscious process, and when wishes take over to direct the operation, it ceases to be dowsing.

c) "REMANENCE." This is the memory or continuing influence of an object in the place from which it has been removed. Some think of it as a scent; others, as a residual vibration or electromagnetic effect. Dowsers have frequently been distressed to find that the box, cave or hiding-place to which their instruments have unmistakably led them is now empty. In many cases the treasure has been confirmed as having been there at one time, but has since been removed.

d) VAGUE QUESTIONS. Another problem is failure to be specific enough. A friend of Elliot's once asked his help in finding some art gallery keys that she had hidden before leaving on a vacation. After dowsing a sketch of her gallery and apartment, asking "where are the keys," he suggested she look in the top left drawer of the gallery desk. "No," she answered. "There are keys in there, but those are the spare keys to the flat." Dowsing the apartment, he then suggested three other places to look. One, behind the books on a bookshelf, some 3 feet to the left of the fireplace in the living room; two, in the right-hand drawer of the worktop in the kitchen; three, in the long hanging cupboard of the bed room, 5 feet from the door. The first was a place where she did occasionally hide things, but the keys were not there. In the worktop drawer of the kitchen were two long-lost spare keys for the front door of the flat, but not the missing set. In the long hanging clothes cupboard she found a basket on the wall behind the clothes, within which were the missing keys.

Though it took Elliot four tries to locate them, the case is both remarkable and instructive. He found keys *only*—several sets of them, but remanence also tripped him up. "I have no doubt that the keys had been in the top drawer of the desk quite often," he explained, "but they were not there when I was searching. What I should have asked was, 'Where are the gallery keys *now?*' "

"How To's"

"How to" guides and handbooks on dowsing are springing up like mushrooms after a rain. Colleges and extension courses are beginning to teach it in a number of states.

No matter how good the guide books, however, nothing beats the first-hand instruction of a seasoned practitioner. In September 1978, I made my way to the "home of the dowsers" in Danville, Vermont (pop. 300), where people from all over the country gathered, as they have for almost two decades, for their annual rites, to compare notes, share know-how, and try their hands at "the ancient art." For four days, in that tree-shaded crossroads village, six hundred dowsers, and about six thousand dowsing instruments, filled and overflowed churches, high school, American Legion, and Masonic meeting rooms. At the town hall, sandwiches and literature were served up in about equal amounts. A huge banner floated over the street: WELCOME DOWSERS!; and around the corner, in a small storefront, the national dowsing headquarters worked overtime.

"What we want to get, first, is the 'feel' of that tug, the pull that *we* don't control," one instructor told prospective dowsers. "Try different tools and techniques, then use what suits you best." A few said that the instrument serves simply as a magnifier, accentuating what the *body* receives.

The elaboration of dowsing tools was a sight to behold. Most old hands, I noticed, seemed to stick with the tried and true tools of the past, simple and unencumbered, often homemade: rods bent from coat hangers, wands of light whalebone, a single bead or wedding ring, hung on a string, for a pendulum. "Park your instruments entirely, if you want to," some told us. "Learn to dowse with a pencil, or try 'deviceless dowsing' and learn to work with nothing at all."

With Danville, we are just beginning to catch up with the rest of the world. Most dowsing literature, up to now, has come from abroad. The American Society of Dowsers has two thousand members in twenty-eight chapters. Its first-class quarterly digest, *The American Dowser*, has earned a place beside others, such as the Irish *Diviner, Radiesthesia and Radionics* from New Zealand, and the *Journal* of the British Society.

For the Birds?

Awesome though dowsing feats may be, some are convinced that humans have no monopoly. It is said that donkeys are so adept at locating underground water that Mexicans call dowsers "burros."

Tennessee oil dowser Earl Pyle recalls:

> About a year ago Sarah and I were eating breakfast. It was zero weather and had been that way for a day or two. Everything was frozen and I am sure trees must have been frozen all the way through. A big red-headed woodpecker landed on a maple tree right beside us, and began to walk up and down the trunk. All of a sudden, he began to let the chips fly from the center of the tree. By rights, it should have been frozen through.
>
> He slammed away for maybe five minutes, and got halfway through the tree, and then he began to eat a worm from the center. After he went away, I looked. Down about a foot away from where he had pecked this hole, there was a small, round hole, like something had gone into the tree. I am sure that bird would have no way of knowing how far up the tree that worm had gone, even if it went into that hole.
>
> What I don't understand is, how did he know it was there? I am sure that worm was frozen so solid it couldn't have made a noise for the woodpecker to hear it. I am sure it was frozen so tight he couldn't have smelled it. Something told him exactly where to go. It was dowsing ability!

Ours may be a technically-oriented society, but we are at last beginning to discover how many "superstitions" and "old wives' tales" check out scientifically. Medical schools now look at acupuncture. Laboratory technicians now explore the chakras of the Indian yogi. Scientists now study the effect on people's behavior of the phases of the moon. Some have even begun to listen to the old man with the divining-rod, and to savor his philosophy.

Running through the remarks of the veterans, you will often pick up a heavy sense of personal responsibility, and a strong ethical note.

"You can't set a price on your dowsing," says Earl Pyle's brother Willie. "Some can afford to pay, others can't. You just have to dowse for one and for all, wherever there is a need."

Glendale, California, dowser, Legory O'Loughlin, may have capsuled this philosophy best in the motto of the regional group which he leads: "The aura of dowsing shines brightest when helping humanity."

4

HEALING:
The Marvel of PK

At a national symposium on healing, I met an animated young woman from Washington, D.C., Lynn Brallier. She was in physical therapy, working on a Ph.D. I asked her: "You're in nursing; what do you think about psychic healing?"

"I've always been an absolute skeptic," she began.

But as I moved among my patients and colleagues, I kept hearing about this healer from Baltimore, Olga Worrall. People talked about the different ailments and diseases she cured, and the people, old and young, who came to her. She doesn't take any money; she works strictly for free. Does most of her work in the Mt. Washington Methodist Church; holds services there Thursday mornings at ten. Calls it "The New Life Clinic." They come from everywhere to be healed. She doesn't do the healing, she says; God does. She is only the channel for His healing power.

I didn't believe a word of it—the healing business, I mean. I work in a clinic and you can't hand me that. Of course, people are better off when they have faith and stick to their treatments.

One day it got to me, though, and I had to see for myself. I got a friend to go with me up to Baltimore.

We got in all right. The service had just begun. It was the usual, with some singing and such. Olga said a prayer. People did go down to the front then, and one by one, they'd "Thank God," but from where I was sitting, I couldn't really make out what was going on.

Actually, I was kind of disappointed, to have come all that way and have nothing—bang! bang!—to show for it. "Maybe if I got closer," I said to myself, "I could get a better feel of things."

So I went down front and was just getting ready to ask a few questions, when Olga walked over to me, put her hands over my head, and closed her eyes.

A burst of heat, such as I've never felt before, surged down my spine. I could feel it moving down, down, down, every inch of the way. I forgot all about questions and what I was there for.

Making my way back to the car, I kept asking my friend, "Whatever happened? What did she do?"

On the drive back to Washington, I reached up to adjust the rear-view mirror, which was slightly askew. "Look at you!" My friend shouted. "Lynn! Look what you've done! You reached *up!*"

I hadn't even noticed, but she was dead right. I hadn't been able to lift that darned arm as high as my shoulder for years!

The use of Psi for healing may be the most important and remarkable of its applications. Certainly its range of uses in the health field is spectacular. We'll touch on a number of these in this chapter, but first we must ask, What is "psychic healing?" It is physical healing (reversal of symptoms, rapid healing, or both) that cannot be explained in purely medical, physical, or psychological terms. To get at the explanation—the Psi factor presumably—it is necessary to eliminate these other factors.

For this reason, accounts such as Brallier's don't make it for the Psi scientist. There are too many possibilities other than Psi: subconscious hopes and expectations, for example.

We include such materials nonetheless, i.e. reports from credible witnesses which are not conclusive by hard scientific standards, but impressive enough to warrant serious study. We include also a body of experimentation where factors such as expectation and suggestion have been eliminated.

There are several ways to approach the problem. For example, to investigate the healer, to follow up on the one being healed, and to test the healing process itself.

Checking Out the Healer

Let's start with Olga Worrall, whom Lynn Brallier told me about. I learned that Olga was "the most-tested healer" to come down the pike. No number of testimonials and claims can equal controlled observation by serious investigators, so when I met her, at a platform appearance in January 1977, I asked her pointblank where she'd been tested. "At the Menninger Clinic in Topeka," she began, "by Robert Miller at Emory University, and—oh, honey—I've been everywhere. I don't even remember all the places!"

Since psychics are prone to exaggerate, I took it to be hyperbole or a brush-off. It was neither, as I soon found out. I can't remember all the places, either. A complete listing would have to include University of California at Los Angeles; Rosary College in Buffalo; McGill University, Montreal; Kent State University in Ohio; and Stanford. She's also been studied at King's College in London, at Hiroshi Motoyama's Parapsychological Laboratory in Japan, and the shrine at Lourdes, France.

She was tested in the physics lab at Agnes Scott College, for example, in 1974. This was a key experiment, using the Atomic Laboratories Model 71850 cloud chamber, to determine whether some kind of energy is given off by a healer's hands. She placed her hands at the sides of the chamber, without touching the glass, then visualized energy flowing from her hands, much as she does when treating a patient. Observers saw a wave pattern develop, although, before she had placed her hands in position, the contents of the chamber had been quite uniform. The waves were parallel to her hands, and the motion seemed to be perpendicular to the palms.

After several minutes, she shifted her position 90 degrees, to see if the pattern in the cloud chamber would be affected. The waves then changed direction, and were soon moving perpendicular to the original path.

A follow-up experiment was conducted to see whether she could affect the cloud chamber from a distance. The instrument was in a physics lab in Atlanta, and she was in her Baltimore home, some 600 miles away. A camera had been mounted to record proceedings.

When the chamber was steady, the researchers telephoned Ms. Worrall to ask her to hold her hands at the side of the chamber "mentally," beginning at 8:50 P.M.; to concentrate her thoughts and energies for several minutes; then, to change the orientation 90 degrees.

At 8:53, a definite change occurred: the mist began to pulsate, and dark waves, parallel to the length of the table, moved back and forth. They continued for seven minutes but did not change direction. At 9:10 P.M., when they called her again, she said she had begun to concentrate as instructed, and felt a cool sensation, like a breeze, flowing over her hands. She explained that in the midst of the proceedings, however, in order to make the most of the energy, she had decided not to shift her hands.

The test was repeated. Turbulent undulations, at the rate of one per second, were perceived. Photos, which I have seen, were taken before, during, and after the experiment. As a further check, members of the research team tried it themselves, placing their hands around the chamber, but with no results.

Olga says she's had psychic ability at least since she was three. "I've never known anything but. I thought it was just the way people are, until I found out other kids didn't see what I saw.

"My parents knew what I had, including my knack for healing, but wanted to keep it dark. I found out why my parents wanted to shield me: There's simply no let-up, morning and night.

"I'm not against 'doctors,'" she declares, "even though I cure patients after their physicians have failed. I have a doctor myself and will not accept a patient who refuses to see one. The doctor gives bodily therapy; I supply spiritual therapy. I don't care who gets the credit, as long as the patient gets well."

Biochemist Bernard Grad, at McGill University, asks not only "Can healers heal?" but, "If so, what do they do? What happens when a healing takes place?" Grad started in 1957 when Col. Oskar Estabany, a Hungarian now living in Montreal, said he could heal animals and humans, just by placing his hands on the afflicted place. "It all sounded very strange," Grad explained to me. "My specialty is research on living bodies, and I'm *very* curious."

Since the Colonel seemed balanced and serious, I asked him how he did it. He mentioned a number of manifestations, among them a terrific development of heat in the part of the body he laid hands on. He told me, "I believe there is a movement of energy down my hands, to the sick part."

Now, a lot of people would have stopped right there. I knew it was getting off base, as far as conventional scientific wisdom goes, but I'm a born inquirer. I just *had* to know. Besides, I saw a way of testing it.

The odyssey of Grad's meticulously plotted, step-by-step sequence of experiments is one of the most cited chapters in psychic inquiry. I have made two trips to his laboratory in Montreal to build my profile of him. Grad established, first, in tests with Col. Estabany and dozens of wounded mice, that healing *does* take place. The results were "statistically significant": the rate of healing was faster in the group of mice treated by the healer than it was in the control group. (The term "statistically significant," as determined by mathematical techniques, is used when the outcome of an experiment cannot be explained by coincidence.) The experiment was repeated, by Grad and at the University of Manitoba, with the same results. Other experimenters tested the Colonel, and agreed that he could heal.

To re-test his findings, Grad conducted experiments with rats, mice, seeds, and plants using different research assistants, different healers, and different designs—all with the same results.

Not only did this pioneer work and that of others turned on by Grad's experiments demonstrate that a healer could really heal, but it laid to rest the cliché that "it's all in the mind." With the mice, and later with rats, plants, and seeds, it became unequivocally clear that the healing was healing, not hope, faith, or expectation. What rat, mouse or barley seed would expect to be healed?

Checking Out the Healee

Another approach to healing is to follow up on the person being healed. Was he/she really cured? Or did he grab back those crutches the minute he got out the door? There is plenty of evidence that some of the most convincing on-stage "instant cures" have been imagined, temporary, or faked.

Animal experiments have, for this reason, proved to be exceedingly useful. Animals do not imagine or fake cures. Their temperatures and wounds can be measured, their non-subjective state of well-being assessed. Every mouse and rat in the laboratory that exhibited measurable benefits from the laying on of hands is clear evidence of its efficacy.

Checking out human healees—in or out of the lab, particularly the latter—is much more complex. We must look at such subjective variables as attitudes, perceptions, and expectations. Does the healee heal himself? (We'll look at that later.) Some theorize that context may be a factor in healing. Does the frenzied atmosphere of the shouting, jam-packed crowd itself generate a kind of physical energy, for the healer to work with and mobilize? Some suggest that such cumulative mass energy was a key to the dramatic healings in Kathryn Kuhlman's congregations. It is an intriguing topic for future research.

In the meantime, investigative writer Allen Spraggett has made a beginning in this direction, by trying to push beyond the "hallelujah moment" to what happens afterward. Following up a cross-section of "miracle cures" by Kuhlman, he interviewed patients' doctors and inspected their medical records.

One of those he checked on was George Orr, a seventy-six-year-old resident of Butler, Pennsylvania, "healed" by Kuhlman. Years before, Orr had been blinded in his right eye in an industrial accident. In his 1970 book on the healer, Spraggett cites the documents from the testimony at Orr's compensation hearing, and the decision that "the claimant is entitled to compensation . . . for the loss of an eye."

At a Kuhlman service more than twenty years after the accident, the evangelist declared that physical healing was just as possible today as was spiritual salvation. The statement stabbed something awake inside George Orr, Spraggett reports. "Right then," Orr recalls, "I prayed, 'God, please heal my eye.'"

"The next moment, I felt a tingling in my right eye, as though a mild electric shock were passing through it. Then it began to stream tears. They ran down onto my jacket. I was embarrassed, because I couldn't control it."

When the service was over, Orr had trouble negotiating the aisle. He couldn't walk straight. "I have the strangest feeling," he confided to the young man with him. "Something has come over me that I don't understand."

On the drive home, Orr was aware that something was different. He kept blinking his bad eye, which was still running tears. Then, suddenly, he covered his good eye with his hand. In that moment, he realized what had happened. "I can see! I can see everything!" he exclaimed.

Some healer-effect studies have been conducted by medical professionals acting in the double capacity of healer and researcher. Their results may be excellent and their conclusions sound, though the limitations of evaluating one's own work are obvious. Two such healer-evaluators are Hans Engel, M.D., president of the Los Angeles Academy of Family Physicians, and Professor of Kinesiology, Valerie Hunt. As a scientist, practitioner of psychic medicine, and observer of his own cures, Dr. Engel bridges the gap between the hard science of medicine and psychic healing. He began by treating patients in the office of UCLA medical psychologist and psychic researcher Thelma Moss, researching the effects of his own healing and keeping careful records. He discovered that he was most effective in treating those suffering from chronic physical pain. (Healers often seem to be more effective in one area than another.) Engel now accepts only patients who are desperate for relief but have failed to find it through any other therapy.

Here is one of his cases, reported by Mark Jonathan Harris:

Estella's pain is so intense that she has been driven to a suicide attempt. A year ago, she was an active nurse on a busy hospital ward, but a surgeon operated on her herniated disc, irreparably damaging her femoral and sciatic nerves. She has learned to accept the resulting paralysis of her limbs, but not the constant, unremitting pain. Now she has come to the tall physician with the Viennese accent.

"Are you following what your other doctors say?" he asks, lifting Estella gently out of the wheelchair and placing her on the naugahyde couch.

"My other doctors don't hold out any hope," she answers. "So far, you're the only one I've found."

"Well, let's try a few 'magic passes,'" says the doctor.

He closes his eyes, and begins to pass his left hand slowly over the small of her back, about two inches above her body, searching for a cold sensation in his palms and fingers, "like moving your hand half an inch over an ice cube," that indicates the location of the pain.

"This is where it hurts, isn't it?" feeling a chill in his fingertips, though his hand still does not touch her body.

"Oh yes, I feel your hand," she says, as a wave of heat suffuses her lower back. She closes her eyes in relief. "It's so good," she begins moaning softly.

The doctor closes his eyes again, and slowly moves his hand over her back, concentrating intently as he attempts to transmit energy toward the pain. He feels the energy leaving his hand, as Estella's moans grow louder. He continues to direct the "force" until he no longer feels the cold sensation in his fingertips.

"How does it feel now?" he asks, withdrawing his hand and shaking it to restore his own circulation.

"Better, much better," she murmurs gratefully. "It's like a sweet hurt. You have to go through pain to understand it."

The doctor glances at the patient with an embarrassed shrug. "I have no idea how it works," he says. "This is as far out as you can get and I'm skeptical as hell, but for some patients it seems to be effective."

As for statistics—again, not an outsider's but his own—in 1978, Engel's research showed that in 15 percent of the cases, the healing was complete, and in 15 percent of the cases there were no effects at all. "The one thing I can't explain," Dr. Engel admits, "is how I can tell people where they hurt, but 80 to 90 percent of the time, I can."

Dr. Valerie Hunt herself has been healed and now is devoted to research of what she has experienced personally. In 1976, hospitalized with an acute but mysterious viral infection, she called on Rosalyn Bruyere, a healer in Glendale, who works by observing "visual manifestations of a person's energy field." Bruyere arrived at the hospital at one o'clock in the morning, and immediately became alarmed at the state of Hunt's "aura." (The controversial "aura"—see Chapter 11—is an emanation that, many believe, surrounds human beings: a filmy envelope of light with one or more colors. Imperceptible to physical sight, it can only be seen clairvoyantly.) Hunt recalls:

> She worked for about two hours with me. She was changing the field of the virus, which, once it gets started, tends to perpetuate itself and increase. It was intensely painful, but when she left, my "aural" field was back. By the next morning, my internists and physicians noted tremendous changes in me all over—blood pressure, temperature, and heartbeat.

On her recovery, Dr. Hunt knew she must recall the psychic abilities she had had as a child but had repressed as a scientist; she became a psychic healer herself.

Hunt may be the first scientist to have recorded the energies of the aura electronically. Using sophisticated electromyographic equipment during a study of Rolfing techniques (a painful type of deep massage), she recorded small amounts of very high frequency energy from the "chakras" (energy centers of the body described in Eastern philosophies). This she compared with psychic Bruyere's reading of the aura. "In two hundred hours of recording," Hunt reports, "there was direct correlation between what happened to the energy fields and what Rosalyn saw. When she reported that the energy entered the feet and ran up the knee and went into the heart chakra, that's what happened in the data. There is a direct correlation between the color Rosalyn sees, where it's located, and the frequency of the energy which comes off the body." The results were the same with another aura reader.

Hunt has recorded both healers and non-healers, and finds that healers radiate a higher frequency and have more coherent energy fields. She now wants to match the particular frequencies of certain illnesses with the frequencies of specific healers, to see if that is why some healers can cure some diseases, but not others.

Checking the Process

In addition to testing the healer and the healed, others are investigating the process itself. Exactly what happens when healing takes place? Bits of answers are evolving. Working with Estabany and other healers, M. Justa Smith discovered that human thought can generate a force that heals, a force that is "marvelously selective in its effect on body processes." For example, her research in Buffalo showed that a healer could increase the activity of trypsin, an enzyme produced by the pancreas to assist in the digestion of protein.

At New York University, Dolores Krieger, working with hemoglobin, the component of the blood that transports oxygen, found that subjects in test groups who received a healer's "laying on of hands" registered an increase in hemoglobin; control groups with no such treatment did not.

Graham and Anita Watkins in North Carolina learned that mice, placed in a location where healing had previously taken place, revived faster than those which were placed somewhere for the first time. There seemed to be a lingering effect, similar to the "remanence" we have seen in dowsing.

Is there something that "comes from" the healer, that can be identified and measured? To check this, Grad had healers and others hold bottles of weak saline solution, with which he watered seeds and plants. No matter how he designed the experiment, water "treated" by healers always produced measurably better results. Something seemed to "go" from healers to subjects, even non-human subjects, to produce these good effects.

Douglas Dean, plethysmograph technician with the "executive ESP" team above, asked Grad to send him six bottles of saline solution, some handled by a healer, and some not. Measuring the difference between the two samples, he confirmed Grad's work and thesis. The differences were still present when he measured the contents of the bottles three years later. In another experiment, Grad gave Dean four bottles of distilled water. Dean was not told which bottles had been "treated" by healers (one had been held by Olga Worrall). A chemistry laboratory determined that those held by the healers contained less hydrogen-oxygen bonding than the others. Said Dean, "It was as if the healers had heated the water up and broken some of the hydrogen bonds." The four bottles were subsequently sent to the University of Delaware for a totally different measurement. Again, two of the bottles showed a difference—a definite "heat of dilution" effect; that is, less bonding than the two "untreated" bottles displayed.

If something does come from another person, Grad asks, what about "vibes?" Are there good ones and bad ones, or is this just a faddish notion? As a test, he took two identical bottles of water. He had a normally happy man hold one for thirty minutes, and a hospitalized depressed patient hold the other for the same length of time. Plants watered from the bottle held by the normal person grew and thrived; those exposed to the water from the other one languished.

The implications of this finding are mind-boggling. Who's handling *your* food? Who's touching *your* belongings? And who's in a position, even unknowingly, to send "bad vibes" your way? Think of prisons and hospitals. Think of restaurants. Think of your own home and kitchen and the energies therein. Could this be one key, at least, to the catalog of mysterious human ailments?

In any case, in experiment after experiment, no matter how he cuts the pie, Grad's results are always the same: Whenever a healer is a factor, direct or indirect, there are always measurable results.

To attribute the healing to some kind of "energy," as Grad does, is a theory many parapsychologists do not buy. Psychiatrist

Jan Ehrenwald, for example, says "More naive practitioners pin their hope on the operation of assorted vibrations, electro-magnetic waves, radiations, or ethereal fluids transmitted from the healer to the healee."

Nonetheless, Grad does see the phenomenon in terms of energy. He told me:

> My central focus "is energy—life energy—what it is, where it is, where it moves, how it works. I think my overriding interest grows out of my own personal perceptions. Long before I went to school I felt "energy" all around me—everywhere—in the air, in the ground. I had such experiences almost daily as a child. Now, in the course of my studies, I have come to recognize two kinds of energy: positive and negative. I've had confirmatory evidence of this.
>
> It shakes up your whole view of the universe, that there's energy moving through everything: wood, paper, glass, walls. All the man does is hold a bottle of water! All the plants and animals do is drink it!
>
> What's more, it's informational. The energy *itself* is an information-bearer, self-regulating, programmed. Where healing calls for the slowing down of cell growth, as in my goiter experiments, thyroid development is inhibited. Where healing requires speeding up, as in the wounded mice tests, the process is accelerated. Slow down, or speed up for healing—the same agent does both! The *energy itself somehow knows!*

Psychologist and researcher Lawrence LeShan's theoretical explanations of healing are unconventional, but his credibility and results warrant serious consideration. If he could teach *himself* to heal, he reasoned, he'd know there was something to it. If he could teach *others* to heal, it would establish healing as a dependable phenomenon, and would hopefully provide some answers as to how it worked.

He had spent fifteen years full time on a project in psychosomatic medicine. Screening the literature, and eliminating 95 percent of the cases and claims, he assembled a list of "serious psychic healers" who seemed most authentic and successful. Among them: Olga and Ambrose Worrall, Harry Edwards, Rebecca Beard, and Agnes Sanford, Edgar Jackson, Stewart Grayson, and Kathryn Kuhlman. Further study suggested two types of healing: the first, where the healer goes into an altered state of consciousness, in which he views himself and the healee as one entity, "tuning in to become one with the patient." In this, it is essential that there be a deeply intense caring and viewing of the healee and oneself as one, as being united in a universe, in the "Clairvoyant Reality" in which such a unity is possible. Though these healers used different techniques to attain this altered consciousness, there always came a moment of such complete "knowing" that nothing else existed. In some way, this sense was transmitted to the patient. "I could use the word 'telepathy,'" LeShan notes, "or else could point out that, for a moment, the healer's assumptions about how-the-world-works were true and valid. . . . Knowing this at some deep level of personality, the healee was then in a different existential position . . . the healee knew it too."

In this first type of healing the healee's self-repair and self-recuperative systems appear to begin operating at a level closer than usual to their potential. Thus, the healer was not "doing something" to the healee, but permitting something new to happen. As others have observed, and the Grad experiments with mice also demonstrate, the effect of the treatment seems to be a rapid acceleration of the *normal* healing process.

The second type of healing, quite different from the first, LeShan found, was a turning-on of energy, which flowed from the healer to a troubled area. The energy is sensed by the patient as a change in temperature, usually heat, sometimes as a buzzing or tingling, occasionally as a cool sensation. In the first type of process, the healer unites with the healee; in the second, he tries to cure him.

Attempting the first approach, LeShan experimented and practiced for a year and a half, until he could enter the state he calls "the Clairvoyant Reality." Though he was not always successful, he did get some good results: positive biological changes in the healee's body, positive psychological results, and, sometimes, telepathic exchanges between the patient and himself. Occasionally he could feel the palms of his hands begin to tingle, and the urge came to do the second type of healing—that is, *willing* a change. His successes were frequent enough and impressive enough to persuade him to continue his research.

By September 1970, LeShan felt sure enough of his procedures to hold a training seminar for others. By the 1971 seminar, he recalls, all the students became quite proficient at entering the altered state of consciousness and, continuing to practice it after the seminar, became "an amazingly strong healing circle." He concluded that it would be possible for most people who followed such training and procedures to become fairly effective at psychic healing, and to improve the ability with practice. He has since perfected his methods, and trained many dozens.

Psychic Medical Kit

Applications of Psi in the medical field are varied. How varied can be seen in the following examples:

DIAGNOSIS. The psychic diagnostician of all time must have been the "sleeping prophet" of Hopkinsville, Kentucky, Edgar Cayce, whose many thousands of diagnostic feats have never been matched. Cayce could diagnose, from a distance, every known and unknown kind of ailment, for people he had never seen and did not know. So voluminous and remarkable is the record of his "readings" that a foundation was established, in 1931, to preserve, organize and study his work: the Association for Research and Enlightenment, at Virginia Beach, Virginia. One of the inexplicable features of the performances of Cayce—and Arigó as well—was that they were simple and unlettered men, yet they could convey technical and medically sound information, clearly intelligible to trained modern practitioners.

Nor were their reports general and vague, so as to leave room for interpretation. Rather, they were crisp, clear, and unequivocal. A man came to see Arigó, in Brazil, saying he thought he had leprosy. At once, Arigó shot back, "No, you don't have leprosy. You have syphilis, and you shouldn't lie to me!" A medical research team, present at that moment to check Arigó's procedures, found that he was correct. When another patient waiting in the line stepped up, Arigó told the team to check his blood pressure, which he said was 23/17 centimeters. When they compared it with the blood pressure cup, Arigó was right on the button.

PRESCRIPTION. Again, both Arigó and Cayce were masters in prescriptive medication. Both habitually prescribed remedies and medicines that were not in current use. For stomach ulcers, for example, Arigó startled everyone by prescribing for *other* parts of the body, such as the liver, nervous system, and even parasites, which had apparently caused the stomach complaint. Cayce's medications are still being studied by specialists today. His castor oil packs, to pick a homely example, applied externally for a wide range of medical conditions, were never accepted by orthodox medicine. Yet such simple treatments are being adopted today by some doctors and clinics who recognize their efficacy.

ANESTHESIA. One of the most frequently mentioned characteristics of psychic healing is the absence of anesthesia, made unnecessary because of the absence of pain. As Henry (Andrija) Puharich, a doctor who made something of a specialty of investigating psychic surgery, observes, "We have solid evidence that a healer like Arigó could place a sharp steel knife into the eye of a wide-awake, unanesthetized patient and perform delicate eye operations without causing pain. I personally have witnessed hundreds of such operations, where Arigó used a knife, scissors and other instruments to cut into the flesh, and remove tumors or perform other procedures. I have never seen a patient complain of the slightest bit of pain under these circumstances." Puharich adds, "I personally underwent an operation by Arigó that was painless, and no other anesthetic agent or method was used."

BACTERIOSTASIS, or prevention of bacterial growth, must be common to psychic healers, since few of them bother with disinfectant. To quote Dr. Puharich again, "I have never seen a healer doing surgery who observes the rules of antisepsis and sterilization. They all work under what may be called 'dirty' conditions. In spite of this, I have never seen a case of post-operative infection." John G. Fuller's biography of the Brazilian healer *(Arigó: Surgeon of the Rusty Knife)* backs up this view.

PSYCHIC SURGERY. Few aspects of the healing repertoire are more controversial than psychic surgery, which has flourished especially in such places as Mexico, the Philippines, and Brazil. The United States got into the dispute when a stream of ailing Americans began to flow to the Philippines for treatment. A stop was put to the exodus as reputable observers began to return from the Philippines to declare that the surgery they had witnessed was a fraud. Other equally respectable witnesses couldn't explain how such operations took place, but tended to feel that at least some of the practitioners were authentic.

A British researcher, who had accompanied a Japanese parapsychologist to the Philippines, exclaimed to me on returning, "What does it *matter* if the parts 'removed' in the surgery are actually chicken parts, if the person operated on gets *well?* These procedures were designed for a simple people with a very different outlook and culture base. The authenticity of the *procedures* doesn't concern them. What they care about is whether it *works.* "

A quite different view is expressed by Gabriel Cousens, a physician, who witnessed an operation performed by the noted psychic healer and surgeon Doña Pachita, in Mexico City, July 5, 1974. Cousens saw her replace a vertebra in one patient and remove cancerous tissue from the bladder of another:

> There was no question in my mind that she was opening the skin. There was no question in my mind that I was smelling blood. I could see the wound on the person's back; my eyes were about three feet from where the operation was taking place. I could see the opening in the abdomen of the second lady, and I could see Pachita's hands going into the bladder area, into the abdominal cavity. There is no question in my mind that things were taken out through these incisions, and things put back in. I had no doubts that I had seen authentic "psychic surgery."
>
> I didn't understand the use of the knife, except that it was very gross and bloody. Yet the pain was minimal.
>
> I examined the woman from Texas, and found there was a scar, and found that it "healed" more rapidly than any scar I had ever seen immediately after "surgery." There were no stitches. It looked reddish, but not particularly inflamed, and as if it were, perhaps, a month old.

MANUAL HEALING. It is interesting to note that many psychics known for other Psi abilities are able to do healing as well. Among those we have mentioned in other connections are Harold Sherman, Alex Tanous, and Bob Ater. It is interesting, also, to see how much variety is represented in terms of techniques. Some use color; some, music or sound; some, massage. A great many (*e.g.,* the Worralls and Kuhlman) do their healing in an explicitly religious context, calling on God, Jesus, or the power of prayer.

The American Indian healer Rolling Thunder, a Shoshone medicine man, explained to parapsychologists studying him, "It's not me doing the doctoring. It's the Great Spirit working through me." He always exhorts "The Great Spirit, who is the life that is in all things: Creator of all things, I ask that this prayer be heard and carried on the wind."

Others, quite as explicitly, avoid the religious context. "I don't work like any other healer," says Charles Cassidy of Los Angeles. "If you have any preconceived notions, forget 'em. I don't sing songs. I don't chant. I don't light candles or burn incense—let the others do that! I don't say prayers, either. I just act as a channel for the power that comes through me."

Psi reporter David St. Clair describes how Cassidy works:

> He lowers his head and places the thumb and forefinger of his left hand on his closed eyes. For two full minutes, this gray-haired, green-eyed, Archie Bunkerish–looking man communicates with something, somewhere. His presence is so domineering that the patient on the bed wouldn't dare as much as talk during this time. True to his word, there is no music, no candles, and no "stage setting." It's just that one, solitary, unpretentious man.

St. Clair took Alberto, an osteopathic surgeon who "needed an operation," to Cassidy.

> He stretched out on the bed, and after the silence, Cassidy went and sat beside him. He put his left hand on Alberto's abdomen—the only thing he ever touches, even though he knew it was the knee that needed work. Now, I have been in many "psychic" places and seen many "psychic" things, but I was not prepared to see a current of light run down Cassidy's arm and into Alberto's body. I was not prepared to see my friend's body light up, like a white neon tube, and stay that way while I rubbed my eyes and glanced around the room to see if other things were glowing.
>
> Alberto told Cassidy at times during the healing that he felt himself growing taller, that he felt his fingers working on his knee, and that at one point, he felt a screwdriver "screwing something into my knee-cap." That night, his knee was better than it had been for weeks. He never needed the operation.

Each healer has his or her individual technique. In my several visits with Etel DeLoach, I wanted to check out the comment of a fellow healer who said that her hands are "like a bumble bee";

they move so fast you can hardly follow them. DeLoach, whose abilities have been studied by Douglas Dean and Bernard Grad—she now gives extension courses on healing at Johns Hopkins University—gives this summary of her approach:

> There are many ways to heal, and I think that this "energy"—I don't know if that's the right word, but that's all we have right now, unfortunately—can be directed in so many ways. It can be directed by my touching my hand over you. It could be directed to you even by a glance. You could have a wound on your leg, and this has happened many times, I won't touch it, I'll just stare at it. There will be some energy going from my eyes, and I will notice what I call "the healing light." It's like a faint beam of sunlight in an irregular pattern, moving around the wound. As this light moves, somehow in my vision I see the wound closing and healing, and new skin taking over. Usually by the next day, the wound is healed, no matter how bad it was.

Professor of Nursing Dolores Krieger is an ambassador of the philosophy that we can heal one another by "therapeutic touch." Our paths crossed at the First Congress of Nurse Healers—which she helped organize—on one of her swings around the country teaching others, especially nurses, how to heal.

HEALING AT A DISTANCE is more common than many people realize, and is by no means confined to the headliner greats. Claire Balian, in Westport, Connecticut, has told me she prefers distant healing. "It works just as well when you hold someone in your healing circle mentally," Balian explains, "and they don't have to pack up and come to you. My specialty is the elderly, and for them, not having to go anywhere is a boon."

Olga Worrall says that on a number of occasions she has "pulverized" kidney stones, gallstones, and such things, over the phone." It's happened so many times now, she says, she "feels like a gravel factory!" She's been telephoned by doctors in several emergencies, and by concentrating on the stones, has enabled them to cancel the operation.

MENTAL HEALTH. The healing inventory would not be complete without some reference to cures of the mind. Two California women have teamed up in an imaginative way to handle mental health problems. Ann Armstrong, a Sacramento sensitive who has been a research subject for parapsychologists Andrija Puharich and Charles Tart, probes a patient's problems psychologically. In so doing, she is able to pinpoint where and what the difficulty is. Her colleague, Mary Jane Ledyard, a clinical psychologist with training in hypnotherapy and Reichian techniques, then takes over and conducts the necessary treatment. Ledyard also passes on her methods in classes for other health care professionals.

SELF-HEALING is so important, and currently so significant, that we shall devote the entire next section to it.

Self-Healing and Holism: The PK Revolution

In 1964, the distinguished editor Norman Cousins was hospitalized with a serious collagen illness. With limbs incapacitated and jaws almost locked, he learned that he had one chance in five hundred to live. Cousins wasn't ready to die, however; he embarked on an intensive self-directed program one element of which was "to laugh himself back to health." With the help of his doctor, he gobbled reruns of "Candid Camera" every day, while watching his ailment subside. Two weeks later, he left the hospital for some sunshine in Puerto Rico, and the healing which took him back to his desk.

This is more than an inspiring story, or the bestselling book *(Anatomy of an Illness)* that grew out of it. It is a harbinger of new directions in medicine, and hopeful things ahead.

We are in the midst of a revolution, the PK revolution. That isn't the name it goes by, because few people think of healing as a form of PK—psychokinesis, mind over matter—the mind willing the body to get better or worse. A number of journal reports, on the other hand, do support the thesis. Using the powers of the human mind on living matter would appear to be the most widespread and immediately significant application of Psi.

The revolution sweeping the country is known as "holism," the holistic approach, from *holos,* Greek meaning "whole." This "new medicine" involves the discovery that the person is more than a body—namely, "body, mind, and spirit"; if something goes wrong with the body, its owner can do something about it; and what happens in one part of the body influences the rest. "When I'm handed an arm or leg to fix," therapy specialist Elsa Ramsden told me in Philadelphia, "I can't fix it by itself. Wishes, beliefs, attitudes, relationships are all involved."

Rosita Rodriguez, an Austrian sensitive, who studied with the renowned though controversial Tony Agpaoa in the Philippines, says: "Everyone can heal her/himself. It's like in the Hawaiian Kahuna, where the 'lower self' gets the message, and sends it to the parts of the body that need healing. We have to learn to utilize this stuff."

To spell out some key premises of holistic medicine:

1. *The body naturally pushes toward wellness,* positive wellness, not mere absence of disease.

So what's new or different about this? Nothing, except that today's medicine is just the reverse. Its focus is patients and victims, symptoms and disease. Millions for medical research on cancer, emphysema, or heart problems—but how much to study *healthy* human beings and keep them that way?

"The cure is worse than the disease" is more than a saying. *Doctor-prescribed drugs have become a major cause of death.* Adverse drug reaction is the eleventh most deadly killer in the United States today; $4.5 billion is added to the hospital care bill annually because of drugs that misfire, and three hundred thousand patients are admitted yearly to hospitals for this reason alone.

At the 1977 American Medical Association convention in San Francisco, I was surprised to see a scheduled section on "Diseases Contracted in Hospitals." As Norman Cousins concluded, "A hospital is no place for one who is seriously ill!"

2. *You are responsible for your own health, and I for mine.* Lest this sound like a prescription for self-doctoring, it is not. With medical responsibility distributed more effectively, it becomes a partnership. The physician still has his essential and appropriate role. "If both patients and doctors clearly recognized that the physician's proper role is simply to diagnose and treat disease," says clinical research psychologist Kenneth Pelletier, "then the medical profession could again receive the respect and recognition its work deserves."

In short, the "new look" is a team approach: The doctor is on your team, but it *is* your team.

3. *The power of the individual over health and longevity is far greater than we have realized.* Effective techniques are so simple

as to be unbelievable. Studying seven thousand adults, Lester Breslow, Dean of the UCLA School of Public Health, found an astonishing correlation between one's overall wellness and seven old-fashioned personal habits:

- regular meals, no snacking
- breakfast daily
- no smoking
- moderate drinking
- normal weight
- moderate regular exercise
- seven or eight hours' sleep a night.

Bland and simplistic though this little list is, it truly packs a wallop. The health of those who practice seven of these habits is measurably better than that of those who practice only six. Persons with six of the habits are measurably better off than those who observe only five, and so on. Moreover, a thirty-five-year-old man who practices three or fewer of the items on the list can expect to live to age sixty-seven, whereas a man who habitually keeps six or seven of these rules has a life expectancy of seventy-eight!

Similar results were turned up by Dr. Robert Samp, of the University of Wisconsin, who pinpointed these life-giving forces: serenity, optimism, interest in others, interest in the future.

The negative factors, the villain of the piece, trigger illness and disease. Prime offenders are stress and tension. Consensus has it that between 60 and 80 percent of Western diseases are caused partly by stress, which also aggravates any illness. Each civilization has its own kind of pestilence, biologist Rene Dubos once noted, and ours seems to be stress.

"One can become aware of the flow of energy within himself and use it," Jack Schwarz once told me. He can control his body functions much as do the yogis in India. He can thrust an unsterilized knitting needle through his biceps with no pain, bleeding, or subsequent infection, the wound closing when the needle is withdrawn, and healing completely within a day or two.

4. In all of this, *prevention, rather than cure, is the keynote.* A civilization filled as ours is with noise, speed, deadlines, competition, traffic, unemployment, disappearance of resources, and the threat of nuclear warfare is pervaded, as Pelletier notes, with free-floating stress. The key is, apparently, not the stress, but how your mind and emotions respond to it, and so affect your body and its

functions. When it reacts negatively, the resulting afflictions can include hypertension, arteriosclerosis (now the #1 killer in the United States), migraines, respiratory diseases (such as emphysema), arthritis, and cancer, which accounts for one death in six and is now the most feared.

Stress doesn't have to be lethal, as stress authority Hans Selye told me. Indeed, some executives thrive on stress. Send them to the islands for a "rest" and they go berserk. It depends on how you handle it.

PK medicine levels its guns at stress reduction generally. It uses many and varied techniques, from deep relaxation and autogenic (self-generated) therapy, to Taoist thought, yoga, and the broad smorgasbord of meditative techniques, including TM (Transcendental Meditation), "holistic meditation," Zen, and prayer. It leans also on biofeedback, a technique by which one can bring into awareness, and exert some control over, so-called "involuntary" functions such as heartbeat, muscular tension, and so on. As Barbara Brown observes, "If nearly seventy-five percent of illnesses are caused by mental activity, then it would seem eminently more reasonable to use mental processes for their cure." Or, in the words of holistic doctor Irving Oyle, "If you can think yourself sick, you can think yourself well."

The New Medicine

How much of the "new medicine" is genuinely new? Certainly the Taoist and Zen techniques belong to the "Wisdom of the Ages." The ancient Chinese had an aphorism: "The superior physician treats the patient before the illness is manifested; it is only the inferior physician who treats the illness he is unable to prevent."

There has been a universal quest through the ages for the essence and meaning of "the healing energy." Says Mary Coddington, who has documented and traced the course of the quest, the Chinese organized their medicine on the energy, not the physical, level. Cultures around the world have recognized the fundamental life-energy in such terms: The Egyptians called it "Ka"; Hindus and yogis, "Prana"; Hawaiians and others, "Mana"; American Indians, "Orenda." The Chinese call it "Ch'i," the Japanese, "Ki." Among its properties: It can heal; it penetrates everything; it has properties similar to other types of energy but is a distinct force unto itself;

it emanates from the human body; it can be stored inside inanimate materials; it can cause things to happen at a distance; it can be used for good or evil.

The controlling establishment in many Western cultures have ignored this "healing energy." It is amusing that scientists in these same cultures are now studying the chakras, or energy centers, of the Hindus, and practices of the American Indians, and that American medicine has begun to apply the Chinese techniques of acupuncture, based on Ch'i.

Preliterate peoples everywhere, moreover, have known that the cause and cure of illness are part and parcel of the whole web of life; of humans relating to humans, as well as to the natural environment. The "horse and buggy doctor" of our forebears took the pulse of the whole family and the web of conditions, not of the patient's heartbeat alone. The most up-to-date medical program is, accordingly, now reintroducing general practice to counteract the materialistic fragmentation and overspecialization which our modern age has developed.

Positive wellness, not mere absence of disease; responsibility for one's own wellbeing; prevention more than cure: How can these principles be translated into actual practice? It has already begun. "Wellness checks" and "wellness clinics" now operate in a number of places. John Travis, in his center in Marin County, California, administers a "wellness inventory."

There is an explosion of holistic centers, organizations, conferences, courses, and programs across the country. Thus, the new/ old PK medicine, it would seem, has something for everyone. For *patients,* it promises self-realization and a major piece of the control. "The patient is the treatment" declares Barbara Brown; "the aim is to cease being patient." It takes *doctors* off the hook, and relieves the unrealistic expectations that generate disappointment, disillusion, and malpractice suits. For other *professionals* in the healing field, it shifts the emphasis from pill-pushing, bandaging, and tranquilizing, to wellness, prevention, and healing.

Up to now, the "miracles" have been once-in-a-lifetime, headline events in human history, shock-moments in the Bible. The miracle of our age may turn out to be the discovery of our own innate psychokinetic powers, to heal others, and to heal ourselves.

5

DETECTION:
The Phantom Sleuth

Ever since I set forth on my investigation, I have had an urge to visit The Netherlands. A country with a population only slightly larger than Illinois, it has spawned a disproportionate number of top-flight sensitives, whose abilities have made headlines and history around the world. And, from all I can gather, its people take the whole psychic business in stride.

Holland has also made something of a record academically, in the Psi field. The first laboratory for scientific research of the paranormal was established in Amsterdam by a doctor, Floris Jansen, in 1907. The first academic parapsychology lecturer in the world was appointed in Holland, Dr. P. A. Dietz, at the University of Leyden, in 1932, and a "Special Professorate" in parapsychology was established for Dr. W. H. C. Tenhaeff, in 1947, at the State University of Utrecht. In addition, the first international conference for parapsychologists was held in The Netherlands, in July 1953.

When Tenhaeff became emeritus at Utrecht, it was decided to establish a "Professorate Ordinarius," which in our terms means an official post, appointed and financed by the government. (The choice was Martin Johnson, a scholar from Lapland, who served as my host and guide when I finally made it to Holland.) The founding of this chair amounts not only to open endorsement of the Psi field by The Netherlands, but also to its academic recognition as an accepted department of contemporary science.

Dutch Masters

Perhaps the place to begin is with a trio of Dutch sensitives, each of whom has spectacular gifts: M. B. Dykshoorn, Peter Hurkos, and Gerard Croiset. All of them psychically versatile, they are best known as psychic detectives, who for years have helped police unravel missing-person cases and crimes. Dykshoorn and Hurkos—both of whom I have talked with—now live in the U.S. Like many psychics, all three are from modest, even humble, beginnings, homes with no outward manifestation of special qualities. Hurkos and Croiset dropped out of school at an early age, and Dykshoorn picked up what he could from books and evening school courses.

Marinus B. Dykshoorn has, as he explains, solved people's problems, business and social; made many predictions that proved accurate; found buried treasure; cured physical ills—by "pulling the pain out of them." But his most renowned work is as a psychic sleuth: finding buried bodies, tracking down criminals, and reconstructing, in detail, "insoluble" crimes.

"I was born psychic, but no one knew it, least of all myself," Dykshoorn, known as "Rien," explains.

At first I was not even aware I was different from other people, but I soon found out that I was. Images, impressions, sights, sounds, smells, and even tastes, came flooding into my mind spontaneously, unheralded and uninvited. I did not need to concentrate on another person to know about him, I knew *instinctively*. The psychic impressions flooded up from my subconscious and there was no way I could stop them, or even control the flow.

My earliest memories are, I suspect, psychic memories. By this, I mean that many of the things I recall most vividly from my early childhood did not happen to me, but happened to other people. I became aware of them, and so remember them, through my psychic abilities, which were as strong in me then as they are now. For example, when I was no older than five, I witnessed a suicide, and while my memories of my actual life at that time are quite fuzzy and indistinct, I can recall that now with vivid clarity.

I was standing at the window of my parents' home in the small

Dutch town of Honselersdijk, looking out over the scene of our street. It was winter, and the snow was falling heavily. I could barely make out the houses facing ours. There was nothing to watch but the snow falling.

But, as I watched, I saw a man enter a barn. Inside the barn, I saw him take a length of rope and hang himself from a beam.

But it did not happen, and I had not seen it at all. I had seen the snow falling on the street and nothing else. You could not see fifty yards through that snow. Furthermore, our house was in town. There were no barns to be seen, even on a clear day.

I ran and told my father what I had seen, but his reaction was to become angry. I was "imagining things," he said, and my imagination must have struck him as diabolic. A daydreaming five-year-old ought to have been conjuring up more pleasant images.

I was punished because, to be truthful, this was not the first outlandish story I had recounted to my parents out of my "imagination," and the punishment only added to my confusion.

But the worst shock came later, for both my father and myself. No one had hanged himself that day in our district, and no one had done so in the recent past. It was two weeks *later* that it happened, at a farm several miles from our home. A man hanged himself in his barn from a beam, exactly as I had described it to my father, and it was the same man I had seen in my "dream."

Not only is this a classic Psi account, with its puzzling contradictions, but it is typical also of the response to a child, on the part of friends and family, when psychic characteristics begin to emerge: shock, anger, even punishment.

The ability to find things, the insight into the lives of relatives and neighbors, knowing what was going to happen—these have always brought Rien trouble. "If I found something in the house, it was always automatically assumed that I had hidden it, or that I was responsible for its having been lost in the first place. Or, if I found a birthday or Christmas gift for myself, it was assumed I had carried out a systematic search for it, and so I was punished for it again."

Not until many years later, when Rien began to be of help to the police and others, was his "gift" (as he and many other sensitives call it) anything more than a nuisance.

His first criminal case involved royalty. He reconstructed the assassination of Willem the Silent (first Prince of Orange, and founder of the Royal Dutch dynasty, no less), a murder that had taken place in 1584, over three and a half centuries before. The Director of the Prinsenhof Museum in Delft wanted to know whether Dykshoorn could fill in any of the details of the assassination, or of the particular people involved. He tested Dykshoorn first with information he already had. "Of course, I was even more curious than he was," Rien recalls, "because I wanted to know whether I could do it."

Any Dutch schoolboy knows that Willem lived in the Prinsenhof when it was a royal palace. He was assassinated there by one Balthasar Gérard, under instructions from Philip II of Spain. Angry crowds burst into the palace, dragged Gérard into the open square, and roped each of his limbs to a different horse; he was "drawn and quartered."

Dykshoorn recalls:

> We went into the chamber where the killing was known to have taken place. I concentrated on the action, and immediately I knew what had happened. Willem had been shot once in the throat, and another shot had missed. Both bullets lodged in the stone wall.
>
> On the wall of the chamber was a small glass-fronted case, protecting two neat holes from the potentially damaging fingers of sightseers. "These holes were originally much lower down."
>
> "If you are a trickster," the Director replied, "you have certainly done your homework. How else has the room changed?"
>
> "The floor was much lower. This is not the original floor. The level we are on would have been about chest-high in those days."
>
> "Excellent!" the Director exclaimed. "You're absolutely right!"
>
> The psychic continued his concentration. "Gérard really did do it. Philip had promised him instant elevation to the Spanish nobility if he succeeded.
>
> "Gérard gained an appointment with Willem to request permission to leave the country for Spain. Without such a permit, he could not have escaped to collect his reward, so he waited until Willem had signed the document before firing the shots."

Rien went to the wall.

> "There was a doorway here, lower down. Gérard escaped through it and hid under a dung heap outside. When the guards found him, they brought him back inside and walled him up in another chamber.

They hoped to preserve him from the mob, at least until he could be tried and made to confess. But some of the crowd noticed the new brickwork. They tore down the wall and took him."

The Director paid Dykshoorn one hundred guilders on the spot "for clairvoyant services rendered."

Solving a robbery case in Germany by telephone from Holland established Dykshoorn's international reputation. He was besieged by journalists, radio stations, magazines, and TV. Headlines called the long-distance clairvoyance feat "telefonvision."

By this time, Rien had developed his own working "instrument" borrowed from dowsing: a wire. Dykshoorn's explanations and procedures are indistinguishable from the accounts of dowsers, including frequent reliance on "map dowsing."

As his reputation spread, clients from all over northern Europe came to him seeking help. Sample assignments:

For a large Dutch shipbuilding concern, he was given a contract to discover which of thousands of steel plates were faulty.

It was a complicated problem, says Rien. "For hours I pored over the blueprints of ships and factories and warehouses, and riveting sites and even storage bays, relying entirely on the reactions of my gift, while the executives took detailed notes. We finally came up with a list of locations at which I believed they would find faulty plates.

"The plates had obviously been rolled from a faulty ingot, and through a coding system each plate had chalked on it the ingot batch from which it had been rolled, and the date it had left the rolling mill. I took a calendar and asked the executives to call off the days, going backward in time. When the reaction came, I told them the date on which the faulty ingot had been rolled."

The report from the ship company stated that they had found faulty plates at each of the locations he had listed, and at no others. The chalked code also showed that the damaged plates had been rolled on exactly the date he had named.

For a West German war graves commission, he was asked to locate the temporary graves in which two German soldiers were buried in World War II, and to identify the bodies.

He dowsed a map of the general locale, then a more detailed map of the area his divining rod indicated. Finally, when the place had been pinpointed, "I concentrated on the scene, and in my mind I saw the place: a cemetery, two unmarked graves. I calculated distances, described landmarks."

"On July 20, 1954, Herr Oeschle wrote to me as follows: 'From your instructions, I have succeeded in finding, in Lommel, the burial places of the two German soldiers who, in September 1944, were drowned and buried as unknowns in the cemetery for fallen German soldiers.' "

Rien is sometimes overwhelmed by the physical sensations that accompany his vision. Before the eyes of observers, he may take on the characteristics of the person he is tracking down, traits which are often uncannily recognizable as distinctive of the criminal or victim. "I shuffled; my right eye twitched. I felt again the familiar sensation of pain that was not my own. The manager was astonished. 'That's *him!*' he cried. 'That's exactly the way he walked: you *are* him!' "

In another case, Rien recalls, "I soon began to choke and splutter, and my throat seemed to fill with water. I knew then the old man had drowned."

When asked to analyze the disappearance of several of the Devil's (Bermuda) Triangle victims, Rien reported:

In each case, my psychic impressions were the same. I felt a tremendous, crushing pressure on my body, as though all the air was being forced or sucked out of my lungs. I could not breathe and I could not move. It was as if I was completely paralyzed by this feeling of enormous pressure.

I saw instruments going crazily awry, needles spinning wildly and uselessly around the dials and gauges. I heard radio static and garbled words, and under the enormous pressure everything seemed to blur into a greenish-white mist. I can't describe this; it may have been a hallucination brought on by the tremendous pressure on my brain and lungs.

In each case I had the impression that the sea itself opened up into a huge crevasse or trough, as though suddenly ripped open by some incredibly powerful elemental force, and that each vessel or plane was sucked down into the sea, which closed over it.

This, I believe, is the explanation: in two large oceanbound areas of the world—the Devil's Triangle and another area east of Japan, the "Devil's Sea"—tremendously powerful magnetic fields are created at various times of the year, usually between December and March, by the earth's own corrections to what we call "True North."

These magnetic fields are created by the earth itself, and whenever an airplane or ship enters one of these fields at that time, it is acted upon by the magnetism. Its metal parts, which are subject to magnetism, are drawn toward the magnetic center of the earth. The reason there has been no wreckage is that this magnetic force is incredibly powerful—more powerful than anything we can imagine—and everything is drawn deeply into the ocean bed.

This is what I have learned from my psychic impressions of the case. I don't know that it can ever be proved, but I believe it. For what it's worth, one of the Grumman pilots radioed in his last moments, "We seem to be entering white water," and in 1927, before vanishing, a Japanese freighter radioed "Help! Come quick! Like a dagger in the water . . ."

"Of one thing I became certain," Dykshoorn concludes, "each of the people on whom I concentrated died as a result of the crushing pressure."

Another Dutch sensitive, who also gravitated to the United States, is Peter van der Hurk, known in America as *Peter Hurkos,* psychic to Hollywood stars. While Dykshoorn takes pains to state that he was "born psychic," Hurkos' talents did not blossom until he was grown. Their appearance, moreover, was something of a trauma, brought on by the shock of an accident.

An apprentice house painter in The Hague, he fell four stories from a ladder, on July 10, 1941, suffering a serious brain injury, and was not expected to live. For four days he lay in a deep coma in a hospital, and when he came to, found himself totally transformed. He had amnesia, for one thing; but for another, he was now a full-fledged psychic: he could "see" inside people and things, and knew the past, present and future. Moreover, he could now paint at an easel and play the piano and organ, though he had never had such skills before. Suddenly, he was also an expert at psychometry: by merely touching an object, he could tell where it had come from and whose it had been.

He became a world-famous crime-busting detective, and in his police work he was summoned to help with such cases as The Boston Strangler and the Sharon Tate Murders. In this latter case, he was listened to politely, and then dismissed. After the murder gang was finally uncovered, his biographer, Norma Lee Browning, records,

I re-read my own notes with disbelief. I had forgotten how accurate Peter had been. On the very first page of my notebook are scribbled Hurkos' words: "small. little man with beard. Charlie, and another skinny person Charlie, tall Charlie. I keep seeing 'Charlie,' Charlie more than any other." Charles Manson was one of the Charlies, of course, the other was Charles "Tex" Watson, the skinny, six foot one. Other names kept recurring, too: David, Billy, Sally, all of whom figured in the crime. "The leader of the gang is small, thinks he is Jesus Christ and has been in trouble with the police already." (Manson had spent half his life in institutions). ". . . very sadistic, crazy nut, tough, hard and vulgar."

From the beginning, Hurkos had insisted on several points, all of which turned out to be accurate: that the murders were committed by a gang, a ritualistic cult that included both men and women; that they were involved in sex and narcotics; that the victims were caught unaware, and so on.

A number of people have researched this Dutch psychic, including biofeedback authority Barbara Brown, and physician Andrija Puharich, who found him "as good in the lab as in real life." One who followed Hurkos' fortunes for two-and-a-half years points out that the parallels between him and Edgar Cayce (the man some claim to be "the greatest psychic who ever lived") are eerie indeed. Both had peculiar births and later head injuries; both were largely unlettered, but what they did learn they acquired by sleeping on their books; both on occasion spoke in alien tongues and communicated with plants and flowers in an uncanny way; both looked inside persons and things to see past, present and future; both had an astonishing gift for retrocognition (detailed knowledge of the past). Both of them suffered periodically from headaches, strain, and erratic moods, and both seemed consistently afraid of their special abilities.

Gerard Croiset, the only one of the trio who remained in The Netherlands, though he has visited the U.S. and been tested here, is the best known around the world of these three. He receives letters addressed simply to "Croiset, Europe," and bears such grandiose titles as "The Wizard of Utrecht," "The Radar Brain," and "The Man with the X-Ray Mind." Though he is known on both sides of the Atlantic as a clairvoyant, medium, psychic, mind-reader, psychometrist, telepathist, sensitive, and psychoscopist (a European term for one who "sees"—*scope* as in *telescope*—psychically), his mentor, Professor Tenhaeff, calls him a "paragnost," from the Greek meaning "beyond knowledge." The most gifted of the dozens of paragnosts Tenhaeff has studied since 1926, Croiset has probably helped more people psychically than anyone else, and may well be the world's most-tested clairvoyant.

Until he was discovered, in his late twenties, by parapsychologists and police, his life was a disaster. Born in the town of Laren in 1909, Gerard had little or no home life. His parents were in the theater, his father a prominent actor who continually toured and his mother a wardrobe mistress. When he was eight years of age, this child, who had proved to be a nuisance, was placed in a foster home, where he was extremely unhappy. He lived with six different sets of foster parents, but since none of them understood him, he was constantly in conflict and forever being punished. One cruel foster father disciplined him by chaining his leg to a stake in the floor.

He was a sickly, undernourished child, who suffered from rickets. Frequently ill, he was alone a great deal, and spent most of his childhood in a fantasy world, daydreaming and playing with imaginary friends. Moving around so much, he had almost no schooling, and when he did attend, was an odd, maladjusted pupil.

When his father deserted his mother, she remarried and Gerard went to live with her again; he could not get along with his stepfather, and ran away from home several times.

In early adulthood, he fared no better. The imaginative youth was always bored or restless, unable to endure routines or hold a job for long. In 1934, he married the simple, uneducated daughter of a carpenter, Gerda ter Morsche. A year later their first son was born. His in-laws helped him open his own grocery store. But he ran it more as a charity than as a business: he gave goods away, and went bankrupt. Finally, suffering from severe depression, he had a nervous breakdown.

In the summer of 1935, the Croisets paid a call on Henke de Maar, a watchmaker. Picking up a measuring-stick from a table, Croiset immediately "saw" a stream of events from de Maar's youth. Excitedly, he burst out: "I see an automobile accident . . . a body lying on the road of a grassy place . . ."

De Maar listened, aghast. "Everything you say is true! Do you have such feelings often?"

"Very often," answered Croiset.

"Then you must be clairvoyant!"

"That's how it all began," Croiset recalls. "Other people heard about me and brought their troubles to me."

Of interest to us in this account is how every chapter in Croiset's unhappy youth seemed to color his later Psi performance. His conversations with imaginary playmates and daydreaming evolved into telepathic communication and prediction. Uncongenial though his farm chores were, many of his images still revolve around haystacks, dungheaps, fields, and trees. The painful chaining of his leg was translated into an interest in people with foot troubles. He nearly drowned as a child in one of Holland's ubiquitous canals, which seems to have sensitized him to children. One of his specialties is looking for missing children, who may have tumbled into canals.

The most famous experiment involving Gerard Croiset is the renowned "chair test," a major contribution to modern parapsychological research. This experiment in predicting the future has been repeated perhaps several hundred times by scientists in a number of countries, and under the most exacting safeguards.

A chair is selected haphazardly from the seating plan for a future meeting at which seats are not to be reserved; say, the third seat from the left in the fifth row. The meeting is often held in a different city, Croiset not being told where it will be. The seat number is chosen in one of several ways: by lot, by the experiment director or a disinterested party; sometimes by a Geiger-Müller counter. Whatever the method, Gerard predicts, from one hour to twenty-six days before the meeting—it is immaterial whether this time period is long or short—who will sit in the chosen chair.

Croiset's tape-recorded impressions of the person, always precise and detailed, are transcribed and placed in a sealed envelope, or locked in a safe, and not opened until the meeting. After the audience has been seated, they are then checked, point by point, through carefully controlled questioning of the person in the chair. His predictions have proved so accurate that they cannot be explained as accident or coincidence.

One historic chair test took place in Verona, Italy, in March of 1956, in the boardroom of the Museum of Natural History. Professor Anton Neuhäusler, a German parapsychologist, picked the chair for the test at random. It was assured that Croiset could not pick up information telepathically from the professor, since the participants had not yet been invited. Immediately Croiset gave his impressions, which were written down in German and put into a sealed envelope. The Verona chair test was supervised by a Dr. de Boni and a Professor Zorzi, who opened the envelope at the beginning of the test the next day. Until then, its contents were known to no one except Croiset.

Here are some of the correspondences between the impressions Croiset had given the day before, and the person who sat in the selected chair. "A girl will come and sit on the chair. She has dark hair and wears a dark dress and a light-colored blouse." Rita Venturi, who sat on the chair, had dark hair and wore a dark blue coat. Under her coat she wore a white blouse with light blue stripes. "In the immediate surroundings of her house is a lady's hairdresser salon." Correct. "She lives on the fourth floor." Incorrect: Croiset confused the building's first and second floors. "She has beautiful handwriting." Correct. "She loves animals and has a picture of a squirrel. I do not know if she made this drawing herself, or recently looked at a drawing like it, which made a deep impression on her." Correct: Rita admitted that she loved animals. One of her friends had recently given her a picture of a squirrel and she was very happy with the present. "When she walks home, she sees at the end of her street a round building, with arches." Correct: At the end of Rita's street was a small square having a building with many arches, the only building in the neighborhood like it.

"Has she at home a Russian samovar, or Turkish pipes with loops twisted into one another?" Rita, and her mother in the audience, both remembered that she had recently seen such a pipe set at a friend's home, and that they had admired it. "She wears black pumps; the upper leather is slightly damaged, with a crack in it." Dr. de Boni showed everyone that Rita wore black pumps. She denied the crack, but at the end of the evening admitted to Dr. de Boni that there were cracks in the leather in the tops of both her shoes, and showed these to him. She had not admitted this in public because she was embarrassed at wearing such old shoes to the meeting.

"Did she yesterday experience some emotion because of a cigarette box? Did she let it fall to the floor?" The day before, she had bought a cigarette case as a present for a friend. When she had unwrapped it at home, the case fell to the floor and she feared it had been damaged. "Who is the old gentleman with the moustache? Has she a portrait of him in her room?" In Rita's room was a picture of her grandfather, an old gentleman with a large moustache. "Did it recently happen to her that a dead animal from a butcher shop fell in front of her feet?" A few days before, she had been walking past a poultry store; a dead chicken hanging from the rack fell to the ground in front of her.

I labor these details intentionally. Many of those who are critical of psychic experiences and predictions say that they are so unspecific and vague that they could apply to anyone. These details, by contrast, are so many and so explicit that it would be difficult to confuse this girl with anyone else.

Though Croiset "earns his living" at healing—about a dollar for a few minutes' treatment—for the last twenty-five years he has been best known as a detective. "Never before," says his biographer, Jack Harrison Pollack, "have there been so many psychic investigations for police purposes officially undertaken." Police authorities and even judges in Holland have openly called on Croiset for decades.

For such cases he makes no charge whatsoever, but he has exacting scruples as to whom he will help. He will not waste his energies in finding a diamond necklace for a millionaire and is generally cool toward robberies, but will donate endless attention to solving a cruel murder, or to finding a lost child.

In February 1961, a four-year-old American girl disappeared, blonde Edith "Googie" Kiecorius. More than 350 New York City police took part in the search; one of the widest in New York history, it extended as far as Chicago. Finally, Croiset was approached by R. J. Vogels, the vice-president of KLM, the Dutch airline, who offered to fly him to New York immediately.

The child-loving Dutch sensitive replied,

Of course I will help but I will not fly to New York. I have never been there, and if I went, I would choke on all the impressions. If you give me a map, I will stay here and work quietly on the case. I can already tell you it is not in the center of the city. If you are standing with your back to the Statue of Liberty, it ought to be on the left-hand side of New York City. There the child must be. I see a tall building, but that does not mean a thing: there are many tall buildings in New York. I see an orange rectangular advertisement sign, then a garage, rolling shutters, then a square and a park. I see a railroad nearby and rails above the street level. Beyond it, some rubbish, and after that, some water. There is a river quite near. The man who took the child is small. He has a rather sharp face. He wears something gray. I see a gray house; that is where the child is, or has been.

Startled by the specific details, Vogels asked, "Is the child alive?" "No, I am afraid she is dead."

After many calls back and forth, Croiset furnished further information:

What a mass of houses! It is enough to drive you crazy. Now, I have a warm point. I see a woman sitting in front of a window. Two houses further, there is a laundry, and also a shop where clothes are pressed. I see that house again, I think it has five floors. The man I described yesterday is between fifty-four and fifty-eight years of age. He has a small, sharp, tawny face. The child must be in a gray house. On the second floor, I get a strong emotion. In this room I see the child with the man.

As police worked with these details, the ravished body of the four-year-old was found, on the second floor of a dingy building just around the corner from her uncle's house.

A man named Fred Thompson, who had rented the eight-dollar-a-week furnished room, was arrested, and confessed to killing the child. He wore a rumpled gray sports jacket, with gray checked sleeves and collar, a bleached shirt with gray and white checks. He was fifty-nine years old, was small, sharp-nosed, and had a tawny complexion. Thompson's second-floor room, where Croiset had experienced his "strong reaction," had dirty white venetian blinds pulled down over the windows, which may have been the "rolling shutters." Other details also proved correct. Note: Not a line about Croiset's secret role in the case was printed in any American newspaper, though it appeared in the Dutch press routinely.

Examples such as this could be repeated many times over. As in this one, Croiset frequently works at a distance, often solving cases on the telephone. One day, for example, he received a phone call from someone in a town some miles away, with only this information: "A man has disappeared. Can you help me find him?"

Croiset said that the missing man had committed suicide by jumping into a canal from a bridge. He described the locale with such accuracy that police were able to find his body that afternoon. Authorities would probably have turned to Croiset in any case, for it turned out that the suicide had murdered his family that morning.

Psi as a Tool

As can be seen from these accounts, one of the major uses of Psi is as a detection tool. Before proceeding further, however, a word of caution is in order. Astounding as the record of some of these accomplishments may be, no clairvoyant is infallible. The insights of Psi detectives have sometimes led authorities down the wrong trail, and even to an innocent suspect. Psychics usually get their messages in pictures, not words, more often dealing with images than with names, numbers, and figures. There may be more than one "yellow house with white shutters and a mail box at the corner," more than one "tall bearded man driving a blue car." Too many tips, particularly erroneous ones, are less than helpful to harassed police.

Since Psi clues are filtered through the misty recesses of the psychic's unconscious, there are subtle associations and connections which he or she may not recognize. Many of Croiset's associations come from his grocery store experience: "Do you like to eat raisins?" he once asked a puzzled client. "No," she replied. "Well, I see that Smyrna raisins played a part in your life." "Oh, I was born in Smyrna," the woman conceded, "but I don't care for raisins." For ex-grocer Croiset, "Smyrna" meant "raisins!"

There may also be a problem with timing. Is the psychic picking up on a past, present, or even a future event? When Scotland Yard flew him to England to investigate the notorious Moors Murders, Croiset described a grim murder in detail. Unfortunately, as it happened, the incidents he described were of a *future* crime, not the one being investigated. Since no one realized his description was precognitive, they did not heed the warning.

Nevertheless, if one proceeds with caution, recognizing the possible hazards, Psi may yet prove to be the most valuable instrument we have for ferreting out needed and hidden information.

Despite widespread resistance and skepticism about Psi as a working tool, it is increasingly called on in the military, government agencies, and commercial enterprises.

Ernesto Montgomery, for example, was employed by the British in World War II as a psychic spy. A clergyman, and former member of the Jamaican constabulary, he used "out of body" techniques—"soul travel" as he called it—to gain political and military information, and to spy on the enemy. Psi spies were, in fact, as his biographer Clifford Linedecker notes, used by both sides in that war; not surprising when one recalls that Stalin habitually consulted soothsayers, Hitler had a psychic division, and Winston Churchill was a fairly well developed psychic himself!

"He Catches Shoplifters by ESP"

As for Psi in the business world, my leads took me on a merry chase. It seems there was a man who had "caught hundreds of shoplifters in eastern Canada, using uncanny psychic powers." It was said that Reginald S. McHugh, employed by Koffler Stores, Ltd., to help with security in their Shoppers Drug Mart chain, could tell who was going to shoplift before he or she took anything. Sometimes, he could tell in advance what a thief would take!

"Is this super-detective for real?" I started out—to assure myself of the man's integrity and effectiveness. A quick check with employers, employees, security, and top brass took care of that right away.

"I'll say he's legitimate!" the owner of the first store where Reg worked, Murray Grossman of Scarborough, Ontario, said at once. "We hired him on speculation, but kept him on his record."

"I would trust him altogether," the head of Wilmark Security Services, Michael Walsh, told me.

The vice-president of the parent company, Bernie Glazier, volunteered: "I've never looked into *how* he does what he does. I only know he delivers."

Even a shoplifter vouched for him! "He's on the level, all right, and I ought to know. I'd been shoplifting for a very long time. Until he came along, I'd never been caught."

When I asked "What is he like?" the same words kept coming back to me: "phenomenal," "uncanny," "almost infallible." The consensus: "He's not just good, he's different."

Then the stories began.

- Once Reg (most of them began with "once Reg") warned the manager of the Eglinton Square Mart that he had "seen" a youth remove two containers of insulin from the refrigerator in the dispensary, put them into the left pocket of his pants, and then disappear into thin air. An hour later, store personnel saw the youth come down the aisle and pocket the insulin exactly as predicted. This time, however, he was apprehended, and upon questioning, disclosed that he had not been near the store earlier that day.

- "I was in a jam," the merchandise manager at the Mart in Willowdale recalled. "We had apprehended a shoplifter who was giving us trouble. He made such a fuss we weren't sure of ourselves. 'If only Reg were working out of our store now,' I said to myself, 'he'd know what to do.' At that moment, Reg appeared. 'I had a feeling I should be here,' he said calmly, and took over from there."

I obtained several confirmations of Reg's talent from a film crew with Mediavision, Inc., who had shot a segment of an international documentary on psychic phenomena.

While mapping strategy with the camera crew in a back room having no windows, they told me, McHugh had jumped up excitedly: "Wait! I feel vibes! Soon a dark woman in a long orange dress will come in and steal a blue box with yellow stripes on it." He ran out to alert the store detective.

Ten minutes later, an East Indian woman, wearing an orange sari, entered the store, went to the counter in front of the dispensary, and picked up a small box, which she slipped into her purse. As she left the premises, the detective apprehended her, and brought her to the back room of the store for interrogation. When asked to empty her purse, she complied, and a blue-and-yellow package of throat lozenges, not yet paid for, tumbled out.

The crew was astonished. "If only our cameras had caught *this!*" exclaimed the startled associate producer, Tony Bond. (When I talked with him, long afterward, he was still upset that he had missed it.)

The next day, disguised as store employees, with their film equipment concealed in shopping carts, the crew shot McHugh in action. Wearing a microphone under his collar, he softly directed them to appropriate spots in the store with cues for positioning themselves. He told them to expect "about seven" incidents that day. While the cameras rolled, he correctly predicted seven shoplifting episodes—several of which were caught in the act, and after each of which he made an apprehension.

"Shoplifting takes place so quickly," Bond explained, "that unless you know who's going to do it, there's no way to film it. It would be an absolute fluke, with all those aisles and displays, if you were to catch someone in the act—and we did that several times!"

Did this add up to Psi? I had to remind myself repeatedly that these were not scientists, but people who told what they saw, or thought they saw. And, certainly, sprinkled in among all the glowing testimonials were cautious comments, even some skeptical and negative ones.

Reg had been, I found, an undercover agent, which might account for at least some of his feats. He is also an expert at public relations, with a flair for the dramatic, even exaggeration, and a highly polished showman's style. The very smoothness which made him so attractive to many—he wined and dined me at the best restaurant in the area when I caught up with him in New Brunswick—turned others off. But my personal conclusion, after interviews with over forty witnesses from Ontario to the Maritimes, is that the man is a genuine sensitive.

As a psychic detective, Reg has worked in three capacities. First, as an in-store investigator in a number of drug marts, where his reputation developed. "Our shrinkage rate was amazing. In his first two years of work, Reg cut store losses from 3½ percent of sales to ½ percent. Good at prevention, too: teenagers would warn one another 'Stay away from Shoppers—you can't get away with anything there.' " (Merchandise manager Jim McWilliams, at the Fairview store.)

Second, with his wife, Kit, as head of their own security firm, Combined Investigation and Security, where they trained their own team. The McHughs always kept their eyes open for psychic abilities in their own personnel. Solid training and experience are essential, they declare, but the psychic dimension is "about five times as effective as conventional methods" and can add significantly to one's success. A rival executive declared: "His people are the best of the lot; the best in the business."

Third, as East Coast Director of Loss Prevention for Koffler Stores, where he now rides herd on sixty-five stores in the Atlantic Provinces and Quebec. "We were having a terrible time with shoplifting in the Atlantic Region, so we sent Reg there to put out the fire," said Murray Byrne, Director of Security for Koffler.

The familiar Reg pattern may now be developing in that location. On the first day of training, Reg told his new investigator for Prince Edward Island, Vera Doyle, "We won't have any apprehensions in this store for several days. When we do, the first shoplifters we'll catch will be three senior citizens."

"And that's just what happened!" Vera reported to me. "After no one at all—just like that!—three people over seventy, and all on the same day!"

Reg's work with in-house theft also caught the executives' attention. As owner Marty Sone of the Weston Road Mart observed,

> Internal theft accounts for 80 percent of our losses. A shoplifter is in the store twenty minutes; an employee, all day every day, and surrounded with opportunities.
>
> We once had an in-house leak we couldn't pin down. It could have been any of ten employees. When I took the problem to the head of Loss Prevention, he told me "Only one person can solve it— Reg McHugh."
>
> Reg was working elsewhere at the time, but agreed to come in and speak individually with the staff. When he got to the third interview, he said, "She's the one!" So much faith did we put in his judgment, that she was fired. We wondered if we'd done the right thing. Then the others began to come forward and tell us, "You got the right one."

Bobby Katz (Westwood Mall in Malton, Ontario) told a similar story: "Reg broke up a ring of salespeople in my store. When we discovered the leak, we had forty on the payroll. He cracked it in two hours. Three of my force had a good thing going, siphoning cosmetics out of the place."

Were the references *too* enthusiastic, the reactions *too* glowing? Could all of these witnesses in scattered boroughs and agencies have somehow been in cahoots? What's more, even if I established the *what,* I hadn't drawn a bead on the *how.* I approached Nancy Sword, former security agent, now Assistant Director of Loss Prevention for Koffler's. "How does Reg do it?" I plunged in at once. "By extra good powers of observation?"

"Pure observation wouldn't make it," she responded at once. "Not for what he does. I know, because I've been the route, and I was one of the better investigators."

"Then how *does* he work?"

"I'll tell you how. He has his feet up on the table in the back room, the light bulb shining on his head. He jumps up. 'Aha! There's one!' He runs into the store and comes back with a shoplifter. It's as simple as that."

"I've worked in the same stores after he did," she went on,

"and he's an awful act to follow. Some of us work all day to get a single apprehension. Tell me you don't believe in ESP, and I'll show you Reg's record!"

The time had come to check with the mystery man himself. This meant a trip to Moncton, New Brunswick, East Coast headquarters for Koffler Stores. We talked nonstop for a weekend: how does he do it; why is he so good?

Skip the trimmings, it comes down to two things: a crackerjack police investigator background, and extra help from "out there"— or "in there," if you prefer.

As a child in Jamaica, Reg was already dreaming about becoming a super-cop. His seafaring father, whose ship had a Canada-to-West Indies run, told him about the Royal Canadian Mounted Police. This was all it took: he knew what he wanted to be.

His route was circuitous. After attending the University of Kingston, he shipped out to Canada, where for nine years he did a bit of everything—jobs in several plants, driving an oil truck, a coal truck, a taxi; working on the railroad; and—best of all—his musical chapter, plying the entertainment circuit even as far as New York with his own band.

On May 1, 1954, the impossible dream came true: Reginald S. McHugh became the first black Mountie! His education and physique qualified him, the Royal Canadian Mounted Police added training and discipline, marksmanship, and karate—but no fanfare, no horse, and no uniform! He was to be an *invisible* Mountie. So secret was his assignment that only the Narcotics Squad knew he was on the force: Undercover Specialist in Narcotics, Secret Code #255.

After five years he surfaced from underground, this time in the uniform of the Montreal Provincial Police. Before long, though, his secret service activities came back to haunt him, as one by one, persons he'd arrested were released from prison, and made threats on his life.

With this, he moved to Toronto, where he met and married Kit. He also launched a new career. Working two or three stores at a time as a plainclothes investigator, he was confirmed in his hunch that his underground training was just what was called for.

Then, "things began to happen." As Kit explained, when I talked with her in Montreal, it was a harrowing experience. "Reg began to be nauseated at work; so often, in fact, that we wondered whether he'd be able to carry on. Then, suddenly, we put two and two together: the only times he got sick were when he came near a shoplifter! And the closer he got, the stronger his vibes!"

"But what is it *like?*" I kept asking Reg. "How does it feel?"

It's hard to explain. I can just *feel* someone stealing. I'd be at my office and bug Kit about going, say, up to Fairview Mall. She'd say, "What are you going up there for? You've no reason!" She'd go with me, though, to see what was up. The moment we'd hit the Mall I'd say, "There's the woman I am going to apprehend." I'd tell Kit, "Feel here," and she'd feel my heart racing. This is the way it is when I get "vibrations."

One morning, I got vibes of a girl stealing in the Jane/Finch store, but I didn't go after her. "I won't worry," I told myself, "I know she'll be back again this afternoon," and she was.

I'll be in one end of a store, and see someone in the aisle with something in their hand. When I shake the fuzz away, there's no one in the aisle, so I sort of understand that this is something that is *going* to happen.

When I'm looking at a shelf of goods and an item suddenly—if temporarily—"disappears," I know that it's going to be stolen. Once in a while I'll pass my hand over a clerk's daily record sheet and get vibes. I say "This is the one we're going to fire." That happened three or four times last year.

One day, I saw a woman take something but I couldn't quite see what it was, so I concentrated on the back of her head, like an eye, and thought, "Why don't you turn around and show me what you have?" The woman turned around, took what she had in her purse, casually held it up, and put it back.

When she left the store, I stopped her and asked why she had done that "crazy thing." "If I told you," she said, "you'd really think I'm crazy."

I said, "If I told you why I want to know, you'd think *I'm* crazy."

Then she said, "I heard an inner voice say, 'Turn around' and 'show me.' "

My report on Reg McHugh appeared in an article called "The Case of the Psychic Detective." From the editing, cuts, and my conversations with the person they assigned to check out the piece, it was clear to me that the magazine's researcher remained skeptical to the end. Some of my solid witnesses had second thoughts about being quoted.

Imagine my surprise, then, when the double-checking turned up *three* more detectives who use ESP to catch shoplifters, two of them in the same Koffler organization!

The first, Ron Carpenter, had on a smaller scale followed Reg's own psychic pattern: nausea at work, plans to see a doctor, concerns for his career. "In desperation, I talked it over with Reg. He said 'A very good sign' and encouraged me to go with my inner feelings. Since then, I have done exactly that. The other day I was turning a shoplifter over to the police when I picked up a strong message, which I scrawled on a note to the officer at the desk: 'DOPE IN BOOTS.' "

Police did a quick search and Ron was right. There *was* dope: hashish and marijuana in his slip-on (no laces) Wellingtons.

The other sleuth in the outfit was a woman, Irmgard Schmidt, now making the same sort of record for herself that Reg made a few years back. "She's the only one to come up with a record like Reg's," says Barry Phillips, in whose store they've both worked.

When I interviewed Irmgard, I asked her pointblank: "Do you get psychic help?"

"What else?" she replied.

Breakthrough in the United States

U.S. police have been traditionally resistant to psychic involvements: to turn elsewhere for help is an admission of weakness; to listen to psychics is to be taken for a kook.

There are indications, however, that the situation is changing. A western state—not California!—has been experimenting with the use of "crime attack teams," composed of police detectives, psychologists, and psychics. This "innovative crime work," presently classified, is being funded by the federal government, matched by state funds. I've talked with a consultant and a psychic called in on the project, which will be a landmark demonstration if it pans out.

Other changes: an abrupt rise in the open use of psychic methods for detective work, police resorting to psychics, and the reportage of such incidents in the general press. If you lived in San Francisco in the winter of 1979, for instance, you could have read in the *San Francisco Chronicle* about a licensed detective who keeps Psi in her kit. As the headlines announced, "WHEN ALL ELSE

FAILS, SHE USES E.S.P." When private eye Jenita Cargile, it
explains, comes across a case that's too tough to crack by normal
detective work, she takes another tack: she uses her psychic powers
to catch the crooks. "Cargile, a good-looking grandmother who
cruises around Los Angeles in her telephone-equipped Cadillac,
specializes in tracing missing persons—particularly those who do
not want to be found. Cargile is one of the few licensed woman
private detectives in America, and has an astonishing success rate.
In the last four months she has located 100 of the 125 people
she has been tracking down."

Few signs of the changing tide are more definitive than the
case of the New Jersey housewife-turned-detective, now the darling
of authorities everywhere. "Here are some of the medals and awards
police departments have given me," Dorothy Allison says proudly,
displaying a framed case of badges and stars. "I get along very
well with policemen," she told me. "I've got FBI affidavits; I've
got affidavits for everything. I'm an honorary member of I don't
know how many departments. There is only one department I have
trouble with. As I will tell you right in front of them, in both
cases I did for them, I was 100 percent correct. But don't forget,
I am very competitive. They're looking at me almost as a super-
cop."

It hasn't been easy for her. Over dinner in Manhattan she remi-
nisced,

> I had eleven years of hard work before the police would believe me.
> Then, in 1968, I told the Nutley [New Jersey] police about a little
> boy who was stuck in a pipe and drowned. I led them to where his
> body was. From that day on, there's been no peace for me. Police
> call me from different towns, always police, and I thought, "God, if
> I am good at this, then I will dedicate my life to it," and that's exactly
> what I have done.
>
> Now, I'm doing this eighteen hours a day. I don't have any personal
> life—too many people missing. What kind of a personal life can I
> have, with mothers crying at the other end of the phone?

"Do you meditate to calm yourself down?" I asked the turned-
on Allison.

> I have no time for meditation. I'm not the sit-down type. That
> isn't how I found my bodies. (I did that twenty-four times!) I've found
> seven killers in the last year. . . .

Randolph Hearst phoned me when his daughter disappeared. On July 20, 1974, I was finding a missing plane in Pennsylvania, and went in to the state troopers. I hadn't even been thinking about Patty Hearst, but I announced "Patty Hearst is in Pennsylvania." They looked at me as though I was crazy. She had been kidnapped already, but no one knew where she was then. I said "I have to call the FBI!" They wouldn't even let me use their phone! They can't have everybody using their phone. It's the greatest thing that ever happened, because that's how I have proof that I called the FBI about it. I don't know if those troopers believed me or not, but Patty was found there in September. Later, the FBI called to say I was right. I have an affidavit for that.

As for her future plans, it is Dorothy Allison's dream to build a home for runaway children. She has worked for so many children who have left home and disappeared, that she feels home is the most important gift she can give.

Psi Squad at the Ready

Bevy Jaegers is a psychic crime detector with a difference: She trains others in the art, and has a live, working "Psi squad" to show for it. She would rather be known as a teacher of Psi, she makes clear, than as a psychic. "My whole philosophy is that ESP can be taught. It's a natural skill that can be cultivated."

Remembering Dorothy Allison's emphatic statement that psychics are "born, not made," this was a challenging contradiction.

Bevy was not born psychic, nor did she fall on her head. She worked on it slowly, step by step, until she had mastered the art. Now she has helped to solve cases of robbery, burglary, art theft, kidnaping, shipwreck, arson, missing persons, mysterious death, and murder—including murder by police! In a letter I just received from her, she writes, "Have a new murder coming in from a place called Steamboat Springs, Colorado, a hammer murder of a young girl. Sounds like a messy one."

Jaegers pioneered the teaching of Psi in the St. Louis public school system.

She also holds classes in her home when she can. It's convenient for her, comfortable, and she can kick off her shoes while she lectures. During coffee breaks, she plies her students with "sinful" pastries. "Using ESP depletes the body sugar; we need to bring your balance back up."

There were a dozen students in the class I attended, almost as many men as women, most of them from the greater St. Louis area, one from Seattle. We were each tested at the start, pushing a button on a small machine when we thought a hidden light was turned on. Most participants scored somewhat above chance. "You fit in well with the people who come to take this course," Bevy told us. "You are aware that you have some ESP."

There are two categories of sensitives, she began: natural psychics, and those who have learned.

I am in the second category. Learning ESP is something that hasn't been going on before; only in Russia in the last ten years. Things are now changing rapidly. In the work you are going to be doing here, you will be utilizing an ability you already have. I can't give you anything you don't already have. I will try to help you wake up what you have. I have not found any individual who does not have some amount of ESP.

In this class, I will try to teach something else. People are always telling me "I had a hunch that something was going to happen, and then, when it happened, I kicked myself because I hadn't said so." I want you to develop the guts to say it, to say what you think, especially in this class. I had things come to me thousands of times before I learned to *say it the way it comes through.*

Don't edit. By that I mean, don't change your impressions, patch them up, or censor them. No matter how crazy or irrational an impression may be, report exactly what comes through!

This training program is the result of having learned myself, through years of experimentation. I have taught hundreds of people, utilizing the same methods I have used to get myself to where I am today. I suggest you do one thing on you own time, involving the Russian system of color testing. Back in 1960 or 1961, the thing that got me interested in ESP to begin with was a news release out of Russia about a woman called Rosa Kuleshova, who could tell colors by feel, no matter what they hid them under—thousands of pounds of concrete. They tested her for years before releasing this.

This was the first thing I tried to do, and I used to use it in teaching, but it takes too much time. Get color charts, enamel ones, because they are bright. The value of it is, you are teaching your brain to do something it hasn't done before. It was of great value to a woman I found in 1965, who could knit intricate patterned sweaters, though she was totally blind. Even Rosa Kuleshova could not match that. Something was operating that involved, not the use of the eyes, but something else. This "something else" is what we are talking about here.

There is the *conscious,* the *unconscious,* and the *superconscious* mind. The conscious gives the orders, the unconscious receives them and puts the process into action, going to the superconscious for the answer, which hopefully is then fed back into the conscious mind. All answers are in the superconscious: it contains all information. There is *no* information which is not accessible and available through that link. The superconscious is also linked to the "pool of cosmic consciousness," the collective unconscious, to all intelligence, to all time and space. Here, all minds are linked with all other minds. It contains all information that ever was or will be. Your superconscious will give you the direct answer, so let it come through.

What we're doing here today is *programming* the unconscious to get the information you want, letting it come through exactly as it is, without doctoring it. You can learn to extend your senses. As we'll see, it is not *extra*-sensory perception, but *extended* sensory perception—that's a much better word for it, as a matter of fact!

For two days she put the group through exercises and tests. There was no attempt to distinguish between telepathy and clairvoyance. We could have picked up information from her telepathically as easily as from the objects we held in our hands. She had many of the answers in her head. Her goal, however, was straight line—to develop ESP.

I had positive feelings about the comfortable atmosphere, and about the continuous flow of background information, but doubts about the ratings given our performances. She was more than generous, I felt, in her assessment of our "hits" and partial hits, particularly the latter, and a bit lavish with her praise. Was this a teaching technique, to encourage us green novices to hang in there? An attempt to bolster her own hopes? Or both? I couldn't help wondering: Were the advanced sessions more stringent in procedures and evaluations?

In any case, over the two days, most of us registered improvement. A few did get genuine hits, and once in a while, several in the group picked up the same clues or details.

Her parting shot: "Practice, practice, practice!"

After she had taught several classes, Bevy gathered some of her graduates together to form a "Psychic Rescue Squad."

Since the name of our group was taken for an ambulance-type unit, we changed the name to the "United States Psi Squad," a group that police from anywhere in the world could get in touch with, when they're stumped by a case.

The California police, for example, called on the squad in the bizarre Chowchilla case, where a busload of children was kidnapped with their driver and hidden in a trailer buried in a quarry. Ed Cleary, the squad member who got the message, called around: "We've been asked to work on this case. They want to know how many people are involved, who they are, who was responsible, and where they are."

Another member of the squad told me,

We all went to work and wrote down all our impressions of what had happened. We had no physical evidence at all, but we gave them what they wanted. Out of about twenty possible points, we got eighteen completely correct. Bevy "saw" them in the quarry, and "spotted" the green truck. I got the man who had fled to Canada. We reported it to the California police and they closed the thing up in record time. Whether they had other help on the case, we don't know—just that it all turned out the way we'd called it!

Members of the original group included police, a social worker, an engineer, architect, and "just ordinary people." Explains Bevy,

When we're asked for help in finding a missing person, we ask for objects belonging to the person—a coat, knapsack, photo, even a cigarette butt. We pass the items around to our group members, and each person "psychometrizes" the objects—lets his psychic mind react. Just holding a sweater or a watch belonging to a missing person may trigger a mental image of some kind, which could help in locating him or her.

She showed me a bit of lace from a nightie and a piece of towel (the murder weapon), which helped police solve a strangulation case.

The impressions we get from the objects may not make sense to *us,* but we write them down exactly as they come. I once got the word "ROADY." I had never heard the word in my life. I felt like reporting it as "rodeo," but later I learned that "roady" has a meaning: it has to do with the individual who works for a rock group, and who provides them with drugs, in addition to being a front man for the group. So "roady" was right on!

Since authorities may be thrown off the track by a psychic's errant or misinterpreted lead, the squad concept may become a useful corrective. When a number of people get the identical clue, you feel better about it.

I'm from Missouri!

On my first trip to St. Louis, before taking the class, the following happened to me. It could have happened to anyone, I presume. Was it telepathy? Clairvoyance? Was it psychic?

Some members of the squad had just asked me what I now thought of Psi. "I don't know," I responded. "I'm still thinking and asking. Guess I'm from Missouri. You'll just have to show me!" (Pretty funny, they thought, since they're the ones from Missouri.) "The only thing I know," I went on, "is that *I'm* not psychic, and have no such ability at all."

That did it!

"You sit down, right there!" one of them commanded, pointing to the sofa. I sat and flipped on my tape recorder, to take down the lecture.

"Just sit there and relax!" said another. "Forget everything, and take ten long deep breaths."

At this point, Bevy came up with a rock, a rather pretty one, pink and sand-color, mottled, and put it in my left hand. (The left hand is the "receiving" one, she explained.)

"I want you to give me the name of the person connected with that rock!"

"The only thing that occurs to me," I said immediately, "is the word 'Jack.' "

"How does the rock feel?"

"It is very cold. In fact, I am shivering. Yes, I'm shivering a lot! Now it's going up and down my spine! I feel as though I'm getting a chill."

"Is there a good experience connected with the rock, or a bad one?"

"It must be bad, because I'm getting a chill, all over!"

"Is there a last name that goes with the other one?"

"A name comes to me, but it couldn't be that: 'Ripper.' Once you say 'Jack' you think of 'Ripper.' "

(Voices) "Don't think! Keep your conscious mind out of it!"

"What city?"

(Silence from me)

"Ask your subconscious, 'Where does the rock come from?' "

"Maybe Florida."

"What makes you think it is Florida? What do you *see?* Don't use words, use pictures."

"I haven't seen any pictures yet; trouble is, I'm too verbal." (Pause) "I now see flat land and palm trees. Is that because I thought of Florida first?"

"You are responding like a student who hasn't had any training."

"Right! I haven't!"

"If you *see* flat, *say* 'flat.' Don't say 'flat' because Florida is!"

"I wish I could park my brain."

Voice: "You can do this." Another voice: "That's what this is about."

"I'm having to fight my head, because I'm so used to reasoning it out . . . I have to put the rock down because it's too cold." (I do so.)

Voice: "The first thing that crosses your mind is generally the right answer."

(Picking up the rock again) "I *still* feel it's cold and *I* feel cold. When I pick it up, I shiver. It's not healthy. Obviously, if you get cold enough, you'll not be able to tell about it!"

(Bevy) "We can't leave you now; you'll have to go ahead with it. I realize we're kind of rushing you through this. It's different from what we ordinarily do."

"It's sinister, probably connected with death in some way, or severe illness."

"Whose illness?"

"I think of Jack Kennedy."

Shrieks!

Voice: "Shall we tell her where it came from?"

Bevy: "The rock is from Dealey Plaza, Dallas, Texas, where Jack Kennedy was assassinated."

6

PROTECTION:
A Beginning

A mother dreamed that in two hours a violent storm would loosen a heavy chandelier, which would fall on her baby's crib. She "saw" the baby lying there, dead. Terrified, she woke her husband. "A silly dream," he consoled her. "See—the weather is clear. Go back to sleep."

She continued to worry, and brought the baby to her bed. In exactly two hours a storm came up, and the light fixture fell where the baby had been.

This account comes from Dr. Louisa Rhine's unique and formidable collection of spontaneous Psi cases: more than 15,000 of them, which she has assembled and organized over the last thirty years. At least half of the incidents have to do with premonitions—predictions and warnings about the future. Some years ago, she discovered that 68 percent of the forecasts in her files occurred in dreams; the others, while people were awake.

Most reported precognition experiences focus on serious and shocking, rather than happy, events. They warn of danger, like the mother's dream above, accidents, disasters, and death. One survey gives the ratio of 4 unhappy events to 1 happy one. Pleasant forecasts, such as weddings, births and reunions, do not seem to trigger the psychic mechanism as traumatic ones do. And though President Lincoln had the well-known dream of his assassination a few weeks before it occurred, people seem rarely to recognize attacks on themselves.

If a single individual, like Louisa Rhine in North Carolina, has come into personal contact with so many thousands of premonitory incidents, how many such warnings must there be in all, taking place every day, every year, around the world?

Fate and Free Will

This mother's dream, and thousands—millions?—like it, raise the urgent question: Can such warnings avert disaster? This mother saved her baby. A California girl changed her plans and saved her parents from a runaway car. There are examples without end of people who turned in a ticket, changed a flight, or in some way altered their plans, thus avoiding what befell the others in that situation. "I just *knew* something was going to happen," they say afterward.

Winston Churchill had several such experiences. One night he was going out in a car during night air raids in World War II, to boost the morale of London's civil defense forces. Since he always sat on the near side of the car, his driver held that door open, as usual. Churchill started to get in, then inexplicably stopped, and for the first time, went around to the other side.

As they drove along the Kingston bypass, a bomb landed near the off-side of the car, the explosion lifting it onto two wheels. Righting itself, the car sped on.

Had it turned over, both the driver and Churchill would undoubtedly have been killed. Churchill joked that his "beef" on the side near the bomb had held the car on the road.

When the driver related the story to Mrs. Churchill, she was intrigued. "Winston, why did you get in on the off-side of the car?"

At first he shrugged it off, but when she pressed him, he admitted, "Something in me said 'Stop! Go around to the other side!' "

How effective are such premonitions? Can they truly protect us?

In 1956, a Psi researcher, W. E. Cox, looked into the question, and concluded that where there are warnings, an "accident avoidance" phenomenon does seem to take place. He obtained from American railroads a record of the number of accidents since 1950. Comparing the number of passengers on each train on the day of the accident with the number on the previous six days, and on the corresponding day in each of the four previous weeks—eleven days in all—he found that there are fewer passengers on a train destined to be wrecked than on one that will have a normal trip.

Many of the trains carried fewer passengers on their accident days than on any of the other ten days in the study. For example, the Illinois train "The Georgian" had an accident on June 15, 1952. Only 9 persons were on the train at the time. On the six previous days there were 68, 60, 53, 48, 62, and 70. On the corresponding day of the four preceding weeks there were 35, 55, 53, and 54 passengers, respectively. There were thus about one-sixth the normal complement of passengers on the accident day.

On Dec. 15, 1915, Train #15 of the Chicago, Milwaukee and St. Paul Railroad was wrecked, with 55 passengers aboard. The average number of passengers on the other ten, non-accident, days was over 100 every day. It was Cox's conclusion that, though there was no way to follow up with the "absent" passengers themselves, potential passengers were probably experiencing "subliminal premonition."

This whole business raises some very fundamental questions, scientific, philosophic, and religious. Among them is the breakdown in conventional logic. The mother who saved her child from the chandelier not only obtained information about an event which had not yet happened, but by an act of will, she changed it! For some people who cannot endure such an irrational sequence, parapsychologist Douglas Dean suggests an alternative explanation, which he notes is perfectly legitimate, but brings its own disturbing logic: What if the *dream* was so forceful that *it* changed the weather, and cracked the ceiling holding the light fixture? Such immense energy, particularly in dreams, is reminiscent of Jung's "archetypal energy," which supposedly can create events.

Incredible? Well, the Transcendental Meditation group seeks federal funding for an expansion of a 1978 project which, they claim, gave a lift to the state of Rhode Island when a hundred devotees concentrated their thoughts in concert for a month: There were fewer accidents, fewer crimes, lower sales of liquor and tobacco, and even better-than-average weather! Their statistics are not in doubt, though their conclusions are. *How* do we know that the lower crime rate or tobacco sales were the result of meditation?

Dean's suggestion does not solve the problem, however. It merely changes the explanation from one form of Psi, "precognition," to another, "psychokinesis" or "mind over matter."

If one has a premonition, *heeds* it, and there is no disaster, how can we know that it was, in fact, a premonition? *The disaster must occur to confirm it!* As Louisa Rhine reasoned in 1961, we can't tell if a disaster would have occurred if we "interfere." We cannot prove it would have happened.

Which brings us to the question, Are future events set, or are they only tentative? Now we're talking more than parapsychology. We're at the bedrock of the human situation, raising the ultimate question: Are all events predetermined and set, or can we change them? Predestination? Or free will? If free will does exist, what is its nature and what are its limits?

> Others apart sat on a hill retired,
> In thoughts more elevate, and reasoned high
> Of providence, foreknowledge, will and fate,
> Fixed fate, free will, foreknowledge absolute,
> And found no end, in wandering mazes lost.
> —Milton, *Paradise Lost*

The Registry Route

When Eryl Mai Jones predicted the landslide that wiped out her school (Chapter 1), she unknowingly made a contribution to parapsychological research. A London psychiatrist, Dr. J. C. Barker, started it off with the provocative question: If so many premonitions that we know of have proved accurate, why haven't they been used to prevent disasters? If there had been psychic warnings of the Aberfan tragedy, he wondered, would it have been possible to save the many who died?

Barker telephoned Peter Fairley, Science Editor of the London *Evening Standard,* and asked him to send out a newspaper appeal to those who had premonitions with respect to Aberfan. Within two weeks, seventy-six replies were received, most from the London area. The psychological research unit at Oxford University launched a similar appeal through another London newspaper, *The Sun.* A third publication, *News of the World,* also did some investigation, including interviews of people who forecast the landslide. There was a total of two hundred replies.

Using criteria established by parapsychologist G. W. Lambert, Barker evaluated these premonitions with reference to five questions:

1. Had the dream, vision or feeling been put down in writing, or reported to other persons, *before* the event?

2. Was the time-interval between premonition and its fulfillment short enough to indicate a close relationship?

3. Was the event, at the time of the premonition, something that did not seem likely to happen?

4. Did the description concern an event that would be literally fulfilled, not just vaguely foreshadowed in symbols?

5. Finally, were the details of the vision identical to those of the disaster?

On the basis of these criteria, Barker discarded sixteen of his seventy-six replies, then carefully investigated the remaining sixty. Here are some of the warnings he turned up:

- On the evening of Tuesday, October 18, a thirty-one-year-old man living in Kent was resting in bed when he suddenly "knew" that on Friday there would be a frightful disaster. The next day, he remarked to a girl in his office, "On Friday, something terrible will happen, connected with death." What it would be, he had no idea, but he felt depressed for the rest of the week.

- During the night of Thursday, October 20, several persons in England dreamed about "blackness." In her dream, one woman saw "a mountain flowing downward" and a small child running and screaming.

- At nine that same evening, Mrs. C. Milden was in Plymouth, England, at a meeting. Suddenly, a vision appeared before her, as if on a film, showing an old school house in a valley, and an avalanche of coal rushing down a mountainside. At the bottom of the mountain, she saw a terrified little boy, with a long fringe of hair. All around him, rescuers were digging into a coal slag, looking for bodies. One of the workers wore an odd-looking peaked cap.

- At 4 A.M., Friday, October 21, a London woman woke up, and thought that the walls of her bedroom were caving in. At almost the same moment, a Mrs. Sybil Brown in Brighton, south of London, had a terrifying nightmare of a screaming child in a telephone booth. Another child was being followed by a "black, billowing mass." Mrs. Brown woke her husband and said, "Something terrible has happened. He reassured her that there had been no bad news, but

she couldn't sleep the rest of the night; the child's screams rang
in her ears.

- At about the same time, in the early morning hours, an elderly
  man living in northwest England had an unusual dream. He saw,
  spelled out in brilliant light, A B E R F A N. The word had meant
  nothing to him, until he heard a radio broadcast later that day.

At 9 A.M. on Friday, Eryl Mai went off to school. As she left,
the clock in her house stopped ticking (a common Psi phenomenon).
Also at 9 A.M., the man from Kent came into his office and said
to his co-workers, "Today is the day it is going to happen." A
few minutes later, Eryl Mai joined her classmates in school, while
the teachers prepared to call the roll. About half a block away,
three older boys were sitting along a wall, waiting for their classes
to begin at 9:30. At 9:14, a secretary in a distant British aircraft
plant, Mrs. Monica McBean, had a sudden feeling that "something
drastic" was going to happen. In a vision, she saw a "black mountain
moving, and children buried under it." Shaken, she left her desk
and went into the ladies' lounge, where she sat down, trembling.

A few moments later, it happened: the disaster that had been
seen in dreams and visions days, even weeks, in advance. Half a
million tons of coal waste, loosened by two days of heavy rains,
began to rumble, then roar down over the village in a black, billowing
mass 40 feet high. Trees were uprooted, houses and cottages collapsed. The three boys sitting on the wall at the senior school disappeared, and the junior school was buried beneath the moving
mountain.

Rescue workers dug in the rubble all day and night for the
bodies. On Sunday, Mrs. Milden was watching a television broadcast
of the operations; on the screen appeared the terrified little boy
with the long fringe of hair she had seen in her vision. One of
the rescue workers nearby wore an oddly peaked cap.

A mass funeral was held on October 25 for the 144 victims.
The small bodies of the 116 children were buried in a common
grave. Among them was little Eryl Mai Jones, between her classmates Peter and June, just as she had predicted.

Dr. Barker decided to set up a kind of central clearing house,
where people might write or telephone if their "seismic sense" told
them that something terrible was about to occur. A computer could

be used to eliminate trivial, misleading or false information, based on the criteria given above, and to detect "peaks or patterns" in the flow of pre-tragedy data. If the computer signaled an unusually large number of premonitions, pointing to an event at a specific time or place, an "early warning" system could go into effect and the proper officials could be alerted. In the case of the Aberfan landslide, the pieces of the puzzle would have fit neatly together.

In January 1967, Barker and Fairley set up the British Premonitions Bureau. In February 1969, the Bureau moved its operation from the *Evening Standard* to the London *Times.* By May 1970, about a thousand predictions had been received.

Robert Nelson, who had been assisting Stanley Krippner in his dream laboratory experiments at the Maimonides Medical Center in Brooklyn, heard about the British bureau and decided to start a similar agency in the United States. The Central Premonitions Registry was activated in New York City in January 1968, with Nelson's wife, Nanci, assisting in its operation. The fact that he was on the staff of the *New York Times*—as Manager of the College and School Service Department—was just what the project needed: he had continuing and immediate contact with day-to-day news bulletins through the unequalled facilities of the newspaper by which to monitor events.

Modeling the Registry after the London Bureau, Nelson laid down two requirements for an authentic case of precognition: It must be recorded in writing and given to someone before the actual event; and it should be sufficiently detailed and unusual enough to make coincidence unlikely.

Nelson returns a form to each person who reports, asking that she or he send clippings confirming the event's occurrence, and any backup information for the prediction. A "hit" is, of course, any insight that coincides with a subsequent reality. Katherine Sabin of San Diego, for instance, "saw" San Diego in "a big fight or battle" which might occur in October/November and seemed to be some sort of "an attack by a foreign power." In November 1968, a Mexican vessel began firing on an American tuna boat based in the San Diego area.

Although premonitions of tragic events predominate, occasionally there is a lighter one. One filed June 10, 1969, by Rex Coile, a New England textbook salesman, predicted that the N.Y. Mets would win the World's Series. At that time the odds against their doing so were more than 100 to 1.

Before the Apollo XII moon shot, a regular informant, Alan Vaughan, notified the New York Registry that "unless something in the fuel system or electrical system is corrected, there will be an explosion, which could kill the astronauts."

What Vaughan was describing, in a kind of "telescoping effect," was the situation of Apollo XIII, when a short circuit ignited the electrical insulation in an oxygen tank and caused an explosion. Fortunately, though the astronauts were in very serious trouble, they were able to return safely, after the tank burst as they neared the moon.

While studying at a parapsychology lab in Germany, researcher/psychic Vaughan, had such a strong premonition that Robert Kennedy would be assassinated, that he sent registered letters with this warning, to both the London and New York registries. Kennedy was shot two days later.

At this point, a few words about Kennedy forecasts are in order. The Kennedy family has become one of the great recurring themes of modern forecasting. So "in" (and so common) have such predictions become, that if one has not received at least one Kennedy premonition, he/she is not in the club. It was the detailed forecast of President Kennedy's assassination that put the best-known contemporary prognosticator, Jeane Dixon, on the map. In both 1952 and 1956, before she knew who Kennedy was, she had already predicted that a blue-eyed, youngish man, a Democrat, would be the victorious candidate in 1960, but that he would either die or be assassinated in office.

Psychic investigator and author Herbert Greenhouse has attempted to explain this phenomenon:

When the President of the United States is about to die, the tragedy is sensed by thousands, perhaps millions, of Americans. As the nation's leader, symbol of the nation itself, the chief executive shares a psychic bond with the people he serves. If danger threatens him, a feeling of uneasiness spreads through the land, and there are countless dreams, visions and other extrasensory warnings of what is to come. . . . a feeling of despair seems to grip the national psyche, as if there is subliminal knowledge that the tragedy is inevitable. Those psychics who are consciously aware that there will be an assassination attempt generally feel helpless to prevent it. Almost no one will listen to them, least of all the man who is threatened.

Can registries avert disaster? None of them, unfortunately, has been given a *real* testing, nor has the precognitive principle upon which they are based. From present experience, there is no way to know whether the registry idea is a practicable one. Once it is established, no matter how good the facilities, a registry cannot run by itself. At a minimum it takes *publicity,* first of all, and lots of it, to reach great numbers of people in many geographic areas and from all walks of life. All the registries, so far, have had limited access to the public, usually through only one organization, person, or publication at a time.

Second, it takes a large and efficient, probably computerized, *data-bank,* with cross-filing of persons, places, topics, dates and events.

Third, there must be an effective *screening system,* which can distinguish bona fide premonitions.

Fourth, it is also imperative to make constructive and *imaginative use* of the data collected. Fortunately, Nelson, with his parapsychological background, is making use of his data for further research. He and parapsychologist Lawrence LeShan plan to analyze the forms returned by those who regularly contribute "hits."

In sum, the premonitions registry approach requires money— a substantial amount—and staff who have parapsychological savvy.

Front-Page Prophecy

If media treatment is any indication, the demand for future prediction is insatiable, not only in the tabloids, which instantly convert such fare into headlines, but in prestigious dailies.

Some predictions, in retrospect, are almost too embarrassingly far off to read. For example: "The E.R.A. will be passed by three more states and will become national law in 1979." In short, there are many misses, many near-hits, many borderline uncertain calls, and sometimes, spectacular hits.

Since scientists have not claimed this as a major concern, others have attempted to help close the gap. In lieu of hard data, the *National Enquirer,* scarcely disinterested but trying hard, conducted a bit of research on its own. It asked a six-member panel—three professional investors, three psychics—to predict stock market trends for the next six months, on the basis of which they were to select $1,000 of winning stocks. All six participants looked at a newspaper financial section and, using imaginary money, each made a purchase. The selections were notarized, and six months later were examined. Stocks picked by the psychics' team had gained a total of $62.75. Those chosen by the investors showed a $9.95 loss.

"We didn't do too well at all," observed broker Chris Morton, of Merrill, Lynch, Pierce, Fenner and Smith, Inc. "The psychics beat us fair and square."

In the final breakdown, Chicago psychic Olaf Jonsson's picks showed a loss, but the four stocks chosen by New York psychic Shawn Robbins rose $4.75, and the four picked by Bevy Jaegers increased in value by a total of $138.13.

Jeane Dixon is unique in the attention her forecasts receive, yet she has consistently declined invitations to parapsychology labs, so no scientific assessment can be made of her abilities as a prophet. Enough anecdotal evidence has accumulated over the years from responsible persons to suggest that Mrs. Dixon's reputation has a foundation; she fares less well, however, in her annual lists of predictions for world events. Researcher and psychic Alan Vaughan notes that this is a general pattern with precognitive psychics: they may get detailed impressions of an individual's future, but flounder in areas where they hold firm opinions, as in prophecies of world events.

"Every year," David Hoy's *ESP News* for January 1979 explained, "I publish a list of my predictions for the new year. The record will show that I am hitting with a higher degree of accuracy each year." In February 1979 he announced, "Months ago I predicted to a national newspaper that the next Pope would be non-Italian and would be from a communist country. They decided not to print this, because it would be 'too explosive.' I also made this prediction on many radio stations, so it can be documented."

Some of those who release their predictions also cite their rate of success. These usually run around 80 to 90 percent. The scoring in such cases, unfortunately, is usually done by the psychics themselves. Self-evaluation always poses a problem: One's subjective evaluation of what constitutes a hit may be totally honest, but skewed.

In sum, a lot of good forecasting may be taking place, along with much bad, but since there are as yet no accepted guidelines for determining hits, what is objectively good and objectively bad isn't yet known.

Warning Alert

When is a premonition worth paying attention to? Some are so slight, so "subliminal" per Cox's phrase, as to seem totally meaningless, yet they sometimes turn out to be all-important warnings, as we have seen.

There is also the premonition that is unnaturally vivid or hauntingly repetitive, those "living color" experiences that insistently replay themselves again and again. Such was the case with Jeane Dixon's warnings about John Kennedy and Alan Vaughan's about Robert Kennedy.

It would be foolish to ignore warnings such as these. In such cases one should contact immediately the Central Premonitions Registry, Box 482, Times Square Station, New York, N.Y. 10036. If a number of urgent premonitions about the same incident are received, the proper authorities will be notified.

Voices from the Past

Using Psi for prediction is far from new. Precognition records go back at least to Greek civilization. The Greeks relied on the premonitions of priestesses in the oracle temples, the most famous being the Oracle of Apollo at Delphi. Hundreds of confirmed Delphic predictions have been preserved. King Croesus of Lydia tested the accuracy of many oracles and gave the prize to the one at Delphi, who correctly announced that Croesus was cooking a lamb and tortoise in a brazen pot—a most unusual project for a king! When he consulted it further about a military campaign he was contemplating, the oracle said, "A great army will be destroyed." The king assumed this meant the enemy, and discovered too late that it was his own. (Rule #1 for Psi inquiry: Be as explicit as possible!)

A central theme of the Bible, New Testament and Old, is prophecy—of plagues, droughts, floods and destruction. Precognitive dreams are a colorful facet of Biblical history; best known perhaps, Joseph's interpretation of the Pharaoh's dreams (not to mention his own).

Moving nearer the present is the wave of warnings and precognitive dreams associated with the *Titanic* calamity. On April 14, 1912, with 2,207 passengers aboard, the greatest ocean liner ever built rammed an iceberg and went down. The fact that the vessel was believed to be unsinkable added fuel to the emotional shock-fires of dismay. The visions which the event triggered—in advance— were "more real than reality."

Psychic researcher Ian Stevenson has analyzed nineteen premonitions of the sinking, within two weeks before its occurrence, in England, the United States, Canada, and Brazil.

On March 23, J. Connon Middleton, a London businessman, booked passage. The next week he had a disturbing dream. He saw the *Titanic* "floating on the sea, keel upwards, and her passengers and crew swimming around her." Next night, the dream was repeated. He was not struggling in the water, but "floating in the air above the wreck."

Middleton began to have pre-disaster symptoms. He was uneasy and depressed, and tried to put the two dreams out of his mind. But because his business in America was urgent, he did not cancel his passage.

A few days later, he received a cable from New York urging him to postpone his trip. He did. Unaccountably, from April 3 to April 10 several other persons, including banker J. Pierpont Morgan, canceled their bookings.

Before the ship sailed, Middleton told friends and family about the recurring dreams, which they corroborated later.

As the magnificent liner steamed past the Isle of Wight on her maiden voyage, members of the Jack Marshall family stood on the roof of their home, waving their handkerchiefs enthusiastically. The mood was suddenly broken when Mrs. Marshall grabbed her husband's arm and screamed, "It's going to sink! That ship is going to sink before she reaches America!"

Her family tried to calm her, but she became more hysterical. She "saw" the *Titanic* going down and the passengers dying in the Atlantic. "Don't stand there staring at me," she cried. "Do something! You fools, I can see hundreds of people struggling in the icy water! Are you so blind that you are going to let them drown?"

As the ship disappeared over the horizon, the film of the future unrolling in her mind, she shouted "Save them! Save them!"

Herbert Greenhouse, author of *Premonitions: A Leap into the Future,* asks how an effective registry might have saved the vessel. He concludes: "When enough people know about the Central Premonitions Registry and the Premonitions Bureau, and when there are not hundreds, but thousands of warnings sent in, disasters such as the Aberfan tragedy, and the sinking of the *Titanic,* may be prevented. Planes, trains, ships, even spacecraft, will cancel trips that seem to be ill-fated. Fires, floods, explosions, the collapse of bridges and buildings, may be averted, if there is an early warning signal."

Not the least of the *Titanic* drama was a book written by a New Yorker, Morgan Robertson, titled *The Wreck of the Titan.*

She was the largest craft afloat, and the greatest of the works of man. . . . Spacious cabins . . . decks like broad promenades . . . unsinkable, indestructible, she carried as few lifeboats as would satisfy the law. 75,000 tons—deadweight—rushing through the fog at the rate of fifty feet a second . . . hurled itself at an iceberg . . . nearly three thousand human voices raised in agonized screams.

The *Titanic* was built in 1911. The "largest craft afloat," it made its first and only voyage in 1912. *The Wreck of the Titan* was written in *1898!*

It would appear that there's been plenty of precognition around, individual and collective, since time immemorial. The problem, on which we have made but the barest beginning, is how to harness it effectively.

As Louisa Rhine wrote long ago:

If the precognitive ability is developed and directed, as in time it is reasonable to expect that it will be, its operation, even on a limited basis, could obviously be of untold value to humanity—particularly if, with greater understanding of the processes of ESP, a way is found to bring it into better focus.

From present indications, if imperfect ESP impressions, especially those suggesting danger ahead, could be clarified intelligently, preventive action could follow, to the untold advantage of mankind.

Page from the Dowsers

Can Psi help us protect ourselves? In yet another area, we can take a page from the dowsers. By identifying and deflecting "harmful influences," as in highway accidents (Chapter 3), it now seems that dowsers may be on the track of something big.

One advanced practitioner in this sort of thing is Enid Smithett ("the only Smithett in Britain") who, with her husband, the late P. B. Smithett, coordinated the British Society of Dowsers, and issued its journal for many years.

Enid's husband's forte was organization and publicity. Hers is dowsing itself. In this, she is an artist, using a color wheel—a "Mager rosette." She touches a color on the wheel with her left hand, holding the dowsing pendulum in her right. Not only does she locate water, as other dowsers do, but if it registers "black" it is "bad water," not potable. If the pendulum says "yes" when she touches purple, she knows it is good. The lines and points of her underground power maps are in color, "ley lines," for example, changing as they come together and cross at "power points."

" 'Ley lines' are a fairly new development in England," she told me. They are in America, too. The theory is that at various underground spots, there are "power points" or centers, from which energy or ley lines radiate. The force at those centers is subtle, but powerful; it can be energizing and good, or very bad. You can sometimes see where the power centers are, some say, by markings in the grass: a circle of lush and healthy green growth if the energy is beneficial; a brownish and burnt-out circle if it is not. The ancients must have known all about this, from clues that remain: important structures—particularly religious ones—shrines, mammoth rock arrangements, are often located directly over "good" power points. Coventry Cathedral, destroyed in the World War II blitz, was built at just such a spot, British dowsers told me. "You can still go there, to the ruins, and be energized. The rebuilt cathedral, at a new site, has none of that feeling or effect."

One of Enid's specialties is "clearing sites" of harmful influences, map-dowsing with her pendulum to locate underground effects. This she has also taught to an accomplished student, John Trigger, whom

I met. Together they took on the assignment of "clearing the atmosphere of harmful influences" of a girls' school in Rugby. From the day of its completion, everyone in the building had been dogged with confusion and misery. The first headmistress died shortly after the school was opened. The second is now dying of cancer. The girls were perpetually restless, hated the atmosphere, and quarreled constantly. Teachers were fired.

Dowsing a sketch-map of the school, Trigger located and filled in the pattern of ley lines. Then he did something which, to this neophyte, was beyond belief: He placed a small amethyst on the "power point" where the ley lines crossed and were concentrated, *on the map!* Both the dowsers and those at the school swear that, from that moment, all negative symptoms stopped. The school ambience switched 180 degrees, to one of comfort and amiability. There have been no unpleasant incidents since.

John showed me his working sketch of the school, with the amethyst firmly taped to it. "Some people use peridot," he said, "but this works just fine for me. I keep a small bag of amethysts handy."

"What if I were to pull the stone off the map?" I asked.

"Don't you do it!" John and Enid exclaimed.

At this point, there flashed into my mind that there had been a similar and equally baffling procedure in Bob Ater's highway accident experiments (Chapter 3). After Bob had identified the cause of a particular danger spot in Ohio by map dowsing, and Jim Perkins of the Highway Maintenance Department had confirmed it, Perkins drew a blue line on the map, which rests under the glass on his office desk. From that moment on, the unexplained accidents, which had caused twenty-four injuries and four deaths in two years, stopped completely.

A blue line on a map, miles away, preventing accidents? A lavender stone on a sketch curing physical and psychological problems? How far out can you get? "If I accept this, I'll accept anything," I warned myself.

I asked Ater about all this when I got back to the United States. "Crazy, isn't it?" I inquired.

"Not at all!" he surprised me. "Amethyst . . . blue . . . they're at the same end of the spectrum. Experiments with color show that blue tends to neutralize noxious influences." (*Yankee* magazine for September 1979 notes that some dowsers carry blue bias tape with them when they are traveling, for use if they discover "harmful rays" on dowsing the bed in their motel!)

Gordon MacLean often placed blue tape, or blue-painted wires, at strategic places on the floor, or on the ground—even around a bed. ("Leave a gap at some spot in the bed loop," he advised. "Don't connect the two ends.") Until he was called on it for esthetic reasons, MacLean once even painted blue stripes across a lawn!

Cataclysm and Catastrophe

The notion that one can learn whether a tomato has been sprayed by consulting a pendulum is something, but to be able to predict, and possibly to prevent, disaster for thousands—millions?—is almost too awesome to contemplate. A few adventurous scientists, however, are looking into the possibility.

Taking an innovative tack, Arizona scientist Jeffrey Goodman studied the earth-change forecasts of psychics in different parts of the country; he compared them with one another, then with the projections of scientists in the relevant fields. He chose his panel of psychics on the basis of proven past performance, then carried out experiments and field tests with each of them on his own.

The convergence of their predictions was startling. As Goodman notes, when a group of six gifted psychics each independently relates the same essential story, then there is more than pause for thought.

All of them saw the 1980–1990 period as a time when the earth's internal "burners" will be turned up from their normal simmer to medium heat, in preparation for the 1990–2000 period, when they will be turned up to "high!"

"From 1980 to 1990, my psychic group foresaw major earthquakes on both the eastern and western coasts of the United States."

According to Aron Abrahamsen, a sensitive in the Pacific Northwest, there will also be inundations by the sea on both coasts. More specifically, the California cities of San Diego, San Clemente, Los Angeles, and San Francisco will experience widespread destruction from quakes. As a result, according to what several of the clairvoyants "saw," the ocean will make inroads on the land towards the end of this period.

There was virtual agreement on the contours of the new coastline: it would cut in from Baja California, to ease inland. To the north, it would pass through the cities of Pomona (east of Los Angeles), Bakersfield, Fresno, Turlock, and Sacramento, then return to the present coastal position at Eureka. Abrahamsen gave his information to Goodman in December 1972. Unknown to either of them, Ray Elkins had made the same forecast in April 1970. Abrahamsen "saw" the land going under; Elkins spoke of its "splitting away." Clarisa Bernhardt "saw" islands forming off the state of California, as did Elkins, Bella Karish, and persons hypnotized by Susan Harris.

Predictions about upheavals in California are hardly news, but these sensitives joined in predicting that, following a severe earthquake, *New York* will also split away from the mainland, the lower part of Manhattan sinking into the sea. In addition, they projected earthquakes and other disturbances in many parts of the world.

Such convulsions are mild, though, compared to the destruction anticipated in the following period, which Goodman labels the "Decade of Cataclysm." Volcanic eruptions (Vesuvius, Pelée) will trigger earthquakes in India, parts of Europe, and the United States. A magnitude of 10.0 is top on the Richter Scale. The psychics "saw" quakes of 11.0 and even 12.0, almost half a million times stronger than the 1964 earthquake in Alaska, at 8.4.

The new western U.S. coastline will then run from Seattle to Sheridan, Wyoming; North Platte, Nebraska; and Amarillo, Texas, thence west to Phoenix, Arizona and finally to a point south of San Diego. Bernhardt pictures "a beautiful riviera, which will stretch across the southwest United States." On the eastern seaboard, North Carolina and New Jersey will be inundated. Florida and Louisiana will sink into the sea. The Great Lakes will flood portions of Wisconsin, Michigan, and Illinois. In all, the United States will be reduced from its present three-thousand-mile coast-to-coast width to one less than two thousand miles.

Goodman then looked at the prophecies of Nostradamus, Edgar Cayce, the Bible, and the legendary expectations of the Hopi Indians and other ancient peoples. Cayce and Nostradamus, for example, both declared that the planet will undergo a period of major earthquakes and volcanic activity before the year 2000. Cayce also projected Nebraska as a coastal area, the sea apparently covering all the western part of the country.

When Goodman compared the psychics' predictions with those of the scientists, he discovered that the fanciful projections he had assembled were "well within the range of geologic possibility!" The shifts and upheavals predicted by psychics followed the lines of *existing* underground formations. The major difference between the psychics' and the standard geological projections was the *rate* at which the geological change will take place: sudden and catastrophic according to the former; gradual and long-term, say most of the latter. (There are sharp differences about this among geologists: "catastrophism" *vs* "uniformitarianism"—gradualism.)

Stephen Plagemann, a physicist, and British astronomer John Gribbin, editor of the science journal *Nature,* agree that rare planetary alignments can set off extensive earthquake activity where stresses have been building for a long time. There are even those who contend that psychic energy may be integrally related to planetary change.

In *We Are the Earthquake Generation,* Goodman notes, with a dark chuckle, "Ironically, the investigation of the ability of the animals to sense earthquakes, now scientifically in vogue—you know, 'Consult your local goldfish' or 'A cockroach could save your life'—seems to bring us back full circle to psychics and their ability to predict earthquakes."

Three points are relevant here: the use of psychics in ferreting out leads and possibilities; the almost unbelievable convergence of psychic pronouncements with one another, and with scientists' projections; and, distasteful though such scenarios may be, the knowledge that such projections, if applied appropriately, may help arm us for coping with, or even for avoiding, some of them.

After talking with Jeffrey a couple of days, I confronted him. "My home faces the Golden Gate Bridge in San Francisco, and sits almost plunk on the San Andreas fault!"

"You'll have *plenty* of warning," he assured me. "These things happen in a definite sequence—in order: one, two, three. Once a few of these things start happening—in India, Japan, and Martinique—you'll know what to expect and prepare for."

As the former Director of the Geophysics Laboratory at the University of North Carolina, David M. Stewart, concludes: "Some psychics do predict earthquakes far beyond statistical chance. Some psychics have records significantly better than the best endeavors of scientists with millions of dollars' worth of equipment. Psychics are not always right; neither are scientists. Perhaps, if they work together, the results would be more useful than either could obtain alone."

7

SCIENCE: The Paradox

The paradox is that while science dares Psi to prove itself, Psi is, in fact, helping science.

The psychic dimension has been contributing to science since science began: the unexplained hunch, the missing piece or solution, the clue that leaps out of nowhere, the inspiration in a dream. Where does the clue come from? We don't know, but we do know that inventors and intellectual explorers have relied on these hidden resources through the ages. Kekule von Stradonitz solved the chemical problem of the benzene molecule when, in a fatigue-engendered daydream, he saw a snake swallow its tail. "Of course! Rather than a chain of carbon atoms, the molecule is a ring!"

While struggling unsuccessfully to perfect the sewing machine, Elias Howe dreamed one night that he had been captured by savages. Their king told him that if he did not produce a machine that would sew within twenty-four hours, he would die. Sweating and frantic, Howe tried to deliver, but the deadline came. The savages approached and raised their spears above him. As he watched in horror he saw that each menacing spear had a hole in the tip. That was it! The hole should be in the point of the needle, not the middle or the top. The problem was solved.

History is full of such happenings.

In this chapter, we'll consider a few of the ways in which science has drawn on the psychic—in archaeology, for example, in physics, biology, and space.

Psychic Archaeology

Archaeologist Jeffrey Goodman, who studied the earthquake predictions (Chapter 6), has also used clairvoyance to psych out the past. What Goodman was seeking in this instance was the location of man's earliest ancestors in North America. In the course of his inquiry, he'd had two incredibly vivid dreams. In one, on April 30, 1971, he saw himself atop a large boulder, looking down on a dry creek bed. "That's *it!*" he shouted. "That's the place!" He knew, in his dream, that buried there were many artifacts, entire skeletons and jewels.

In the other dream, several weeks earlier, he was working at a dig he'd selected, partitioned off from the rest of the area. He saw, in his dream, a geological map that matched in structure the Four Corners area, where New Mexico, Colorado, Utah, and Arizona meet. He went to the man in charge of the site and told him that he planned to have Jay come help. "The only thing that seemed wrong was that, while I had a cousin Jay, the last thing in the world he was interested in was digging."

Reflecting on these dreams, so different in emotional content from any he'd had before, Goodman felt strongly that, somehow, he was being given a message. On the advice of friends, he contacted a Pacific Northwest sensitive, Aron Abrahamsen; "a real psychic, as good as Edgar Cayce," they said. He wrote to Abrahamsen, asking him specifically, "Where can some of the earliest evidence of man in North America be found?"

What followed was one of the strangest and most intriguing Psi adventures on record, an adventure still continuing.

In less than two weeks, the psychic's reply arrived, a tape made while in a state of meditation. Goodman recalls, "The guy knew what he was talking about. He was using the right terms in the right ways. Aron Abrahamsen, as I learned, had been an aerospace engineer, a project leader for a contractor involved in the first moon landing, but here he was talking about pre-history and excavations like a seasoned archaeologist!"

Abrahamsen named three sites: Kino, Mexico; Pueblo, Colorado; and the mountains near Flagstaff, Arizona. Since the region nearest Goodman, "the mountains near Flagstaff," was so large, he wrote back for more specific directions. He also asked if his April dream was related in any way to the Arizona site.

The psychic sent the information he needed, and told him to have confidence in *both* of his dreams, the first of which Goodman had not mentioned!

As soon as he could manage it, Goodman made the five-hour drive from Tucson to Flagstaff, where he visited with the head archaeologist in the local museum. "There are no early-man sites in the Flagstaff area," he was told.

"The next day I set out in the field," Goodman recounts, "to try to locate the area Aron had spoken about. Instead of being equipped with a staff and entourage, my only companion was a tape recorder with Aron's tapes. All about me were very large, jagged peaks, covered by dense stands of stately Ponderosa pine trees. But by the end of the day, I hadn't seen anything that resembled what I had seen in my dream."

Goodman retired to the University Library in Tucson, to study geological maps and reports about the Flagstaff area. He knew the key was to find sedimentary deposits somewhere in the volcanic mountains near there. Without sedimentary deposits there would be no sandstone cliffs, such as he was seeking. Without the cliffs, there could be no site.

"After searching for hours, I found what I was looking for. One map showed that, deep within the mountain range, there were three places where sedimentary deposits were faulted up. One spot had a dry creek by it, just as in the dream. The fault, the dry creek, the volcanic area and the sedimentary rock cliffs: all the components of my dream were there! I couldn't wait to drive back and field-check the area.

"Early the next day I set out to find the actual place where all these components came together. My four-wheel-drive vehicle got me close enough so that it took only one hour of hiking to reach the general target area. Soon after I began looking about, I suddenly started to tremble. I saw a big boulder above the creek. This was the boulder I had seen before, in my dream!"

He checked out the details of the location, then raced to the creek and began to dig.

Digging like crazy with a little folding shovel I had with me. . . . Only after I skinned my hand raw, did I calm down enough to realize that what Aron said I sought was buried very deep.

So, I was content to draw a map of the spot and return to Tucson. I mailed the map to Aron for a check reading. He said that I had found the right spot, gave me some more encouragement, and then proceeded to deliver a detailed geologic history of the area for the last million years, along with instructions for excavation.

His geologic history included descriptions of earthquakes, faulting, ice flows, volcanic eruptions, flooding and fire. Upon returning to the library, I quickly verified that Aron's rather complex history was accurate.

Aron wasn't simply reading my mind. He was either really tuning in on the area, or engaging in some back-breaking historical research of his own.

The story of Goodman's excavation is an alternation of frustrations and discoveries. Among the former were the hurdles of getting a permit to make the dig, lack of money, bad weather, and what loomed even larger, the opposition and disagreement of authorities. They were firm in their belief that the earliest humans in North America lived no earlier than fifteen thousand years ago. They also rejected the notion of dragging the psychic into scientific research.

The dig began in June 1973. By the end of 1975, Goodman's modest operation had managed an excavation 10 feet square and 30 feet deep. In the course of the digging, he enlisted all the help he could find, including two undergraduates, his wife, two daughters . . . and a "philosopher/carpenter" named Dennis, who answered to the nickname of "Jay!"

Imagine their excitement when they turned up the first object that had "retouch"—a technical term, meaning patterned edge-modification—in short, a human artifact!

Others followed. One was a small scraper tool, used because of its sharp edge. When the edge became dull, the user resharpened it by removing a series of slivers, producing a new sharp, scalloped edge. "Nature never produces such a pattern," Goodman explained as I fondled his precious find. "When I found this," he went on, "I knew for sure that we were on to something. Aron had done it! Either he had pinpointed artifacts in one, ten-foot square below the earth's surface, from his room many hundreds of miles away, or it was a million-to-one lucky strike."

Following the psychic's detailed play-by-play directions, they uncovered a variety of artifacts at different depths: "Cores, flaked debris, flakes, blades and tools." Several specialists agreed that the specimens did look man-made. Moreover, scientific dating techniques established them as having been created not fifteen thousand years ago, generally believed to be the earliest human habitation on the continent, but much earlier—by Goodman's estimate *possibly as much as one hundred thousand years ago!*

Since then, he says, "about fifty archaeologists" have come to inspect the specimens, Goodman says. Though not all are convinced, those I consulted took the Goodman find seriously. Richard Mac-Neish of the Peabody Foundation for Archaeology said, "I want to know more about the context in which the specimens are found: those chipped objects do look man made."

The plot continues. In 1979, Alan Bryan of the University of Alberta brought his own team to the site, which in 3 weeks of digging turned up another tantalizing piece, a stone some believe was intentionally engraved by humans.

Of fifty-eight of Abrahamsen's predictions, fifty-one have, so far, proved accurate.

Psychics have contributed to archaeology in many places over the years. George McMullen, a bush guide in British Columbia who calls himself "an average guy," has an extraordinary ability to go back in time. He has helped guide archaeologists in Canada, the United States, Israel, Egypt, and Iran. He and an American photographer and psychic, German-born Hella Hammid, led scientists to the identical place, in Maria, Egypt, when they were asked separately "What is the most important archaeological site in town?" After two weeks of digging, the native crew came up with what the psychics had "seen," a building, a round bread furnace, floor tiles, and so on.

The director of the project, Stephan Schwartz, former special assistant for research and analysis to the Chief of Naval Operations, reported on the underwater findings outside the Alexandria, Egypt, harbor, to the Eighth Annual Underwater Archaeological Conference, in Albuquerque in January 1980. It was a case of combining psychic information with orthodox science, he explained. Strabo wrote about the royal palace of Anthony and Cleopatra in 24 B.C., but no one knew exactly where it was. Thanks to the help of the psychics, Schwartz and his team are now checking out what answers to the description of the long lost site. "I saw the ancient city ruins," he exulted, "with my own shining eyes."

Schwartz has collected notable cases of psychic archaeology in his book *The Secret Vaults of Time*. Among them is the account of architect Frederick Bligh Bond, who with his friend Captain John Bartlett received and took down in "automatic writing" the entire plan of the lost and buried ruins of Glastonbury Abbey, which Bond was hired to restore.

His informants? None other, Bond reported, than the deceased monks who had lived there and loved the Abbey, before Henry VIII refused to recognize the Pope's authority, thus dooming their Benedictine tradition! By the reign of Elizabeth I, nothing but the Abbot's kitchen, a few ruined walls, and some half-buried foundations remained of what had once been the most important church in England. When his investigation was completed, Bond had entirely reconstructed the detailed plan of the Abbey, and discovered its hidden foundations, along with forgotten and unknown chapels in unthought-of locations, as well as buried stone work and passageways.

Bond's records of the psychic messages from the "Watchers" include meticulous descriptions, and painstaking instructions for locating the hidden remains: "Ye did not go far enough beyond the bank . . . ye must dig a full five feet." They also reflect the differing personalities of these long-gone informants. For example, there was the simple and endearing Brother Johannes Bryant, who admitted that he wasn't meant to be a monk but who served as Bond's main connection with the incorporeal group that eagerly awaited the Abbey's restoration, and the tolerant and analytical Brother Gulielmus.

Another is the case of the Polish clairvoyant, Stefan Ossowiecki. Born with psychic skills, he later apprenticed himself to "an old Jewish yoga, who had spent all his life in India, studying secret knowledge."

Ossowiecki's most useful application of his talents was in the interest of psychic archaeology. In the first such experiment, in a Warsaw suburb in 1935, he was asked to identify the contents of a paper-wrapped box, while a small group of friends looked on. After fifteen minutes of deep thought, he replied:

I see a metal foil box. Its surface is reflective. The inside is brownish, wrapped in paper and cotton. Something like wood or stone, something petrified. This is something very old, and it originated several thousand years ago, before the birth of Christ. This was unearthed by some scientific expedition. I see people in white pith helmets directing this excavation. Around, sand and rocks.

This is in some hot country. This object was a portion of some bigger object, and served or was connected with, some cult or religious procedure . . . wedding, or funeral.

Yes, this was connected with a funeral, but what is it, in fact? It's some figure . . . or idol. I don't understand. I see some fires, like torches, some strange people who bow in front of this, or are praying. What is it? This object has some fibers, knots, in places as though it were covered with strips of fabric.

(Pause)

I can see now what this is . . . it is a petrified human foot!

It was!

A little over a month later, he was *again* given the package. On this occasion, he recited pages of details about the woman whose foot it was. His information checked out with the authorities.

In 1936, Stanislaw Poniatowski, an archaeologist seeking "an appropriate clairvoyant," came to Warsaw to test Ossowiecki. So great was their rapport, so effective the research design, and so amazing their results, that the two worked together intensively for six years, the scientist keeping a detailed record of the readings.

The story ends in tragedy, since both of them were murdered by the Nazis; the scientist sent to a concentration camp, the psychic shot down in a massacre, his body burned. But by the time of their capture, they had conducted thirty-three experiments before a group of leading scientists and observers. One of the more remarkable things about this unique research, observes Schwartz, is that this was at the very time when Drs. J. B. and Louisa Rhine were finding it difficult to get American scientists to take their parapsychological research seriously. Professor Poniatowski established an advisory support group, 75 percent of whose membership is still listed in basic references. It is doubtful, Schwartz concludes, whether any other research program in the twentieth century—except perhaps the Manhattan Project—could make a similar claim.

Schwartz also tells how Professor J. Norman Emerson, in March 1973, admitted to the archaeological establishment in Canada, that he had received information about archaeological sites from a psychic. "By means of the psychic and parapsychological, a whole new vista of man and his past stands ready to be grasped. As an anthropologist and archaeologist trained in these fields, it makes sense for me to seize the opportunity to pursue and study the data thus provided. *This should take the first priority.*"

These and other such examples seem to bolster Goodman's startling claim that "ESP is replacing the spade as archaeology's primary tool."

Psi and Sci: Stretching the Boundaries

Anthropologist Margaret Mead once told the American Association for the Advancement of Science, "The whole history of scientific achievement is full of scientists investigating phenomena the Establishment did not believe were there." The realm of the psychic is one such area.

As we have seen, psychology has had to yield to the insistent demands of the paranormal realm for attention and study. Psychology plus Psi equals parapsychology, now a recognized body in the A.A.A.S. with its own specialists, organizations, and professional journals. The utility of the yeasty fringes of established disciplines is underlined explicitly by Professor Hans Bender of the University of Freiburg, in the name he has given his parapsychology research center, "The Institute for Border Areas of Psychology."

Even physics has succumbed to the pressures of Psi at its gates: physics plus Psi equals paraphysics, a new field that "studies the physics of the paranormal."

Many would find it impossible to believe that Psi could invade that most solid bastion of hard sciences, namely physics, yet today physicists—a minority of them, at least—are among the most avid followers of parapsychological developments. Some of them work with parapsychologists and regularly appear on psi-related programs. I attended a New York conference in November 1978 on "New Dimensions of Consciousness," at which two headline speakers were Viennese Fritjof Capra, doing research in theoretical high energy physics at the Lawrence Laboratory of the University of California, and Hungarian Eugene P. Wigner, who had received the Nobel Prize in Physics in 1963. Capra declared:

> New discoveries in physics now contradict the old paradigm of the world as solid matter, a machine of separate parts. Findings in physics today are revealing the errors of using this as a model. The world is

fluid and ever-changing, and totally interrelated. . . . The cosmos is alive, organic—spiritual and material at the same time.

Wigner asserted that the universe cannot be accounted for by conventional physics, which erred by trying to leave out consciousness, explaining the universe in terms of objects alone. "We need a larger compass, to include life and consciousness." Other participants included biologist Lyall Watson, mathematician Charles Muses, and Karl Pribram, head of the Neuropsychology Laboratory at Stanford. Also on the program were pandit Gopi Krishna, authority on Kundalini, David Spangler, a former director of the Findhorn Community in Scotland, and Pir Vilayat Inayat Khan, head of the Sufi Order of the West. Neuropsychologist Pribram was the featured speaker at the 1979 Parapsychology Association meeting.

There are so many points at which psychic energy and matter (or physical energy) merge, we cannot begin to look at them all. One such area of burgeoning research, drawing hard scientists into the parapsychological ken, is psychokinesis (PK), a phenomenon in which mind affects matter. Physicist J. Hasted of the University of London inserts strain gauges into pieces of metal and other objects, to measure in *physical* terms what happens when they are bent, or misshapen *psychically,* by will alone. He has correlated such effects with movements of a subject's hands and body—for example pointing at metal as one tries to bend it without actually touching it. Rhythmic signals result from rhythmic motions, explains Hasted; peaks on the chart correspond to arm movements. He has also determined how localized or extensive are the effects, within the target objects, of the mental energies directed at them.

There are many other experiments with statistically verified results that demonstrate the influence of human thought over things. For example, Swedish engineer Haakon Forwald's twenty-year study measuring the PK force of mental efforts on precision-designed cubes, and Ingo Swann's raising and lowering the temperatures on insulated instruments at the City University of New York, or changing the readings of a magnetometer inside a multi-shielded quark detector buried 5 feet below the floor in concrete. The implications of such experiments for future use are enormous—even threatening. Who will control how such mind-force is used?

With its perspective of the cosmos as an unbroken and interrelated whole, Psi is, in any case, helping us to see that the concept of knowledge as a set of discrete sciences is a construct, a fiction, and presently dysfunctional. What must happen—is happening—is to bring the separate specialities, physical and nonphysical, back together. "Paraphysics," a NASA aerospace engineer observes, "is a blending of physics, electronics, biology, biofeedback, and the new science of subjective awareness, with the methodology already established in some areas of psychic research and systems engineering."

Biofeedback specialist Barbara Brown suggests that: "There is some hope that biofeedback can be used to bring at least some psychic ability under voluntary control. If this becomes a reality, it will likely become the most explosive, far-reaching discovery that biofeedback can make."

William Tiller, Professor of Materials Science at Stanford University, notes that "From experiments on telepathy, psychokinesis, manual healers and traveling clairvoyance, we seem to be dealing with *new energy fields* completely different from those known to us via conventional science."

Rexford Daniels, task force chairman of a subcommittee of the President's Advisory Council, also notes the contribution of Psi research, which poses the possibility of a *new force* in nature. "We found eight different individuals or groups who had happened upon an unknown force which penetrated everything; could not usually be measured by conventional electronic instrumentation; did not attenuate according to recognized formulas; and could cause instantaneous reactions at incredible distances. Each group interested in it had a name descriptive of its use, such as: a second force of gravity (gravitons), hydronics, eloptics . . . dowsing, radionics, and so on."

A provocative possibility is that, in a time of waning energy supplies, Psi itself is a *new energy source!* The internationally recognized Soviet physiologist, Leonid Vasiliev, has stated, "The discovery of the energy lying behind Psi events will be as important, if not more important, than the discovery of atomic energy." A major emphasis of Russian research has, in fact, been trying to uncover the nature of these energies for practical application.

Another place where the psychic and the physical meet is in "thoughtography"—the phenomenon in which mental images are imprinted directly on film or plates by thought only. The term originated in Japan in 1910, when a sensitive being tested by Tomokichi Fukurai accidentally recorded a thought impression on a plate. When the professor asked the subject to repeat the performance, he was able to do so. Fukurai experimented for three years, using other sensitives as well. Similar tests were carried on in France, England, and the United States.

The best known such experiment was a long-term series in Denver beginning in 1964, in which psychiatrist Jule Eisenbud tested the abilities of a Chicago bellhop, Ted Serios. With scores of trials before dozens of witnesses, Eisenbud was able to demonstrate that Serios did imprint images on film with his mind alone: pictures that he thought of or that were suggested to him, as well as hidden targets, written on slips of paper by witnesses and not seen by either Serios or Eisenbud—e.g., the Statue of Liberty, the Great Wall of China.

Staring at a camera, he would signal the photographer when to trigger the shutter. In one series, attempting to produce images of vehicles on Polaroid film, out of 117 photos, 8 showed identifiable vehicle images and 10 were "blackies," in themselves considered to be evidence of something unusual. In another series, Serios tried to reproduce Jefferson's home, Monticello. In 56 attempts, there were several "blackies" and 6 pictures of columns or cage-like structures, which scientists deemed similar to the building.

At a University of Virginia laboratory, Ian Stevenson and Gaither Pratt conducted two separate studies that successfully replicated Eisenbud's findings.

Not all thrusts and projected uses of Psi into other fields are firmly established, of course. For example, the theory that human thought can influence the condition and growth of plants. Some are convinced that it can, and have demonstrations (the development at Findhorn) and experiments (the lab work of Cleve Backster) to prove it. Such efforts have been challenged, however.

Another example is Kirlian photography (Chapter 11). While Americans debate—Is Kirlian photography valid? Is it Psi?—the Russians are reported to be using the technique on a very large scale, for diagnosis and disease prevention, in research centers and hospitals all over the U.S.S.R.

Some refuse to accept any projection whose workings we can't explain. John White and Stanley Krippner, however, in their compilation, *Future Science,* point out that "invention has often preceded full scientific demonstration and understanding of the invention's energy-source." Our use of electricity, they note, is so commonplace that we take it for granted. However, even yet, we don't know what it is. "What is electricity?" Thomas A. Edison was once asked. "I don't know," the inventor replied, "but it works."

Psi in Space

By now you may be wondering, as I did, how much farther can we go? The answer, I found, is *much farther*—to the far reaches of space.

Bored with the interminable *minutiae* of experimental procedures at the Stanford Research Institute, psychic Ingo Swann conceived of his own, non-boring experiment: a psychic probe of outer space. During March 1973, he noted with growing interest the approaching bypass of NASA's *Pioneer 10* spacecraft with the distant planet Jupiter. Wouldn't it be interesting, he reasoned, if a psychic probe of Jupiter could be compared to the actual feedback from *Pioneer 10?*

It would be easy enough to do. All one had to accomplish was a psychic viewing of conditions on Jupiter. To give the undertaking more substance, Swann invited Harold Sherman, who lived 2,300 miles away in Arkansas, to "go" with him on the 500-million-mile trip. Sherman enthusiastically agreed.

Their journey began on April 27, 1973. Sherman made his "launch" from his home in Mountain View, Arkansas as Swann "took off" from "the somewhat unaesthetic experimental chamber at Stanford Research Institute." The simultaneous probes ran for thirty minutes. The responses of both subjects were carefully recorded by senior research physicist Harold Puthoff and laser specialist Russell Targ.

The convergence of the psychics' probes was remarkable. One of them observed "trillions of silver needles, ice crystals . . . I am wondering if they are not icy cold." The other reported "Very high in the atmosphere there are crystals. They glitter. Maybe the stripes of Jupiter are like bands of crystals, like rings of Saturn, but closer to the surface . . . inside the cloud layer, those layers of cold crystals."

One noted, "It is a gaseous mass of myriad colors—yellow, red, violet, some greens, like a giant fireworks display. It billows and leaps with a changing vivid yellow, red and green incandescence, as though reflecting great magnetic fires."

The other commented, "They look so beautiful from the outside, like glittering rainbows of many colors, but inside they look like rolling gas clouds, eerie yellow in color . . . toward the surface the horizon looks orangish or rose-colored, but overhead it is a kind of greenish-yellow."

Not only did Sherman and Swann agree in their reports, but they were not far off from the data later fed back by *Pioneer 10,* which proved to be so much at variance with existing hypotheses about Jupiter that conventional theories had to be radically reassessed. Had the psychics taken their cues from existing literature, as some claimed they had, they would have been far off base.

Challenged by a science editor ("In this business, a psychic is a fraud until proven innocent," Swann notes wryly) they then turned their attention to Mercury, about which almost nothing was known. Fortunately, within the same month, the space probe *Mariner 10* was to fly by Mercury, and radio back scientific data. A New York researcher, Janet Mitchell, monitored and later published a full account of their "trip."

Prevailing opinion was that the planet had no atmosphere, and because of its small size, no magnetic field. Both psychics, however, reported a thin atmosphere, and a magnetosphere. On the sun side of Mercury, Swann "saw" magnetic belts pressed closer to the surface, and on the far side, "belts pushed out into space, trailing the planet, in the opposite direction."

To the astonishment of scientists, *Mariner 10* revealed both an atmosphere and a magnetic field. "The most significant discovery about the atmosphere," *Science News* reported on April 6, 1974, "was the existence of a helium 'tail,' streaming out from Mercury, in a direction away from the sun. It was significant because, shaping the tail, was another unexpected feature, a magnetic field."

To satisfy their own personal curiosity, Sherman and Swann later "visited" Mars. No matter how cleverly and carefully scientists had designed them, they told me, the *Viking* Mars probe could only observe the tiniest area of the planet. "We saw much that they didn't see," Ingo confided. "I plan to release the details myself, later.

"Among other things, we 'saw' five kinds of life, and the ruins of intentional constructions."

"But there is no way to confirm this!" I exclaimed. "If the space probe didn't find it, and the scientists didn't release it. . . ."

"That's just the trouble," Swann readily agreed. "All we can do now is sit back and wait for science to catch up."

8

GENERAL UTILITY:
A Third Arm

We've seen how Psi can find oil, launch an industry, avert catastrophe, cure fatal disease, solve murders, broaden science, make millions, probe space. Is it then, a tool only for the rich and the great, for the once-in-a-lifetime crisis or the epochal turning point? Is there nothing in it for us ordinary mortals, on an average run-of-the-mill day?

Duke of Paducah

David Hoy has built his career on the principle that Psi is an ever-present, all-purpose tool which can serve everyone. "According to Hoy," it can do practically anything. He spreads the word at colleges and clubs, on phone-in shows, radio and TV, and receives eighty to a hundred thousand pieces of mail a year. But most of the time he answers questions, such as "Where's my lost watch?" "Can I get a better job?" "When will the baby come?" "Will we really have to move?" "Is the sale going through?" and "Has our puppy been stolen?"

"How did you get started with all this?" I asked him in his museum-like home in Paducah, Kentucky.

I had written a book on how to improve your ESP. I was discussing it on the radio one time, and a woman called in and asked about a

pair of lost scissors. I said, "Does your phone sit on a little black
stand?" She said it did, and I said, "Open the third drawer, and your
scissors are under some books." She called right back to say that I
was right. It caused a sensation. The response was incredible. People
started calling in from all over, and that led to other radio and TV
programs.

How do you develop ESP? I think there are two fundamentals.
One is, to *keep a record* of the experiences when you have them—
things as simple as "knowing" the outcome of a ball game, or buying
something at the store when you've had a hunch someone wanted
it. This builds confidence, when you have been right enough times.
Second, the more willing I am to state the first feeling I get, the
more right I am.

Hoy is criticized for his flamboyance, in lifestyle, taste, and
manner. When they invited me to visit them, his wife Shirley said,
"We'll treat you royally," and they did. The restaurant they'd
planned to take me to the first night was closed, so they had cartons
of Chinese food sent in. The change of plans and disappointment
did not stop them, though: the "emergency" food was served up
with Chateau Lafite Rothschild, 1971!

A recent newsletter shows a picture of Hoy with Elizabeth Tay-
lor. His 1978 Christmas present to subscribers: an appointment
book calendar with his picture on *both* front and back: "I'll be
looking at you from the covers, urging you to use your ESP all
year through."

This razzle-dazzle, however, gets his points across—some of
the same ones that many others make, namely that Psi, which can
be cultivated, has many uses in everyday life. It can help your
business firm, for example, or your selling techniques. Hoy drew
up a study course, incorporating Psi materials, for a men's hairstyle
corporation several years ago, and received rave letters of appreciation: "an increase of 70 percent in our business."

So what does he *do?* Predictions, for one thing. When Hoy
was in Indianapolis for a talk at Indiana Central College, he appeared on Kokomo station WWKI. As the UPI reported, "A prediction made Wednesday in Kokomo by psychic Dr. David Hoy came
true so rapidly his hosts were startled."

He had forecast that the Kilauea volcano in Hawaii would erupt
soon. The Halemaumau crater of Kilauea let go early next day.
After reading a UPI newsbrief from Honolulu, his interviewer, Rick

Rainbow, called United Press International to confirm it. He then called Hoy, in Indianapolis. "I had that strong feeling several days ago that the volcano would erupt," Hoy said. "I had not made that prediction before, but when I had that feeling, I wrote it in my notebook."

Businessmen take Hoy's ESP newsletter he says, because of its information about stocks. In July 1977, he had a stockbroker in to analyze his predictions for the preceding year. Eleven of thirteen stocks had gone up, one had remained the same, and one was not yet known. While the average stock declined 6.8 percent (the Dow Jones average fell in that year from 917.57 to 854.56), the stocks picked by ESP gained 62 percent. Knowledge of stocks? ESP? Or both?

But first and foremost, Hoy's specialty is personal counsel. "He's called 'the people's psychic,' " Shirley told me, "because he helps them with practical, everyday things"—such as the following:

• After two years of searching for my pearls which you said were in my home, in a drawer back in the corner under something *blue*. . . . My maid found them in a kitchen drawer with all the lids, way back in a corner under a *blue* lid.

• I spoke with you while you were in Atlanta. I asked you if I would be financially able to travel outside the continental U.S.A., and you said yes, that a woman had left me money. Of course you did not know that my mother had passed away four months ago.

• I talked to you on WHO radio and you told me where to find my missing earring. . . . I fished out the earring from under the washer-dryer set after talking to you.

• My daughter had disappeared from home. You told me that she would return a little wiser, and that later on she would go to California, with my permission. . . . It all came true and she finished school in California. I believe in your powers of ESP.

One can't help wondering how many of David's hits can be explained, not by ESP, but as lucky guesses—though it's hard to imagine *guessing* that a lost earring "is under the washer-dryer set" or that the lost keys "are in a yellow building" or the pearls "are in a back corner under something *blue*."

I pressed the Hoys a bit about this. He encourages people to tell him how things turn out, and the amount of return business is another measure of success. Shirley pulled out question forms #200–299, from June 19 to 30, 1978. Out of one hundred, thirty-eight were repeat clients, and thirteen said their questions had been answered correctly. The one hundred inquiries #800–899 from August 24 to September 5, 1978, had forty-five repeat clients, eighteen of whom reported highly correct and helpful replies from Hoy. But in an operation of this magnitude, I feel it's important for the Hoys, and for the Psi field, to have a more accurate measure of performance.

I've written a respected Psi investigator in the hope that some testing can be arranged. Shirley, also, seems eager to have some followup research. "We have at least forty thousand documented cases of people asking David questions, and his answers attached. This is the laboratory I'm so proud of. (I organized it!) If only someone could come in and find out about the people we haven't heard from, like, 'Whatever happened after we wrote?' "

In a small way, I tested the Hoy service from the other side. When a friend in Connecticut, a graduate student named Ed, told me he was in turmoil because a professor of his had lost his valuable research paper, I suggested he write David Hoy. That was in March 1979.

David replied almost immediately: "The paper isn't lost. I feel it is still in the professor's effects. It has been misfiled—under your name, rather than the name of the paper. Within the next three weeks, the paper will be located and returned to you. I want you to be sure to let me hear back from you. I appreciate Dr. Bartlett's putting us in touch."

In July, my Connecticut friend wrote me: "Good news! The lost manuscript has been found. It *was* in the professor's office. It *had* been misfiled! Not under my name, but another student's, and it's been three months, not three weeks. . . ."

Was this a good guess, or a hit? In the opinion of my happy friend: "To predict the right building and room and situation from a thousand miles away is not bad!"

Every psychic brings a unique perspective to the work. Hoy's comes in part from his early experiences as a Baptist missionary.

Another source of Hoy's orientation is his background in stage magic. He's a master magician, a member of the Society of American

Magicians, and the International Brotherhood of Magicians, and lectures at gatherings of these professionals. With his stature, goatee, and imposing voice, he's a natural.

Aside from showmanship and flair, the art of magic gives him a sense of what is trickery and what is not. He has analyzed the performances of psychics and would-be psychics, ferreting out what is phony in their acts.

I sat in front of him on the floor of his living room one whole evening, while he demonstrated the tricks that some "psychics" use.

"So much parades under the label ESP," he explained, "that is really sleight-of-hand. Just put the label 'psychic' on a trick, and you're half way to fooling anyone. A Nobel scientist is easiest to fool with a magic trick; the hardest is any kid here in Paducah."

I told David, "I've concluded that one difference between a trickster and a psychic is that a magician is infallible. *Not*-failing is his stock in trade. A psychic is *not* infallible: he never knows when he'll 'have it.' "

"That's right," he agreed. "But remember this: magic needs props. Psi *never* does."

In sum, Psi is for David Hoy a kind of extra arm, to use when you need it. "The point I'm always making," he says, "is to use ESP as an *aid*—an extra tool in your life. It can't be used as a substitute for skill, or hard work, or education. . . . Work, knowledge, plus ESP: if all three are applied in unison, it's virtually an unbeatable trio."

Sage of Mountain View

Harold Sherman (of the planetary space probe) would agree that Psi is for everyone, any time, but he packages it differently. The titles of his books convey his message: *Your Mysterious Powers of ESP, How to Picture What You Want, How to Make ESP Work for You.*

He and his sparkling wife, Martha, left the bright lights of New York and Hollywood, where he was a writer, for two hundred acres of rolling natural beauty in the foothills of the Ozarks. Their hideaway, Ark Haven, has been their home and much-loved work center ever since. I've drunk in that pure air in their guest cottage in the woods, where I revelled in my first close-up encounter with whippoorwills. Across the road lives Harold's dowser brother, Thomas, or Arthur, as Harold calls him.

Harold's first experience with the psychic was sudden and dramatic:

> I had switched on the electric light in my room hundreds of times. There was no apparent reason why, that afternoon in the late spring of 1915, I should suddenly be seized with a feeling of apprehension as I took hold of the bulb. "Don't turn on the light," a voice in my inner ear seemed to say.
>
> I stood for a moment, hesitant, my fingers on the switch. I had been seated at my typewriter desk, typing, and the sun had dropped behind the western horizon. The giant shadow of dusk was moving over the landscape.
>
> "All right," I decided, wondering why I was surrendering to the impulse. "I won't turn on the light just yet. I can still see." So I resumed my seat and my typing, but it soon became difficult to distinguish the keys. I rose once again and put my hand on the bulb. *"Don't turn on the light!"* The impulse was stronger this time—a positive warning!
>
> I instinctively let go the switch. I had never felt this way before—almost as though some invisible presence had spoken to me, not in an audible voice, but in words which rang out in consciousness.
>
> It was absurd to let an inexplicable urge like that paralyze me, and yet I could not bring myself to go against the impulse. Again I pulled my typewriter desk nearer the window, and turned it about, so that the dwindling light would fall on the typewriter keys. In this manner, I was able to type for perhaps five more minutes.
>
> By this time, the light simply had to be turned on. I was not going to put up with any more nonsense from this strange whim of mine.
>
> My hand was on the switch above the bulb when I heard heavy footsteps come running up onto our front porch. There was no one at home but me. A fist pounded excitedly on our front door, and then the bell commenced ringing furiously.
>
> I hurried downstairs and flung open the door. An electric light linesman burst in. "Don't turn on the lights!" he gasped. "There's a high voltage line down across your wires outside . . . and there's no telling what might . . . ."

It was not until more than two decades later, however, that Sherman's talents won public attention. He had moved to New

York, where, in keeping with themes of his writing, he attended meetings of the National Geographic Society. On one occasion, the famed Arctic explorer Sir Hubert Wilkins was a speaker. Wilkins had just been assigned the task of searching for a crew of lost Russian flyers.

Wilkins remarked how wonderful it would be if we didn't have to rely on radio, but could simply pick up thoughts. At that, Sherman spoke up. He had been experimenting with telepathy, with promising results. How about setting up an experiment with Wilkins sending him thought-messages from the Arctic? To his astonishment, Wilkins accepted.

The plan was to communicate regularly on a scheduled basis, across two to three thousand miles, three nights a week, for a period of five and half months. Wilkins was to serve as the sender, Sherman as the receiver.

Immediately following each telepathic "sitting," Harold sent his recorded impressions, protected by government postmark, to two individuals for filing. One was the late Gardner Murphy, then head of the psychology department at Columbia University. Meanwhile, Sir Hubert kept a detailed daily log and diary at his end. Later, the sets of records were compared. They now comprise one of the classic examples of Psi literature.

During the telepathy experiment, for example, Sherman picked up some strange images. He "saw" Sir Hubert making an Armistice Day address. As he later explained: "I quickly jotted down what I felt to be the highlights of this talk. . . . When I had finished, I noted: 'These thoughts are running through your [Wilkins'] mind, *if not actually uttered in Armistice address.*' And, what to me was even more astonishing, that I should have received 'mental picture impressions' of the Armistice Ball held that evening! I recalled how I had said to my wife: 'Imagine my recording that Wilkins attended this affair—*in evening dress!*' "

After the "sitting," Harold felt dissatisfied and thought he must have been completely off the track, influenced by reading in the papers of Armistice observances.

"Then came a large envelope from Wilkins. I dreaded to look at the pages of the Armistice Day material. A nerve reaction hit me, which I felt in the pit of my stomach, something like the sensation everyone experiences when he is expecting bad news."

When he did look, Sherman learned that bad weather had compelled Wilkins' plane to land at Regina, where he was drafted to help with an Armistice Day celebration! Moreover, Sir Hubert *did* give a talk, expressing the very thoughts that Sherman had recorded, in almost the same words. The report also confirmed another incident Sherman had "seen": the pinning of a medal on the explorer's coat lapel.

But imagine Harold's surprise, when the day's diary concluded with these exact words: "My appearance at this affair was made possible by the loan to me of *evening dress!*"—the only time on the expedition that Wilkins had occasion to don such attire.

One of Harold's key premises, running through his speeches and writings: You can make ESP work for you. "You're getting such messages all the time. Make use of them!"

Some years ago, a couple was visiting the Shermans in New York. Thieves broke into their guests' car, parked in front of the apartment, and stole the new suit the man had just purchased.

Meditating on this occurrence that night, and feeling strongly about it, I suggested to my Subconscious: *No one will ever attempt to steal anything of mine, but I will be made aware of the theft in time to prevent it!* I repeated this suggestion until I felt my Subconscious take hold of it; then I gave it no further conscious thought.

A year and more passed. I had become editor of the *Savings Bank Journal.* I was asked by the publisher, Milton Harrison, to stay downtown to dinner for a discussion of business. As we were about to take the elevator, I acted on impulse, returned to my office, got a copy of the magazine, and placed it in the inside pocket of my winter overcoat. I had no need for this copy since I already had taken my two regular file copies the day before.

My overcoat was an undistinguished, plain, gray one, similar to many others. I hung it on a coat rack some 50 feet from a table at which we were seated. . . . Suddenly, in the midst of our conversation, an inner voice said to me, *"Quick! That man has your overcoat!"*

I found myself on my feet, cutting through between the tables. The man had finished buttoning the coat and was in the act of paying his check. I said, "I beg your pardon, sir. I believe you have my overcoat."

The man pulled back defiantly. "I have not!"

Instantly, upon impulse, I grabbed the coat lapels, and turned them back. There was the *Savings Bank Journal!*

Full of apologies, the man took off the coat and handed it to me. "Well, it looked exactly like mine," he said, and took a few steps back toward the coat rack as though to get his own coat. Suddenly, he made a bolt for the door and dashed out.

About the incident, Harold points out:

> Having received my suggestion, over a year before, my Extra Sensory faculties had stood guard all that time. . . .
>
> Most people give the wrong instructions to their Extra Sensory faculties and as a consequence get the wrong result. If I had *feared* that I would some day be the victim of a theft, and had strongly pictured this possibility, this would have been the same as ordering my higher faculties of mind to create a susceptibility in me for such a happening. It is not likely my mind would have reacted in a way to protect me, as it so obviously did in conformance with my prior instruction.

The overcoat incident was not a matter of life and death, Harold admits, but *some* warnings are.

> On another occasion I had taken a cab, and during the ride the motor began to cough and sputter and almost stop. The driver fussed with the choke, a cloud of fumes came out, and the cab continued on its way. This had happened infrequently before on other cab trips. But this time, when the motor began to act up again, I suddenly became concerned. An inner voice said to me, *"Get out of this cab!"*
>
> The driver protested. "It'll be okay, mister. I think I've got it fixed now."
>
> The motor was still sputtering. "Pull over!" I ordered, with great urgency.
>
> He swung to the curb, still objecting. I pushed open the door and jumped out. Just as I did so, there was an explosion and the cab burst into flames. The driver leaped to safety from the other side, and we both watched the cab become an inferno.

Actually, Harold explains, your intuitive level consciousness is trying to serve in every life situation you are facing, but your conscious skepticism and unwillingness to depend upon it usually causes you to reject, in whole or in part, its proffers of extrasensory guidance.

If David Hoy is a secular minister, Harold Sherman is a religious one. Hoy, who was actually ordained, says "The aim of life on earth is to live and enjoy it to the best of your ability." Sherman, who has no professional ties with religion, declares "God is the Great Intelligence which dwells within you. Apply this mental

method to your own specific fears. Drive them from your consciousness and your life forever. Come to know and feel the presence of
God—within you!"

Harold even has a church—or at least, a camp meeting!—his
ESP workshops, to which hundreds of followers come annually.
Leading psychics and healers, writers, doctors, and other practitioners in the field share Harold's platform—I almost said "pulpit."
In the healing area, for example, he has had Dr. Gerald Jampolsky,
psychiatrist and director of the child center in Tiburon, California,
which works with dying children; Dr. Robert Miller, who has researched noted psychics and healers; Dr. Elisabeth Kübler-Ross,
death-and-dying specialist, and many more.

"Let Me Count the Ways"

It would be difficult to give a complete inventory of the uses of
Psi. They are so many, so varied, and often so personally original.
A California mechanic I know of "psychs out the engine" when
a car is brought in for repairs. He simply holds a small pendulum
over each auto part in turn, and when the pendulum spins, knows
that's the thing that needs fixing.

Education and Conditioning. Edgar Cayce and others are said
to have learned their school lessons by sleeping on their books.
This might not work so readily for the average person, but many
feel, nonetheless, that Psi can help with the educational process.
It doesn't take much understanding of the psychic to know that
opening oneself to the possibilities brings better results.

Dr. Georgi Lozanov, director of the Institute of Suggestology
and Parapsychology in Sofia, Bulgaria, a government-supported bureau with thirty staffers, has research findings that point to the
beneficial learning results of suggestion, relaxation, and selected
psychic techniques.

Elizabeth Toles, a fourth-grade teacher at an elementary school
in Memphis, Tennessee, uses her psychic perception to determine
her students' problems and talents, and helps them accordingly. Miss
Toles notes, "Sometimes, it takes a teacher a whole year to know
the strength and weakness of each student, but I know right away."

Business. As we saw in Chapter 2, drawing on extra help and
ability is commonplace in the business world. Al Pollard's successful

"think tank" seminars and workshops for business leaders are veritable showcases for the use of the psychic. When he formed his own management firm in Little Rock, he saw the possibility of sharing his insights with others. "I had long been interested in the psychic field, and its potential for application in business," he says. "This was a unique opportunity to show others how it could help them professionally."

The combination of expectation and PK ("What you visualize is what you get!") is a tried and true formula among success-peddlers. As one sensitive puts it: "Psi puts your mind in control of circumstances, events, and your future."

Creativity. Parapsychologists are beginning to consider the relationship between creativity and Psi. Though the final results aren't yet in, in a study of randomly chosen high school students, Charles Honorton found that those who scored highest in a creativity test also scored highest on an ESP predictive test. In research at UCLA, Thelma Moss discovered that artists score higher on ESP measures than non-artists.

Some creative individuals are aware of drawing on a paranormal realm of knowledge. Singer Della Reese notes, "When I want to be especially creative, I don't try to do anything. I just open myself up and let go. . . . I think we all get communications we don't understand."

Creator of the Learjet and other inventions, William Lear says, "In designing an airplane I use an awful lot of intelligence from 'other sources.' "

In eight years of research, neuropsychiatrist Shafica Karagulla found that breakthroughs in creativity, what she calls "Higher Sense Perceptions," are essentially psychic. "The remarkable and swift insight that comes with some types of Higher Sense Perception can encompass a vast wilderness of facts and come up with the right conclusion. . . . My discovery that there are many people with HSP abilities, already quietly making outstanding contributions to society, in science, in business, in medicine, in industry, and in many other areas of leadership, surprised and astounded me. However, Higher Sense Perception is just beginning to be respectable, and many people see no reason for discrediting their work by admitting they have these amazing abilities. Some of these people we call 'geniuses.' Others we simply designate as very gifted individuals, or as great leaders in their field. Society is very definitely benefitting by HSP ability, whether we admit that it exists, or not."

Sports. The classic *Zen and the Art of Archery* points out the necessity of letting go, and turning the whole business over to cosmic forces:

> The arts, as they are studied in Japan . . . are not intended for utilitarian purposes only, or for purely aesthetic enjoyments, but are meant to train the mind . . . to bring it into contact with the ultimate reality. Archery is therefore practiced not solely for hitting the target; the swordsman does not wield the sword just for the sake of outdoing his opponent; the dancer does not dance just to perform certain rhythmical movements of the body. The mind has first to be tuned to the Unconscious. . . . The archer ceases to be conscious of himself as the one who is engaged in hitting the bullseye. . . . rid of the self, he becomes one with the perfecting of his skill, though there is in it something of a quite different order. . . .
>
> Man is a thinking reed, but his great works are done when he is not calculating and thinking. . . . When this is attained, he thinks yet he does not think. He thinks like the showers coming down from the sky. He thinks like the waves rolling on the ocean. He thinks like the stars illuminating the nightly heaven. He thinks like the green foliage in the relaxing spring breeze. Indeed, he *is* the showers, the ocean, the stars, the foliage.

Now, researchers are beginning to document what Eastern mystics have long since known, the relation of Psi to sports. Michael Murphy, the founder of Esalen Institute, and Rhea White, a parapsychologist—sports fans, both of them—have put their findings together in a book about the psychic side of sports. Together, they have come across over forty-five hundred instances in which athletes have reported experiencing psychic phenomena during their performances; instances in which professional football players "knew" what the opposing team was about to do; golfers were able psychokinetically to affect the trajectories of poorly hit balls; martial arts masters could force assailants away with some unexplained power, without touching them.

The two found, among athletes, reports of uncanny predictions, out-of-body experiences, and altered states of consciousness, all produced during the euphoria of athletic experiences. Though the athletes don't seem to know what's happening, they know that it happens. Says Murphy, "I gather that top athletes are people who are accustomed to altering time . . . to a higher state of focus and concentration . . . to altered perceptions of many types, and to going with the inner flow of things; but I don't see any of this on the sports pages . . . our culture seems to screen it out."

Take a pass Brodie once threw to Gene Washington. The moment he released it, he "knew" it was going to connect. "It looked for a moment," observed Murphy, who had seen the play, "as if the safety would make an interception, but then it seemed as if the ball went through or over his hands, as he came in front of Washington."

Said Brodie, "Our sense of that pass was so clear and our intention so strong, that the ball was *bound* to get there, come wind, cornerbacks, hell or high water. . . . Such things seem to exist— or emerge—when your state of mind is right. It has happened to me dozens of times. I've seen it happen too many times to deny it."

Individual/Social Welfare. There is massive evidence that the thoughts of one person can benefit another (or harm him, for that matter). There is evidence that prayer, concentration, or wishes of a healer, or even of an interested party, do bring personal benefits. The experiments of Bernard Grad and a whole series of others attest to this. The realms of healing, to which we have devoted an entire chapter, are further documentation.

But what about the effects of *group* "energy" on others? It stands to reason, that if *one,* by sending special thoughts, can effect beneficial results, *many* can bring larger ones. Yet there has been little acceptable testing of this sort of situation.

Since time immemorial people have assumed that collective psychic endeavors will bring good effects. This conviction has been built into cultures the world around; into religions and ceremonial practices, rain-dances, harvest festivals, blessing of the fishing fleet, World Day of Prayer. Sometimes a heartfelt group gesture has seemed to bring results.

We may be on the brink of analyzing such phenomena. Granted, it is difficult to separate the variables, and to determine cause and effect. Would it have rained anyway, if people had not danced? Would the war have stopped if people had not prayed?

While we look for these answers, practitioners continue to urge the use of Psi for your personal benefit. Use it to quit smoking or to lose weight, says Hoy, who dropped a hundred pounds by taking his own advice. Use it to sell your product, shine in interviews, get a better job or a raise. Use it to improve your self-image, your public image. Use it, even, Sherman and Hoy advise, to improve your sex life!

All of which brings us back full circle to that all-purpose tool, the pendulum. There has been too little hard testing of the uses of this instrument, or the many claims made for it. *Is* the food or medicine the pendulum warns against *really* harmful? *Does* the knowledge it unveils prove out? There are hundreds of pendulum addicts around the world who will testify that it works.

Is this substance radioactive? Can you tell what it's made of? "You *can* dowse for the radioactivity of rocks and minerals," says Dr. Z. V. Harvalik. In the *American Journal of Dowsing,* he tells how.

Is your plot of earth good for the seed you wish to plant? Col. F. A. Archdale of the British Society of Dowsers explains the use of the pendulum to test compatibility of plants and soil.

Use your pendulum when you are in danger, advises Hanna Kroeger.

> A pilot in a single engine plane had an accident in icy conditions, away from civilization. He calmed down and prayed. . . . In the snow he marked off the directions, North, South, and so on. Then he took his key as a pendulum. Slowly, the pendulum showed "Northeast." He asked it, "How many steps?" It counted 165. The man dragged his injured feet the distance, and found shelter from ice and snow, in a cavern, which was thickly covered with pine needles and dry leaves.

Do you have a leak, broken pipes, a blockage somewhere, faulty ducts, drains or cables? Get at them, urges Gen. Scott Elliot of Dumfriesshire, with the help of a pendulum.

So you've found and marked the spot where water is hidden? What about the rig you've brought in: Will it do the job? "Dowse the rig!" says Jack Livingston.

In fact, declares the newsletter of the Southern California Chapter, American Society of Dowsers: Dowsing is *not* super-human; anyone can do it! Here is their partial list of its uses:

Locating:
- airplanes (lost)
- persons (lost)
- coins (lost)
- water (selected types)
- ships, subs (at sea)
- water pipes, leaks, etc.
- property lines
- archaeological finds
- caves
- golf balls, etc.
- mineral deposits
- snakes
- fish and game
- buried treasure
- graves

Determining:
- weather calculations
- earthquakes, faults, etc.
- location of distant objects
- bilocation (maps, etc.)
- signatures (genuine?)
- sex of unborn babies
- pregnancy
- soil (contaminants, etc.)
- biometric measurements
- suitability of foods
- north, south, etc.
- paintings (originals?)
- sex of eggs
- potency

In short, it would seem that the only limits to the uses of Psi are the limits of the human imagination!

PART
II
THE QUEST

9

THE GREAT CONTROVERSY: Is Psi So?

In the great Psi controversy, where do people come out? Where does society stand? Offhand, the answer would seem to be simple: there are believers, non-believers, and undecideds—the people in between.

On second thought, however, it is not quite that simple. "Believers" include both the super-gullible, who will believe anything, and the cautious, who, after careful thought and investigation, have painstakingly come to the conclusion that there is something to Psi. So too with "non-believers," some of whom reject Psi on principle, while others among them hold the same position after serious inquiry.

Further complicating the picture are people who take both pro and con stands, depending on the circumstances. Some are publicly anti-Psi, for example, but privately pro.

A personal encounter with a prominent newsman pointed this up for me. As the head of a national newspaper syndicate, he was considering a Psi-information column. He asked me to bring in some sample columns. For three quarters of the hour I was with him, in his skyscraper office on Madison Avenue, he declared that he *personally* had absolutely no interest in the subject. What's more, he didn't believe in it.

When I got up to leave, however, he followed me to the door.

"Well, there was one strange thing that happened to me," he said hesitantly, "at the time my wife died." Whereupon he spelled out in great detail an overpowering psychic experience, which still troubled him.

I suspect that there are many closet pros, who professionally are officially against, but personally are pro-Psi. On another occasion, I was visiting the parapsychology laboratory of an internationally known researcher in the field. Had I not known who he was, I would have assumed, from his conversation, that he was the most articulate of anti-Psi voices. The most cool, cautious scholar I have yet talked with, he made no positive statements about anything, hemming every sentence in with exceptions, cautions, and qualifications. He ended the interview with this statement: "I wouldn't be surprised if the whole subject of Psi would blow over, simply evaporate, within the next ten years!" This, from a man who runs a well-known parapsychology program!

On the way to the plane, he took me to lunch. Sitting there in a corner of the cafe, the sun streaming in on the table with its freshly-cut flowers, he leaned back in his chair and stretched. "Now I'll tell you about *my* psychic experiences," he said, and throughout the meal, held me spellbound with one of the best batches of Psi adventures I've yet heard.

Some time back Dr. Elisabeth Kübler-Ross, the psychiatrist who has studied death and dying extensively, asked an audience, "How many of *you* have had an 'out-of-body' experience?" She was flabbergasted when twelve to fifteen persons raised their hands. At her next lecture she did the same, and again at the next. Every time she asked the question, at least a dozen people admitted that they, too, had had the same exotic and uncanny experience.

I told my husband about Kübler-Ross' discovery. "Isn't it amazing that in her audiences, the out-of-body experience is par for the course?" The statistic must have startled him. In his next lecture he tried it himself. Though his gathering was made up of teachers, medical specialists and engineers, once again, a number of hands went up. Afterwards, a consultant to the Bechtel Coporation, oil producers in Saudi Arabia and hardly an airy, visionary type, described to my husband in detail a dramatic out-of-body incident that he and his wife experienced together.

We have no idea how many people there are, pro or con, or

even how many are involved. We can look at some of the categories we know about, however: blind believers, avid skeptics, the undecided.

Blind Believers

Blind believers are overboard followers who keep the Psi Show on the road, literally, with floor shows, fairs, demonstrations—on stage, radio, and TV. These undiscriminating, across-the-board supporters will believe anything, and buy anything, thus keeping chicanery in the marketplace and trash on the shelves: books, magazines, tabloids, catalogs, crash courses, mountains of ads, and psychic horror tales. Who can tell which ads, such as the following, are good or bad, helpful or wacky, sincere or fake?

VIMALA BEADS
Made with devotion at the Abode of the Message. 99 clay beads of unusual beauty and magnetism!

Pyramid Centre: the largest selection of pyramid products in the East today. 12″ open frame Steel Pyramid, with a compass and Experimental Guide Book.

The Handbook of Astral Projection
See the World and Beyond. . . .

The Brain Wave Synchronizer
A photo-electronic instrument that tunes to the natural frequency of the brain. 1980 professional model. Shorter induction time. Deepen the hypnotic level.

WITCHCRAFT!
Harness its powers and gain serenity, spiritual awareness, psychic proficiency, wealth.

THE MOST COMPLETE LINE OF OCCULT SUPPLIES!
Candles, Oils, Incense, Herbs. Special discount to Witches, Mediums, Spiritualists.

Faster than Ouija Board!
Smooth-rolling ball bearings speed flow of automatic writing
—without awkward pauses
—*The Planchette.*

For some people, at least, there is an urge and a need to believe, which can be served more dependably by tricksters and sleight-of-hand artists posing as psychics than by psychics themselves. As we have seen, it is the *business* of showpersons and magicians to be foolproof. Not even the greatest of psychics can make that claim.

It is incredibly easy to fool others, and to be fooled. To make this point, the sponsors of an educational Psi program injected a phony into the lineup before a generally knowledgeable audience. "Mr. X" was presented as a parapsychological investigator just back from Russia, having learned some special procedures for developing his powers. When he objected that he didn't feel confident, and wasn't good enough to perform, the chairman overruled him: "At least, you can show us something of what you learned!"

At this, the audience joined in: "Please! Please!" Mr. X shyly agreed. He would see if he could identify the color of a board behind a screen. He made several tentative starts, then fell back. Finally, with an extra effort, he blurted out "Yellow!" The tension broke and everyone cheered.

Mr. X performed several such feats, in the same manner. Each time he made it, they cheered.

When the audience had thoroughly hanged itself, the chairman announced that Mr. X had never been to Russia, but did have some theater in his background. The feats, he explained, were brought off with the aid of a little electrical gadgetry, and a confederate in the audience.

Thus, to their chagrin, having trusted a supposedly authoritative presentation, a sophisticated audience fell into the trap: after two halting apologies by a diffident young man, they were ready to believe *anything*.

Much the same psychology undergirded the great age of mediumship, which, beginning in the mid-1800s, swept over America and Europe, and continued for some decades. Claiming they were specially endowed, and able to communicate with the dead, mediums attracted an eager and hopeful public.

It was not just the half-baked, the uneducated and the credulous who turned up at séances and "spirit circles." Among those who followed these mediumistic developments to one degree or another were Harriet Beecher Stowe, William Lloyd Garrison, James Fenimore Cooper, Arthur Conan Doyle, William Cullen Bryant, and Horace Greeley.

Historians usually date the modern spiritualist movement from the discovery, at the end of 1847, by Margaret and Kate Fox, of unexplained rappings, which disturbed their home in Hydesville, New York. Word of the rappings, interpreted as "messages from the other side," spread, and in 1849 a public demonstration was staged in Rochester.

From this small beginning, hundreds of imitators sprang up across America, spawning thousands of followers who called themselves "spiritualists." Most of the manifestations were rappings, but other techniques blossomed: automatic writing, slate writing, voices, table tipping, and human levitation.

William Lloyd Garrison, writing of a séance he attended in 1867, conducted by a twelve-year-old-girl, noted that there were

> bells ringing over the heads of the circle, floating in the air and dropping on the table; spirit hands touching the garments of all present; pocketbooks taken out of pockets, the money abstracted and then returned; watches removed in the same manner; the contents of one table conveyed by invisible power from one end of the parlor to the other; the bosoms of ladies partly unbuttoned, and articles thrust therein and taken therefrom; powerful rappings on the table and floor . . . a basket containing artificial oranges and lemons emptied, and its contents distributed around the circle, and the basket successfully put upon the head of everyone present, in a grotesque manner; striking and tickling of persons by spirit hands; and so on and on.

Though rundowns of such acts seem no different from sideshows, a number of mediums were tested and found to be gifted indeed. When the distinguished physicist Sir William Crookes tested medium Daniel Douglas Home's ability to move objects at a distance, he pronounced it genuine.

Mrs. Lenore Piper, the eminent medium from Boston, was investigated intensively by psychologist William James, who reported to the American Society for Psychical Research, in 1886: "I now believe her to be in possession of a power as yet unexplained."

Some time later an Irish medium, the accomplished Mrs. Eileen Garrett, came from London to the United States in order to work with parapsychologists. Bewildered about the nature of her own talents, and the way in which they worked, she put herself in J. B. Rhine's hands for extensive sessions at Duke University. Mrs. Garrett later founded the Parapsychology Foundation in New York.

Thus, there were some reputable mediums; but as the decades wore on, deceptions and chicanery aplenty were revealed, until a cloud of resentment and suspicion built up and hung over them all.

Under the pressure, in 1888, Margaret Fox publicly confessed that she and her sister had produced the "rappings" by cracking their toe joints, but almost instantly retracted her statement. Cornell Professor of American History Laurence Moore suggests that actually, the medium may never have known *what* she was up to.

The debacle of mediumship cast a lingering shadow of doubt over the whole psychic field, a shadow from which parapsychology has not even yet fully recovered.

Another problem plagues the serious psychic quest: the overeager attempts of novices to expand their psychic abilities and break into the inner charmed circle of psychic masters. Over three years ago, clinical psychologist Allan Cohen told me: "There are already two thousand documented cases of individuals needing psychiatric help, specifically because of symptoms caused by prematurely and forcibly trying to develop psychic powers—that is, trying to become psychics."

Toronto psychotherapist Howard Eisenberg, awarded the first academic degree in parapsychology in Canada, observes that some individuals who are particularly susceptible to suggestion, and relatively naive about the recognition and control of altered states of consciousness, may work themselves into a situation where they require a knowledgeable therapist to help free them from an essentially self-suggested state.

California psychiatrist Ernest Pecci has developed a specialty in "salvaging psychic casualties." He also warns against pushing into the unknown Psi jungle without guidance and help.

Everyone I've consulted warns would-be psychics to stay away from Ouija boards.* It is rare to find consensus on anything in this field, but at least everyone I've asked about this agrees. It's hard to imagine why there are such strong feelings about such an apparently innocent gadget, but it seems that those who open themselves indiscriminately to incoming "messages" may open themselves up to much more. For the same reasons, some of my consultants have cautioned equally against the practice of automatic writing—waiting eagerly with pencil poised for a message from beyond.

In sum, they advise: If you find you have psychic tendencies, don't panic; these are normal. But don't push them, either. Avoid the wrong kind of *meditation,* such as extreme concentration exercises designed to produce or accumulate "psychic power"; the wrong

---

* From "Yes" in French and German: "oui" and "ja."

kinds of *motivation*—cheap thrills, an ego trip, a quick buck, or drug-induced experiments, which too often end in "bad trips"; the wrong kinds of *gurus or counselors*—phonies who resort to a panoply of gimmicks, neon signs on highways, high charges for services that can't be precisely evaluated. Check credentials and reputations, as you would in any business undertaking; look for people with good references, who "feel right" to you. Pascal Kaplan of John F. Kennedy University, which makes a specialty of parapsychological education, observes that "What we need now is a kind of Psi consumer protective agency, to inform and advise us on things psychic, and to protect us against ourselves."

Finally, if the field attracts you, educate yourself. Consult your local library for bona-fide parapsychological organizations and professional publications. Check colleges, universities, and adult education programs for reading lists and courses. (And don't overlook the notes and bibliographical suggestions in this book.)

As a chaser to gullibility, I highly recommend the tragic yet hilarious exposé *The Psychic Mafia,* in which a master charlatan in the mediumistic field, M. Lamar Keene, tells all. He and his colleagues, with a few ectoplasmic props, milked untold thousands from credulous clients—not in the 1850s, but in our day. Not only did they commit such gross sins as delivering fake messages from "the other side," but pilfered from wallets and handbags as well.

When I exclaimed, to a woman knowledgeable in such matters, how amazing it was that these clients were deceived in so many and such obvious ways, she replied, "That's nothing! I've *explained* to some of them just what's going on, how they're being lied to and cheated, and even some of the tricks. But even after they have been personally robbed, they keep going back, year after year. They *want* to be fooled!"

Avid Skeptics

There are also the super-skeptics who, no matter what the evidence, reject Psi on principle. *Not* believing is, for them, as much an article of faith as believing is for their opposite numbers.

Some of the actively "con" group have gone so far as to *institutionalize* their skepticism into anti-Psi organizations, journals, and lobbies. Paul Kurtz, the former editor of *The Humanist,* established perhaps the most trigger-happy of these: the "Committee for the

Scientific Investigation of Claims of the Paranormal." It sponsors a journal, *The Skeptical Inquirer*. The organization boasts a distinguished roster of scientists and others who have no use for the psychic. Among the most vocal of its members are Martin Gardner of *The Scientific American* and "The Amazing Randi," a magician. Magicians, incidentally, are increasingly called into parapsychological research, to cover possibilities that a scientist is not trained to catch. A number of parapsychologists are themselves amateur magicians, e.g., Arthur Hastings, Stanley Krippner, Russell Targ, and W. E. Cox.

Even I, who am so peripheral to the parapsychological scene, have been a target of the committee's wrath. For a *Reader's Digest* article on Psi, I wrote:

Paul Kurtz, Professor of Philosophy at the State University of New York, Buffalo, speaks for many scientists, when he says "We are disturbed that only positive results are published. The public rarely hears about negative findings, which are considerable."

That issue of the magazine had barely hit the stands when Kurtz and company called a press conference at the Biltmore Hotel in New York, to protest my article and the "irresponsibility" of the *Reader's Digest* in carrying it.

No one called me to ask for my comment; the committee had the last word in headlines and articles. But there is an intriguing postscript to this story. Immediately following the press conference, I received a letter from Marcello Truzzi at Eastern Michigan University, co-chairman of the CSICP and, like myself, a sociologist. He wrote to tell me he was resigning as co-chairman of the committee and editor of its journal.

"I am not resigning because I now agree with you," he took pains to explain, "but because of incidents like this. I found myself in the midst of a protest meeting before I'd even heard of your article!"

On another occasion, just hours after an evening NBC documentary on psychic experiments, produced in conjunction with the Institute of Noetic Sciences, the Committee's chairman was on a top-of-the-morning TV show to protest the program publicly. Shortly afterward it was announced that the Committee had sued, though nothing came of it.

What is of significance for us is the issue of open communication and genuine "scientific investigation." I can only applaud bona fide communication about, and investigation of, this difficult subject; the more the better. I do, however, deplore claims and trappings of such procedures where there are none.

Perhaps editor Truzzi's own spinoff journal, *The Zetetic Scholar,* "an independent scientific review of anomalies and the paranormal," will help fill that bill. Its consulting editors include experts from many fields, and an even wider spread of opinion, including members from the original committee, and a former, very active, president of the Parapsychological Association.

There are two other avid opponents of far greater import. One of these is the churches. Organized religion is far from uniform on any subject, of course, including Psi, and a tiny fringe, such as the spiritualists, even hold psychic views. But for a great many churchpeople, Psi is the work of the Devil, anathema in any form.

More subtle, but far more effective than church or committee in restraining psychic inquiry, is the Scientific Establishment itself, which is faced with a category of data it is not equipped to handle. Its traditional view, standing foursquare on the mechanistic-materialistic scheme of reality—only what can be measured is real—is fundamentally threatened by the *non*-material, *non*-measurable psychic realm. Its reflex response, thus, is to reject or ignore parapsychological findings.

One tack of the Establishment is to save its plums for the orthodox faithful and withold favors from deviants. When psychologist Charles Tart prepared to write up a carefully controlled "out of body" experiment, the man who lent him the lab refused to let his name be mentioned in the credits, lest it blacken his reputation.

I have talked with a number of researchers who have discovered that their funds have suddenly dried up and their promotions been forgotten after they dipped their toes into these uncertain waters. Some of the most promising plans on the drawing board have been shelved for lack of financial support.

The Undecided

A third category is, of course, one somewhere between the two above: people who have to be shown, but who, if given sufficient evidence, are willing to change. It is this third category whom this entire book addresses.

Though I bemoan the dearth of careful and systematic criticism, the skeptics do have a case. Let's spell it out.

First, on the face of it, Psi doesn't make sense. Everything about it contradicts the prevailing scientific view: Here are phenomena that can be perceived, but not through the senses; known, but not measured; which defy all laws of direction, causality, time and space. In the prevailing context, the very idea is absurd.

Second, psychic manifestations as reported are very often undependable. Most firsthand accounts are informal and subjective. Spontaneous events that take people by surprise tend to be hazy in the telling. Anecdotal accounts—a target of the critics—are a far cry from the disciplined procedures of the lab, where the attempt is made to eliminate bias and identify all the variables.

Third, there is a great body of psychic phenomena that has never been tested; that, possibly, cannot be tested! For example, such subjective happenings as insights and dreams. Premonitions and warnings can be compared later with what actually happens— *if* recorded ahead of time. But, as with any one-time Psi incident, they cannot be repeated, as experiments traditionally require. Whatever it is that takes place when a Psi event happens cannot be measured on any instrument yet devised.

Fourth, even in the laboratory, insurmountable difficulties develop. An Alabaman told me about her daughter: "She can do everything—tell what's going to happen, describe hidden objects, identify colors without touching them, blindfolded. But when we took her to a laboratory to have her tested, nothing happened. Absolutely nothing! Her whole psychic apparatus, whatever that is, turned off, and she was no more psychic than that table."

Researchers have particular difficulty with replication—that is, getting the identical results each time they repeat a psychic experiment. For example, in 1968, when Cleve Backster reported the results of his experiments with plants—plants have Psi ability!—it caused a sensation. He'd discovered that they react to human thought, sense threats to their welfare; they even sense threats to the welfare of other living things. After attaching a polygraph to a philodendron, he found that the instrument responded to the plant much as it does to a human. Just the *thought* of touching a match to a leaf made the needle jump. And when brine shrimps were dumped into boiling water in another room, the plants "cringed" empathetically. From his observations of this "primary perception capability" on the part of plants, Backster hypothesized an unknown kind of common linkage among all living things.

But—were Backster's experiments valid? Other researchers were divided. Dr. Aristide H. Esser, head of the research laboratory at Rockland State Hospital of Orange, New Jersey, asserts that he has been able to replicate portions of Backster's work. Marcel Vogel of IBM said he had confirmed all of the effects, as reported. However, K. A. Horowitz, D. C. Lewis, and E. L. Gastiger, at Cornell, reported that they were unable to replicate the work. Nor could R. B. Johnson of the University of Washington, or John Kmetz of Science Unlimited Research Foundation in San Antonio.

Fifth is the serious matter of fraud. We've seen how much of the mediumistic phenomenon in American history was, and is, chicanery. Even some of the so-called "greats" have tarnished their reputations by occasionally stooping to trickery. Uri Geller is a case in point. He is first and foremost a showman, with the trouper's commitment to never disappointing anyone; never failing.

When a sensitive, even a talented one, pressures himself, or lets himself be pressured to be always right, he has been backed into a corner from which there is no escape. Many observers, scientists and magicians among them, have caught Uri in trickery. He once bragged to a friend of mine that he did tricks!

Arthur Ford, that famous and most respected of mediums, may also have resorted to a little extra help. His biographer notes that he kept files of distinguished persons and likely clients. Just such a collection, a mutual friend tells me, was found under his deathbed. These, and a remarkable memory, are said to have pulled him through many a demonstration emergency.

Fraud has, unfortunately, surfaced even in the lab. In 1974, the then director of J. B. Rhine's Institute for Parapsychology, Walter J. Levy, Jr., was caught by his colleagues faking experimental results. He was summarily fired, of course, but if it could happen here . . . ?

In short, if there is such a thing as Psi, it is evasive and ephemeral at best—difficult if not impossible to measure, to replicate, and to pin down. Even those who have worked in the field for years admit that they don't know what it is, or how it works.

First-Person Struggle

I am more than a bit sympathetic with the problems of scientists trying to cope with a topic as controversial and skittish as Psi. I shared their frustration as I tried to research and verify the claims of a respected dowser in Southern California, Ralph Harris. So frustrating have my efforts been, in this instance, that this is the first time I have written anything about it.

The co-founder of the Southern California chapter of the American Society of Dowsers, Harris' accomplishments have been cited repeatedly, complete with pictures, in the press. One incident particularly struck me: how Harris helped General Patton win the African campaign. Patton, it seems, had said "The only thing that can defeat us in Africa is lack of water!"

Here's a brief account of that story, from the Los Angeles *Herald-Examiner* for February 8, 1976:

> When General George Patton landed in Africa, he was as worried about water as he was about Gen. Erwin Rommel. The retreating Germans had blown up all the wells.
>
> A lanky captain from California, who had never lost his Virginia twang, offered a brash solution: if the General would find him a forked willow stick, Ralph Harris would find enough water for 600,000 men!
>
> General Patton liked that kind of flair. He had an entire willow tree flown in. Harris cut himself a divining rod and walked into the desert to dowse for water, accompanied by a skeptical geologist colonel. Harris, now a real estate broker, says he found a vein of water 300 feet wide, that yielded 2,000 gallons of water per minute, just 400 feet below the surface, "and you never saw such a happy man as Patton!"
>
> From then on, Patton ordered Harris to locate wells as the troops advanced.

What a story! Why hadn't we heard about it before? I went to the library, but could find no trace of it, even in *The Patton Papers*. I went to see Mr. Harris in Glendale, California. He was glad to tell me all, and equally willing for me to tape it. Here are some excerpts from that account:

> See, I finally go to General Patton. You know, a captain has a hard time to see a general. It finally made me pretty mad. I said, "Dammit, we need water here . . ."

Well, I got to see him, and he said, "What do you need?" I said, "I need a forked willow stick. I can get you water, you get me a forked willow stick." He said, "I'll fly you a whole goddam tree!"

They said, "Have you gone crazy down there, General? What do you want with a willow tree?" But he said to the Air Force, "Go get one," so I got my forked stick and went out there with this colonel, a geologist. He gave me a rougher time than Patton.

Well, the colonel and I drove out there in a jeep. In North Africa, the water runs in veins. They run in the direction of northwest to southeast.

Anyway, we went out there and located, and I said, "Drill here." He drilled it, and he brought in two thousand gallons of water a minute; a beautiful well, right in the middle of the sand (it blows all over out there). Meanwhile, I went out and located another one.

What did General Patton say?

Oh, he hugged me. He said, "Now there's no way I can lose this war!" It was a great experience. I got twelve wells under the colonel; then, of course, he got killed on the thirteenth. His name was Colonel Bradshaw. I got fourteen wells in all. I'm sorry the colonel got killed. General Omar Bradley or General Stone would verify this for you— Stone was a one-star general in World War II.

The last time I saw General Patton was in Sicily: water running off that island! I said, "General, need any water?" He said, "Oh, here's my water captain! No, don't need any water: got too damn much water here!"

The story was as good as ever. But how could I check it out? Stone was gone; Patton was dead. The colonel had been killed. As Harris told me: "The records of all this were blowed up with the colonel."

"Then whom shall I talk to?" I asked Harris.

"Omar Bradley's your man. You'll have to get his address through the Army. He's way over eighty now."

A bit of detective work led me to New York, and finally to the Bulova Watch Company, where Bradley was honorary chairman. "He's moved away from New York," they told me. "Try Fort Bliss, Texas."

On five-star letterhead, an aide-de-camp answered my letter: "Due to General Bradley's responsibilities and current health . . . the General is unable to fully respond to your inquiry."

I then turned to military records and libraries: to the U.S. Military Academy, Department of the Army; to the U.S. Military Institute at Carlisle Barracks, Pennsylvania. No luck.

I next tried Command General Staff College at Fort Leavenworth, Kansas, whose librarian replied, "We are unable to confirm this story. Our belief in it was severely shaken by the discovery that neither Capt. Ralph Harris, nor Gen. B. G. Stone are listed in the Army Register for 1943. Also, accounts of the battle for Morocco and Tunisia stress the constant rain and mud plaguing the participants. It's a fun story, but unlikely."

So much doubt had been cast on the tale by this time that I began to wonder whether Harris, or even I, had imagined it.

The event was abruptly revived, however, at the national convention of the American Society of Dowsers in 1978, when Christopher Bird, a respected researcher/writer in the field, recounted the complete dowsing-for-Patton incident at a plenary session.

When I excitedly asked for documentation, a land surveyor, Louis Matacia, got up to announce, with some emotion, that I would "never in the world get any information out of the military"; that they would, in fact, go out of their way to sidestep, deny, or avoid the subject of dowsing.

Matacia, it turned out, is the one who introduced dowsing to U.S. soldiers in Vietnam, something I mentioned earlier. He first tried the technique with bent coathangers in Virginia, and was so successful in ferreting out military secrets by that mysterious technique that his methods were picked up and passed on to soldiers in training.

When I tried later to contact Matacia, however, he was unwilling to comment further. Some of his colleagues suggested that he had been given such a hard time himself that he had resolved to steer clear of the subject. My final efforts to throw some light on "The Patton Incident" by consulting knowledgeable dowsers brought the following suggestive input. From Christopher Bird:

> I don't think you *ever* will confirm the Ralph Harris story. It was only one incident in a virtual maelstrom of activity. Hundreds of funny incidents happened in the war, none of them recorded by military historians. I doubt whether the U.S. Marine Corps would *officially* confirm Louis Matacia's efforts to teach dowsing to Marines. He spent at least two weeks of his own time on it, without a dime's worth of remuneration, and at one point took himself plus six other dowsers for an all-day teaching session to Camp Lejeune, N.C. I have all the

documents on this but the USMC itself never made it *official*, so for the high command it doesn't exist. That fact doesn't make it any less true.

I have found that, in investigative reporting, appeal to *authorities* for confirmation of facts is a waste of time.

The head of a large and successful chapter of the American Society of Dowsers had this to say about Matacia:

I had much correspondence with him about his getting into the military with his dowsing ideas. It's too long to relate here, how one particular officer was demoted, and so on, because of his condoning and cooperating with Matacia on dowsing.

About Harris:

He is a retiring type, and I doubt if he had any idea of his military past creeping into public records, where he'd stand to profit, or get recognition. So many have come to me privately to say, "There is a humble man. He helped me in this way. . . ."

About the African incident:

Every time I ask the question with the pendulum in my own dowsing—whether Harris worked for, with or by General Patton—I get the same answer: he did.

Honest research can be long, hard and tough. *Was* there a Patton incident or not? Sometimes you just have to give up on checking . . . or bide your time.*

---

* As this book is about to go on press: Ralph Harris has died but General Patton's daughter, Ruth Ellen Patton Totten, has enthusiastically confirmed the dowsing incident. "I *know* it's true because Ma told me. She thought it was very amusing. My old man was a dowser himself—it runs in our family very strongly. We all took dowsing for granted. Daddy wrote to Mother and said it was so interesting to find somebody else who believed in it."

"People laughed at me when I tried to check it out," I explained.

"Sure they do!" she agreed.

"A crazy story, they told me."

"It's *not*. It's true! *And you may quote me.* It wouldn't be in the records because people are ashamed of admitting they have extra-perceptive possibilities. Sometimes people think *we're* crazy. . . . There were no willows in Africa so Daddy sent for one in England. They flew it to him," Mrs. Totten declared.

The Case for Psi

Evidence: Scientific. Despite the difficulty of "proving" such incidents, for those who care to examine it, there is plenty of evidence that Psi is so. The fact of Psi has long been established in the laboratory in voluminous research by investigators—600 to 700 bona fide experiments in ESP, a leading parapsychologist assures me. While another psychic researcher was protesting that "no other phenomenon in the history of science has had so little recognition for so much experimental research," a physicist, Raynor C. Johnson, was declaring that the evidence for telepathy, clairvoyance, and precognition "are indubitably hard facts, as well-founded and reliable as the basic facts of physics and chemistry."

So confident does the parapsychology community feel about this that a few years back its professional association resolved to quit trying to prove Psi to the skeptics, and to get on with the business of discovering how Psi works.

Evidence: Statistical. The statistical evidence is best represented by the fifty years of research by J. B. Rhine and associates. His Parapsychology Lab at Duke University once ran a series of 1,850 trials, with results above chance of 10^{22} to 1. In the words of an outside report team, "10^{22} equals 10,000,000,000,000,000,000,000— a number so big, that even in these inflationary times, there is no word in common usage to name it."

Evidence: Pragmatic. The pragmatic evidence for Psi includes the many people who knowingly or unconsciously use it for practical purposes in their everyday lives. Part I of this book is filled with such witnesses.

Evidence: Spontaneous. The most imposing body of evidence, however, in both quality and quantity, is the eternal river of Psi happenings that has flowed down the ages—in other civilizations and throughout primitive tribes: the historic "coincidence," the epochal prophecy, the uncanny knowledge of shaman and medicine man, the phenomenal insight or vision of mystic or seer, in all cultures and all religions. Add to this the coincidence of similarity— of knowledge and experience in different places and different times.

That river still flows. Over half of those questioned recently in a scientific U.S. survey claimed to have had at least one ESP experience—many had had more. You can't meet with a group—any group—in which someone has not been involved in a psychic happening: knowing something will happen, and it does; picking up someone's thoughts or knowledge of an event; being warned in a dream.

For the average person—parapsychologists included!—no number of statistics or experiments is as convincing as having it happen to *you!*

Louisa Rhine cut off active collecting of spontaneous cases at 15,000—though hundreds have continued to come in. "At some point in my work," she told me, "I would start to read a letter and would know exactly what was going to happen next. Such distinct patterns developed—fifty letters, say, telling exactly the same story—that I could begin to identify standard types. When something is reported to me now, I already have hundreds of such accounts."

My own mailbox bulges with testimony from many countries and in many languages, of people who unexpectedly awakened to find Psi working in their lives. People in the Philippines, Argentina, Indonesia, in Paris, England, and Bombay. The dean of a university, a convict in Folsom prison, a New England dowager, a Piute Indian on a reservation, a distressed woman in Japan, an elderly man in Brazil, a mental patient, a professor, a high school sophomore.

If the world of Psi, as some would have us believe, is all a giant hoax (frauds on the platform, shenanigans in the lab), were my far-flung correspondents also engaged in some sort of massive conspiracy?

Of this vast accumulation of human experience, Stanley Krippner has observed: "It is fairly easy to take isolated bits and pieces of the phenomena of life and sweep them under the rug year after year, but they start to accumulate and the bumps get enormous. You can't ignore them any more."

10

IN SEARCH OF
WHITE CROWS:
Scientists at Work

Sigmund Freud, says his biographer, once wrote, "If I had my life to live over again, I should devote myself to psychic research, rather than psychoanalysis."

This marvelous piece of the unknown, the psychic, is still a lure. It has drawn humans into its web since the dawn of humanity. It draws scientists today.

But why? Psychic researchers travel at their own risk. Hazards and booby-traps are everywhere. It cuts them off from the very ties that sustain them: friends, colleagues, and accepted beliefs. There is next to no money and moral support; there are threats to career advancement. Why would anyone ask for that? What keeps them going?

The First Fifty Years

The commitment to explore psychic phenomena seriously can be marked, if we need a marker, by the founding of the British Society for Psychical Research in 1882. As for the scientific, or parapsychological, stage of exploration, it is barely fifty years old; its birth usually put at about 1930, when J. B. Rhine was just getting into his research at Duke University.

One notable contributor to the story of Psi research was the maverick psychologist William James, who helped found the American Society for Psychical Research in 1885. James saw that the reality of Psi must be proved by incontrovertible evidence. He pointed out, however, that if any single manifestation could be shown to be psychic, in principle such phenomena would be validated. "A universal proposition," he said, "can be made untrue by a particular instance. If you wish to upset the law that all crows are black, you must not seek to prove that no crows are. It is enough to prove one single crow to be white."

James was intrigued by the study of mediums, and of these, he intensively investigated the Boston sensation, Mrs. Piper. As her prowess continued to astound him, he felt she might be the person who could supply the proof. He dubbed Mrs. Piper his "white crow."

But while in James' time psychic research centered upon mediums purportedly receiving messages from "the other side," it began to dawn on observers, as time went by, that such messages might—with no deception whatever—be coming from *this* side. What if mediums were picking up information, not from a dearly beloved wife or godfather who had "passed over," but *telepathically* from the minds of those attending the séance? Wasn't it possible, even probable, that the message from or about Aunt Sophie had surfaced from the mind of her inquiring nephew, from the deeper recesses of his memory, from early childhood experiences and hearsay?

So, the whole focus of inquiry shifted toward telepathy. This was where matters stood when the two University of Chicago biologists, J. B. Rhine and his wife Louisa (who eventually became a full partner in the enterprise), came on the scene. It was the question they addressed. In Louisa's words, telepathy was "the first objective and obvious starting-point" for anyone determined, as J. B. Rhine was, to establish by scientific investigation, the reality of Psi.

The budding parapsychologist contributed an innovative way of testing psychic phenomena: the application of mathematical probability theory to massive accumulation of data; and an experimental design for gathering such data, based on card-guessing.

Rhine built upon the work of a member of the British Society for Psychical Research, Ina Jephson. She had discovered that when playing cards she sometimes knew what a card would be before she saw it. She began keeping records of this apparent manifestation of Psi and found that her hits were too frequent to be chance.

Through the Society she got hundreds of people in other countries to guess cards as she had, for psychic hits. She published the results of her survey in 1928.

Meanwhile, statisticians had developed a formula showing what could be expected by chance alone. This made it possible for scientists to know, almost definitively, when their results are "better than chance"; i.e. when they are "statistically significant."

Rhine put the new statistical testing together with card–guessing, but added some twists of his own. He devised his own set of laboratory test cards with the help of a perception expert, Carl Zener, so as to provide a neutral target pattern. Each "Zener card" has one of five symbols: star, cross, circle, square and wavy lines; a deck consists of five of each card. These lend themselves to an infinite number of trials, and simple tabulation. Subjects are asked to name which card a sender is thinking of, which card will be turned up next, which card has just been turned up, and so on. Using all twenty-five cards in the deck constitutes a "run." Five hits or correct guesses can be expected in a single run if chance alone is operating.

Equipped with this simple, but as it proved, effective and durable experimental model, J. B. Rhine set out to establish the reality of Psi in the laboratory, beginning with telepathy.

Though the idea of telepathy was becoming widely known, in the lab it turned out to be the hardest nut to crack. The Rhines did succeed in their mission—ultimately—of demonstrating telepathy scientifically, but not for many years, and not until they had first taken an unintentional detour, and confirmed the authenticity of clairvoyance and precognition.

In 1935, the Parapsychology Laboratory at Duke University was formally established under William McDougall, with J. B. Rhine as its Director. At the heart of its work was their innovative process and innovative device. Basing their researches on an unheard-of number of tests, the Rhine staff subjected all experiments to statistical evaluation as they went. Their lab procedure was unprecedented, and effective. Though they used a number of designs, and appropriate props to go with them (dice calling, for example, in testing for psychokinesis), it was their reliable and constant companion, the Zener deck, and the statistical formula that did the trick. With these they pinned down the fundamentals of the struggling new science, and roughed out its contours. By sticking to their last they have been able to hammer home their clear and definitive message: a "science" without built-in statistical controls is no science at all.

It is my impression that their hosts and colleagues at Duke University have not all enthusiastically welcomed the Rhine presence over the years. How galling it must have been, for those who did not even approve of such experiments, to have the "Duke Lab" better known in some circles than the university itself! Ask it softly: How many first heard of the university because of the lab?

Thus, when the Rhines retired from their longtime connection in 1965, there was no institutional fanfare. Though the Parapsychology Laboratory at Duke had, as such, ceased to exist, many other centers were springing up and other researchers coming to the fore. However, the Foundation for Research on the Nature of Man, which J. B. Rhine then set up on the same theme with which he began, continues to thrive. A private research institution with its own parapsychology lab, it is housed in a former dean's residence near the university. Though into their eighties, the Rhines were busily catching up with a self-assigned backlog of writing when I visited them in their own tree-shaded work center, near the Foundation, in May 1979. The following February, J. B. died.

Even in such close historical perspective as this, it is startling to see how much impact one couple and one laboratory have had. In the course of their half-century quest, they were instrumental in:

1. spearheading parapsychological research in America;
2. establishing the laboratory approach as optimum;
3. developing a framework of widely emulated techniques;
4. building evaluative statistical procedures into the process;
5. raising a generation of parapsychologists to follow them.

In the words of Psi reporters, Norma Bowles and Fran Hynds:

The Rhines' leadership, even dominance, of the field of Psi, was long unchallenged, and the stamp of their personalities is even now clearly evident. Almost every major researcher in the field was trained by them, or at least did some work in their lab. The Rhines' basic theory about Psi was strongly impressed on these researchers. It is, that Psi is to be found, to a greater or lesser extent, in every individual, and that it is totally different from everything else.

What We Know

I have in my files the back-and-forth correspondence of two serious Psi investigators. One contends that, for all the hundreds of painstaking experiments through the years, we still know next to nothing about Psi. The other bristles at such a statement: "We know a great deal!"

Is this glass half empty or half full?

What do we know about Psi? Here are some specific research findings.

Telepathy. People can and do communicate by means other than the five senses. In experiments at the Newark College of Engineering, Douglas Dean and Carroll Nash found that the body responds to telepathic messages without knowing it. A subject was asked to relax in a room while the blood volume in a finger was measured by a plethysmograph—an instrument that detects minute changes in blood volume in the tiny vessels close to the skin. In another room, the sender (Dean) thought of a series of names: five from the telephone book, five of his own friends, and five who were emotionally important to the subject—a spouse, child or close associate.

The subject did not know exactly *when* a name was being sent, or which one. There were, however, significant changes in the blood volume when names important to him/her were concentrated on. In one series of ten experiments, one name called up an unusually high response, thirty-eight out of forty-three times it was sent. It was the name of the subject's boss. (Telepathy? Possible clairvoyance? Or both? In any case, definitely ESP.)

At Maimonides Dream Laboratory in Brooklyn,* it was discovered that telepathy also works in dreams. This finding documented Freud's observation of "the apparently intimate connection between telepathy and dreams," and "the incontestable fact that sleep creates favorable conditions for telepathy."

In an experiment in 1966, a sender projected to a subject the

---

* Since the experiments cited here were performed, the laboratory has moved from Maimonides to Princeton Forrestal Center in New Jersey. It is now the Psychophysical Research Laboratories, Inc., Charles Honorton, director.

content of a randomly selected Japanese painting, Hiroshige's *Downpour at Shono*. The subject, William Erwin, asleep in another room. dreamed about "an oriental man," "a fountain," "water spray" and "walking down the street while it was raining." It was found in this and many other successful experiments, that acting out, or in some way dramatizing, the content of the picture—in this case holding an umbrella or taking a shower—brought more dramatic results.

In addition to the laboratory work in telepathy, there is a massive input from psychiatrists, who have often noted the close, and sometimes embarrassing, telepathic ties between themselves and their patients. Psychiatrist Montague Ullman describes such an incident:

> In his dream, the patient offered a chromium soap dish to a man who blushed when the patient said, "Well, you're building a house."
> The patient could not report any associations to the soap dish. However, the therapist remembered that a year and a half earlier, a chromium soap dish had, by mistake, been shipped to the new house into which he had just moved. In a belligerent spirit, responding to the mounting building costs, he never bothered to return it; but a week before the patient's dream, several architects had come over to inspect the house; and one had spied the soap dish lying unused in the cellar, and had embarrassed the therapist by calling attention to it.

Berthold Schwarz reports that, from December of 1955 to December of 1973, he saw 3,764 patients, and during that time recorded 3,077 examples of physician/patient telepathic exchanges. Many had to do not only with the doctor, but his wife and their children throughout the entire course of their childhood. He published 505 such vignettes, in which the content sometimes extended to other patients and other people. On the strength of such frequent telepathic incidents, Schwarz says, "I gradually came to realize that one could not fully understand a patient without taking into account this psychic matter—genuine or spurious.

"Psychiatric studies over the past fifty years have revealed how telepathy is related to the subconscious mind. The dream and altered states of consciousness can also be ideal vehicles for telepathy."

Clairvoyance. People can and do pick up information about remote or hidden objects, persons, or events. Many dozens of tests have pinned down the phenomenon of clairvoyance—"remote view-

ing" as it has been known at the Stanford Research Institute. One
of the best known and most convincing of this type of test was
the Pearce-Pratt series in the Duke Laboratory, mentioned in Chapter 9. Here, Hubert Pearce racked up one of the largest scores
in experimental history, by identifying cards handled in another
building by Pratt. Scores of similar experiments have been conducted
in other places. In 1938 and 1940, for example, extensive work in
clairvoyance was carried on at the University of Colorado with
thirteen subjects who were tested individually with the standard
ESP deck of cards. The most outstanding of the subjects, C. J.,
was tested for 25,000 trials (1,000 runs) and produced a "critical
ratio" of 29.35, one of the largest "C.R.s" in the history of parapsychology, and thus some of the most striking evidence for clairvoyance.*

In another kind of test, physicists Harold Puthoff and Russell
Targ of the Stanford Research Institute asked Ingo Swann to describe a hundred geographic targets, at different points on the globe,
based on their geodetic coordinates—that is, simply the latitude
and longitude. In one experiment, they explained to Ingo:

> A skeptical colleague of ours on the East Coast has heard of your
> ability to close your eyes and observe a scene miles away. He has
> furnished us with a set of coordinates, latitude and longitude, in degrees,
> minutes and seconds, and has challenged us to describe what's there.
> We ourselves don't know what the answer is. Do you think you can
> do it right off the top of your head?
>
> "I'll try," says Ingo, appearing unperturbed by a request that we,
> as physicists, can hardly believe we are making. For us, this is a crucial
> test. We are certain there is no possibility of collusion between the
> subject and the challenger. The coordinates indicate a site that is
> roughly three thousand miles away, and we have been asked to obtain
> details beyond what would ever be shown on a map, such as small
> man-made structures, etc.
>
> Ingo closes his eyes and begins to describe what he is visualizing,
> opening his eyes from time to time to sketch a map. "This seems to
> be some sort of mounds or rolling hills. There is a city to the north.
> I can see taller buildings, and some smog. This seems to be a strange
> place, somewhat like the lawns one would find around a military base,
> but I get the impression that there are either some old bunkers around,

---

* "Critical ratio" is a technical statistical test used to determine whether the observed
deviation is significantly greater than the expected random fluctuation above the average.

or maybe this is a covered reservoir. There must be a flagpole. Some highways to the west. A river over to the far east. To the south, more city."

He appears to zero in for a closer view, rapidly sketching a detailed map, showing the location of several buildings, together with some roads and trees. He goes on: "Cliffs to the east, fence to the north; there's a circular building, perhaps a tower, buildings to the south. Is this a former NIKE base, or something like that?" He hands over a detailed map. "This is about as far as I can go without feedback. . . . Since I don't know what to look for, it is extremely difficult to make decisions on what is there and what is not. Imagination seems to get in the way. For example, I get the impression of something underground, but I'm not sure."

But imagination was not a factor on that decisive day, as we learned a few weeks later when we received a phone call from our challenger. Not only was Swann's description correct in every detail, but even the relative distances on his map were to scale!

On another day, the target, selected blindly by the experimenters, turned out to be what they thought was the center of Lake Victoria in Africa. After checking it psychically, Swann replied, "I'd say this coordinate refers to a piece of land to the east of a large body of water."

"No, that would not be correct, since the coordinate we gave you is actually in the middle of Lake Victoria."

Swann: "I don't believe it. Where the hell is a good map?"

Since the S.R.I. library did not have one, they went out to a bookstore and purchased *The Times Atlas of the World*. The staff was chagrined to discover that the exact coordinate given in the experiment referred to the peninsula jutting out into Lake Victoria, just east of Ukerewe Island—in fact, exactly where the psychic perception said it was.

Precognition. People can and do sense what is going to happen before it takes place. Chapter 6 was devoted to precognition experiences. For many people, precognition is so obvious a phenomenon that to test it in a laboratory is somewhat ridiculous. Scientists have tested it, however, in a great many ways. The Duke Lab pinned it down, by guessing cards that would turn up next; 4,500 runs of 25 trials each, for instance, gave odds of 3 million against coincidence. Physicist Helmut Schmidt, who had worked at Boeing Aircraft, introduced mechanized techniques for testing precognition: a subject guesses which of four lamps will be lighted. Three of his subjects, a housewife, a medium, and a truck driver, had scores increasingly divergent from chance. Repeated testing of these subjects in 60,000 trials gave 1 million to 1 odds against mere coincidence. Icelandic parapsychologist Erlendur Haraldsson replicated Schmidt's experiment with eleven persons, and found that when he gave them immediate feedback, their scores improved. Knowing they were registering hits as they progressed was apparently an aid in attaining them.

Years of experiments had convinced researchers at Maimonides Dream Laboratory that information could be relayed in dreams via telepathy. But what about precognition? Could a sleeping subject be induced to dream about an incident that had not yet taken place? The Laboratory brought young British psychic Malcolm Bessent from England for tests, in 1969. On eight different nights, Malcolm went to sleep in a soundproof room, while an experimenter in the control room watched his brain-wave patterns for signs of dreaming. Malcolm's only instructions were to try to dream about what would happen in the morning, when a picture would be chosen at random and a sequence of actions would take place based on the theme of the picture. No one in the laboratory would know the content of his dreams except this one experimenter.

On the first night, he dreamed that he was in a mental hospital, surrounded by people who were drinking out of glasses, while doctors and psychiatrists wandered through the scene. A female patient broke loose and ran down the corridor. The dreamer sensed a feeling of hostility in the atmosphere.

"Malcolm, wake up!" came the voice over the intercom, from the control room, where the fact that he was dreaming had registered. "What's going on in your mind?"

"I saw a large concrete building . . . a patient escaping from upstairs . . . she had a white coat on, like a doctor's coat, and people were arguing with her in the street. . . . Medical people . . . white cups on a tray."

The picture was chosen afterwards: one of the staff members chose at random a series of numbers, referring to a page in a book of key words of dream descriptions. Dr. Krippner's initial role in the experiment was to select a painting in the laboratory that matched the target word or phrase. The first word chosen was "corridor." The painting that matched it was Van Gogh's *Corridor of the St. Paul Hospital.* Krippner then created for Malcolm a series of actions dramatizing the target word: two grim-faced men wearing white hospital uniforms walked in, slipped a tight-fitting jacket over his head, gripped his arms firmly, and guided him into the corridor. Krippner later handed him a pill, with a glass of water, and ordered him to swallow it.

When Krippner devised the late morning drama, he hadn't the faintest idea what the psychic had dreamed about the night before.

One night, when Malcolm was awakened from a dream he answered, "All I can think of is a bowl of fruit." The target picture the next morning was Cokovasky's *Fruits and Flowers.*

On the fifth night, Malcolm dreamed that he was in a room surrounded by white. Every imaginable thing in the room was white. The light was very bright; the predominant colors were pale ice-blues and whites. The target picked afterwards was "parka hood," and the picture was *Walrus Hunter.*

At the end of eight nights of experiments, a panel of judges not connected with the Dream Laboratory was asked to examine the dreams and see how closely they corresponded with the targets. The results were judged positive, and statistically significant.

Psychokinesis. People can and do move or affect objects, even distant ones, without touching them.

Note that this fourth of the parapsychology quartet is qualitatively different from the other three. Whereas the others have to do with various aspects of *knowing,* psychokinesis involves physical *change:* in position, or structure.

Gertrude Schmeidler tested Ingo Swann's PK abilities. Using four thermistors (extremely precise temperature-monitoring instruments), some of which were exposed, others inside sealed thermos bottles, she would ask him to "make it cooler" or "make it hotter." He then had 45 seconds to concentrate on each. Swann could alter the temperature reading on random command.

Schmeidler conceded, "Theoretically, it seemed impossible to do what we did with Swann. I did not know whether the experiment would be a success or not. It seemed like a miracle. It still does."

At the Varian Hall of Physics at Stanford University, Swann was also, by concentration, able to alter the magnetic fields of shielded meters. These were encased in an aluminum container and a copper canister, as well as a superconducting shield, and buried in concrete five feet below the floor.

When Uri Geller appeared on British radio and TV, it was reported in homes all over England, Scotland, Ireland, and across the English channel that spoons bent, cutlery twisted, broken clocks and watches started running again. One woman, stirring soup, said that the handle bent in her hand. When Uri broadcast in Germany, Hans Bender told me, "It was like a wave over Europe. Extraordinary public reaction—a unique event." Bender of the University of Freiburg made studies of the "Geller effects," based on interviews and questionnaires. It was his hypothesis that the excitement generated by Geller sparked PK responses among people who were interested.

London physicist John Hasted, who tested Uri Geller's phenomenal metal-bending ability, found that what is "phenomenal" is not Uri Geller, but the phenomenon itself. He has tested numerous subjects since then, many of them children, who can bend metals without touching them, by the force of will alone.

Swedish engineer Haakon Forwald confirmed that subjects can influence the fall of dice psychokinetically, as the Rhine lab demonstrated.

Among the most impressive results in PK testing involves the effects of psychic energy on living tissue. Use of the word "psychokinesis" for healing is controversial, but the findings are not. Since we have already presented the work in the area of healing by Montreal biochemist Bernard Grad, and his successors in other labs (Chapter 4), we shall not repeat them here. Let us simply note that in the entire PK series, in every instance in which a healer or person with healing intentions was involved, plants, seeds, or animals registered physical benefits.

This is a summary, then, of what is generally accepted as the core categories of the parapsychology field. Let me add a postscript.

Even when we have sorted them out, other mysteries remain. One *touches* an object from the scene of the crime—a belt, a shoe— as in psychometry (literally "psychic measurement") and receives a *visual* image. Does one sense trigger another? What are the linkages and relationships?

Moreover, isn't the term "extra-sensory" (i.e. outside the senses) rather odd when Psi phenomena are sensed? Perhaps those who insist that Psi is not "extra"-sensory but, rather, *extended* sensory perception, are onto something.

How We Know

Most of the data cited here are from laboratories. The lab makes a unique and indispensable contribution to our knowledge. For all its difficulties, the controlled laboratory experiment is designed to eliminate all extraneous factors that might color the findings and affect the results. An apparent PK effect may come from any number of non-Psi factors—a passing breeze, a change of room temperature, movement of the building, of people on another floor, the crash of a garbage truck outside, the beat of traffic. Repeated trials in a controlled environment can rule these out.

Such lab features, however, must not overshadow the fact that the laboratory cannot do everything. There are other kinds of information to be gleaned, and many circumstances where the lab experiment is neither possible nor appropriate.

Other types of research include the following:

• *Study of cases.* The spontaneous case is the phenomenon in its natural setting, with the context, qualitative content, detail, and effect, which can neither be caught nor reproduced in the laboratory. It is the record of the live, one-time-only sort of happening: the horrified dream of an Aberfan or *Titanic,* the "Stop!" or "Don't take that flight!"

The breadth of a large number of cases—e.g., Tyrrell's collection of apparitions, the Census of Hallucinations, L. Rhine's thousands of spontaneous happenings, Ian Stevenson's census of "remembered" incarnations—makes possible the broader, overall perspective: What is typical? What is not? How many types of Psi phenomena are there? and so on.

• The *in-depth interview* lends still another perspective—first-hand witnessing of doctors, neighbors, family, friends, or subjective experience of participants or psychics: How did it happen? How did it feel? What did others see, hear?

• *Questionnaires.* Another net for assembling a broad sweep of information—attitudes, beliefs, experiences, and practices.

• *First-hand observation,* the oldest and simplest form of data-gathering, brings researchers to the site—of the haunting, the surgery, or the healing. Knowing what to look for is the key here. Without special expertise, mere witnessing is not much use, and may be misleading.

• *Participant observation* casts the researcher into two roles at once: joining in the activity, yet registering pertinent inside information. The technique may yield fine data, or deceive. Again, it is rather hazardous without training, as in evaluating a séance. An atypical kind of participant observation was Robert Monroe's attempt to monitor objectively his own subjective out-of-body experiences, as reported in his *Journeys Out of the Body.*

• *Testing ready-made groups,* such as the reactions of an audience, those attending a fair, hospitalized patients, and so on. By far the most popular situation of this type is the researcher or professor using his students in the classroom. Students have, for example, been tested for Psi in Iceland, Holland, Texas, and the Soviet Union. For J. B. Rhine, one of the attractions of the Psychology Department of Duke was the availability of students as subjects.

• *"In the field":* research must often take place "on site." One goes to mountains, desert, or farm land to check dowsing or archaeology leads, or to a troubled house to look into reports of poltergeists ("noisy ghosts" given to rattling and throwing china and other pranks). Instruments are sometimes taken to the field. Thus Julian Isaacs took his "PK machine"—which we tried out in Edinburgh research meetings—to queued-up British housewives, to screen for their paranormal metal-bending ability.

Beyond Proof

As the mountain of experiments has piled up, scientists have moved beyond the search for *proof* (Is telepathy a fact?) to the search for *conditions* under which Psi operates (Where? When? Who?).

• *Where?* Anywhere. Distance doesn't seem to matter, nor do physical barriers. Psi has been recorded between people at adjoining desks, and on a space flight, with sender and subject 212,000 miles apart. Psychic Harold Sherman and Arctic explorer Sir Hubert Wilkins conducted their five-month telepathy experiment when separated by thousands of miles. Even psychokinesis (mind over matter) has registered at great distances—*e.g.,* Olga Worrall rippling a cloud chamber in an Atlanta laboratory, from her Baltimore home 600 miles away; Ingo Swann affecting instruments thoroughly shielded in terms of known physical forces.

• *When?* Any time. Planned, unplanned, unexpectedly, spontaneously, morning, noon, or night. In laboratory situations, subjects usually do better at the start of an experiment, and then taper off, or turn off entirely—the "decline effect." Giving the subjects immediate feedback—ringing a bell, lighting a light if their answers are correct—seems to help sustain their effectiveness.

However, Psi is not always "here one minute and gone the next." In some situations, the effect seems to be lasting. A shirt, tie, or sock may retain a tell-tale message. With "remanence" in dowsing, we've seen how "memory" or continuing influence of an object in the place from which it has been taken is sometimes a problem. The Watkins, in North Carolina, discovered that ailing mice, placed in the area where other mice had been healed, mended more quickly. Is it possible that past healings are a factor in the spectacular cures at places such as Lourdes and St. Anne de Beaupré?

How long does this "lingering effect" last? The limits have not been tested. Of the experiments with healers holding bottles of water, Bernard Grad says, "I have no evidence that the healers' effect on the water disappears."

• *Who?* Anyone . . . everyone. When it was assumed that Psi was a rare and special gift, the aim was to study very talented mediums and other selected sensitives. As it began to seem that everyone or almost everyone has some Psi ability, labs took to bringing in an assortment of volunteers: housewives, occupational categories, and sometimes even casual visitors, some of whom turned out to be psychically talented.

Who? People who expect a Psi experiment to work do better at it. Gertrude Schmeidler has demonstrated the "sheep/goat effect," in which believing "sheep" score higher than doubting "goats." People who feel close to one another are more likely to relate psychically than those who do not; 80 to 85 percent of reported precognition cases involve people in close relationships: fathers, sisters, children, sweethearts, wives.

For some, Psi will work only under exactly right circumstances: temperature, noise (or lack of it), deep relaxation, a pre-somnolent or trance state. For others it can come anytime, at the drop of a hat. Ingo Swann jolts laboratories accustomed to waiting for psychics to get settled: He sits down, lights a cigar, and, blowing smoke rings, is into it.

Psychic ability is not the special province of either sex. As of now, the sexes show equal potential; certainly the "world's great sensitives" have been both male and female. Psychic researchers echo the usual academic pattern, with males predominating numerically; but where women have entered the field, their record has been outstanding. At the St. Louis parapsychology association meetings in 1978, a panel of young women researchers paid tribute to the contributions of women in the field. Drs. Gertrude Schmeidler and Louisa Rhine, as we have seen, are still making major contributions. Eleanor Mildred Sidgwick, a brilliant mathematician at Cambridge, served as president of the British Society for Psychical Research as long ago as 1908. Eileen Garrett, one of the greatest psychics ever studied, was so committed to research that she established the Parapsychology Foundation in New York, which publishes the *Parapsychology Review,* and sponsored the first International Conference of Parapsychology Studies in Utrecht, Holland, in 1953.

There is some evidence that children are more likely to exhibit psychic ability than adults. In his reincarnation research, Ian Stevenson tries to interview children before their memories have faded. Psychiatrists and others are discovering that many children have had strong psychic tendencies punished or conditioned out of them. From his investigation of psychic children, Samuel Young is convinced that Psi is "by no means confined to a few exceptional children, but permeates every child's experience."

From his research, Berthold Schwarz finds that children and parents are psychically sensitive to one another when they are in a state of rapport. He has described more than a thousand such examples involving his own family. Helene Deutsch, Dorothy Burlingham, and others have published observations of telepathy in mother-child relationships.

Who? There are many reports of spontaneous incidents in which animals seem to have Psi. One is the well-publicized case of Sugar, the cream-colored cat who found his way to his owners after they had moved from California to Oklahoma.

Though the results of laboratory experiments with animals have not been extensive, they have bolstered the evidence for "AnPsi" or animal Psi.

"A cockroach or goldfish may save your life?" U.S. Geological Survey scientist Ruth Simon has found that, before an earthquake, cockroaches change their behavior. The Japanese have long kept goldfish as an early warning system. Of this practice, University of London biologist Lyall Watson explains that "when the fish begin to swim about in a frantic way, the owners rush out of doors to avoid being trapped by falling masonry." A. J. Kalmijn of the Scripps Institute of Oceanography says that ordinary catfish can sense earthquakes six to eight hours before they happen. Soviet scientists have established animal warning centers in the quake-prone Uzbekistan area.

Scientists at the Stanford School of Medicine Primate Center announced in December of 1976 that they had "a dozen psychic chimpanzees who had amazed them by predicting two earthquakes."

We don't know yet whether animal warnings such as these are triggered physically—by earth vibrations, say—or psychically. Whether plants, also, have Psi—a very ancient belief—is still being debated. There is enough evidence from recent experiments, at least, to warrant further exploration.

Alex Tanous, now being studied by Karlis Osis at the American Society for Psychical Research, introduced me to "Jasper the psychic cat," when I was a visitor there. (JASPR is the acronym for the Society's *Journal*). The cat, he told me with a chuckle, is said to know when invisible entities come around, responding visibly to their presence, as he patrols vestibules, stairways, and library. The Secretary of the British Society told me, in London: "We have a fine place here, but I do wish we had a cat like Jasper!" Personally, I have enjoyed a fine relationship with this cat, but I didn't see him switch his tail at any entities when I was there.*

* On reading this, my copy editor noted: "Coming home one evening, I was surprised to be greeted by my cat, who should have been 'locked away' from the foyer's Oriental rug. When he twined around my ankles, I didn't feel him, and when I looked again, he wasn't there. I told my companion what I'd seen, and we both knew. . . . We found the cat's cold, stiff body in the room where he should have been, unexpectedly dead. His name was Jasper."

Things About Psi You Didn't Think to Ask

• *Emotional involvement* often heightens Psi performance.

• *Shock events* such as catastrophes and major disasters seem to trigger Psi. Serious events predominate—at least they are reported more often: four unhappy events to every pleasant one, says one study. Another shows death as the number-one precognition subject; accidents are next. Accidents, being more unexpected than illness, seem to generate more shock.

• Psi often breaks through in an *altered state of consciousness:* a state induced by meditation, deep relaxation, yoga, psychedelic drugs, hypnosis, fasting, fatigue, religious experience, trance, biofeedback, sleep—including pre- and post-sleep states—and dreams. The largest number of precognition cases occur during dreams.

• Psychic performance can also be enhanced by creating *special devices and environments,* some suggested by psychics themselves. One of the most successful of these is the Ganzfeld technique. Its aim is to eliminate all extraneous (non-Psi) stimuli, and produce maximum relaxation and receptivity.

The subject, alone in a soundproof room, is seated in a comfortable lounge chair. Half of a translucent ping-pong ball, edges padded with cotton, is fastened over each eye. The view is hazy, with a soft rosy glow. Earphones are provided and register a soothing, uniform sound. For a designated period, the subject describes, into a microphone, all pictures and thoughts as they pass through the mind. The subject's voice is recorded and monitored by an experimenter in another soundproof room.

While in this setting, thoughts are beamed to the subject. Sometimes the message is the content of a randomly chosen picture. He/she is then shown an assortment of pictures, and asked to choose which one was being beamed. One of the suggestive byproducts of Ganzfeld testing: the subject sometimes "sees" pictures *before* they are given to the experimenter to send!

Charles Honorton, director of the Psychophysical Research Laboratories, at Princeton, estimates that in the combined Ganzfeld experiments at his and ten other laboratories, there is only 1 chance in 100 billion of the experimenters getting similar results by chance.

• There is evidence that Psi works *indirectly,* or once removed. In healing experiments, for example: when put into contact with wool or cotton cuttings that had once been held by a healer, animals recovered or improved more rapidly than control groups did.

• There is *negative* as well as positive Psi! *Misses* as well as hits can be "statistically significant." Such scores are not the results of chance: persons who characteristically miss in experimental guessing are, in their unconscious avoidance, expressing Psi through such "Psi missing."

What We Don't Know

So, we know *that* Psi is, but we don't know *what* Psi is, or *how* it works.

There is no shortage of theories, partial theories, and attempts to understand Psi. These are numerous, varied, complex, simplistic, tentative, exploratory, and, needless to say, not at all agreed upon. None of them to date is comprehensive enough to explain everything. Furthermore, one's basic assumptions color one's theory. For example, if one believes in survival of bodily death, one is not likely to entertain a materialistic explanation of Psi. Again, one's theory will be affected if one assumes that only *living* systems are involved in Psi.

All knowledge is in transition today. Change physics or psychology, biology or astronomy, in any basic way, and you change Psi theory. Psi itself, moreover, challenges basic assumptions in many fields. Disrupt one, you disrupt them all.

One can scan the many theories, however, for common approaches and similar themes. These fall, understandably, into the same broad categories as the theories outlined in Chapter 3. At one end of the spectrum is the body of materialistic explanations, which hold that the psychic is *physical:* radiations, emanations, thought-waves, energy-waves, electromagnetic force fields, and other types of emissions, all within the basic varieties of forces recognized by present-day physics.

More specifically, there are electromagnetic theories of Psi, a number of them, some so sophisticated as to posit an interaction between the hypothetical neutrino and tachyon, with electromagnetic waves. There are bio-electric, bio-energetic, and bio-plasmic theories of Psi. Many new fields of investigation have developed, which focus on physical elements, among them the overlapping areas of "paraphysics," "psychotronics," and "psycho-energetics."

The first of these, at the borderline of physics, explores the material bases of the psychic. The second, technological extension of electronics and biochemistry popularized by a Czechoslovakian scholar, reflects the Eastern European view that psychic research is, at bottom, a materialistic science.

The third, psycho-energetics, is the Russian equivalent of parapsychology; understandably it is interpreted as essentially physical. The Russian term for telepathy is "bio-communication"; for clairvoyance, "bio-location" or "introscopy"; for precognition, "proscopy."

A Russian scientist, Alexander Gurvitch, startled scientists in the 1930s by announcing that all living cells produce an invisible radiation. The discovery of the specific nature of the "energy" underlying Psi is the great goal of Soviet investigation. Present Russian inquiry includes research on force-field detectors at the Leningrad Laboratory for Biological Cybernetics, where extremely sensitive high-resistance electrodes are being used to check the "electric aura."

Others who seek the essence of psychic phenomena in energy fields, magnetism, and radiation, are experimenters with healing, the aura, or Kirlian photography (Chapter 11). Those who see psychic "powers" as the extension of physical senses are also in this camp.

Austrian psychoanalyst Wilhelm Reich claimed to have discovered a primordial cosmic energy, "orgone," which is universally present and demonstrable (electroscopically, for example, by means of a Geiger-Müller counter). In living organisms, its manifestation is biological energy. Though Reich's "orgone energy accumulator" was branded a fraud by the U.S. government, similar attempts to trap cosmic energy are much in vogue in some circles today, and his theories are still being pursued.

At the other end of the continuum are those who see Psi as of a different order altogether. Among them are the Rhines, who have insisted that these phenomena are essentially *non-physical.* In this camp, of course, are also the mystics, sages, and poets, voices from ancient cultures and religions, who also speak of a realm apart. The invisible, as they see it, *is* reality; what we see is illusion. Physicist Capra asserts that modern physics leads us to a view of the world which is very similar to the views held by mystics of all ages and traditions; one that provides a consistent framework that can accommodate our most advanced theories of the physical world.

Here too are some great allies in philosophy, medicine, and psychology. William James, for example, held a "spiritistic" hypothesis of interaction "between slumbering faculties in the automatists' [mediums'] minds, and a cosmic environment or other consciousness of some sort, which is able to work on them."

In the non-physical camp are scores of thinkers and investigators who focus on *consciousness*, rather than on forces. We have spoken already of a "cosmic pool of consciousness," available to each and all in the universe, in which all individual consciousness resides. Lawrence LeShan calls it the "Clairvoyant Reality." Unlike the sensory reality, the focus is on the oneness, the relationships, not aspects or parts. In the clairvoyant reality, events *are;* they don't happen. Past, present, and future are one. Time doesn't flow in a direction, it just *is*.

Here too was Carl Gustav Jung, who recorded his own reminiscences and journeys into the unconscious in *Memories, Dreams, Reflections,* and left the pregnant concept of the "collective unconscious" and "synchronicity" for later researchers to probe. Translated, the latter refers to a meaningful connection between events that are not caused one by the other, but springing from a common source, of which we have only unconscious awareness. Examples, said Jung, are extra-sensory perception, psychokinesis, and prophetic dreams.

And now also, at this end of the continuum, are Jung's descendants: Alan Vaughan, for instance, who in his book on "the baffling world of synchronicity," *Incredible Coincidence,* moves the longtime debate on the source of Psi into today's context.

Along the axis between the two poles is ranged an assortment of Psi theorizing, including the theory that it is *partly physical* and *partly psychic,* or that it is *sometimes* one and sometimes the other. Materials Science Professor William Tiller holds that the psychic is a unity of both:

It is clearly arbitrary to partition nature into the domains labeled (a) physical space-time, (b) nonphysical space-time, and (c) nonspace, nontime. In our very distant future we are likely to find that there is only *one* energy, which has manifold expressions, depending on the state of consciousness which interacts with the energy. However, we presently have a scientific foundation which has already segmented

and delineated uniquely different energy characteristics as perceived
by our biological senses, and by our extended instrumentation-senses.
Thus we must continue along the path already laid down by our scientific forbears, until we have reached the level of consciousness where
the unity can be known.

Eagerness to nail down the facts and to tie up the answers unequivocally is understandable and good, but parapsychology is, after
all, just barely under way. William James may be right about "our
moral and human impatience with the phenomenon." In this elusive
sphere, he reminds us, we must expect to mark progress, not by
quarter-centuries, but by half-centuries, or whole centuries.

With a nudge of encouragement, Tiller adds:

> [Psi] is far too important to deserve any less than the best of our
> abilities, to provide a firm and reliable foundation of understanding
> in this area. The technique of analysis and experimentation, and the
> standards of quality synonymous with conventional science, serve as
> a meaningful guide. Let us be open-minded and flexible in our seeking,
> but let us also require extensive proof, before we rest to enjoy the
> satisfaction of a completed task.

Where the White Crows Have Led Us

It has now been established, in thousands of tests, that people
can and do influence objects by "mind over matter"—by *will* alone.
This brings us smack into the central dilemma of Psi research: If
human beings can move or change physical objects *with their
thoughts,* how do we know that the dedicated seekers are not, by
taking thought, *themselves* producing the lab results they seek?

We know that those who want or expect Psi to work in an
experiment get better results. Does *this* explain the problems that
parapsychologists and critics have had with replication?

K. Ramakrishna Rao, President of the Parapsychology Association (1978–79), has observed:

> The experimenter's personality, and his attitude toward Psi in general,
> and the subject in particular, his mannerisms, his mood, his enthusiasm,
> his perceptiveness, the clarity with which he presents his tests, the
> confidence he instills into his subjects, and a host of other factors

are likely to make up the psychological complex that accounts for his success or failure.

In research gatherings everywhere these days, there is rising concern over "the experimenter effect."

Thus the effort in the parapsychology lab is to screen out "the human factor," to eliminate "human contamination." Lab specialists now shuffle cards by machine instead of by hand; run "double blind" experiments in which no one, not even the experimenter, has knowledge of the targets; and select targets, not by whim, but by scientific random methods.

One of the major advances here is the "random number generator" (RNG), an automatic source of randomness considered scientifically and mathematically reliable. One such machine, invented by physicist Helmut Schmidt, makes use of the haphazard deterioration of the subatomic particles of strontium 90. The machine selects numbers randomly: these can refer to a target—card, picture, place, whatever the experimenter programs for. This eliminates the possible human element of choosing targets subconsciously.

The RNG has also been used to demonstrate precognitive ability.

But guess what *else* it has demonstrated! That human beings can not merely anticipate where the counter stops, but *influence* where it will stop! By putting their mind to it, some people can affect the flow of its "random" output, so that it is no longer a succession of *chance* results, but, in significant measure, *willed* results! Human beings can thus *think* changes in the operation of a "scientifically reliable" and "humanly uncontaminated" machine.

The immediate reaction of Psi scientists to this was "One more evidence of PK, a 'giant step' for Psi." But what does it *mean* that a human being can *think changes in the behavior of the atomic "building blocks" of the universe?*

The physical realm has for centuries been believed to operate automatically, mechanically, impersonally. Yet here is evidence that we are unconsciously but inextricably involved in running the universe. The RNG machine is not the only such evidence; the accumulation of instances mounts daily.

If this be so, then it has momentous implications for *every* science and *every* laboratory, not just the field of Psi. The "experimenter effect" is radical and definitive. We must now deal, not only with the traditional concern of parapsychology, "knowing" (ESP), but with its new challenge, mind impinging on matter (PK).

We now have evidence running over, that *Psi is so.* Thus we have found our white crow.

But it is clear that this isn't The Answer. The crow has led us to its nest, but from where we now stand we can see dim outlines of higher ridges and slopes beyond.

11

TRUE OR FALSE?
The Fuzzy Fringe

While I was on my rounds in preparation for this book, a psychic I respect volunteered some emphatic advice: "Whatever you do in your book, don't mention ghosts!"

Startled by such vehemence, I asked, "Why not?"

"Because if you do, no one will believe anything else you say."

Still pondering this admonition, I paid a visit to the Director of Research at the American Society for Psychical Research in New York, Dr. Karlis Osis. He was deep in a project with the sensitive Alex Tanous, and was showing me his lab set-up and instrument recordings.

"You work so hard," I concluded. "What do you do in your spare time?"

Without an instant's hesitation, he replied, "I hunt ghosts!"

"Ghosts" are part of what I call "the fuzzy fringe." Quite apart from whether the ghosts themselves are fuzzy, the "fringe" includes all the controversial and far-out topics that, rightly or wrongly, attach themselves to the Psi field. They are of all kinds and qualities, ranging from auras to the zodiac. One of the things that drives many parapsychologists up the wall is the way their critics tend to lump the whole blooming assortment together: psychokinesis and "pyramid power," telepathy and Tarot cards, ESP and UFOs.

The fringe, which least interests parapsychologists, and about which there is least consensus, is what most interests occultists. That figures. "Occult" mean secret, mysterious, and hidden; the more it is studied, the less hidden it becomes! What separates parapsychology from occultism, parapsychologist Rhea White observes, is not so much the subject-matter, which may even be the same, but the *methodology*.

This chapter will try to make sense of the peripheral jungle.

Ghosts, Haunted Houses, and Things That Go Bump in the Night

One of my biggest surprises has been the number of Psi scientists who take ghosts seriously. Ghosts are, of course, universal in history and pervasive in literature. They were also the first subjects of early psychic research. The first systematic exploration of the phantasmal appearance was instituted by the British Society for Psychical Research in 1882. Of 5,705 persons selected at random and canvased as to phantoms they might have witnessed in the previous twelve years, 702 had had such an experience.

A much larger international survey was undertaken in 1889; 32,000 opinions were received, 17,000 of them in English. This "Census of Hallucinations" emphatically ruled out chance. Similar investigations in France and at the American Society for Psychical Research produced even larger percentages of positive responses.

Such studies tied in, of course, with the central concern of both societies: after-life phenomena. The perennial interest in human survival continues; it is now staging a vigorous comeback among parapsychologists.

Sixty years after the launching of its first "phantasm" investigation, the British Society invited G. N. M. Tyrrell to give the Myers Memorial Lecture. Tyrrell's lecture, published as a book, *Apparitions,* is also something of a classic.

Apparitions are of four types, he explained:

1. apparitions of the living;
2. crisis-apparitions, which appear at the time of death or an accident;
3. apparitions of the dead;
4. continuous apparitions, which appear repeatedly.

In common parlance, "ghosts" usually refers to apparitions of the dead, and to those which repeatedly return.

Apparitions of the Living. Some of the best-known early experiments were conducted by S. H. Beard, with the help of Edmund Gurney, a tireless researcher and founding member of the British Society. Beard started off by attempting to project an apparition of himself to his fiancée, L. S. Verity. In this, he succeeded. She did see his apparition at her bedside, in full evening attire. She was so astonished that she screamed, waking her sister. What impressed the researchers was that her sister saw the apparition, too! The test was performed successfully several times.

How can such a phenomenon be explained? One theory is that apparitions are conveyed by telepathy, which produces a hallucination. That is, a *psychic* occurence triggers a *physical* or apparently physical result. Apparitions of the dead are explained in the same way, as "delayed telepathy": a thought is conveyed to the percipient during the agent's lifetime, but remains dormant until it is activated by some thought or incident after the agent's death.

This theory becomes sticky, though, when more than one percipient is involved. How does a third person, like Miss Verity's sister, not involved with the agent, receive the same image and have the same hallucination? And, as Tyrrell asked repeatedly, how does each percipient see the same hallucination (entity) in proper perspective from her or his unique location in the room, as if indeed something were actually there?

Whatever the theory, the testimony of other witnesses is considerably more impressive than the report of one person alone. Eleanor Sidgwick reported to the British Society a case of collective observation that is now well known. It involved a Mrs. Wilmot, who was extremely anxious about her husband on a transatlantic crossing during a storm in which another ship had already been wrecked. In her anxiety, she appeared to her husband in his stateroom. Ignoring the man in the berth above, she checked the situation, went to her husband, whom she kissed, and departed. What made the case so celebrated was the other passenger also saw the apparition. Here is Mr. Wilmot's account:

Upon the night following the eighth day of the storm, I dreamed that I saw my wife, whom I had left in the United States, come to the door of my stateroom, clad in her nightdress. At the door she seemed to discover that I was not the only occupant of the room, hesitated a little, then advanced to my side, stooped down and kissed me, and, after gently caressing me for a few moments, quietly withdrew.

Upon waking, I was surprised to see my fellow passenger, whose berth was above mine, but not directly over it, looking fixedly at me. "You're a pretty fellow," said he at length, "to have a lady come and visit you in this way."

I pressed him for an explanation, which he at first declined to give, but at length related what he had seen, while lying, wide awake, in his berth. It exactly corresponded with my dream.

Mr. Wilmot's sister, on board also, verified the accounts as given at the time.

Crisis-Apparitions. We have seen one of Tyrrell's examples of crisis-apparitions in Chapter 1: the case of the woman in Birmingham, England, whose uncle clearly appeared at a concert she was attending, at the moment of his death in Australia. A fair proportion of such cases, Tyrrell reports, were *collectively* perceived. "It is obvious that the probability of two or more percipients having similar hallucinations at the same moment corresponding to the same distant event, and very closely, if not exactly, similar to one another, is enormously less than the probability of one percipient having such a hallucination alone. In some auditory cases, as many as five percipients have shared the experience."

Two common features of crisis-apparitions that Tyrrell points out: They are so like human beings as to be frequently mistaken for them until they vanish; they do not occur when people are expecting them, or are worried or anxious about the "agent's" welfare. Rather, they usually "burst in upon them" while they are pursuing ordinary occupations, or are simply lying in bed.

Apparitions of the Dead. Incidents involving the deceased have been accepted for countless centuries as evidence of human survival. One of Myers' cases, F. G., while in a hotel room in St. Joseph, Missouri, was shaken up to see an apparition of his sister, who had died of cholera nine years before. What struck him particularly, as he looked at her, was a long, red scratch on her cheek.

When F. G. reported the apparition to his parents, his mother nearly collapsed. She later explained that, in "touching up" her daughter's face before burial, she had accidently scratched the girl's cheek. To hide the disfigurement, she had applied an extra layer of makeup. She had been so upset about the incident she had told no one.

Quite recently, journalist John G. Fuller has tracked down and documented the appearance of ghosts following two different air crashes, one in the Everglades, and one out of England. His findings, reported in best-selling books, *The Ghost of Flight 401,* and *The Airmen Who Would Not Die*, were that the dead airmen were seen repeatedly by several witnesses. In the English case many messages came to Eileen Garrett, the medium, from the deceased.

Continuous Apparitions. The most familiar example of the apparition that returns or hangs around is the ghost that "haunts" a particular house or location.

How do you know if a house is haunted? The Psychical Research Foundation, an independent research organization in Durham, North Carolina, has run down a number of reported "hauntings." In one investigation, which used the familiar technique of comparing a reputable psychic's impressions with those of the family, the English sensitive Douglas Johnson corroborated the residents' report.

Gertrude Schmeidler has used a team of psychics in a similar but elaborated technique. In one case, two of the psychics spotted the haunting just where the family had; four of the psychics agreed with one another, and with the family, as to the nature of the "haunt's" personality.

Graham Watkins based his researches of haunted houses on the idea that animals change behavior in a house that is haunted. He brought a cat, a dog, a rat, and a rattlesnake, into a Kentucky investigation, to see how they would respond. The dog backed out of the room, snarling, and could not be induced to reenter. The cat leaped from its owner's arms when brought into the room, and hissed and spat at an empty chair in the corner. The rat did not react at all, but the rattlesnake assumed a strike position, again focusing on the corner chair. None of the animals reacted in any way whatsoever in a control room. Perhaps the animals did see a ghost. The humans surmised that "some sort of tragedy" had occurred in the "target" room—the principle of "Psi memory" we have noted earlier, the "lingering effect" of an event, perhaps similar to the workings of psychometry. An Italian parapsychologist,

Ernesto Bozzano, wrote in 1920 that 80 percent of 304 haunted house incidents he had studied were linked to a death. The apparitions did seem to represent the body of the deceased, although they often were not identified until old photos and portraits were brought out of storage.

What do parapsychologists make of this whole business? There is not yet a consensus. In the 1950s, Duke University sociologist Hornell Hart concluded that apparitions represent some type of ultraphysical vehicle, which can be liberated from the human body during life or at death. In 1970, Raymond Bayless presented the thesis that animals manifest themselves in the same four apparition forms as humans.

More recently, William Roll postulated the existence of a "Psi field" that pervades and emanates from all objects. Parapsychologist D. Scott Rogo believes that apparition theories have been too simplistic. Not one, but several mechanisms, both physical and nonphysical, are probably involved. Physical evidence includes the fact that apparitions have sometimes been seen collectively, that they have been known to move physical objects, and that their reflections have been seen in mirrors. Supporting the non-physical theory are the facts that they are not always seen collectively and that they walk through walls. The different types of apparitions may, in fact, be different phenomena.

A "ghost of a different color" is the "poltergeist," a German word meaning "noisy ghost." Whereas most apparitions are quiet and subdued, the poltergeist tends to be dramatic: objects appear and disappear suddenly, are rattled, moved, and heaved. Furniture may be tipped over, fires lit, or stones thrown against the house. Poltergeists rarely cause injury, but they may cause physical damage. Whereas hauntings often continue over a period of years, the appearances of poltergeists usually last only for a short time—a few weeks at most.

Mysterious happenings such as these have been reported for hundreds of years. They are said to be referred to on an Egyptian papyrus. When a poltergeist appeared in the house of Samuel Wesley, father of Methodism's founder, John Wesley, in 1717, it was presumed to be the work of the Devil.

In 1960, parapsychologist A. R. G. Owen reported the case of eleven-year-old Virginia Campbell, who had just moved to Scotland from Ireland and had had to leave most of her possessions behind. Strange occurrences began to take place all around the unhappy girl. Her teachers saw the hinged top of her school desk open by itself while Virginia tried futilely to keep it closed. At other times, another desk and linen chest rose in the air; two witnesses, both doctors, tape-recorded raps, sawing noises, and other sounds that seemed to come from her bed as she lay still.

Witnesses to a headline-making case in a Florida warehouse included insurance investigators, policemen, reporters, writers, TV crews, curious onlookers, and even a magician; this active poltergeist was particularly fond of breaking glass objects. Parapsychologists William G. Roll and J. Gaither Pratt investigated the Florida sensation; they have written about it in journals and popular publications, including Roll's book, *The Poltergeist.* Parapsychologists are summoned more and more frequently to poltergeist cases. Roll, now a specialist on the subject, is one who responds.

A German authority on the poltergeist is the Director of the Psi laboratory at the University of Freiburg, Hans Bender. In his work he sets up equipment "on location" for observations and recording via video, sound recording and other instruments. In a few cases, Bender told me, he had caught unexplained physical movements on film.

Parapsychologists have begun to call the phenomenon "RSPK" for "recurrent spontaneous PK."

Our present understanding of the "noisy ghost" comes largely from the work of Roll and Bender. The incidents are now believed to be essentially examples of psychokinesis produced by the *living* rather than the dead. They are usually associated with a particular person. In the Florida warehouse case, Julio Vasquez, a shipping clerk, was always present when the mysterious breakages took place. Vasquez was laid off from his job, because of the incidents, when the work of the warehouse came to a virtual halt. At Roll's invitation, he went to Durham for extensive testing. At this time, a vase in the Psi lab was broken—as far as we know, the only poltergeist occurrence in a laboratory to date. In each place where he was later employed, poltergeist goings-on occurred.

The person at the center of these phenomena is frequently young—often adolescent—with unstable emotions. There is almost always a built-up and powerful, but repressed, anger and hostility.

Poltergeist agents he has worked with usually have limited powers of verbal expression, says Roll, and a crippling inability to express their rage. They are rarely aware of their repression, or of having caused the disturbances themselves.

Roll has found complex patterns in the apparently random acts of destruction: objects near the agent move more often than distant ones; their trajectories indicate a definite design, a kind of moving force field.

The ultimate effects of some poltergeists may be for the good. Britain's now-favorite psychic, Matthew Manning, was once known as the "poltergeist prodigy." At age eleven, in a fit of depression over some approaching examinations, he did a pretty thorough, if unconscious, job of breaking crockery, disrupting furnishings, and generally turning his household upside down. The event served to alert him and others to his remarkable Psi abilities. These turned out to be, among others: clairvoyant writing and drawing (marvelous works of art!), medical diagnosis, PK, and precognition. With this, he became involved in laboratory experiments around the world— bending metal, disrupting computers and electronic gadgetry. At last, bored with metal-bending and academic demonstrations (still in his early twenties), he turned to higher goals: the application of Psi abilities and knowledge to healing, and other human benefits.

Auras and Human Energy

The "aura" is a field of energy which many believe surrounds the human body—some say it surrounds every living thing. The word is a favorite among sensitives, but has so many dubious connotations that parapsychologists tend to avoid it altogether. Auras are not even mentioned in some parapsychology reference books.

But few topics are more worked over in the popular literature. What do auras mean, how do you interpret them, can they be seen? Much is made of aura colors, as indicators of one's personal well-being: blurred and dirty colors, for example, are said to signal ill health. Some psychics hold that there is more than one (often seven!) within the "aural envelope," each with distinctive properties, each revealing physical, psychological, and spiritual conditions. Blue means trust, calm, peace, says one manual; green—humanitarianism; red—anger, passion, and sexual energy; dark red—lust and madness. Yellow is thought; and yellow-green, selfish desire. Brown is earthy; gray shows depression and illness; black ranges from so-phistication to self-destruction and murder. Breaks in the aura reveal physical ailments at those specific points.

Healers and other sensitives who say they work with such guide-lines have made some accurate diagnoses and effected some remarka-ble cures. As for research, however, in this uncertain area, few parapsychologists have done any.

The celebrated California dowser Verne Cameron designed an ingenious "aurameter" in 1952. With this gadget, it is said, one can discern the shape and movement of an aura, and tell when it changes; one can locate invisible, intangible etheric forms that have been thought or imagined into being. With this instrument he also discovered "wings" in our auras: "lines of force which protrude from the shoulderblades down to the hips, extending horizontally, on top, from the center of each shoulderblade, and usually running straight back anywhere from four to twenty feet. The under edge is curved, similar to a shark's fin, and the whole wing usually thins down to a point or tip. With but one exception, I have found that the wings stand parallel, with the tips about three inches apart."

Cameron also discovered a halo! "A sixteen-inch diameter seems to be about normal, but in the case of one young woman, the diame-ter was about twenty-two inches. I was told afterwards that she was pregnant, but whether or not this was related to the size of the halo, I cannot say."

Lestor B. Wood, a knowledgeable dowser in Breckenridge, Texas, first showed me how the aurameter works. Until that moment, no one had told me that I walk around every day with a gorgeous pair of angel wings!

Did those who painted the gold and rosy auras around religious figures and saints know something we don't know? Is there some-thing to the angel wings and haloes that permeate the art of the ages, after all?

Much Psi literature identifies the aura with ancient knowledge and religions, with the seven "chakras" or energy-centers in the body, for example, as taught by yogic philosophy. It is also identified with the seven planes of consciousness through which human beings are said to move.

Parapsychologist Hiroshi Motoyama, in his Tokyo laboratory, has attacked this problem with his instruments. He explains,

According to yoga theory and practice, a human being has, beside the body and mind usually known by us, a kind of subtle body (actually several higher bodies) which can be grasped only extra-sensorily. The centers of this subtle body or system are termed "chakra." These chakra accept "prana," or a higher dimensional non-physical energy, from the universe on the one hand, and convert it into a kind of physical energy, which is in turn supplied to the internal organs and peripheral tissues through the spinal cord, nervous system, and blood system. The chakra also supply the prana in its highest dimensional form to the subtle system through passageways called "nadi."

The nervous system and blood vessel system, through which physical energy flows to the internal organs and peripheral tissue, are termed "gross nadi," while those nadi which carry higher dimensional energy to the subtle system are termed "subtle nadi." These subtle nadi correspond to the meridians of acupuncture.

My machine is able to pick up energy from an awakened chakra which I believe to be the origin of paranormal phenomena. In the ordinary person, the chakra are only working on the physical plane, but for those with inborn Psi ability, or for those who have progressed through yoga practice and so on, the chakra are awake and are working on higher levels.

His experiments, Motoyama concludes, suggest quite clearly that so-called "siddhi," that is, paranormal powers, are not just products of the imagination, but rather are a different kind of power, whose influence can, in actuality, be exerted on the outside world.

Examining his machines and researches in Tokyo is the closest I personally have come to the meeting of East and West: ancient Eastern philosophy and Western gadgetry!

And yet, for all the popular focus on auras, solid experimentation in this area is so far small indeed.

The problems we face in studying the aura were voiced by parapsychologist Charles Tart: "What are we trying to measure?" he asks. "The physical aura, that extends beyond the surfaces of the body, but is not routinely visible? The psychological aura, or mental concept, that occupies the space around a person? The psychical aura which sensitives detect? The projected aura, or one's subjective impression of what exists out there, which is only in the mind?"

We need to check observers against one another, he suggests: perhaps have ten sensitives engage in perception comparisons. In short, says Tart, it is altogether too simple to ask the question, "Is the aura real?"

Psychic Energy on Film?

The aura debate extends into the manipulation of film by human energy. One such exploration is Kirlian photography, named after the Russian couple, Semyon and Valentina Kirlian, who developed it. Unexposed film is placed on a flat metal plate; the object to be photographed—such as a hand, finger, or leaf—is placed on the film. High-voltage electricity, at very low amperage, is pulsed through the metal plate. The electricity passes through the film and exposes it. When developed, the film shows an outline of the object, with a halo of light surrounding it. If the film is color-sensitive, the halo has many colors, and appears much like the auras that sensitives see.

Since an extended "corona" of every living object is caught by the process, it has been greeted by many as a way—at last!—of photographing the aura or "etheric body." Experiments with the technique have colorfully and dramatically fed that impression. Experimenting with Kirlian techniques since 1970, Thelma Moss at UCLA has produced and recorded changes in the corona as the body changes. Such photographs, she and her associates believe, capture not only the energy surrounding the body, but changes in the physiological and emotional states of those being examined. Moss has studied extensively the changes in healer Olga Worrall's hands as recorded in Kirlian photos. These show an even "corona" around the fingers before the healing, but bright flares and plumes of "energy" pushing out from the fingers when a healing is contemplated or is in process. Douglas Dean has also used the Kirlian method on psychic healers. He and others have found that, during healing, the coronas are larger and more vivid than usual.

Moss has, with Kirlian techniques, produced the Soviets' so-called "phantom leaf" effect. A portion of a leaf is removed. The damaged leaf is then photographed. The resulting image shows the *entire* pattern of the original leaf, not just the truncated part of it, with its whole outline intact—presumably a "lingering effect" of its total energy pattern.

Proponents of Kirlian photography claim that the photos show nothing less than the workings of Psi: undeniable material evidence of an energy that surrounds all living things and changes as they change.

Much of the excitement surrounding these experiments and revelations has been dampened, however, by the resulting controversy. It is a wet blanket, indeed, to be told that these remarkable "auras" may be nothing more than photos of an irrelevant element, produced by changes in body temperature or by *sweat!* A Drexel University research team has reported in *Science* that there are at least twenty-five variables that must be controlled for, to take meaningful Kirlian photographs. And William Tiller observes, "We should not be at all surprised or dismayed to find a perfectly reasonable physical explanation for the generation of light and for the color observations."

Thus, what the Kirlian debate may finally boil down to is not whether the coronal effects are there, but *whether they're Psi.* The Soviets, from all reports, find Kirlian effects very real and exceedingly useful. As for a connection with the psychic, however, that's still unproved.

Astrology and Psi

Astrology is routinely linked with the Psi field by many, a connection most establishment parapsychologists would deny.

There are areas of overlap: *e.g.,* the unexplained "knowing"—through psychic insight, such as premonition, or through astrological charts; the unexplained relationships, often at great distances, of people, things, and events—telepathy, clairvoyance, PK—or, astrologically, with heavenly bodies.

In probing the intricacies of human character, or making predictions, psychics and astrologers both have been credited with remarkable hits—the former, presumably, through psychic abilities; the latter, through astrological knowledge. When an astrologer gets a "good reading," a prominent parapsychologist asks, "Does this confirm the validity of astrology, or does it prove that a highly sensitive person can use an astrological chart as a focusing device? The chart may facilitate the astrologer's unconscious observation of subtle clues, to combine with ESP so as to produce a fairly valid statement about the individual."

One of the most accurate in the casting of horoscopes, himself a student of the art, David Womack, reports,

I began to see that my better predictions had come out of my head, not from the stars.

I now think that all fortune-telling is the same thing—the working of the subconscious mind rationalized as pattern interpretation. The patterns themselves don't have anything to do with the predictions, except to provide a point of reference for human belief, and an organized basis for asking questions.

Our minds are capable of limited glimpses into the future. That's why we sometimes dream about future events, or have hunches we call "premonitions." Modern psychic research . . . has proved that the mind has certain powers. . . .

"What's working in the predictive side of astrology," Womack concludes, "is not the planets, but the mind. It's psychic, rather than planetary."

Given the present stance of Psi researchers, there's been little serious exploration of the relationship between Psi and the stars.

Studies by others have reported a positive correlation between planetary or lunar activity and conditions on earth. At Northwestern University, biologist F. A. Brown, Jr., kept rats in a closed room for several months under constant light, temperature, and air pressure. Even so, the rats' peak activity was related to the position of the moon, being greater when the moon was beneath the horizon and less when it was above.

In a study of nineteen hundred murders in the Miami, Florida, area between 1965 and 1970, it was found that the murder rate began to rise about twenty-four hours before the full moon, reached a peak at the full moon, then dropped back before climbing again to a secondary peak at the new moon.

An endocrinologist in New York City, Dr. William Wolf, has observed that hemorrhages in throat operations were 82 percent higher in the second quarter of the moon than at other times.

As we noted earlier, some scientists believe that planetary alignments trigger earthquakes. John Gribbin, an astrophysicist, and Stephen Plagemann, a NASA physicist, write that "to the surprise of many scientists there has come evidence that . . . the astrologers were not so wrong after all; it seems that the alignments of the planets can, for sound scientific reasons, affect the behavior of the earth." On the basis of such evidence, they predict that the coming rare alignment of planets in 1982 will trigger off regions of [unprecedented] earthquake activity.

Michel and Françoise Gauquelin have pursued a number of studies on the relation between moon and planets at one's birth, and the career later chosen. Though their results were not striking (they were "statistically significant" but only slightly so), they did discover some interesting correlations between time of birth and personality types.

In an examination of over twenty-seven thousand birth records from France, Italy, Belgium, The Netherlands and West Germany, sixteen thousand of which represented well-known personalities, it was found that the celebrities tended to be born just after the moon, Mars, Jupiter, or Saturn had risen or culminated at midday. The Gauquelins also identified "Mars," "Jupiter," "Saturn," and "lunar" temperaments.

The "lunar" temperament, for example, characterizing people born when the moon was on the horizon or at the meridian, was likely to be "amiable, having many friends, simple, good company, good-hearted, accommodating, disorderly, absent-minded, generous, imaginative, easily influenced, fashionable, worldly, nonchalant, poetic, dreaming, obliging, rather snobbish, superficial and tolerant." They rarely found this temperament among athletes, soldiers, physicians or scientists. The most flexible of the four types of personality, it typified many kinds of writers and a greater variety of professional workers than did temperaments associated with Mars, Jupiter or Saturn.

In 1968, the Belgian Committee for the Scientific Study of So-called Paranormal Phenomena attempted a replication of that portion of the Gauquelin study that dealt with British and French sports champions. The Committee was surprised by their own findings, which were almost identical to the Gauquelins': significantly more athletes had been born when Mars was rising, or culminating at midday, than at other times.

Of these researches, the distinguished British psychologist, Hans J. Eysenck, has concluded, "This work has been replicated and re-analyzed so many times by skeptics and cynical observers and physicists elsewhere, with positive results, that it must now be accepted as entirely factual, and exposing some interesting questions to orthodox modern science."

The few parapsychological investigations of Psi and the stars are suggestive. In a pilot study with ESP cards in New York City, Andrija Puharich found that the proportion of correct guesses increased on nights when the moon was full. Keeping records of his precognitive dreams in Vienna, Franz Matauchek had more hits with numbers to be drawn in the Austrian lottery on nights of the full moon, than on any other.

Egged on by such discoveries, Stanley Krippner checked the records of the first eighty subjects who had been tested in his dream lab. He found that on nights when the moon was in its full quarter, there had been only two misses: twenty-one of twenty-three sessions had been hits. In the other three phases of the moon, only half of the trials had been hits. However, his own follow-up study, and one by a Soviet psychiatrist, found just the reverse, namely that "the full moon is the time when Psi abilities are diminished. These abilities are increased in the new moon." The question remains provocative. *Different phases for different people. Use*

The Many Faces of Divining

What of other modes of probing human character and existence, and divining the future: the I Ching, Tarot cards, numerology, palmistry, hand analysis, the crystal ball, tea leaves, and so on? Each has its own history, sometimes ancient: the Chinese *Book of Changes* (the I Ching) dating back to over 3000 B.C.; the Tarot, called by some "the oldest book known to man." Each has also, in addition to its miraculous, possibly well-founded claims, its devoted adherents, distinctive rationale, and esoteric knowledge.

Though parapsychology generally rejects these divining modes as irrelevant, their relation to the psychic is obvious: Probing the hidden and unknown, past, present, and future, is the goal of the diviner, and (as telepathy, precognition, clairvoyance, and so on) the central subject of the parapsychologist's quest.

Very little study, however, has been done by parapsychologists in this area. Charles Honorton and Lawrence Rubin once conducted an experiment in which they attempted to relate Psi to the I Ching. Their results were similar to those of other Psi experiments: Subjects who believed in the existence of Psi obtained answers to their particular problems from the I Ching at statistically more significant levels than did those who were skeptical about Psi.

Aside from the question of how successful diviners actually are, much of the debate centers about whether the devices *themselves* are endowed with special properties that can reveal answers, or whether they serve *merely* as tools or props to aid in psychic detection. Advice on the care of the instruments often seems to support the former, such as the following instructions by a knowledgeable interpreter of Tarot cards:

> A new deck of cards does not respond as easily to the reader's vibratory influence as does a deck that has been used for a long time. . . . Hence, the more you, as the reader, handle your cards, the more accurate your readings will be. . . .
> Exclude the vibrations of other people or objects by wrapping the pack in soft velvet or silk, of a deep purple color. . . . The wrapped cards should be placed in an unpainted and unvarnished box, made of white pine.

From his analysis of the Tarot, David Hoy speculates that its actual workings "appear to lie somewhere between the prop theory and the mysterious properties theory. . . . A good deal of the art of Tarot divination probably does rely more on the skill and insight of the reader, than in the magical properties of the cards themselves. But this does not mean that the reader deals the cards into a spread and then interprets those cards arbitrarily, to match his insights into the inquirer's situation. For each card in the Tarot deck there is a traditional divinatory meaning that must be read as it is, and never changed to fit a particular situation."

"But What About . . . ?"

As one moves about the Psi-and-consciousness lecture/workshop circuit, things fall into a pattern: After a few hours, or a day if it's a weekend stand, there is a new sort of question: "But what about . . . ?"

In this section, we'll look at some "what abouts"—Pyramid Power, the Bermuda Triangle, UFOs, and such—topics, all of them, that parapsychologists wish would go away. "Go away" mainly because of the continual query, "What is their connection with Psi?"

Their connections with Psi are more subtle and indirect than those of divining. If one assumes a theory of general cosmic energy, which many do, "pyramid power" may be, along with Psi, one of its manifestations. Here, the belief is that pyramid-shaped structures focus universal energy of some sort, probably the same energy that is mobilized in the body for PK, yoga disciplines, and healing. There may also be other ways to focus it outside the body. Wilhelm Reich had his energy accumulator, the "orgone box."

The Bermuda Triangle? There is evidence on all sides of forces we don't understand, ESP and PK in humans, "noxious veins" in the earth. Perhaps the Bermuda Triangle, which has claimed over a hundred ships and planes, and a thousand lives, since 1945, is a similar but more potent example of that power. In any case, psychics have been called on to probe the triangle phenomenon.

Whether and in what way UFOs are Psi-related is more difficult. Too little has been established about them to know even what we're dealing with. Psi may be involved, but the subject may belong more properly to astronomy or psychology, or to exobiology, which specializes in the investigation of extraterrestrial organisms. A 1976 poll of the American Astronomical Association found that 28 percent had observed UFOs, and 80 percent considered UFOs worthy of study.

Let's look more closely at these three.

Pyramid power. Aside from the fact that, in a trance, Edgar Cayce discussed them, how did pyramids get into the present Psi context?

A Frenchman named Antoine Bovis discovered that small animals that wandered into the Great Pyramid of Cheops and died there were preserved. He concluded that the pyramid's distinctive shape must have something to do with it. Building a model, Bovis experimented with various types of organic matter, including a dead cat. His conviction: Something about the pyramid causes quick dehydration and obviates ordinary decay.

His published reports attracted Karel Drbal, a pioneering radio engineer in Czechoslovakia. Drbal also experimented with pyramid models, concluding that there was, indeed, a relation between the shape of the space and the physical, chemical, and biological processes within it.

Sheila Ostrander and Lynn Schroeder met Drbal in Prague and publicized "pyramid power" in their 1970 book, *Psychic Discoveries Behind the Iron Curtain.* The authors say that letters from almost every country in the world have since reached them, reporting theories and kitchen experiments.

Today, you'll find "pyramid kits" advertised in every Psi-oriented supply catalogue and magazine. There's even an international bi-monthly newsletter, *Pyramid Guide*. But as for consensus based on solid research, there's not much to go on.

Ottmar Stehle, a scientist with NASA, observes that "pyramids are geometric shapes that focus energy fields. That's exactly what antennae do."

Ruth M. Flynn of the Toronto Society for Psychical Research tested pyramids for plant-energizing and food preservation. She found "no basis at all for the claims made for the power of pyramid shapes. It appears to be mere superstition." Parapsychologist A. R. G. Owen, also of Toronto, conducted pyramid experiments, and likewise came up with no significant results.

Do pyramids have powers? Ostrander and Schroeder suggest you find out for yourself. In their *Handbook of Psychic Discoveries*, they tell you how.

The Bermuda Triangle. The Bermuda Triangle is of more than parapsychological concern. Scores of air and sea vessels and hundreds of passengers have disappeared in its maw, a large area in the western Atlantic between Bermuda and Florida. Because of these unexplained losses—always "disappeared without a trace"; no bodies, debris, oil slicks, flotsam, weather disturbances—the area is also known as "The Hoodoo Sea," "The Devil's Triangle," "The Limbo of the Lost," "The Twilight Zone," and "The Port of Missing Ships."

It is the unsolved-mystery aspect that is its continuing lure:

• In March 1918, a Navy coaling ship, the U.S.S. *Cyclops,* with a crew of 309, disappeared without a trace.

• In January 1948, a British airliner with a crew of 6, and 21 passengers, vanished near Bermuda.

• In 1963, a 600-foot tanker, the *Sulphur Queen,* was lost in the straits of Florida without leaving so much as an oil slick.

• Also in 1963, a DC-3 airliner, en route from San Juan to Miami, went down within sight of the Florida coast.

• Perhaps the most astonishing disappearances, which brought the Triangle to the notice of the world: On Dec. 3, 1945, a whole squadron of U.S. Navy torpedo bombers, five Grumman TBF Avengers with a total crew of 14, took off from Fort Lauderdale Naval Air Station on a routine training mission, which proceeded uneventfully until mid-afternoon. At 3:45, as they were returning home, the pilot suddenly radioed a frantic Mayday call: "We are lost . . . can't be sure of any direction, even the ocean doesn't look right, everything is wrong . . . strange." At 4:25 one pilot was heard to say, "It looks like we're entering white water. We're completely lost." Then, silence. None of the men was ever heard from again. A Mariner flying boat loaded with rescue equipment and a crew of 13 was sent to search for the missing squadron. That plane also vanished.

The Navy then launched the most massive sea and coastline search effort ever organized: 242 planes, 18 sea vessels, and an aircraft carrier with 35 more planes covered an area of 280,000 square miles, in an exhaustive week-long search for some trace of the aircraft and crewmen who had vanished. Land parties scoured hundreds of miles of coastline in Florida and the Bahamas for any clues. Searchers covered the Everglades and the Gulf of Mexico. Nothing, not a stick or a stain, was ever found.

In May of 1970, a documentary film maker, Richard Winer, asked the psychic Dykshoorn to investigate the mysterious area and to contribute his ideas on film; we have already cited parts of his account in Chapter 5.

Almost ten years later, I asked Dykshoorn if he had changed his ideas about the Devil's Triangle. "Not at all!" he exclaimed. "I stick to that. I think it was the difference between the True and Magnetic North. In Miami, where the Triangle comes down, there is a variation of from one to two degrees. There is so much friction built up in the magnetic field, that a plane or ship goes down.

"And what is so interesting, the other Devil's Triangle on the other side of the globe, east of Japan—*exactly opposite this*—has the same thing on the compass. When they get four or five degrees' variation, they get the same trouble there."

There is a similar hazardous triangle in Lake Erie, about which Bob Ater was called in. He came up with a hypothesis much like Dykshoorn's. It is somewhat paradoxical that in each of these cases a psychic has probed a mystery that has defied investigators, and offered a straightforward *physical* explanation.

UFOs (Unidentified Flying Objects). When I was in Japan last year, the top hit tune was called "UFO" (pronounced *oof-oh*). Over seventy thousand sightings have been reported all around the world. The number of unreported sightings is incalculable. "There's overwhelming evidence that UFOs are real," says a reporter who has researched the data. Polygraph tests have been given to witnesses, evidence has been collected in scores of photographs, and physical traces have been found where a UFO has "landed." *Something* is going on, all right, but what it is, mesmerizes and eludes us.

Fifteen hundred true believers gathered at the First International Congress of Unidentified Flying Objects, at Acapulco in 1977. Hundreds more were at the Mutual UFO Network Convention in Burlingame, California, in 1979. They came from every part of the globe, and from every walk of life, among them, astronomers, social scientists, aerospace engineers, clergymen and physicists.

The contemporary UFO movement began with Kenneth Arnold, a salesman from Boise, Idaho. When flying his private plane over Mt. Rainier in 1947, he saw nine glowing disc-shaped objects flying in a chainlike formation. They swerved erratically among the peaks, turning over at times in unison. He clocked their speed at more than 1,000 miles per hour. A journalist, picking up the account, called them "flying saucers." (Incidentally, this term is never used by serious students of the subject.)

Arnold's sighting was the start of a thirty-year investigation, beginning with the first official Air Force probe. Most sightings are not vehicles for creatures from outer space or even actually UFOs, since they are ultimately identified—*e.g.,* as secret weapons, ball lightning, birds, planes, satellites, cloud formations, weather balloons, hallucinations. The 20 percent or so that cannot be identified are finally designated as UFOs.

Cases, as everyone must know by now, are "of the first kind"—sightings; "of the second kind"—measurable changes in the surrounding environment, such as radioactive remains and scorched plants; and "of the third kind"—much less frequent and hard to believe, direct encounters.

Documentation in the third kind comes from witnesses, polygraph tests, hypnotic regression, and from residues of radioactivity found in the bodies of those having encounters. Most dramatic are reports of abductions. Within each "kind," accounts are surprisingly similar—even reports of the third kind, which cite strange, foul-smelling "humanoids." Results of such encounters are always profound: manipulation of consciousness, temporary paralysis, loss of memory, healings, and *increased psychic abilities.*

J. Allen Hynek, a leading astronomer and former director of the McMillin Observatory at Ohio State University, appeared at a Psi-oriented conference I attended. Employed by the Air Force as scientific consultant to its UFO research "Project Blue Book," he found the evidence of UFOs so overwhelming that he has now resigned from all other commitments to devote himself to his own UFO research. It was he who, after twenty years of investigation, wrote what is probably the most authoritative book on the subject: *The UFO Experience: A Scientific Enquiry.* It is his three-fold breakdown of sightings, above, that is in general use, as in the movie *Close Encounters of the Third Kind.*

Hynek's Center for UFO Studies is a place where people can, with dignity, report their experiences, confidentially, if they choose. UFOs have been put on the United Nations agenda, Hynek told us: Kurt Waldheim met with him to make arrangements. *Voyager* spacecraft en route to Jupiter and Saturn carry, on tape, Waldheim's greetings from our planet to the universe. "It's *our* UFO to somewhere else!" Hynek chuckles.

He summarizes the current state of affairs:

1. UFO reports exist and continue to exist; they haven't blown over.

2. Reports are global—from 133 countries; and from highly respected people—pilots and others—with testimony that would be accepted in courts of law.

3. Reports are bizarre, and do not fit the current scientific framework.

Says Hynek, "When the long-awaited solution to the UFO problem comes, I believe that it will prove to be not merely the next small step in the march of science, but a mighty and totally unexpected quantum jump. This may be the most important phenomenon of our era."

One could continue almost indefinitely to list topics, controversial in the extreme, which are presumed to be somehow related to Psi. These range from the *"lost continents" of Atlantis and Lemuria,* cited by Cayce and other sensitives; the ancient *standing stones* and *megaliths,* which, with buried mounds, tombs, and temples, are believed to tie in with astronomical movements and subtle patterns of cosmic or earth energy; methods of tapping and liberating the *Ch'i* or *Ki* or *psychic energy*—by yoga, meditation, relaxation, hypnosis; *materialization, dematerialization, levitation,* and so on and on.

Motoyama showed me a glass ashtray on his desk in Tokyo, recalling that when a powerful psychic was in intense concentration in the "chakra machine" upstairs, the ashtray from his desk was dematerialized and materialized again, with a thump, on the floor of the laboratory above. In his investigation of Rolling Thunder, Doug Boyd cites many instances in which the medicine man dematerialized and materialized objects. The general literature is sprinkled with such incidents. Not so the scientific journals.

Levitation has been approached through studies of anti-gravitation. There is a Gravity Research Foundation, for example, in New Boston, New Hampshire, founded by Roger Babson. It makes scientific studies of gravity and its anomalies. Of greater interest, perhaps, are the current claims of Transcendental Meditation groups that they can train people to levitate.

Spells. One more Psi-related domain we should mention: *spells, possession,* and *exorcism,* referring respectively to "casting a spell" or "bewitchment" of another person; inhabiting or "possessing" another against his/her knowledge or will; and terminating this unwelcome influence or presence. The last two are usually thought of as connected with the dead (or "undead")—discarnates, evil spirits, and such—but they also apply to living persons who invade another's life and privacy. I include these, in part, because such instances have impinged upon me in the course of my inquiry, in the form of requests for help.

There was a phone call from a distressed woman in Connecticut. From the moment Mrs. B. D. met Mr. F., she knew something strange was happening; she had the sensation he was "watching and hovering" over her, and even clinging, somehow. "It was as though he was working on me." In the weeks that followed, the cloying sense of his presence continued and intensified.

She tried talking to others about it, but to no avail, and finally turned to me. I suddenly thought of Edward Jastram, in the Boston area. I had heard him talk of something which, at that time and place, seemed out of context: possession! It had seemed out of context with him, too: he's a physicist, a graduate of MIT, with years of his career spent at Texas Instruments Corporation.

"It should more properly be called 'visitation,' " he'd explained. "I work with it all the time." He described how he located "troublesome entities" with his pendulum, and how he got rid of them. "I just call it 'clearing'—'clearing personalities'—because 'possession' and 'exorcism' have such bad connotations. I just 'clear entities.' "

Could Dr. Jastram help my Mrs. B. D.? I took the leap and referred her to him. Awash with questions, I awaited results.

Three letters and a phone talk with her, and a phone conversation with him, assured me that his technique was working out just fine. Jastram told me, "She *was* very open to such an invasion from the outside. She had great vulnerability from unfortunate experiences, and psychological conditioning from way back. There was not just one, but three entities 'visiting' her. I'm trying to help her deal with this now. She has to learn how to shut them out." Then he added, "Her channels are so open. She has the potential for being a remarkable psychic."

What we must now ask: Where is the line between the burgeoning discoveries of the new Psi science, and the knowledge and arts of the far-distant past?

12

THROUGH THE VEIL:
Psychics at Work

An old wives' tale says that a person born with a caul or veil will be psychically gifted. Ancient tradition holds that there are other physical signs as well. Whether this is superstition or not, psychics Alex Tanous, Ernesto Montgomery, and Peter Hurkos were born with a caul; Jeane Dixon, with a Star of David in her palm.

Inside Psychics

What is it like to be a psychic?

From the stories we hear, it must be glamorous and exciting, marvelously convenient, and remunerative in the extreme. How great it would be to find your lost car keys or necklace merely by picturing them! What a boon, to pick up warnings of planes not to take and trips to avoid! Imagine, knowing which card is coming up next, or what horse will win. Add to this having one's own private pipeline to some hidden Source of Information!

That's not the way the psychics have told it to me. For many of them, at least, it's been a painful, harrowing experience, filled with fear, guilt, bewilderment, and the knowledge that one is not like the rest of the human race. Working through the problems of being different is a theme running through many of their life stories. "My gift gave me no satisfaction whatever until I became an adult," Dykshoorn says with conviction. Many a sensitive would say Amen.

Take Ingo Swann. He's on his feet now, certainly: productive and widely recognized as an artist and distinguished psychic. He was lecturing and showing slides of Psi-inspired paintings—his own and others—when I met him. He lives in New York but is on call for extended lab testing assignments, such as those at Stanford Research Institute, where he was when we last talked. Fairly oozing projects and creativity, he discussed his science-fiction novel *Star Fire*, which was going the rounds, and took me to a recording studio where he was cutting his first album—Psi-inspired also, *Star Children.*

Who would know that he's been through a drawn-out ordeal because of the very talents that now bring him fame?

His psychic adventure started early; out-of-body experiences, for example, when he was only two and a half, and people were still talking baby-talk to him. Via such an incident, he watched his own tonsillectomy: the forceps, an accidental slip of the scalpel on his tongue, the removal of the "dirty brown things," which interested him immensely. "I want my tonsils," he demanded when he came to. They'd been thrown away, he was told. "They have NOT!" he rejoined. He'd just "seen" them put in a bottle on a shelf, behind two rolls of tissue. "You put them there," he pointed. "No, I didn't," said the nurse. When he got home, his puzzled mother asked how he knew where the tonsils had been hidden. He couldn't explain it, but had that same startling separation of body and self many times afterwards.

This was only the beginning of a long string of confrontations with unbelieving people, and events that seem almost like fairy tales. Through psychic eyes he saw tornadoes, horse races, earthquakes. He saw people fleeing villages and towns and killing each other. Wherever his heart and interest took him, he saw frightful and wonderful and bewildering things. On one memorable "trip," he journeyed across the ocean and saw a king—the king of England, sitting alone and crying, in a big room with big chairs in it.

"Will the king marry her?" he asked his mother. Then she began to cry too, which amazed him. He learned quickly that telling her these adventures hurt her, and he resolved not to tell her any more. There was only one person he could turn to, his maternal grandmother, Anna. She was regarded in her Scandinavian community as having the "evil eye." She couldn't do much to help him, though, and told him that ordinary people hated and feared this kind of thing.

The fact is, he believes strongly today, one has to degrade one's natural psychic awareness considerably in order to participate in life and society as it is constructed on this planet. Hardest to bear was his relationship with other children. His private experiences set him apart. Ingo remembers the exact moment when at last he had to choose between "normalcy"—acceptance by his peers—and his incredible glowing adventures.

It was on the Fourth of July, when he was eight. After a children's party, movies and games, gazing out his bedroom window, he took a "trip" to the stars—a recurring motif in much of his work today. He saw them there, by the countless billions, glistening, gleaming in a symphony of sound and color. At that moment, he knew he had to make a choice—a bad choice as he finally realized—but a choice he feels that many like him have had to make. In the eye-blink of his return to the planet, he suddenly knew that he simply didn't wish to be different from others. He chose "normalcy," knowing that this was the last trip he would take. From that moment, such experiences were forced back to the edges of his memory, not to be thought of for years.

How did Swann rejoin the human race? Oddly, he says, with the help of a chinchilla. He saw it first in the window of a Greenwich Avenue pet shop in New York, a small grey piece of fluff with bright sparkly eyes, long whiskers, and amazing pint-size elephant ears. When it realized he was studying it, it started running and jumping over the backs of the other animals, and up the edges of the cage. It was the look in his eye, though, that captured Ingo. In two weeks, he bought him.

For several weeks, the chinchilla lived in a box on Ingo's desk; then, when his master finally gave him the run of the house, it became clear that "Mercenary" was a thinking animal; in fact, that he was picking up Ingo's thoughts. If Ingo began thinking "bedtime," while scratching Mercenary's ears, the small piece of fluff would jump into the air and disappear.

Ingo tested this for several days, then brought in friends to verify it. Whenever he winked at them, they were to think about putting Mercenary in his cage. The response was always immediate.

The discovery that the animal could pick up his thoughts, but that he couldn't fathom Mercenary's, shook him up. The tiny creature's psychic knack hit home. Why couldn't Ingo do the same?

It was this that jolted him back to his own thought-system and potential. Today, when people ask how he produces the amazing effects he does in the laboratory, his mind always turns to the small furry creature that got him back on the track.

Alex Tanous' trip from alienation to adjustment took a quite different route. Now a teacher and counselor in Portland, Maine, he is in demand by the lecture circuit and the media. We first met in Montreal, where he spoke in French and English to a Psi-oriented group. My interviews with him continued in Missouri at an ESP research associates' gathering, and in New York at the American Society for Psychical Research, where he gave me a personally-conducted tour of the layout of the out-of-body experiments he was then engaged in.

Again, with his present confidence and composure, it would be hard to believe that his psychic abilities had caused years of trauma.

Alex' father was a friend of Kahlil Gibran, the famous, and also Lebanese, poet today best known as the author of *The Prophet.* "You will have a son," Gibran once told him, "a man of exceptional gifts, of great abilities, but also a man of great sorrows."

The first indication of anything unusual in Alex' life—it must have made an impression since I've heard him tell about it several times—was a psychometry demonstration when he was eighteen months old. Feeling the edge of a stack of phonograph records, he could always find his favorite, "Mary Had a Little Lamb," no matter where it was in the stack, although no one else could see or feel any difference between this record and the others.

He had many unusual experiences in his youth, such as jumping down a long stairway and feeling himself floating like a balloon. This happens to all of us in our dreams, but Alex was awake. On landing, he'd look at his "other self" at the top of the stairs, and find himself in both places at once—what is sometimes called "bilocation."

He was not cut off from his family as was Ingo, since his father did readings with cards, and his mother was psychically gifted. However, the family belonged to the Maronite rite, an Eastern rather than Roman Catholic church, and his father's reputation had already singled them out as somehow different. When his father died and the family became nearly destitute, Alex' mother was deeply concerned lest his psychic experiences mark him as odd. Thus the support and encouragement he had known previously dried up.

When he reached high school, real troubles began. Torn between his religion and his own nature and inclinations, he withdrew from society. Feeling as though he was carrying a plague, he lost interest in life and in his ability to function normally.

Things came to a head in a football game. He was playing with friends, running with the ball, when a blue-eyed boy named Everett Tilley tackled him. Alex crashed to the ground and blurted out, "You're going to die for that!" Six months later, on November 26, *Alex' birthday,* Everett Tilley died of a ruptured appendix. Today Alex says that the incident was just a burst of premonition. At the time, though, he felt certain he had caused the boy's death. Nearly drowning in guilt, he skirted a full mental breakdown.

One vehicle for Alex' recovery, I gather from my interviews, was academic life and books.

Entering Boston College, he found himself on the verge of flunking out almost before he began. He was given an ultimatum. Remembering that Edgar Cayce had slept on his books to acquire his lessons, Alex tried the same thing—with a twofold effect: he got 100 percent on the exam, but was believed to be cheating! From then on, he would flip through his books, sleep on them, and learn what he needed to know.

He reached the final stage of reconciliation in his role of observer at the Vatican Ecumenical Council, which brought forth the "doctrine of conscience," a rule that now allows Catholics to make up their own minds on moral issues. This allowed him to resolve the conflicts between his psychic nature and his religious beliefs.

His most recent therapy has been working through the pain of his own childhood by writing a book for parents and other adults about children and their Psi abilities, *Is Your Child Psychic?* He hopes to salvage children's talents, and help them avoid what he went through.

We have seen how Rien Dykshoorn was censured and punished throughout his childhood. His hold on sanity finally came with his "wire." On top of social and family problems brought on by his psychic abilities, he had to contend with the psychic forces themselves. He was being continually bombarded by clairvoyant impressions: sights, sounds, smells and even tastes kept flooding into his mind, uninvited. He didn't need to concentrate on another person in order to know about him; he just knew.

Rien finally solicited help, because he could not stem this psychic flow. "You appear," the psychologist told him, "to possess a paranormal or psychic ability, and a remarkably acute one. . . . You will probably never adjust to living with people, however, unless you learn to control it. The strain will become more and more intense."

"Should I try to become a professional clairvoyant?" Dykshoorn asked him.

"Why not? After all, you are clairvoyant, and you can do valuable work. Why shouldn't you earn your living at it?"

Through trial and experimentation, Dykshoorn found that he could divine for water, and since water-diviners were respected there, thought he might support himself in this way. Since most dowsers used a forked twig, he took a thin length of piano wire and bent it into the shape of a forked twig. It would be his divining rod, he decided; his aid to concentration. To this day he can't explain why, any more than he can explain how, it turns his abilities on and off.

It was misery, too, for the unhappy Gerard Croiset, whom no one understood—and for how many more?

This isn't meant to be a tale of woe, but simply a dollop of reality to counter the over-glamorization of the Psi-blest life. There are doubtless exceptions. The story of Kenny Kingston, "Psychic to the Stars," would appear to be as unruffled as a clear summer morning, as content and up-beat as a life can be. "I have a love affair with my work. . . . God instilled *this* gift in me, and as long as I use it properly I'll never lose it."

Other Doors

Birth or childhood is not the only entry to the psychic realm. There are others. Psi crashed in on Peter Hurkos, as we have seen, with a fall on his head—instant Psi. When he awoke from a four-day coma, he was overwhelmed by a flood of psychic perceptions he could not comprehend. He was a young man in Holland, then. He's in America now, and sixty-nine, but the memory of the shock is still vivid.

"What is it like," I asked him, "if you are not born with this ability, but simply wake up one day to find you have it?"

"Terrifying!" he replied with conviction, "and hard. I had a hard time of it those first few years. I was very emotional. Couldn't control it. Didn't know where it came from. Didn't know what it was. I came to America to find out. A doctor in Washington, D.C., and Dr. Puharich in Maine brought me here. That was in 1956. I spent three years with Dr. Puharich, being tested in his lab."

Hurkos is one of the few I talked with who did not cite his own published biography. He is unhappy with it. "Too many author's views; not enough of mine." His own book, he hopes, will appear before long and do justice to his perspective.

There's plenty to tell: three years with the police in Miami, five years with a foundation in Milwaukee, in the 60s to California, where he's given private consultations and worked with Hollywood celebrities. But first and foremost, for many years, is his work with police, especially in murder and criminal cases.

Olga Worrall's story has a different twist. She has been psychic for as long as she can remember, but it was her marriage that pulled her talents into focus.

"My father was a Russian theologian in the Orthodox Church," she told me on one of our visits. "My mother was a Hungarian countess." She smacks of the countess herself, as she mounts the podium in a fur and her pearls, until she opens her mouth and her folksy, down-home comments start to flow. Then, she's just your neighbor down the block. Everything is "Oh boy, this is great!" Everybody is "honey" or "kid," including "you kids in the audience." It's easy to see why she is the darling of the lecture circuit.

As a young woman, she faced a challenge. She had met and fallen in love with an engineer, Ambrose Worrall (of the ailerons incident above, Chapter 2). He was a serious scientist, she kept reminding me, "and I don't know beans about that! Besides, I was afraid, with my peculiar abilities, that marriage couldn't possibly work. I finally had to tell him, 'I can't marry you!'

" 'And why not?'

" 'Because I see *dead* people!'

"Ambrose was jolted for a moment, but he came right back: 'I see dead people, *too!*' "

Neither Ambrose nor Olga had the slightest idea of the other's lifelong psychic gifts, nor had they dared, even with one another, to reveal this important part of their lives. Once they opened the gates of sharing, however, they were astonished to find how parallel their backgrounds had been. Both sets of parents, for example, had ordered them never to mention the "people" or "voices" they saw and heard.

So Olga and Ambrose were married, became a Psi phenomenon, and lived happily ever after—until his death separated them in 1972. (But this has not really separated them, she declares, since she and he now communicate more than ever.)

Marriage for them was a mutually rich and fulfilling partnership, which pooled and optimized the abilities of them both. It was the door to their effective psychic work, and their founding of the New Life Clinic in Baltimore.

Bob Ater is one whose psychic abilities surfaced gradually, in adulthood. In the process he found, as have others, that opening up one talent seems to jog loose another. Here's how Bob explained it to me:

> I was trying psychometry. . . . These pictures and ideas coming into my head were constantly about 95 percent right. I haven't tried to develop it, though. . . .
>
> Many times I've been able to go into a house and go room to room, telling people what happened in that house. I've gone where the lights would flicker, objects would move, pan or can opener would start to swing. Not always but often. Have had lots of experience with ghosts, rappings, all this stuff. I don't go seeking it. . . .
>
> Several years ago I was down at Longmeadow, Massachusetts. Someone asked if I'd like to go with him to the spiritualist church. The medium that day was a local hairdresser. He looked in my direction, looked shocked, did a double-take. He pointed to me and said, "Are you in this business?" I said, "No, just interested." He said, "Well, you've got all kinds of people around you. I can see them." He named names. Several I recognized; one, especially, was my first Sunday School teacher back in Gurnee, Illinois. Elsie, her name was.

I approached dowsing with the idea of finding out how it works, what it's all about, not to prove anything. I just experiment and see what happens. This has gradually led me in many different directions—locating water, then checking out energy, and finding lost people.

The way I got into healing? I'm very curious. As soon as I began dowsing, I began experimenting. . . . Soon, I got so I could feel this energy with my hands. One thing led to another—a steady progression of personal knowledge.

Then I started to discover that there were certain types of people who seemed to walk around with certain types of auras. A certain shape seemed to be typical of certain personalities. I started to find breaks in the aura that indicated certain things—a muscle might be damaged or so, or something was wrong at that point. . . .

Things just started to happen. I didn't set myself out as a healer, but very often, within a few seconds, someone would say, "The pain is gone."

Bevy Jaegers *worked* at it, she stressed to me in all of my interviews. "I *learned* how to do this, and you can, too. I didn't fall on my head or anything like that. I was just curious, and tried to figure it out. I studied hard—everything I could find. And I practiced. Oh, *how* I practiced! And bit by bit, it came. I teach it now, and you don't even have to come to me personally to be taught. I have textbooks, and a kit."

From Séance to Shingle

How do present-day psychics compare with those of the past? A shorthand way of putting it: they've been moving from séances in which, as go-betweens, they received messages from "the other side," to setting up shop for themselves, hanging out their shingle, as it were, for any of a broad spectrum of services: police work, counseling, oil-finding, and so on.

Most of the communication, in the earlier era, was conducted not directly with the departed, but through "controls" or "spirit guides." Sometimes the spirit guides were better known personalities among researchers than the mediums themselves. One of the renowned Mrs. Piper's spirit messengers was a French doctor named Phinuit. He was later replaced by a group of controls named after their leader, Imperator. This same group had served earlier as guides for the English medium-cleric, Stainton Moses, who founded the Spiritualist Alliance, now the College of Psychic Studies.

Another of Mrs. Piper's controls, still a fascination to investigators, was Pelham. A lawyer and writer when he was alive, he often argued with his friend, Richard Hodgson, that survival is not only improbable but inconceivable. Pelham promised, however, that if he died first he would return and "make things lively." He, or a reasonable facsimile thereof, did just that. In February of 1892, when he was just thirty-two, he was killed in a fall. On March 22 he made his first appearance in Mrs. Piper's automatic script, and over the next six years talked with one hundred and thirty persons, thirty of whom had known him. He addressed each in the tone and manner that he had used in his lifetime.

The Irish-born medium Eileen Garrett bridges the older and newer modes. Her first spirit guides were: Uvani, a centuries-past soldier from India; next came Abduhl Latif, a healing enthusiast who had been a twelfth-century physician at the court of Saladin (since Abduhl Latif came through to several different mediums, Mrs. Garrett called him "the traveling salesman of the spirit world"). After him came Tehotah, and Rama, who had never had a life on this earth.

Sometimes, in the spirit of twentieth-century parapsychology, Mrs. Garrett hypothesized that her controls were subconscious split-offs from her own personality. After tests at the laboratory at Duke, where Uvani scored above chance (!), at about the same level as she did, some of the parapsychologists were inclined to agree. Tehotah and Rama seemed to come from a deeper level, in some ways resembling the Jungian archetypes of the "collective unconscious."

Gladys Osborne Leonard's control was a small girl named Feda. The late Arthur Ford's was Fletcher, who in Ford's closing years took complete charge of the sittings.

Trance mediums still exist, Britishers Ina Twigg and Douglas Johnson among them, but the style and methods have veered considerably from the nineteenth-century patterns. Ina Twigg's control is her deceased father. Aron Abrahamsen tells me he has had two spirit guides, the third in a series of pairs. "One is Chinese, named Gautamo, about five feet six inches tall, slender, with a cap, long beard, wide sleeves, very, very gentle—he's older, talks with a real Chinese accent. The other is a Greek named Tropikos, who goes around in a short skirt and kilts. The Chinese is in charge."

Mrs. Garrett developed her extra-sensory abilities so that in later years she worked no longer in a trance but in a waking state. Many mediums today, including Twigg and Johnson, now employ a conscious state which they call "waking clairvoyance," or go into what Abrahamsen calls a "state of meditation."

Mediums report that messages come through different channels. Mrs. Twigg's communications, for example, are often auditory. She hears the message in an inside ear—"clairaudience." Occasionally, the message is by "direct voice," an actual voice heard in the vicinity. A modern version of this is "electronic mediumship," in which spirit voices are recorded on tape. Messages are often visual, sometimes symbolic; and in Douglas Johnson's work, must be interpreted.

One old form of spirit communication, automatic writing, has lost none of its allure. Packaging the messages that continue to flow from "the other side" is itself a lively and profitable business. All in all, it adds up also to a rather extensive literature. The "Betty books" by Betty and Stewart Edward White are among the most popular of this genre. The first, in 1937, from entities called "the Invisibles," was passed on to Betty when she was in trance. After her death, her communications passed through a medium and were taken down by her husband. The best known of these are *The Unobstructed Universe* (1940), and *The Road I Know* (1942). The voluminous "Seth" philosophy, received by Jane Roberts, is another example. *The Book of James* "wrote itself" on Susie Smith's typewriter. Its source was said to be "James Anderson," a spirit who, as Ms. Smith learned later, was really the psychologist William James.

None of these writings has caused more of a stir than the three-volume *Course in Miracles,* a Christian message dictated to a Jewish woman in New York City. Its ethical and way-of-life overtones have won it a surprising hearing, for example, a full-scale feature article in *Psychology Today* (September, 1980), and a following even in some parapsychological circles.

We should hardly be astonished at such a development. The received message or Revelation from On High is a very ancient phenomenon, coeval with prophecy or shamanship itself. It has been revered throughout history: after all, Moses brought down the tablets from the mountain, and Muhammad heard a voice saying "O Muhammad, thou art the Messenger of God"—and Messenger of God he has been called ever since, his message, the Q'ran. John of Patmos was commanded, "Write down the things which thou hast seen, and the things which are and will be." (Rev. 2:19) The Mormons' Joseph Smith received his Word from the Angel Moroni on gold plates.

If there is a difference between these historic messages and the later ones, it may be that many of the older recipients were commanded to write proclamations of global scope, directly from God or an archangel; while many of today's receivers are given chatty how-to's from humans "over there."

In any case, prominent sensitives are less inclined now to mount a séance than they are to go into business. No small number of them have some kind of enterprise, with office, secretary, agent and if volume warrants it, a staff. A spouse may devote full time to coordinating the venture. Martha Sherman, Doris Abrahamsen and Shirley Hoy are three examples. (Muhammad's beloved first wife, Khadija, played a similar role in his work.)

There's a tendency also to specialize: in clientele—tycoons, movie stars, John Does—and in subject matter. Whatever your problem, there's a psychic somewhere to take care of it. We are just beginning to get local listings and directories. The January 1979, issue of *New York* magazine published what it called a "psychic directory," names and fees of the better-known local practitioners; not a bona fide directory, to be sure, but a start.

There is a *Psychic Yellow Pages* in the San Francisco area, the entries selected for motivation, qualifications, and feeling-tone. The compilers are trying to address Alan Vaughan's observation: "Since the psychic and allied fields have no licensing body, no committee to award certificates of competence, no boards to expel malpractitioners, consulting a psychic at random has been hazardous."

Species: Sensitive

Question: Is there a psychic breed? A clear-cut Psi type? When I started out on this inquiry, it seemed that there was. So modest were the backgrounds, so skimpy the education of many of the psychics I knew of, I wondered if these circumstances were, in fact, essential to psychic development. Perhaps academic training and cultural polish drive Psi away? (I still find support for this thesis.)

I looked at the pattern with religion. Cayce was a Bible student. Jeane Dixon goes to Mass every day; according to her biographer, Ruth Montgomery, Jeane considers herself "an instrument of God." Olga Worrall's work is based in a church: "It is not I, but God, who does the healing." Alex Tanous had set his sights on the priesthood.

Were unspoiledness and religion, then, key attributes of the psychic "type?"

As I have moved around since among the Psi-centered population, I have concluded that there is no such thing as a psychic type. I still run into the unpretentious sensitive such as Dorothy Allison; Dorothy was the eleventh child of thirteen, who told me her mother taught her to believe in St. Anthony "because he can find everything." I still see sensitives for whom religion is central: Aron and Doris Abrahamsen, for instance, who are deep into their version of the Christian religion, even have their own group. In personal prayer times they find glossolalia (speaking in tongues) "meaningful and helpful."

Simple background and religion continue to be themes, but they are far from the rule. By the time a gypsy had alerted Jeane Dixon to her abilities, Jeane's father had amassed a fortune and retired at 45. For every psychic consumed with the love of God, there are others—as many or more?—who explicitly dissociate Psi from religion.

There are no common physical traits: psychics come in all shapes and sizes, young and old, male and female. They are found in all races, cultures, and nationalities, in every part of the world.

Let's run down some of the differences among them.

Lifestyle. Harold Sherman fled New York for the woodsy silence of Arkansas foothills. From Beverly Hills, Kenny Kingston advises followers, "Surround yourself with elegant people."

Each day, Edgar Cayce got up early and watched the sun rise out of the ocean. By its light he read the Bible. Usually he got his own breakfast, a biographer notes, because he preferred his own version of coffee—hot, black, and strong. When weather permitted he worked outside until the mail came.

Work Styles. Even among those who cater to the movie stars, there are radical differences in work styles. Kingston, for instance, holds carefully staged séances, preferably the "trumpet séance." These are filled with elaborate protocols and rituals.

> I place each person's name on the chair, where he or she will be sitting, along with a hymn book, and sit and meditate quietly for fifteen minutes to half-an-hour on that afternoon, asking the good spirits to come in that night. At that same time, I burn a tall, non-scented white candle to purify the air and bring in healthy spirits.
>
> For participants:
>
> On arrival, they should enter the circle by passing on either side of the medium's chair, which is pushed back farther than the others. They must not break the circle by going in between their own seats.
>
> I prefer to start my séances punctually at 8:30 P.M. because Clifton [one of the spirit guides] likes that hour. Guests arrive at 8:15 P.M., and after the last person is seated the doors are closed, and must not be opened again.
>
> When everyone is seated comfortably, the white candle is lit, and we all repeat, three times, "No negative vibrations shall enter tonight."
>
> We meditate for about ten minutes, then rub the palms of our hands together, to generate energy. Next we begin to sing. We must sing loudly, to bring up the vibrations.

"What techniques do you use?" I asked the Dutch import Peter Hurkos, also a psychic to the stars in the Los Angeles area.

"I can do it with an open shirt, in the street, anywhere, and I don't close my eyes, go in trance, or shake. I just be a normal human being."

Some, like Rien Dykshoorn, use props—rods, pendulums, cards. Some use nothing, or hold only the police specimen from the scene of the crime.

Some work at first hand, and on the scene. Many work at a distance. Healers, as we've seen in Chapter 4, vary widely in their approaches. Almost all are loners, though some choose or are forced to work as a team. Police sometimes call on several sensitives to pool their input. Ann Armstrong combines her Psi abilities with therapist Many Jane Ledyard.

Receiving. Most psychics report seeing images, shapes, colors, and designs: someone large, lots of red, a winding road, a fallen log, a blue mail box, a brown dog. "Beyond is a windmill, a broken-down fence, and a culvert." Or again, "A three-story red brick building, a fire hydrant in front, an antenna on the roof, white awnings." Less often do they pick up specific addresses or names of towns, persons, or streets. Numbers, when they come through, are frequently jumbled: 384 for 483, or 29 instead of 92.

Not all clues are visual. Dykshoorn says he "sees, hears, feels, smells, and tastes." So powerful are the sensations he picks up that he often suffers: suffocation in the Bermuda Triangle case, nausea or dizziness in others. While seeking an ancient church relic in the Dutch town of Breda, near the Belgian border, he was suddenly stricken. "It began with a sense of disorientation, of dizziness, almost of nausea, that suddenly congealed into physical pain that took my breath away. It was like an electric shock—every joint, every muscle ached. I hunched forward, almost fell, and could not straighten up. In my mind, I was *beyond* reality. I remained aware of my surroundings—the modern buildings, passersby—but I could also see a different town! Different streets, old buildings, unpaved, narrow, haphazard streets and lanes. . . . Breda as it had been some time in the past!"

So complete was his identification with persons he was seeking that Dykshoorn often *became* that person, even down to his handicap or limp.

> An old man . . . had disappeared.
> I took out the divining rod, and began to concentrate on the old man. I soon began to choke and sputter, and my throat seemed filled with water. I knew that the old man had drowned.
> I set out to follow the course he had taken on his last walk. My gift brought him into me: I shuffled, my right eye twitched. I felt again the familiar sensation of pain that was not my own.
> The manager was astonished. "That's him!" he cried. "That's exactly the way he walked! You *are* him!"
> The room was one of many opening into a long, narrow hallway. At each door I felt a compulsion to stoop and peer through the keyhole. "The old man was a Peeping Tom," I said. "He liked to look through the keyholes. You had to speak to him about it."
> "Yes," the manager said weakly.

It is because of this identification that Dykshoorn does not do healing. "I take on the pains and symptoms of the people I'm trying to heal."

As we have seen (Chapter 3), the late Evelyn Penrose also took on the physical ills of those she diagnosed. The discovery of rushing underground water threw her off her feet, gas and oil deposits severely jolted her, gold brought a violent stab of pain through her feet, even when she was riding in a car.

Psi Catalogue. Though many sensitives specialize, few of those I've met or read about have only one Psi capability. Most are endowed with a wide range of talents to select from or develop as they choose. Healers are very often telepathic, for example; clairvoyants may be pre- or retrocognitive, or psychokinetic as well.

A peculiar feature of these incredible abilities: Even the most accomplished Psi artists I know of usually have a "black hole" or blind spot plunk in the middle of their talents. Having received several SOS letters about lost or stolen property just before my last visit with Ingo Swann, I asked him to help me. "I'm sorry but I can't," he answered. "I get many requests to find lost or stolen things, but I'm really very poor at it. I think," he added, "this is very undeveloped among psychics generally." This, from the man who can identify a dot of land in Lake Victoria, and "go" to Jupiter, 500 million miles away!

Individuality. Were I, as of now, to name the "common trait" of psychics I know about, I'd have to say they are *individualists.* The more they get into the public eye, the more they become Personalities, Egos, self-consciously aware of themselves and their views. They are either super-confident of their talents, or working actively to become so. The sales pitches and claims of psychics-for-hire give ample evidence of this.

Among psychics on the make, I found more than a little rivalry, all the facts, foibles, and gossip one could take concerning the competition. I'll name no names here, but as the months went by, I heard names called, sex habits spelled out, and saw the finger pointed at tricks and ethical lapses within the Psi fraternity.

The chief thing you can count on among psychics is their differences. And, while Swann paints pictures, Hoy frames mementoes, and Cayce made pickles, the main differences by far are different attitudes about Psi!

For example, I've been collecting "bad words," such as "gift," "powers," "clairvoyance." The words themselves aren't bad, but for certain individual psychics they are taboo.

Some speak of their abilities as a "gift"—"The Gift," "My

Gift"—as something especially bestowed on them. "My gift," one respected psychic notes, "has dominated my life."

" 'Gift,' *nothing!*" rejoins another. *"What* 'gift?' It's something *everyone* has—so what's special? And don't say 'psychic *powers*'— that's a no-no! Psi *isn't* a power. That puts you in a special and bad relationship to everyone else."

Dixon says her precognitive ability is a "gift entrusted her by God."

"What's God got to do with it?" says another. "It's just how things work!"

One clairvoyant explained to me, "I *never* use the word 'clairvoyant.' It smacks of gauzy curtains and ectoplasm. I'm not into the occult!"

"Psychic ability is just what some people *have,*" Dorothy Allison explains. "You're just born with it. A psychic doesn't guess; she's got to *know*. I don't *study* about the psychic. Don't believe in reading books about it. I don't believe that any book can teach me to do that." The book about her—by Scott Jacobson—came out after I interviewed her.

Says Jaegers: "You *can* teach Psi. I have dozens of students to prove it. I taught *myself*—how about that? Miracles happen as a matter of course, in my classes, all the time!"

Can you learn Psi? The wives of Abrahamsen, Sherman, and Hoy all say they did—just from working with their husbands. Psychic writers think you can. *How to Make ESP Work for You* is one of many titles by Harold Sherman, who assures his broad readership that they have ESP, and healing power too. Tanous' biography ends with a section on how to tap your own psychic powers. Over the years, he explains, "I have developed several concepts to lead others toward psychic experiences. They are disarmingly simple, but they have succeeded on literally hundreds of occasions with hundreds of different people." Parapsychologists I have consulted, incidentally, say yes, you can learn Psi, but probably not enough to apply in significant ways.

One of the major differences of opinion among psychics is in their occupational goals—from just entertaining or making a living, to trying to inform or contribute major types of assistance.

There is no more controversial item than the matter of fees. "If others want to take fees, let them do it," declares Allison, "I take no money whatsoever. That's the way I was raised." Dixon and Worrall (who accepts donations to her church) refuse payment for consultations; Croiset accepts a pittance for healing; Tanous, and a great many others, take only enough to support a simple life. "This ability was given to me; I did nothing to earn it," says one sensitive. "Why should I charge?"

When I asked Hurkos his policy, he said, "May I ask you a question: Do you work for nothing? Does the police department work for nothing? When I work on a case and spend fourteen days, I charge some money!"

As for performance, most psychics have long since settled for less than perfect scores. Those who aim at perfection, as we have seen, are in trouble from the start. Most shrug philosophically, "You can't win 'em all." Hoy's clients sign a disclaimer, to register formal understanding of that fact. Some sensitives announce their own batting averages as a matter of policy. The usual estimate, though a few may put it higher, is 80 to 85 percent.

One fascinating detail about scoring: when psychics miss, it often seems to be only at one remove: the information is about the wrong person, say the woman in the adjoining seat. I've seen Warmoth give a reading in a group "for the lady in the red dress." She declares it is wrong. "Are you *sure?* I 'get' a knee problem so clearly, even a brace. I see something about finances and someone named 'M.' "

"Definitely not!"

"Hold on. I still see it—clearly. *Think!* Something about property and legal complications—I think there was a hearing. Many relatives were involved."

"Wait!" A woman jumps up from the seat just behind her. *"Everything* you've said applies exactly to me! I have a knee brace— had polio. My sister Myrtle bought land, but the deal was contested. There was a hassle. She was sued and her nephew won't speak to her now."

This phenomenon is so common it appears everywhere in the literature.

No Bed of Roses. If the life of a psychic seems easy, here are a few things to note. They are under attack for "making money at others' expense" or on the defensive for fraud. They are often treated by researchers as children, or as objects, part of the lab machinery. They are legislated against: in some states and cities it is against the law to do such things as psychic healing, predicting, astrology, and locating oil. The motives of such laws are, admittedly, the best: to protect the public from chicanery, but the sweep of some of them makes an honest psychic cringe. From a municipal police code in San Francisco County comes the following:

> It shall be unlawful for any person, or persons, to advertise by sign, circular, handbill, or in any newspaper, periodical or magazine, or other publication, or by any other means, to tell fortunes, to practice phrenology, to find or restore lost or stolen property, to locate oil wells, gold or silver or other ore or metal or natural products, to restore lost love or affection, to unite or procure lovers, husbands, wives, lost relatives or friends, for or without pay, by means of occult or psychic powers, faculties or forces, clairvoyance, psychology, psychometry, spirits mediumship, seership, prophecy, astrology, necromancy or other crafty science, cards, talismans, charms, potions, magnetism, or magnetized articles or substances, oriental mysteries or magic of any kind or nature, or to engage in or carry on any business, the advertisement of which is prohibited by this section.

The code section goes on immediately to state that it doesn't apply to

> any ordained or duly accredited minister of any form of religious belief, or to the faith, practice or teaching of any religious body, provided that fees, gratuities, emoluments or profits therefore shall be paid solely to or for the benefit of said religious body.

I had often wondered why so many psychics, and healers, had unfamiliar church connections or "Reverend" before their names.

A Case Apart

Overlooking the sea are some buildings—a large and impressive square structure, a cluster of others on a higher level, including an older, historic one impressive in a different way, and an extensive parking lot.

College or university? Clinic or publishing house? Arts center or library? It is all of these and more: the active, living monument to a psychic who was, and is, in a class by himself, a case apart.

The sign at the entrance reads: "The Association for Research and Enlightenment. Visitors Welcome." It is here that the records are kept, in a Master Archive, and in duplicate in a library, of the 14,256 psychic readings of Edgar Cayce, the man people called "The Sleeping Prophet." Cayce was guided to make his base here, at Virginia Beach.

It is here people come, around the year, from around the world, to read, inspect, and study the records of the most remarkable, and certainly the most influential, sensitive of them all. Here are lectures and workshops, whose participants pour into the conference center every week of the seminar season. Here is one of the largest parapsychological libraries in the world, a Braille library, an ESP testing center, creativity lab, a therapy department, and a large Psi-related bookstore. Aside from this campus, it has a youth camp in Rural Retreat, Virginia, and a medical center, the A. R. E. Clinic, in Phoenix, Arizona. There are a journal, a newsletter, cassette tapes, and circulating files, all of which are available through Association membership.

The center is an elaboration and continuation of Cayce's own interests and analyses:

• *Health and physical welfare,* taking off from 8,985 physical readings, with diagnoses and recommended treatment—hence the clinic, referral doctors, and youth camp.

• *Continuity of human life after death,* a spinoff of 2,500 "life readings" about survival and past existences on earth.

• *Dreams* and their meaning: 667 of Cayce's readings dealt with dream interpretation.

• *Religion and philosophy:* spiritual practices, such as meditation, which stem from his accumulated messages and recommendations.

The Association encourages research and publishes its findings. But it's unlike your usual laboratory project, in that there is a body of "scripture"—the readings.

Ask researchers or even other psychics where they stand on Cayce and you'll get strong, unequivocally conflicting answers. "He was nothing but a fraud." "Much ado about nothing." Or, *"The* pioneer," "The greatest in history."

Born in 1877 to uneducated parents in Kentucky, the Bible-loving farm boy grew up to become a salesman. A seemingly incurable loss of voice, which threatened to end his career, drove him in desperation to seek help from a hypnotist. The event was the turning point in his life. While under a hypnotic spell, he cleared his throat and began to speak in an unaffected voice: "Yes, we can see the body."

"In the normal state," Edgar went on, "this body is unable to speak, due to a partial paralysis of the inferior muscles of the vocal cords, produced by a nerve strain. This is a psychological condition producing a physical effect. This may be removed by increasing the circulation to the affected parts, by suggestion while in the unconscious condition."

"The circulation to the affected parts will now increase," the hypnotist said, "and the condition will be removed."

One of the family leaned over and loosened his shirt. Gradually, the upper part of the chest, then the throat, turned pink. The pink deepened to rose. The rose became a violent red. Ten, fifteen, twenty minutes passed. Edgar cleared his throat again.

"It is all right now," he said. "The condition is removed. Make the suggestion that the circulation return to normal, and that after that, the body awaken."

"The circulation will return to normal," the hypnotist said. "The body will then awaken."

His family watched, while the red faded back through rose to pink, and the skin resumed its normal color. Edgar wakened, sat up and reached for his handkerchief. He coughed and spat blood.

"Hello," he said, tentatively. Then he grinned. "Hey!" he exclaimed, "I can talk! I'm all right." His mother wept. His father seized his hand and shook it again and again. "Good boy! Good boy!" he said.

This was the start of his incredible life work. This was also the pattern of his "physical readings" from then on. He would enter an alternate state of consciousness, and from this give diagnoses of anyone's physical problem, along with suggestions for treatment. He needed only a name and the current location of a client, anywhere in the world, known or unknown to him, to give a searching and technical diagnosis. Though he had almost no formal education, and was far from scholarly by temperament, his remote, unorthodox remedies, and the effectiveness of his results, brought him a unique kind of fame. He was an unheard-of and unequaled medical phenomenon. Years later, he was sought out for information on any number of other topics, from spiritual disciplines to forecasts of world events.

I've rarely had a more pleasant and profitable experience anywhere than my visit to Cayce's headquarters by the sea, for conversations with Cayce administrators, son and grandson. Special screenings of A. R. E. documentaries, and a leisurely browsing in the spacious bookstore and library, gave me a sense of what the dozens of seekers who make their way to this mecca must feel.

According to Charles Thomas Cayce, Edgar's grandson,

> We attract a very interesting subject population. Lots who come, do so because of an experience they don't understand. Another large group come because they wonder if Edgar Cayce was for real. If they can decide he was, they can decide in respect to the whole thing. Also, some parents want to know about the experiences of their children: what are they to do? Sometimes, the experiences can be replicated, and thus researched. . . .
>
> Our major focus here is, and should be, to test the general applicability of some of the information that Edgar Cayce gave. Most of the readings that he gave were for specific people. His focus was almost entirely individual answers.

I asked him, "How do you see the conflict and debate about this institution?"

> One of the major points of confusion about A. R. E., and I think, about parapsychology in general, has to do with the mixing of nonscientific concepts into the research data of parapsychology. The Cayce readings clearly illustrate this. On the one hand, his major interest was in trying to help people understand who they are, and to help them with a physical problem. So when you move past the points about parapsychology and its corroboration, you see that just about every reading is talking about the nature of man. So ESP gets mixed up with religious overtones, karmic memories, and other such concepts.
>
> Researchers say to us, "Why don't you get on with lab-type research, concerning ESP, and so on?" I think that probably there is more of a focus here on the "enlightenment" or "education" facets than on research, much to the consternation of lots of people in the field of parapsychology.
>
> Don't think of us as having a creed, though. Take reincarnation. Though Cayce believed in it, there are lots of A. R. E. members who don't. I think that as far as you could go in terms of a common

denominator among our membership, would be a serious interest in the possibility of there being more to us than the physical being.

In my conversation with him, Edgar Cayce's son Hugh Lynn Cayce explained,

Rigid parapsychologists don't understand what we're doing. We have a mass of data that has accumulated over forty-three years. We are cataloguing all the material, and are inviting people to test it; to find a concept, to find a theory. We are getting doctors in, to check specific remedies. Also working on dreams: for example, the guidance a dream can provide for our health, one of Dad's emphases. These can be tested.

All of the correspondence, all of the reports are wide open. Anybody can come in and check it for themselves. We are being as honest as we can. *I have written a whole book on Dad's mistakes!* It's called *The Outer Limits of Edgar Cayce's Power.* The funny thing is, though, it has sold less than any of our forty books! I did it because I think we can learn from our mistakes, but nobody who comes here wants to know or think about that!

The Psychic Vision

Shafica Karagulla, the brilliant and distinguished neuropsychiatrist mentioned in Chapter 8, was given a book about Edgar Cayce in 1956. It changed her life.

Says Karagulla, "The book was a challenge to my whole medical and scientific outlook. I knew a great deal about the brain and nervous system. I was familiar with the symptoms of brain injuries and epileptic seizure. Hallucinations and illusions of the insane could not explain the phenomenon of Edgar Cayce. Edgar Cayce shattered my theories about the nature of man's mind. . . . The book made a hole in the dike of my scientific mind."

Are we, she asked, like Plato's prisoners in an underground cave, who see only shadows on a wall, reflections and echoes of reality, which we take for reality, but never reality itself? Was Cayce one who had broken out of the limitations of the cave, to the larger world of reality?

So great was her excitement with such questions, that she put aside her plans, direction, and entire career, to probe the nature and meaning of "Higher Sense Perception." She studied Cayce's

records at Virginia Beach, and started to look for others who manifested some sort of "HSP"—her version of ESP. After eight years
of research, she released her findings in *Breakthrough to Creativity*.
Here is the record of others who are edging out of Plato's cave;
the discovery that HSP abilities are far more widespread than anyone
had supposed. She found "thousands of people already using these
abilities and gifts in all areas of life."

She found "Paul" for example, a young man who had trouble
in obtaining stimulating work because of his limited high school
education. Advised to take training in technical writing, he did
so, and landed a writing job in a very technical industry. After a
short course in elementary electronics to learn the vocabulary, he
was soon working smoothly with scientists and top-level engineers
in writing complex articles. Everyone took it for granted he had
a good scientific background.

Pinch-hitting for two superiors at an important conference concerning a government contract, Paul could suddenly "see" the instal-
lation in his mind. In his presentation, every detail was accurate,
the scientific words "flowed" as he described it. The vice president
complimented him afterwards for helping out in an emergency,
and asked where he had had his fine training. When Paul said
that he had none, the executive cried out, "Incredible! For God's
sake, don't tell anybody—but how did you do it?" Paul didn't know
how he "did it." He only knew that he could soar out, survey
large areas, and spot building arrangements at great distances. He
began to explore and experiment, and found he could do other
mental gymnastics as well. Promoted to a higher-level job, he was
given a six-to-eight month assignment in systems planning. When
he turned in the complete assignment in one week, his supervisor
was aghast. It was exactly what they wanted, complete and perfect!

But—no one could have done it in that length of time. "Shut
your office door. Do what you like for the next five months. Just
don't present the program until we ask for it!"

Are we beginning to crack the mystery of creativity and genius,
as we investigate higher sensory perception? Karagulla asks.

What about Nikola Tesla—an Austro-Hungarian of incredible
creativity; his panoply of patents leaves Thomas A. Edison's discoveries in the shade. Did he use "Higher Sense Perception"? Tesla
attributes his discovery of alternating current, and all of his subsequent discoveries to one high moment on a late February afternoon

in a city park in Budapest. He was strolling with a friend, when he abruptly fell into a state of supreme concentration, which the friend couldn't break, even by shaking him physically. For a brief instant, Tesla glimpsed the totality of the electromagnetic functioning of the solar system. At that moment, not only were revealed the secrets of alternating current, but all of the underpinnings of his life's later contributions.

Do the Pauls and the Teslas, and all of those who experience Higher Sense Perception, point to a window of higher, deeper knowing, which is not remote or of another world, but somewhere in ourselves? Perhaps we, in our own beings, with our almost limitless potential, are keyholes to the universe.

13

THE ULTIMATE QUESTION:
Life After Death

In August of 1951, in the town of Chatta, India, a boy named Prakash was born. He cried a great deal, and at the age of four would awaken in the night and run out of the house, looking for his "real" family, "real" home, and "real" town. His own name, he insisted, was Nirmal, and he lived in Kosi Kalan.

His family at last gave in to his pleas, and took him to Kosi Kalan. He led them straight from the bus station to "his" home, where he recognized and identified friends, relatives, and neighbors, and where a "Nirmal" had lived and died.

"I was in the hospital with heart trouble," a woman recalls, "when I felt a severe pain in my chest. I pushed the button beside the bed, and as I did so, I quit breathing and my heart stopped beating. I heard the nurses shout 'Code pink! code pink!' and could feel myself moving out of my body. I started rising upward slowly. On my way up I saw nurses come running into the room—there must have been a dozen of them. I saw the doctor come, too. I drifted on up, past the light fixture—I saw it from the side, very distinctly—and then I stopped, floating right below the ceiling, looking down. I felt as though I were a piece of paper that someone had blown up to the ceiling.

"I watched them reviving me from up there! My body was lying

241

stretched out on the bed in plain view, and they were all standing
around it. I heard one nurse say, 'Oh my God, she's gone!' while
another one leaned down to give me mouth-to-mouth resuscitation.
I was looking at the *back* of her head while she did this. I'll never
forget the way her hair looked; it was cut kind of short. Just then,
I saw them roll this machine in, and they put the shocks on my
chest. When they did, I saw my whole body jump right up off
the bed, and I heard every bone in my body crack and pop. It
was the most awful thing!

"As I watched them below beating my chest and rubbing my
arms and legs, I thought, 'Why are they going to so much trouble?
I'm just fine now.' "

What do these two incidents have in common—a child in an
Indian village, and a woman in an American hospital?

Both are part of the data now being studied in an area formerly
taboo in scientific circles: the subject of life after death.

Research life after death? How can one possibly "research" what
goes on after death? Speculate on, yes, but *research* . . . ? A tricky
question, to say the least.

If human survival is one of the subjects mainstream parapsychology dropped as unprofitable and improbable, what is it doing in
contemporary parapsychology, or in a book about the present state
of the art?

Though we have postponed the after-death question—some call
it "life after life"—it is, as it has always been, the first and foremost
question for every human being: *Is* there life after death? Whether
it can be answered or not, the problem of human mortality is always
there.

Cracking the Taboo

We have come to a historic turning-point in our dealings with
life after death. The attitudes and approaches of our society at
large are veering from total rejection and skepticism of things unseen
and unknown, to openness. More than a third of the American
people say they have had a mystical experience of some kind, in
which they felt "very close to a powerful force that seemed to lift
them out of themselves." A much larger 60 percent of this national
sample report having had an ESP-type of experience, in which

they were sure they had been in touch with someone far away.

Up to now, it's been a clear-cut dichotomy: the religious, non-empirical world, and the secular, scientific sphere, with no communication whatever between them. The amazing thing has been that for neither of them has it been appropriate to pursue openly the question of life after death. For the former, immortality is a given, taken "on faith" and, therefore, not to be questioned. The latter find it suspect by definition, since the whole business is inherently unprovable.

All this is changing in several ways. People from both sides are coming out of the closet. They are talking with one another. There are signs that life after death is even becoming a topic for bona fide research. At an after-death conference I attended, there was a push for "hard findings" and "solid data." A large segment of that overflow crowd was made up of pragmatists and practitioners: doctors, psychiatrists, nurses, counselors, hospital administrators and the like. Part of the powerful consensus that emerged was that research is now called for in a field formerly dominated by mystics, sensitives, and seers, and that top priority should be accorded life-after-death studies.

How has this happened? Why such a turnabout? There are a number of reasons. One is the changing climate in the society at large: there is a growing awareness that there may be spheres we know not of; that there are many paths to knowing, other than the senses, the intellect, and the cognitive. Theodore Roszak declares that "the mind has reached the end of its tether," and is moving out into other realms.

Among these other realms is the enormous panorama of Eastern religions, which pour like a torrent into the gaps and holes left by the inadequacies of our rational Western approach. Exposure to these unfamiliar orientations not only contributes a general openness to new types of awareness and levels of knowledge, but to specific concepts as well, such as "planes of consciousness," karma, and reincarnation, all of which turn "reality" as we know it upside down.

Another reason for the turnabout is the breakdown of the taboo that has surrounded death and dying.

Much of the credit for smashing the taboo goes to the pioneering efforts of that small, intense, and dedicated psychiatrist, Elisabeth Kübler-Ross, who plunged into the hush-hush area by talking frankly with terminal patients, and emerged with a whole new perspective. Our traditional avoidance of the subject is the worst thing one can do, she points out in her now-classic *On Death and Dying.* Dying patients do not welcome the stereotyped avoidance games. On the contrary, at certain stages, they need to face and talk frankly about the most important thing in their lives, their own death.

Yet another reason for the reversal of public attitudes is new information about psychic occurrences of all kinds. Clairvoyance, telepathy, out-of-body experiences, we are learning, are far more common among "normal, sensible people" than most of us realize.

"At the birth of our youngest child," a Bechtel Corporation engineer told me, "my wife died on the operating table, and floated up to the ceiling, where she hovered above the doctors and nurses as they worked to save the baby. After they had given her up for lost, she 'came' to me where I was sitting in the waiting room. In her own voice, and very clearly, she said, 'I am going to have to leave you, but please take care of our baby.' It was awesome.

"She returned to her body, however, and is now healthy and beautiful, but this has happened, and we both know it."

In the past, most people concealed such experiences, or confided them only to the closest of friends. Now, such stories are everywhere.

Part of this "new information" is being developed by scholars. Out of the mainstream for the most part, after-death research and reporting by now add up to a respectable scientific beginning. There is even a serious journal, *Theta,* now over ten years old, devoted exclusively to serious research on "human survival."

Thus, "death and dying," now a cliché, is finally "in." Courses, seminars, books and articles abound. Death-and-dying offerings have been added to curricula in seminaries and elsewhere. One can even get a Ph.D. in "thanatology"! The fastest-growing component of health care services today, "Hospices" enable terminal patients to manage their own death in the context of family and friends. Surely the ultimate in this trend must be the frank and extended TV interview I saw recently: a mother wrestling publicly with this issue, with her small children and husband gathered around her deathbed.

Finding a Handle

The knottiest problem for scientists, however, has nothing to do with social taboos, or even the still-considerable problem of colleague acceptance. It is, rather, *how to go about researching life after death*. How does one design and carry out experiments, or follow scientific protocol, in an area where even the data are problematic?

This is not the first time scientists have had to work with unseen or unknown factors, nor the first time they have had to substitute oblique findings and inference for direct observation. The sub-atomic particles known as quarks are, so far, the invention of physicists. They have never been observed or measured, but they are the best working explanation of certain atomic phenomena to date. The pull of gravity, and mysterious inner programming of the genes, are both "facts" of the universe that we "know" indirectly from their effect, not from first-hand observation. Within our present scientific framework, such well-founded inferences offer the best way to account for certain occurrences. In the same way, the assignment for life-after-death investigators is to find levers and handles, indirect if need be, for its exploration.

Out-of-Body Projection

One of the major handles for getting at the after-death state is the out-of-body experience (sometimes referred to in the literature as "OOB" or "OOBE"). This is a phenomenon in which consciousness separates from the physical envelope, enabling people to view their bodies from the outside, to travel elsewhere—even distantly—and to witness events they could not otherwise see. We have noted several such instances already; the mother who "died" and appeared to her husband when her baby was born; Ingo Swann's bewildering early childhood "trip" to the distressed king of England; Swann's and Sherman's planetary probes to Mercury, Jupiter, and Mars.

The rationale for using the out-of-body experience as a life-after-death handle is this: If the human consciousness can be shown to leave the physical body during this experience, is it not possible that the body is not essential to consciousness? If it is found that consciousness can and does exist independently, and apart from the human body, it would follow that the end of the body—that is, physical death—would not spell the end of consciousness.

The key point here, of course, is whether the out-of-body entity—

whatever that may be—is dependent for its existence on the living physical body.

Though it has recently been incorporated into the sphere of scientific exploration, out-of-body projection itself is nothing new. In 1929 Sylvan Muldoon and Hereward Carrington published the first of three books on this topic, *The Projection of the Astral Body.* As Carrington explained, "The Astral Body may be defined as the Double, or ethereal counterpart of the physical body, which it resembles and with which it normally coincides." The book is a detailed account of Muldoon's innumerable out-of-body experiences, with an analysis of their character, variety, conditions, and significance. From firsthand experience, he describes what astral projection is like, how it feels, and how such a state is attained. Carrington adds a review of OOB literature, ranging from the ancient Egyptian and Tibetan *Books of the Dead* to current accounts.

Muldoon bases his positive knowledge of immortality on subjective experience: "Once you *experience* the projection, you will never doubt." For him the projection of the astral body is apparently, *per se,* proof of life after death. What he does not establish, however, is that the projection is independent of the physical body. In fact, he establishes just the opposite. He tells us that nearly every student of spiritual phenomena knows of the "astral cord," an elastic-like structure, connecting the astral body to the physical. "The nearest one can come, when trying to form a conception of the astral cord, is to compare it with an elastic cable; yet such a comparison does anything but justice to this truly living organ."

Though Muldoon's descriptions and illustrations of the cord would seem to argue against the ability of the astral body to exist on its own, there's a twist. It works the other way around, says he: It is the physical body that is dependent on the astral!

> The phantom body is the condenser of cosmic energy—the very energy you employ in moving about. This energy is the "breath of life"— omnipresent in every living thing. . . . Without this "breath of life," man would really be nothing but the dust of the ground. . . . When the astral body is in coincidence, you are physically alive. When the astral body moves out of coincidence, you are physically dead—*unless* the astral cable, running from the energetic body to the physical body, is intact. That is the purpose of the astral "line of force"; to deliver the "breath of life" to the physical body, while the finer body is projected.

A contemporary version of the Muldoon analysis is the first-hand investigation of a Virginia businessman, Robert Monroe. Startled and traumatized by the unexpected and inexplicable experience of an OOB "trip," then another and another, he was forced to seek help, though he didn't know where to turn. The president of two corporations in communications and electronics, he was intellectually curious as well as personally disturbed.

Monroe first sought medical help, then discovered a psychic "underground" who did know something about the phenomenon. In 1964, at a meeting of about twenty scientists, he asked, "If you were I, what would you do?" A minority advised him to run, not walk, to the nearest psychiatrist. The majority, however, urged him to experiment. He took the latter advice.

Monroe's book, *Journeys Out of the Body,* which appeared in 1971, is provocative. It aims, he explains, to help others avoid the trauma he suffered, and to help expand the frontiers of scientific knowledge. It is his conscientious record of more than a thousand OOB trips, in which he tabulates the characteristics and conditions of every experiment, along with a detailed analysis and commentary. He tells of occasional difficulties in extricating himself from his body; of troubling incidents in which he "dived back in"; of different states and locales as well as familiar scenes and friends whom he visited. He even tells of pinching someone while out of his body!

Based on his long and attentive personal experience, Monroe is convinced that there is a "second body" that can act independently of the physical one. Its movement, however, can be partly controlled by the body. He believes that some individuals, possibly most, separate from their physical bodies during sleep, and that there is survival of the personality after death.

Monroe posits three different "locales":

1. The here-and-now sphere, the only place where OOB verification can occur,
2. The non-material or thought sphere, the natural environment of the "second body," and
3. A physical-matter world, almost identical to ours, which may be a context of racial memory or history.

Human survival, he notes, takes place in Locale 2.

Parapsychologist Charles Tart greeted Monroe's book enthusiastically. "There is almost no scientific information on the OOBE," he declared. "Science has ignored it altogether. As with Psi, in our present world view, this simply cannot happen. There are thousands of OOBEs which are treated simply as 'coincidences,' yet, as records from many peoples, places and times attest, it is a universal experience."

Monroe has erected a fully equipped laboratory on his estate, near Afton, Virginia, where he now works with others in new explorations of time and space. By the time I had heard him explain this later work, in 1978, he had mounted over eight thousand individual OOB experiments with two thousand volunteers. "We have a tiger by the tail," he asserts.

> We are beginning to get a handle on what kind of force is involved. It is a different kind of energy, not the kind scientists test. It is not electrical and not magnetic. I perceive this energy as separate and apart from others. How can we control it? How can we use it? are the questions we must ask.
>
> It affects people differently. Many at my laboratory have had peak and mystical experiences, and returned with a different overview. One man was instantly multiplying eight-digit numbers. Some have had a sense of euphoria. One man got an idea on solar energy from his experience. Another drafted a book on his way home. The gateway opens! It is the beginnings of a new consciousness.

Tart has himself conducted investigations in the laboratory. In controlled experiments, he has studied persons who seemed to be able to leave their bodies in the course of normal events. Some years ago, for example, he discovered a young woman who had had such adventures all through her childhood, several times a week. So familiar was she with the experience that she assumed it was usual for everyone. Almost always at such times, she explained, she would float near the ceiling and look down on her body.

Since she seemed to be a natural for such study, Tart planned experiments for this "Miss Z": to study her brain-wave pattern at the time she "left her body," and to see if she could read a number on a high shelf next to the ceiling, not visible from below.

Tiny electrodes were glued to her scalp, and her body, to record her brain waves, eye movements, blood pressure, and the electrical resistance of her skin. The appliances also served to keep Miss Z from moving physically out of the bed.

On the fourth night of the experiment, Miss Z reported floating to the ceiling, where she correctly read the number on the physically inaccessible shelf. It was a five-digit random number, chosen by Dr. Tart from a book of random numbers: 25132. In interpreting the experiment Dr. Tart said afterward, "Since the odds against correctly guessing a five-digit number when trying only once are a hundred thousand to one, this is a highly significant result."

Since the experiment did not eliminate the possibility of clairvoyance, or even of telepathy (Tart knew the number), the results cannot be regarded as definitive for OOB. Tart did, however, find unusual physiological conditions, patterns in no way similar to those of persons near death. At the time of her OOB experiences, Miss Z displayed a distinctive brain-wave pattern, "an alphoid pattern not seen in ordinary people: a general lower-voltage configuration, showing alpha waves slower than her ordinary alpha rhythm, and no REM ["rapid eye movements" associated with dreaming] at all."

Tart also studied Monroe, with quite different physiological results. "The differences should alert us that we may be dealing with more complex phenomena than we believe," he observed. "There may be several kinds of OOBEs."

For fourteen months, beginning in 1972, the American Society for Psychical Research conducted OOB experiments with Ingo Swann.

In the attempt to eliminate all possibility of telepathy and clairvoyance, the staff finally designed an optically elusive target which would only "look right" if the viewer were positioned directly in front of it: two flickering images were projected onto a screen. From the single correct position the eye composed these into a horse moving to the left; from any other place, there was, in effect, no image. Nor was there any image until the projection machine was activated. From another room, with his eyes closed, Swann "went" to the projection-box and reported seeing a horse moving to the left.

From here, research moved to the question: If a person can "go" out of his body to another place, is there any way to *record* his out-of-body presence? In another experiment at the ASPR laboratory in New York, Alex Tanous was asked to "fly in" from Portland, Maine, to the office of the Research Director, Karlis Osis,

and observe what objects had been placed on a table. Tanous had
had hits in such experiments numbers of times, but on this occasion,
unknown to him, the Society had brought in another psychic, Chris-
tine Whiting, to find if she could "see" someone in the room at
that moment.

As Osis wrote later of that trial, "[Tanous] felt that when he
projected to the place of our stimulus display, he was bent over,
and floating over the display. The psychic who observed the area
that evening did see someone hovering over the target display, who
was bent like a jacknife."

Added Tanous,

Miss Whiting not only described my position and location in space,
she also saw me in a shirt with rolled-up sleeves and corduroy pants.
I was wearing a shirt with rolled-up sleeves at the time, and I was
wearing, not corduroy pants, but pants with many thin stripes that,
even a short distance away, looked like corduroy.

Many people have asked me how I do this, what it feels like.
Well, it doesn't seem difficult to do. I find myself a comfortable position
in a quiet room, empty my mind of extraneous thoughts, and say to
myself, "Mind, leave my body now. Go to New York. Enter Dr.
Osis' office."

Again and again I repeat these phrases, slowly, silently, thinking
about nothing else. At a certain point I find I am without a body. I
consist of a large spot of light, of consciousness, which gradually gets
smaller and more concentrated. . . . After a while, quite automatically
and beyond my control, I return. I would love to remain outside of
my body, for it is very pleasant indeed, but I have no say in the
matter. Before I can think about it I am back, almost as if I had
awakened.

In a long series of unprecedented trials, Osis is now attempting
to *record* physical manifestations at the point where the OOB occurs.
The results, as reported to his colleagues at the 1979 Parapsychology
Association meetings, are, in scientific terms, "promising"; in lay
terms, very exciting indeed!

It was the first attempt to register on instruments the effects
of an out-of-body trip to a designated site. Out of 147 trials, there
were 114 hits. As Osis announced, the experimental hypothesis was
confirmed: "Ostensibly *unintentional* kinetic effects can occur as
by-products of narrowly localized out-of-body vision."

The project was a great deal more than that for me, since I was invited to be present during one of the experiments. Here's how I remember it.

The psychic Alex Tanous was stretched out on a pad in a shielded, soundproof steel booth, where he was connected to instruments, and was in touch with the researchers by intercom. On the other side of the building, with offices, a hallway, and another room in between, Osis presided over the polygraph room, also with an intercom, where instruments recorded Tanous' physiological changes. Adjoining the polygraph room was a room in which no one was present.

In this "experimental room," as it was called, were two boxes. One was a "shielded chamber," an 18-inch cube, suspended from the ceiling by elastic rubber strips, to reduce environmental and street noise vibration. Inside the chamber were suspended two metal sensor plates, 8 inches apart. Extremely sensitive strain gauges were attached to the plates, which would record the slightest sensor movements or vibrations.

The other box, near to it, was an "optical box" with a window about 3 inches in diameter and a target space inside. There is no target, however, until it is created optically, by revolving a flat wheel, divided into four quadrants, each of which is a different color; and by projecting pictures into a system of lenses and mirrors. The illusion is activated by a random number generator, which decides when it will start and stop.

When a person stands in front of the activated box and looks through the window, he sees what appears to be a picture superimposed on one of the colored quadrants; for example, an Egyptian standing on the top right-hand green quadrant. There is no such picture actually. As they say, "It's all done with mirrors." The box is designed to assure that the viewer must stand immediately in front of the window to catch the illusory picture, or, if it is an OOB trial, that he must "go" to that spot to "see" the correct image. The operation of both boxes is recorded in the polygraph room.

When he is in the OOB state, Tanous says, he experiences divided consciousness; Alex 1, his in-body, and Alex 2, his projected self.

As I watched the needles in the polygraph room, Osis asked Tanous, "Are you ready? Can Alex 2 now 'go' into the shielded chamber?"

"Yes. Here he goes!" says Alex 1. A moment of silence, then the polygraph needle jumps.

"Is he in the chamber now?" Osis asks.

"Yes, Alex 2 is there."

"Verrry good," Osis says calmly. "Now, can Alex 2 look into the optical box and tell what he sees?"

"He'll try," says Alex 1. Silence for a few moments as Alex 2 presumably looks through the optical window. "There's an Egyptian standing on the upper right-hand quadrant of the target. It's green."

"Verrry good," Osis purrs. Whether the reading is correct or not will not be known even to the experimenters, however, until after the session is over—thus eliminating the possibility of giving cues telepathically. (They hoped to eliminate clairvoyance by the optical device, in which there was no "picture" to be seen, only the illusion of a picture.)

When Alex 2 has completed his optical assignments, he is then asked to perform some out-of-body exercises in the shielded chamber. "Can you clap your hands?" "Can you turn somersaults?" The action moves the delicate sensors. The pen records circles.

Some parapsychologists believe that in the OOB state, the consciousness or a major part of the human personality is externalized in such a way that it exists apart from the body. Others suggest that nothing leaves the body, but that during an OOBE, the personality is in an altered state of consciousness and that perceptions received at this time are attributable to standard ESP.

Osis theorized that it is probably not a case of either/or, but of both: Some leaving-the-body may take place, at which time ESP and PK are activated. If this is so, while the individual is in the "extrasomatic" OOB state, there will be registrable kinetic effects *at the location* where the experient feels his consciousness to be— what some call "distant PK." Moreover, when the subject is "more out," the registrable effects will be greater. Osis further hypothesized that when the subject is making "hits" in perceptual tasks, the registered physical effect will be greater than when it is less externalized and scores a miss.

What was the scientists' delight to discover that the strain gauges *did* register when Alex 2 was "looking" at the optical targets, and that the gauges registered significantly higher when there were hits than when there were misses. Hypotheses confirmed.

As far as the researchers could tell, Alex regarded the optical portion of the trials as exclusively perceptual tasks. It was the opinion of the scientists that the results could most likely be attributed to his out-of-body presence in the shielded chamber.

There is yet another approach to out-of-body research, since such phenomena can be induced by external means: experiments using chemicals or electrical stimulation. The chief of research at the Veterans Hospital in Topeka, Kansas, Stuart Twemlow, used such procedures. In the belief that scientists should themselves experience the phenomena they are investigating, he subjected himself to laboratory experiments in which sound waves were applied to the brain. In one such experiment, he experienced some of the same sensations reported by the "dead" and the dying, such as moving through a long, dark tunnel.

On one occasion, he "traveled" from a laboratory in Kentucky to his own home in Kansas. On arriving, he moved first to his wife on the couch in the living room. He then floated to the mirror in the hall to check his reflection. There was none.

Though his wife is a skeptic in such matters, she did report later that she was aware of a shadow coming near her at that moment, and sensed that it then moved toward the mirror.

How many unreported and unanalyzed OOB instances there are within the population at large would be impossible to calculate. These would include all the cases induced by religious exercises, yoga disciplines, fasting, drugs, and so on, in addition to an uncountable number of unexpected and spontaneous OOB events.

The Round Trip

The out-of-body incidents discussed here so far refer to experiences of normal, healthy people, sometimes asleep, sometimes awake, but always alive. A different way of latching onto the question of human survival is to study the experiences of people who have been pronounced clinically dead, but who have, somehow, come back to tell the tale. This was the essence of Raymond Moody's research, which brought the after-death experience to popular attention.

A former professor of psychiatry at the University of Georgia Medical School, Moody's report of his findings was the best-selling *Life After Life,* in which he recorded and compared the experiences of those who have died, or almost died, and recovered. This he has followed up with further investigations and observations in *Reflections on Life After Life*. The first report covers in-depth interviews of fifty people who had had such a "round trip" experience. The essence of Moody's findings is the similarity of the many accounts. Again and again the same set of elements was reported: noises ("a whirring" or "buzzing sound"), "a passageway," meeting others ("my grandmother," "a friend who got killed," "spiritual helpers"), and the experience that Moody found had the most profound effect, an "encounter with a very bright light." There was, moreover, a characteristic set of stages through which many of his respondents passed: from hearing "he's dead," then moving into a calm and comfortable deep peace, through the tunnel (or "funnel" or "valley"), and finally back.

"The first few moments following death are a desperate desire to get back into the body," Moody observes, "and an intense regret over one's demise. However, once the dying person reaches a certain depth in his experience, he does not want to come back, and he may even resist the return."

Moody and many others report a final stage on coming back to the body: a changed life stance, a kind of euphoria, finding a new meaning in being alive, a joyous sense of purposes, or the determination to be of service to others.

Many physicians have run into the same phenomena. When Kübler-Ross first saw proofs of Moody's book, she wrote the publisher that, on the basis of her own observations, she could have written the same book herself. She has by now collected hundreds of similar reports.

The significance of these findings for the investigator is their generic quality. If everyone has the same kind of experience, rather than individual and idiosyncratic ones, it can be reasoned that the phenomenon is not internal and subjective, but objective.

Moody concludes that it may never be possible to prove life after death within the context of science alone, but those who dismiss the near-death experience as an unworthy topic for research are off the mark.

At the Moment of Death

Another handle for "researching" the after-death state is to study patients at the moment of death. Do they give any clues to what lies beyond? How do they act? What do they say? What do they "see?"

Karlis Osis and Erlendur Haraldsson, an Icelander who has studied psychic phenomena in India for several years, joined forces to explore these questions. Their report, *At the Hour of Death,* is the first research on the subject conducted on an international scale. They have examined hundreds of cases in India and America, which include Hindus and Christians, to ask: Do the dying of contrasting religions in very different societies experience different things, or is the transition experience the same in them all, thus suggesting a universal death and after-death phenomenon?

There were three studies, actually: a national survey in the United States; a more intensive study in five Eastern states—New York, New Jersey, Connecticut, Rhode Island, and Pennsylvania; and a survey in northern India. In all of the studies the researchers hypothesized that witnesses at the deathbed may be able to glimpse something of what lies beyond, by detailed observations of the dying— their final comments, actions, and emotions. Witnesses in all three surveys were doctors and nurses who had close and extended contacts with the dying. Data was collected by detailed questionnaires and follow-up interviews.

Many of the dying on both continents saw visions, overwhelmingly dominated (four to one) by apparitions of dead and religious figures. (By contrast, only a small percentage of hallucinations in the general population are of other-worldly apparitions.) When the dying see apparitions, they are nearly always experienced as messengers from a post-mortem state of existence. Of the human figures seen, most are of close deceased relatives. (Hallucinations of mental patients and drug-induced visions are seldom of close relatives.)

In both cultures, the apparitions were clearly understood to have come to take the patient away. Rather than expressing the desires or inner dynamics of the dying patients, the apparitions were widely reported to have a will of their own.

One of the unexpected findings in the studies was the reactions of patients to these apparitions. In nearly all of the American patients, and in two-thirds of the Indian ones, once the patients encountered the apparitions, they wanted to "go." In both cultures, some patients bitterly reproached those who attempted to revive them.

There were differences between American and Indian data, however. For example, Indian apparitions were more often of religious figures; American, of close relatives.

In both cultures, much that was reported by dying patients ran counter to current religious beliefs and expectations. No evidence of judgments, salvation, or redemption was mirrored by Christian patients. Visions of devils and Hell were almost nonexistent. The researchers were surprised that in India, the Vedic loci of an after-life (the Hindu Heaven) were never mentioned; nor were reincarna-tion, or dissolution in Brahma, the formless aspect of God, which is the goal of Hindu spiritual striving. Thus cultural conditioning was apparently contradicted by the visionary experiences of the dying.

In the pilot study for the larger research, *Deathbed Interviews by Physicians and Nurses,* Osis reported on the large number of patients who were *elated* at the dread moment of death. Surprisingly, he noted, *"fear is not the dominant emotion in dying patients,* in the opinion of both physicians and nurses in our sample." Some subjects in that large survey showed astonishment: "The eyes of the patients opened wide, staring at something very surprising, reaching out."

The Osis/Haraldsson study concludes: "In our judgment, the similarities between the core phenomena found in the deathbed vi-sions of both countries are clear enough to be considered as sup-portive of the post-mortem survival hypothesis."

Spirit Communication

We come now to the sticky topic of spirit communication: mes-sages, appearances, and other manifestations of life "on the other side." The topic is "sticky" because of its entanglement with phonies, fraud, and superstitious cults. Sticky also, because this is "where we came in"; where parapsychology, with its studies of mediums and spirit messages, began. The assumption on the part of many is that surely we have moved beyond all that by now. Reports of such communication are voluminous, however, throughout societies contemporary and primitive, across social classes, and over time. It is one of the largest residues of human experience that we have. It is also one of the more sparse and fragmentary areas of formal research. The problem, then, is to separate what serious inquiry there is from the mountainous accumulation of spontaneous and anecdotal reports.

So remarkable is the congruence at times between the "spirit message" and the facts, which a medium could not possibly know, that many serious-minded people have meticulously investigated the issue. The objection to the spirit-message hypothesis, which has long since become standard, is that the medium might be getting the informational "hits" from *this* side by telepathy. Critics of the critics, however, rejoin that telepathy could not possibly explain it: Some of the messages contain information that is not known by anyone present, or by anyone at all, for that matter—sometimes having to be researched in order to be confirmed; moreover, some spirit messages are linked to the future, predictions that some time later become true. The debate continues.

A suggestive development in the investigation of spirit voices is the attempt to record them on magnetic tape! Friederich Jürgenson, a Russian-born Swedish film producer, is the person usually credited with the first such attempt, though I've heard of earlier ones. He discovered that spirit voices can be "caught" on tape. When he was playing back the song he had taped of a Swedish finch on his recorder, he also heard what sounded like a human voice. Thinking that the effect was caused by faulty tape, he continued to investigate, and on subsequent tries, caught a message that he clearly identified as coming from his dead mother.

Among the scientists who were impressed with his published report was Latvian psychologist Konstantin Raudive, who joined him to conduct further research into the recording of paranormal voices. Raudive collected and studied over ten thousand such recordings, in several languages. When his book appeared—the English translation is entitled *Breakthrough: An Amazing Experience in Electronic Communication with the Dead*—the phenomenon became generally known as "Raudive voices." Some of the parapsychologists who have listened to the tapes find the voices clear and agree that they do, indeed, seem paranormal.

Investigating Jürgenson's findings, Hans Bender, under controlled conditions, also obtained "extra voices" on magnetic tape. Although no voices were heard by the people in the room when the tape was made, other voices can be heard when it is played back.

An even more improbable instance of auditory spirit communication is that posed by parapsychologists D. Scott Rogo and Raymond Bayless: telephone calls from the dead! Investigating scores of independent incidents and all possible explanations, the two researchers, though challenged by others, conclude that such enigmatic calls *do* occur, and are probably more common than most people would like to think. Some of the calls involved prolonged conversations. When the caller has died recently, they "tend to be abortive, confused, and exceedingly brief."

> A young woman answered the telephone to hear her husband's voice clearly saying only one word, "Goodbye." Then the phone went dead. A short time later she was informed that her husband had died of a heart attack shortly after reaching his office. When she compared the time of his death with the time of the telephone message . . . she found that she had received the call about thirty minutes after her husband had died.

Rogo and Bayless document other cases in which messages from the dead have been received via telegraph, gramophone, amplifying equipment, magnetic recordings, and even answering devices. After two years of study and experimentation, they suggest that the dead may be just as interested as we are in establishing a reliable method of inter-dimensional communication.

The literature is also full of reports of other sensory cues: peculiar or unexplained odors—a wave of gardenia or carnation scent at the moment a certain message comes through; temperature changes—a sudden chill in the room, an "icy pall"; touch—the feel of something on one's arm, back or shoulder, something "brushing by." Research on ghosts and hauntings confirms such manifestations, though it fails to explain them.

One provocative effect of so-called spirit influence is automatic writing. A voice may command "Write," or may take the hand and guide it. There is great variation in the type of reception: The writing may be in unknown tongues, or so minute that a magnifying glass is needed to read it; mirror writing, upside down, or in reverse order, words even being spelled backwards. Mrs. Henrietta Cholmeley-Jones in Westport, Connecticut, who takes down messages of deceased relatives, showed me her automatic writing—all rolling circles and easy curves, in which the words were connected. "You never lift the pen," she explained, "the whole thing just flows from the moment you begin."

There is a whole literature, as we have seen, derived by this means. Variations in the technique have been obtained by table-tipping, the ouija board, and the planchette.

The most baffling case of automatic writing in parapsychology annals began in St. Louis on Pearl Curran's Ouija board, in 1913, when it spelled out: "Many moons ago, I lived. Again I come. Patience Worth my name." Over the years, the words flowed from Ouija board to handwriting, and at last to the typewriter, from this seventeenth-century spinster of rural Dorsetshire: poems, stories, articles, proverbs, and finally novels. Though Mrs. Curran had not traveled, had read little, and was limited in education, Patience Worth's output won praise from the critics, "higher ratings than Amy Lowell, Edna St. Vincent Millay, and Edgar Lee Masters." Henry Holt published three of her books.

Psychic researcher W. F. Prince ran a test. He asked Worth to write a poem and, at the same time, conduct a dialogue between a wench and a lout at a fair. Without interruption, Patience shifted smoothly from one theme to the other, with differences in language and style. Scholars testified to the linguistic quality and accuracy of the work: The use of English words belonged to the date claimed, some of them tracked down as authentic after they appeared. "As evidence for survival," Cambridge psychologist Robert Thouless concluded, "the Patience Worth writings are unique in kind."

The most convincing evidence of spirit communication is visual; that is, "believing one's eyes." Visible spirits and ghosts fill many accounts. Some, human faces and forms, are clearly and unequivocally recognizable.

John Fuller's *The Ghost of Flight 401* reported on a tragedy in which apparitions figured prominently. In this jet-age mystery, many confirmed that they had seen, some of them repeatedly, actual appearances of Captain Bob Loft and Second Officer Don Ropo, flight crew of the Eastern Airlines plane that crashed in the Florida Everglades in December of 1972. Fuller's witnesses included other pilots, stewardesses, and ground crew who worked on Eastern's Whisper-Jets. Fuller later married the airline stewardess who helped him ferret out vital information from her shaken colleagues. She wrote her own version of the apparitions from her special inside view, *My Search for the Ghost of Flight 401*.

I've heard Dr. Elisabeth Kübler-Ross tell a personal apparition story that must surely top them all. She was just completing an exhausting speaking trip and all she could think of was "I've done enough of this now! I've got to phase out this work."

She had given a speech and all the follow-up responses that go with it and was wearily trudging out. As she stopped at the elevator, she was startled by the sudden appearance of a former patient whom she had helped to die. The woman greeted her warmly, but with deep concern: "You can't give up this work for the dying! It's *much* too important."

The woman accompanied her down the elevator and along the corridor. "This can't be happening!" the psychiatrist told herself. "I'm surely imagining it!"

When they reached her room, the former patient exclaimed, "Promise me you won't give up your work!"

Kübler-Ross did the only thing she could think of: grabbed a piece of paper and said, "Give me your autograph."

The woman did so, then turned and, as quickly as she had come, disappeared out the door. The doctor ran after her, looking down the long hall in both directions, but the figure had vanished. Kübler-Ross stood there dumbfounded, with her former patient's signature in her hand.

Rogo suggests that, even with the clear-as-day presence, we may not be seeing it with the physical eye.

Perhaps the apparition, appearing in some sort of fourth dimension, is not actually affecting our optic nerves, but is igniting our clairvoyance. . . . The evidence for this view comes from two factors concerning apparitions: they are seen in totally dark rooms at night, in full detail, and they are often seen as glowing. Now, if these phantoms were physical objects, we would not see them as glowing, or in such detail in a darkened room. So, I believe we might resolve this paradox by postulating that an apparition, when it appears, is actually somehow psychically causing us to see it.

As spirit voices are reported to have been captured on tape, so have visual likenesses. One type consists of pictures "taken at the bedside at the moment of death," in which a pouf of rising gray mist is shown "leaving the body." I have seen such photographs, but am not aware of any study that has been made either of the photos or the phenomenon.

The other more familiar type is of "spirit photos," images that appear unexpectedly on film when it is developed. Typically, there is a normal picture of a person, scene, or group, in which the paranormal image of an outside face or body, appears, sometimes surrounded by a cloud of vapor. There are at least thirty-five references to "spirit photography" in the *British Journal of Photography* around the 1870s. Often these photographic "extras," as they were called, are recognizable as a deceased friend or relative, looking over a shoulder in the photo, or hovering somewhere in the background. In such cases, the photographer or a legitimate subject in the picture has sometimes turned out to be psychic. In the early part of the century, a photographer, William Hope, collected more than twenty-five hundred such photos. Both he and his collection were very controversial, as were others' specimens of spirit photographs.

Professional photographers, journalists, and others have looked into the matter in the past. Not all "spirit photos" have been found to be fraudulent; neither has their authenticity been proved. Among the believers was Alfred Russel Wallace, the co-discoverer with Darwin of the theory of evolution, who declared that such photos furnish perhaps "the most unassailable demonstration it is possible to obtain of the objective reality of spiritual forms."

I've twice seen Olga Worrall show her collection of "ghosty pictures" to audiences. In them, photos of friends and family, including her husband, Ambrose, are supplemented by tipped and tilting glimpses of deceased acquaintances and friends. One of her pictures has a disproportionately tiny child in it, and another, as I recall, a surprised dog.

The most interesting spirit photos that I have seen were taken on site at "ghost hunts": the face of a child in a closet where a youngster had hanged himself, a skeleton showing through the floor of a cellar, identified as an Indian by an anthropologist who knew the history and layout of the region, and a black man in a white serving jacket, peering out a bay window of a Victorian house.

Reincarnation

Reincarnation is the "handle" for after-death research some readers have been waiting for, and others hoping to avoid. We cannot avoid it, however, since for many it is "the" answer to the riddle, and, though some find it unbelievable, it has become an area of scientific inquiry.

The concept of reincarnation came into the mainstream of contemporary Western consciousness largely through the back door of recent interest in Eastern religions. (It has been around, as a small sidestream interest, at least since the Theosophical Society was founded in America in 1886.)

Though reincarnation has become popular in many circles today, the Western version bears little relation to the Oriental views from which it derives. To the Western proponent, reincarnation is a welcome alternative to the finality of death: a succession of varied and fascinating lives. Though there are many variations, however, the classic understanding of reincarnation is an endless and distressing sequence from which there is no escape. Hindus call it "The Wheel."

As one scholar put it:

> Highly reflective minds. . . . contemplated the apparently endless series of rebirths that the doctrine of transmigration conjured up to their imagination, [and] felt acute distress. . . . They have tended to look upon The Wheel with dismay. Beholding it eternally revolving, their hearts have failed them at the prospect of a thousand million rebirths stretching out their length before them.

Edgar Cayce unintentionally gave the philosophy of reincarnation a boost, a rather astonishing development in view of his deep Christian orientation and views. Never aware in his waking state of what he had said in his readings, he was in fact shocked when told that he was discussing past lives of patients. "If reincarnation is true," he fretted, "why isn't it in the Bible?"

Gina Cerminara, a psychologist from the University of Wisconsin, spent two years studying the Cayce readings in Virginia Beach, twenty-five hundred of which concerned reincarnation and karma. She also interviewed many of the people who had received such readings. It is her tightly reasoned contention, spelled out in her book, *Many Mansions,* that the principles of reincarnation and "karma" (the idea that the way you conduct yourself in each life influences your lot in future lives) are the key to the uncanny feats performed by Cayce. Most psychologists, she observes, see genes and environment as the sole causal factors in human behavior, but

Cayce was able to tune in on "karmic causes" as well. From the retributive principle of cause and effect, and from previous incarnations, he could clairvoyantly ascertain the inexplicable ailments and miseries of people living today. For example, he described how a girl lamed by tuberculosis at the hip joint had, as an aristocrat in Nero's court, taken particular delight in the torment of a Christian girl whose side was ripped open by the claws of a lion.

Though Cayce resisted the reincarnative principle, which went against the grain of his Christian upbringing, two decades of readings invariably demonstrating that present physical or psychological suffering was a link in a chain begun centuries ago finally convinced him. As Dr. Cerminara concludes (in the words of the Buddha), "All that you are is the result of what you have thought"—and thoughts can go a long way back.

Aron Abrahamsen is another who uses reincarnation in his life readings, with the help of his wife, Doris. He has done about thirty-five hundred of them, based on information from the "Akashic records," a kind of cosmic filing system of past events and actions, which may be consulted in certain conditions of consciousness.

When I visited him in Everett, Washington, he described how it works. "Before Doris and I do any kind of a reading, we pray expressly for that person . . . then we attune ourselves . . . and then I go into a state of meditation, and when I am ready, when I know that I am at the Records, then I tell Doris I am ready, and she says, 'You will obtain the records for John Doe.' "

"So she is conversing with you while you are in this state?" I asked.

"Yes, and so, when I have the records of that person, of John Doe, I say 'Ready,' and we begin. At that point, I am at the Akashic Records, but I also know I am in my chair. I know, consciously that I am in two places at that point."

"If I speak to him too loudly," Doris added, "it jars him."

"Even at the level she is now speaking [and she was speaking quite softly], that would come as something of a shock."

"He is very sensitive to sound. If the telephone rings, that's a terrible experience for him, and so we disconnect the telephone during readings."

"She's an integral part of the reading process, then?"

"You better believe it!" Aron explained. "The moment she leaves or the phone rings and I know the room is empty, then everything stops."

"When we discovered that, he said, 'Don't leave me if you can possibly help it.' We discovered this many years ago when we first started. I operate the tape recorders and take notes, and I give Aron the energy he needs. He draws on me. I also ask the questions."

"Most people want to know the purpose of their lives," he notes. "This is given in the last part of the reading. They want to know what they can do to improve their lives. So many people don't have a purpose."

Each person, he says, has a "life seal." "I never start a reading until I see all or part of that life seal—a description of themselves in symbolic form: what they're going through, what their talents might be, what their purpose would be. Sometimes general, sometimes very specific. This I get at the Akashic Records—the life seal and the influences."

"Is this a specific place?" I asked him.

"Oh yes, a very specific place. The Akashic Records are at a temple, someplace in the universe. I can't give you directions or position. Somewhere in space. From the records, we then get into their past lives."

"Then you are a believer in reincarnation?" I asked Aron.

"Reincarnation is the only game in town!"

"We don't think that humans become animals or insects, though," Doris put in.

"Once a human, always a human," Aron added. "Reincarnation gives you an opportunity to correct what you have done wrong."

A quite different technique bringing many people into the reincarnation camp today is "hypnotic regression," in which a person under hypnosis is led to remember "past lives." One such case took the country by storm some years back, when the life of a housewife, "Ruth Simmons," was reconstructed under hypnosis, piece by piece, as that of "Bridey Murphy" in nineteenth-century Ireland. The controversial *Search for Bridey Murphy* was a bestseller almost twenty-five years ago.

In 1979, a case in which a psychiatric nurse in Los Angeles, Doris Williams, was hypnotized, brought similar headlines and excitement. Here are excerpts from the story she told me:

I've known Laurie Young for a long time, and I was visiting her. She lives right on the water, and we were talking about the water. And then all of a sudden as I'm telling Laurie about how I fear deep water, I began to shudder.

She said, "You really are scared, aren't you? Maybe when you were young, maybe one of your brothers or sisters held your head under the water. Why don't you let me regress you and we'll find out what happened."

She went through each year of my life, and didn't get a thing. Then she snapped her finger and said, "Now you are in the first life previous to this life"—and there I am! She said, "Where are you?" and I replied, "On the ship," just as if she ought to know. It's just like you open a door and look inside, and there it is.

So she said, "What ship?" and I said, "Why, the *Titanic,* of course."

She asked me, "What's happening?" So I discussed what's happening. I told her all about it: "I'm halfway in the ship. The ship is listing. The life raft I'm hoping to get onto is on my right." Wow, it was real!

When she asked me my name, I told her it was Stephen Worth Blackwell. I was a passenger on the ship.

Doris had never read a book or seen a film about the *Titanic;* she didn't believe she'd been on the ship, but, her curiosity piqued, decided to follow it up. A stranger in the library heard her requesting information and referred her to a book about the *Titanic, A Night to Remember.*

The librarian handed it to me. . . . I stood there looking at the index. It said, "Passenger list . . . 185," so I turned to page 185 and, nonchalantly, not believing a thing, all in control of myself, I went slowly down the passenger list. Sure enough! There out of two thousand, two hundred and seven passengers was one Stephen Worth Blackwell, the name I gave. Now this was too far out for me. I suddenly went into shock, right in the Burbank Library.

Some time later, I got an invitation to an affair at the Los Angeles Biltmore put on by Charles Sachs. He is a *Titanic* authority. The point of the party is just to remember the sinking of the ship. They have it every year. I was asked to be the guest speaker that night, and before dinner they have a huge replica of the *Titanic* run in on a gurney. Well, from the moment they brought the *Titanic* in, I got very ill. I was unable to eat and unable to give my talk! It is *real!*

I went to the party with Zelda Suplee, a Los Angeles woman who knows a lot about parapsychology. She does hypnotic regressions too. She knew about my experience and was fascinated by it. We decided that she would regress me again, to see if it checked out and if anything else turned up.

The first thing she asked was "What is your name?" Instantly, I said, "Why, Blackwell." She should know that. "And what is your first name?" "Stephen Worth." "And your address?" "One sixty-seven West State Street, Trenton, New Jersey." "Where do you work?" "Brown, Shipley and Company. I'm a shipping executive."

My hands were trembling and my voice was quaking. I told her "The ship is listing . . . the water is coming up . . . I'm watching the lifeboats being lowered . . . There is so much confusion. . . . People are crying. . . . There isn't a light in the world and the universe is sad. . . . The ship is lunging up . . . I am being thrown forward . . . now my hands and wrists are broken.

"The women are being put into lifeboats. . . . I feel so sad. People are praying . . ."

When I checked with Zelda later, she told me that she couldn't continue. "She couldn't relive her death. Her hands were hurting so badly—even in hypnosis—that I had to bring her back to release the pain."

"I thought it was a hoax at first," *Titanic* buff Sachs admitted. "But here is this woman recalling things that she couldn't have known unless she actually sank on that ship!"

Sachs even went to Washington to check records in the Library of Congress. "There's no way she could have known some of the things she was telling us. It just wasn't in any books. But it was in a Senate subcommittee report in the archives, Blackwell's address and the name of his company! I wouldn't have believed it!"

San Francisco psychologist Helen Wambach, author of *Life Before Life* and *Reliving Past Lives,* is perhaps the best-known though controversial publicizer of hypnotic regression. She has analyzed over 750 past-life recalls. She reasons that, if such regressive memories are merely fantasies created out of things people have read and forgotten, her subjects would recall being famous personalities, such as Joan of Arc or Alexander the Great, or at least lords and ladies who play the important roles in historical romances. She also reasons that they would have lived in places highlighted by modern history books.

Instead, she observes, "My subjects tended to recall the past lives of peasants." She hypnotized seventy-two people and sent them back to the year 24 A.D., but only fourteen reported having lived in Rome or Palestine at that time. The rest were scattered throughout the world, especially in Central Asia.

Hypnotic regression can be a party game, but it is used increasingly for therapy. Past-life data are being gathered today within the clinical context, when, as part of medical or psychological treatment, troubled patients are hypnotized. They sometimes revert to what they believe to be a clearly recalled previous existence; these newly remembered situations and relationships can offer clues for the clinician.

One such well-known practitioner is a Los Angeles psychologist, Morris Netherton, who describes his technique in *Past Lives Therapy*. The process may take months or longer, but he claims that through the process many phobia patients have been cured. In some of his cases, as with other therapists, actual symptoms show up during the recalled memory. A woman who screamed "He's got a whip!" suddenly showed red welts on her face and shoulders, as if she were at that moment being lacerated. "On the basis of cases I have handled personally," he declares, "and the independent research I have done, I feel that the theory of reincarnation *most logically* explains the phenomena I have witnessed."

Pierre Clement, who has been practicing hypnotism for thirty years in a clinical setting, treats clients with emotional and practical problems. He has also had clients who progressed into future lives! Though the future is "jelled," he explains, "as solidly established as the moon," it is not completely solidified. It can always change.

Psychiatrist Ernest Pecci's work with reincarnation therapy carries over into his understanding of infants and children. He has a growing conviction that the mind is independent of the brain, and brings something to it from the past. Small children, he observes, are incredibly psychic. Even the newborn are preternaturally aware of their surroundings—though few recognize it. He finds it amazing that the newborn know so much with such an undeveloped brain; he feels it is because children have been "imprinted" with their patterns from previous existences, which in this one becomes a dominant or recurring motif.

Does hypnotic regressive evidence about past lives prove anything about reincarnation? Most psychiatrists and psychologists
seem to feel it does not. Parapsychologist Ian Stevenson, at the
Medical School of the University of Virginia, who considers reincarnation a "real possibility," told me that he is suspicious of any
evidence obtained through hypnotic regression.

> If the subject has been instructed by the hypnotist, explicitly or implic-
> itly, to "go back to another place and time" or given similar guidance,
> the new "personality" may appear to be one of another period of
> history. In fact, however, nearly all such hypnotically evoked previous
> personalities are entirely imaginary, just as are the contents of most
> dreams. They may include some accurate historical details, but
> these are usually derived from information the subject has normally
> acquired through reading, radio and television programs or other
> sources.

Stevenson even warns that the "previous personality" may not
go away upon instruction from the hypnotist, thus leaving the patient
with an altered state for several days or possibly longer. In any
case, Stevenson concludes, adults make poor subjects for reincarnation research.

As for children, however, Stevenson considers that a different
matter altogether. When young people display an astonishing knowledge about persons and events that point to a past-life existence,
Stevenson is there to explore it. It was his life-before-life case of
Prakash/Nirmal in India with which we started this chapter.

Stevenson has studied the reincarnation possibility for twenty
years. He has accumulated an international census from many locations and cultures, of hundreds of persons with knowledge of previous existences. His book, *Twenty Cases Suggestive of Reincarnation,*
includes in-depth descriptions of "rebirth cases." Along with the
one of Nirmal are six other instances from India, three from Ceylon,
two from Brazil, one from Lebanon, and seven from Alaska. Each
of those he studied had memories of an earlier life and setting.
One child recalls having stabbed his second wife to death in a
previous existence, which is why his hand and chest are deformed
in this life. One told Stevenson that he'd known he would be recognized on his return to earth by certain moles, which would appear
in the same places on his future body. The person questioned was
named for his grandfather in this life, because he had moles in

the identical spots. One of the twenty cases spoke a foreign language, which could not have been learned by normal means ("xeno-glossy").

Stevenson's working assumption is that existence is not tied to or coterminous with a single physical body. As he explains, "Consciousness has a separate life of its own, moving separately, and continues when the body is gone." He believes that the most promising sources for such inquiry are spontaneous examples, rather than those explored in the laboratory, and most especially examples of children, in whom the memory is fresher and less contaminated by repeated conversation and questioning. In many of his most solid cases, the sharp knowledge of previous details had, by the time of his second investigatory visit, begun to fade.

The mood and modus operandi of such researchers as Stevenson is a far cry from the sensationalized hit-and-run treatment that we are more familiar with. He and his colleagues are demanding a new kind of scientific patience and rigor, which the tabloids and popularizers don't have. In his *Twenty Cases,* for example, he gives a careful account of his checking and cross-checking with all available witnesses; meticulous recording and investigation of all discrepancies; repeated visits to both existence sites, present and previous, including follow-up visits some years later. He has drawn up tables of interpreters and witnesses, along with contradictory information and possible errors. His final sentences reflect the caution characteristic of much current investigation and its care with respect to extravagant claims:

> In such cases we have, then, in principle, some evidence for human survival of physical death. I say "in principle" because I continue aware of particular weaknesses in the present cases. . . . Some (not all) . . . are well enough authenticated to permit a decision on the question, whether or not the events described did in fact happen as the witnesses describe them. The chief contribution of the present cases may lie in their illustration of the *kind* of cases which would provide compelling evidence of survival.

In the careful words of another scientist: "Empirical evidence from the various branches of parapsychology . . . does not *prove* life after death, but is consistent with such an hypothesis, and in some areas, offers the best explanation."

The psychical research society was organized in London to answer the question: Does life go on? The same concern sparked the founding of the American Society. Now, a century after the founding of these pioneer bodies, we have come full circle. Again, the most important question is the ultimate and perennial one: Is there life after life?

14

THE SO-WHAT OF PSI:
The Prometheus Gift

Greek legend has it that the giant, Prometheus, went up to Mount Olympus, stole fire from the gods, and brought it back to the people of earth.

Angry about the theft, Zeus sent the earthlings a "present"—the woman Pandora. Prometheus' bumbling brother, Epimetheus, was delighted and took her as his wife. Prometheus, which means forethought, warned his brother about accepting gifts from the gods, but Epimetheus, which means afterthought, ignored the advice.

We all know what a disaster that was: Overcome by curiosity, Pandora opened the storage urn entrusted to her, and released upon the earth all the evils that attack humans.

So it was with the gift of fire. In the hands of bungling Epimetheus, its warmth and usefulness quickly turned to disaster and ruin.

Psi, like fire—or electricity or atomic energy or even water—can be a gift of infinite blessing, or a force of unimaginable tragedy.

We come now to the final phase of our exploration, where we must ask about our Promethean gift. What is its significance? Is Psi to be used for destruction, or for comfort, aid, and human welfare?

Proceed with Caution

Despite our interest in pointing out the possibilities of the psychic, we must register some cautions. *First,* Psi has not been perfected as a dependable, predictable tool. Though in the chapters of Part I we noted many ways it is already being used—in business, sports, healing, dowsing, the arts, archaeology and so on—we cannot yet count on it.

We can cite case after case of uncanny predictions: earthquakes, accidents, assassinations, the sinking of the *Titanic,* scores of premonitions by people in countries all over the world. But it is only a beginning. We have not yet managed to harness this precognitive power for regular, practical, early-warning use.

Instances of psychic healing are legion, but we cannot depend on this, either. Many people swear by pendulums for everyday help, personal decisions in selection of food and medication, answers to questions about health, travel, business, social relationships. No one, however, as far as I know, has ever checked out the validity of these choices. And though psychics have performed unbelievable feats in finding missing persons, solving murders and kidnapings, they have also come up with off-base information and disastrously misleading clues.

Thus, Psi is a remarkable instrument of incredible potential, which is and has been successfully used. It is also, however, an instrument awaiting development, and in fundamental need of refinement to make it the tool we would like it to be.

Second, our knowledge of Psi and its workings is so limited that we must approach it with care and respect. Medical specialists and clinicians, psychiatrists and psychologists deal regularly with people who have become entangled in its intricacies and flipped out. Altered states of consciousness, we have seen, tend to trigger Psi performance, but where is the line between psychotic hallucinations and "normal" but expanded Psi states?

Hoping "to become psychic" but without proper guidance, some become the victims of gullibility and personal desires. They attempt exercises and disciplines for which they are not prepared, and open themselves to forces they do not understand and cannot control. The psychological mechanism is not only exceedingly intricate, but one which we still know little about. Even the simple Ouija board, say those who are knowledgeable in such matters, may prove dangerous for vulnerable personalities.

"Experts" don't have all the answers, but they are better informed, generally honest, and they can at least advise the rest of us what to avoid—among other things, charlatans and quacks. In Chapter 9 we suggested ways of threading one's way among the good guys and bad.

Third, in the psychic arena, we have two major needs. As I wrote in a guest editorial for *Human Behavior* of March 1978, these are:

1. a *central clearing house,* where anyone can go for Psi information; and
2. a *psychic "hot line"* that anyone can use for immediate help.

The Education Director of the American Society for Psychical Research in New York, Marion Nester, has told me that she concurs with these sentiments. Her organization is one of those that provides information and sponsors events. In addition, it supplies up-to-date releases on parapsychology courses and centers, and maintains a parapsychology library. A central information source is now under discussion. In the meantime, there is nowhere you can turn for an immediate and available file and cross-referencing of what has been done on a particular Psi topic, in the way Edgar Cayce materials have been organized by the Association for Research and Enlightenment at Virginia Beach. With its vanguard interests and unique graduate program in parapsychology, the John F. Kennedy University in Orinda, California, is looking toward the development of a full-scale program in this field.

Nor has anyone yet organized a proper emergency and referral service. This is such a new idea that there are almost no places to turn. I've had to scurry around considerably to find resources for my own SOS requests from readers.

I was pleased and surprised, therefore, at the 1979 Parapsychology Association meetings to hear Keith Harary, who does crisis counseling, announce that he is pushing for a national toll-free number for emergency Psi calls.

Elephants and Anomalies

There's not a person among us who has not experienced at least one "amazing coincidence." I can remember one of mine, though it happened in my childhood, as clearly as though it had happened this morning. We were driving across Iowa, my sisters and I, in the back of the old sedan, and we were all slightly bored. There had been nothing much to see for some time. "Let's play the four-legged game!" one of us suggested. You remember the game—one person or team takes the right side of the road, the other the left. The first to see a hundred animals wins.

I was on the left side, eyeballs peeled, but nothing I could count turned up, only chickens.

"How much will you give me for a chicken?" I finally asked.

"Nothing, silly! You know that only four-legged animals count."

Resigning myself to no score, I went on looking. No results. Once more I ventured, "How much will you give me if I see an *elephant* on my side?"

"We'll give you a hundred and you'll win the game."

I had hardly settled back in my seat when we swung around a curve and there, in front of me and on my side of the road, was an elephant!

It turned out that a small circus had arrived in town and was making its way to the county fairgrounds.

I have always treasured that incident.

Many years later, I'm in touch with a new breed of people, many of whom believe "there is no such thing as coincidence."

How can this be? I've told them my story. I've tried it out on psychics. Their reaction is always the same. It's not that they doubt it, not at all; they believe it and shrug, "So what's new?"

"If *that* is not coincidence, what is it?" I say.

"Just what you'd expect. That's the way Psi works."

"But how?" I persist.

"You 'picked up' the fact that the elephant was just around the bend. You 'knew' it was there. You 'saw' clairvoyantly."

"But why are you sure it was psychic?" I argue. "Maybe I just imagined it . . . "

They always say next, all of them: "But you didn't 'imagine' a camel or a zebra or a giraffe. You 'imagined' an *elephant.*"

But an elephant in Iowa is peanuts compared to the theories scientists are coming up with to explain "simple coincidence." In Psi circles, there are those who contend that coincidences are not special events or even anything extraordinary. Rather, they are the normal working together of related factors. It *seems* like coincidence because we can't see all the elements.

A Parapsychology Association panel debated the meaning of

coincidence at a recent meeting and found no agreement. Some hold that in some subtle way coincidence is essentially a matter of psychokinesis. (I so *wanted* to see an elephant that, "mind over matter," my needs/wishes willed it!)

Psychiatrist/parapsychologist Jule Eisenbud notes that if we combine our incredible Psi potential with what is known about hypnosis and suggestion-at-a-distance, the potential range of human Psi abilities is unlimited. Nothing in the range of remarkable coincidence, he explains, would be beyond accomplishment "by the most innocent-looking observer or happenstance bystander. At the most, he would be doing unconsciously, and with no manifest effort at all, what a movie director goes to great pains to do on a conscious level, that is, deploying props, natural surroundings and events, and the wide capabilities of 'central casting,' to achieve any desired effect."

How is it, Eisenbud asks, "that such possibilities have been so consistently ignored or underplayed, and that the deeper levels of human motivation have not been explored to the fullest?"

Some aver that coincidence is explained by "synchronicity," Jung's term for "meaningful coincidence," and is, unlike PK, not *caused* by any single impulse of will, but is merely *there*—a manifestation of cosmic arrangement or accident or statistical probability. Thus, my elephant and I were part of a subtle ordering tendency hidden in the fabric of the universe.

But how do such vertiginous theories account for another coincidence in my childhood? This one happened to my father. He'd been turning the house upside down to discover the address of someone he needed to reach. His search was cut short because he had to leave for a meeting downtown. When he had parked the car and was headed for the building where the meeting was to be, he passed a second-hand bookstore—as irresistible for him as a candy store is for a child. Since he had ten minutes before the meeting, he could use five of them to browse.

Diving into the store, he passed the first aisle, then the second. Moving down the third aisle, he reached up to a high shelf on the left, pulled down an old volume, and opened it. There, like a bookmark, was a slip of paper, on which was scrawled the name and the address he had been looking for!

Was this a coincidence or was it not? Did my father *cause* the phenomenon, by *willing* the address in some psychokinetic fashion, so that it materialized out of thin air? Was it not-caused, a probability happenstance, or pre-arranged in some synchronistically cosmic fashion? Or did he "know" where it was all along, subconsciously, so that he was "led" to it?

Alan Vaughan, author of *Incredible Coincidence,* is one of those who posits that the hologram may be a link in this cosmic mystery. A hologram, though resembling a photographic negative, is not a picture until a laser beam shines through it, reproducing a three-dimensional picture in space. The point is this: if the hologram is dissected into many pieces, *each piece is capable of reproducing the whole picture.* A person's individual "psychic hologram," says Vaughan, may contain an incredible amount of information. "The staggering implication is that every individual contains within his 'psychic hologram' or blueprint, the picture of the whole universe of consciousness. . . . God not only made us in His image; we contain the whole image."

At least some scientists are coming, via many diverse routes, to the view that the holographic principle may apply throughout the cosmos. Each cell in the body, for example, contains information about the *entire* structure, making possible the cloning of physical bodies from a single cell. Each cell in the brain holographically contains the whole consciousness, neurosurgeon Karl Pribram asserts. The ultimate substrate of matter and energy is consciousness, declares physicist David Bohm: "Present events are manifestations of an infinitely large number of unmanifest germs of events contained in the holographic structure of the universe that knows no time or space."

In the holographic perspective, "amazing coincidence" isn't so amazing. Maybe the amazing thing is that there aren't such "coincidences" more often.

Early psychic study was based on the principle of "anomaly," that is, variations and deviations from the norm. Psi, in fact, defined itself—and still does—in such terms: the study of aberrations; things that cannot be explained by normal means. Thus, parapsychology was not a positive field in its own right, like physics or psychology, but residual and negative, made up of leftovers, unexplainables, and exceptions. The "para" in "paranormal" and "parapsychology" reflects this: "beyond-the-normal" or "outside-of-psychology."

What is developing now, and very rapidly, is the perception

that Psi is not "anomalies" at all, nor is it "outside" or "beyond" or in any way exceptional. Rather, it is *the way things are,* the *essence* of normalcy in our universe.

Prometheus Revisited: The Future of Psi

Who has not heard, by now, murmurs of "psychic warfare" or of a rapidly building "psychic arms race"? The first hint of such unsettling possibilities, after the Cold War, was the way the *Nautilus* incident was handled (1958–59). French tabloids had released the sensational story that the U.S. atomic submarine *Nautilus* was engaged in testing sub-to-shore communications by *telepathy.* U.S. officials hotly denied it. Some speculated that the story was planted by Soviet parapsychologists to gain support for their own program. It was then rumored that the CIA had released the Soviet-planting story to cover up their own leak, and so on . . .

Submarine testing holds considerable importance among Soviets. "If your navy didn't do the *Nautilus* experiment," a Russian scientist exulted to an American reporter some years later, "then Soviet scientists were the first in the world to test ESP from a submarine."

> We didn't use human subjects; we used a mother rabbit and her newborn litter. As you know, there's no way for a submerged submarine to communicate with anyone on land. Radio doesn't work. Scientists placed the baby rabbits aboard the sub. They kept the mother rabbit on shore, where they implanted electrodes in her brain. When the sub was deep below the surface of the ocean, assistants killed the young rabbits one by one.
>
> The mother rabbit didn't know what was happening, of course, yet at each synchronized instant of death, her brain *reacted. There was communication!* Our instruments clearly registered those moments of ESP.

The first large-scale exposition of psychic warfare was Sheila Ostrander and Lynn Schroeder's *Psychic Discoveries Behind the Iron Curtain,* in 1970. "Communist scientists take Psi research seriously," they reported. "It is not a joke."

The zeal and commitment of Soviet scientists particularly struck them. Leonid L. Vasiliev, who had been close to Western European experimenters in the 1920s, and to expanding Psi research at Leningrad University in the 1960s, asserted, "Discovery of the energy behind Psi will be comparable to the discovery of atomic energy."

In their travels through Russia and Soviet-occupied countries,
Ostrander and Schroeder heard guarded rumors that clandestine
military research was in progress. Scientists often expressed the
fear that psychic research would be turned to dangerous uses, and
asked the reporters to carry this message to the West.

The most important difference between Soviet research and
American, the women stated, is that Soviet research is "angled
toward use"—ours is not.

> Their aim is technological application, and the Soviets seem to be
> many years ahead of us. . . . To them it is practical. . . . They are
> working on ways of using Psi: to improve intellectual and artistic
> ability; to communicate in space and under sea; to help locate minerals
> and water; to predict . . . the future; to command another person's
> behavior at a distance; to see at a distance; to see living force-fields
> around the body. That's just the beginning.

Read that statement as a Westerner entrusted with U.S. security;
what do you see? The possibility of sending information to military
forces deployed in space and under the sea, and of picking up such
information from the other side? The possibility of psyching out
essential resources from nature's reserves, and of knowing the outcome of important strategic events? Note also "the ability to command a person's behavior at a distance"—by "mind control"
presumably. If you can do this for *a* person, what about *many*
persons: military headquarters staff, researchers, planners, media
personnel, the Pentagon, the CIA, the U.S. government, whole cities . . .

"That's just the beginning," they observed. The mind can go
on with endless possibilities of psychokinetic disruption of channels
of communication, and potent but invisible influences on the human
body, like undetectable murder and other science fiction enormi-
ties.

Is "ESP-ionage" the real Soviet goal? After five years of collaborative work, Ostrander and Schroeder concluded that the "major
impetus behind the Soviet drive seemed to come from the Soviet
military and the Secret Police; that there were twenty or more
parapsychological centers in the Soviet Union at that time; and
that the government supports parapsychology research to the tune

of 20 million rubles a year." By way of contrast, they said that the United States government budget for such research "is apparently zero."

Many who read the book were disturbed by it. The parapsychology community took it more calmly, on the surface anyway: the book was "flawed"; there were "errors"; its "enthusiasm was inappropriate and excessive." The flurry subsided, but left a residue of uneasiness. Was America being "taken"? One never heard of our government launching, or funding, even a run-of-the-mill piece of Psi research.

In 1978 there came another alarum, *The New Soviet Psychic Discoveries,* by Henry Gris and William Dick.

Was it the rapidity and seriousness of Psi research developments, Gris and Dick asked, that prompted Soviet Premier Brezhnev in 1973 to call for U.S. and Soviet agreement on banning research and development of new kinds of weapons "more terrifying" than nuclear devices? Was the arrest of journalist Robert Toth in 1977, reportedly for receiving secret parapsychology information, a reflection of tighter policies of Soviet secrecy?

The issue was growing more serious. Since the "Iron Curtain" revelations, people had learned of a "remote viewing" experiment with Patrick Price (the West Virginia coal company executive mentioned in Chapter 2). This was reported in detail in the Washington *Post;* Price "flew in" to NORAD headquarters in Colorado, "read" a secret document in a locked file cabinet, and reported its contents to local researchers on the West Coast. The "hit" was verified by the military.

While Uri Geller was being tested at SRI in 1974, there was a sudden and unexplained failure of the ARPA computer network while he was near one of its nodes. This kind of thing was par for Geller, but bewildering to the scientists.

When the Leningrad PK powerhouse Nina Kulagina was reported to have stopped a frog's heart in a lab by taking thought, many scientists around the world felt things had gone too far. In the light of such marvels, *what good are traditional international agreements and policies?* How effective can the mechanisms for "monitoring" U.S.–Russian SALT agreements be if you can psychically tranquilize or confuse monitoring personnel, or send out misleading Psi information about weapon stocks? Why bother with bulky weaponry at all, even atomic, if you can perform wholesale manipulation of moods, and can stupefy whole towns, through mind control?

President Carter has proposed a "final" and "foolproof" $33-billion defense "shell game." Super-weapons would be hidden in cubbyholes in our western deserts and switched rapidly and randomly among hundreds of such "shells" via high-speed tunnels, so the enemy would have impossibly long odds of guessing which shells they must hit to knock the weapons out. But if a psychic can read a secret document in a locked cabinet a thousand miles off, can we feel secure? Can we honestly believe another psychic cannot guess which "shell" contains the target weapon at any given moment? Shades of France's "impenetrable" Maginot Line!

Meantime, year in and year out on this side of the Atlantic, parapsychologists complain "There's no money anywhere; we can't get funding!"

The many questions above quite simply boil down to these:

1. Are people really working on frightful Psi possibilities?
2. If so, why was everyone I talked to in my research for this book so calm about it?
3. Is Russia really running circles around the United States?
4. Isn't the United States doing anything?

Trying to crack this nut was the toughest assignment on my journey through Psi-land. How does anyone get to the bottom of questions like these, particularly an outsider? (Although even insiders, apparently, don't know the score.) If there *is* any information, it's classified.

I'm sorry to report that I can't hand it over to you all neatly tied up and packaged. The best I can give you is the pieces of the jigsaw I came up with.

• "Isn't the United States doing anything?" "Don't kid yourself! They sure are!" I've picked this up from several sources. Brendan O'Regan, Research Director at the Institute of Noetic Sciences in San Francisco, for one: "What do you think is keeping Psi experimenters at SRI in business, like bringing Ingo Swann from New York to do experiments there for a year? All this is classified, though!"

• "What about government funding for Psi research at SRI?" I asked Psi research physicist Harold Puthoff of their "remote viewing" team. "We've had exactly two contracts, one from the Navy and one from NASA." They were in the fifty-to-eighty-thousand bracket.

• "Have you really moved from New York to California to do research with SRI?" I asked Swann. "I'm here for all of this year," he told me in 1978–79. He was back again in 1979–80.

• "How much has been spent altogether in the United States on Psi research?" I asked reporters Fran Hynds and Norma Bowles, the team who made a definitive study of psychic experimentation and had published the statement: "Funding to support Psi research is so small as to be almost nonexistent." "All Psi research, together, adds up to no more per year than the cost of one Army helicopter." (This was in 1977.)

• "What is the total funding for American Psi research, overall?" I inquired again, in 1979, this time of Charles Tart, who was the first to complete a survey of parapsychology funding. After polling all of the major Psi centers, he found that from all sources, approximately $520,000 a year *in toto* is being given for civilian research.

• "How does American government expenditure for Psi research compare with that in Russia?" I asked him. Tart's estimate: Overt Soviet Psi research gets from $50 million to $100 million annually. He leans toward the latter figure. Covert research? No one knows, but it must be at least as much. The same ratio between the two countries, 1 : 100, must hold for covert research as well. "The United States wouldn't just lie down and take it if Russia is going overboard with millions for research?" "I'm afraid that's what it's doing," he replied.

• "What does NASA think of Sherman and Swann's 'journeying' to Jupiter and Mercury and coming up with much of what NASA's later space probes found?" I inquired of a scientist familiar with both projects, who asked that his name not be used. "You'll never get a word out of NASA about *that!*" he exclaimed. "As far as *it* is concerned, the psychic probe never happened."

• "What do you think about the dire applications of Psi?" I asked Ingo Swann, who had written a Psi-fiction cliff-hanger, *Star Fire,* about a super-psychic who took over the delicate mechanisms controlling the missile satellites of rival world powers. "If the Russians said they're using slices of cat's brain in bio-computers, they're probably using human brain by now," he replied.

• "But can what happened in your book really happen?" "I didn't think so when I wrote it, but now, I do."

How can the United States be unconcerned if the situation is so desperate and the potential enemy is bearing down?

Social critic Michael Rossman has concentrated on this question and come up with an answer. It may not be *the* Answer, he admits: "Myself, I don't know what to think"; but given the slippery circumstances, he says it's the best he could do. His book "on the politics of consciousness," *New Age Blues* (1979), is the fullest and most conscientious treatment of the subject I've seen.

It is Rossman's gloomy thesis that we are *supposed* to believe that there is no one of importance who is much interested; that there is almost no funding; and that not much is going on. This "plan," carefully promulgated by the United States government—the military, the CIA?—is designed to throw the U.S. public, Soviet authorities, and even American parapsychologists off the track. The motive? To permit U.S. agencies to proceed, freely and in secret, with Psi. What better strategy if you are trying to manipulate things? The Devil is never happier than when we don't believe he exists, the saying goes.

Rossman also calls up the image of the evil wizard "prying into one's inmost thoughts and manipulating one to do his will, by magic and psychokinesis. . . . The image is terrifying, repulsive, fascinating, a secret fantasy of shameful power—all these at once. . . . In sad fact, the militaries of both sides now seem to be assuming, together, the 'bad wizard' role . . . and to be in advance of the civilians on both sides who are exploring the 'good wizard' role of healing the sick and blessing the crops."

Whether he has better sources than the rest of us, or inclines more to pessimism, I can't say. In any case, the answer Rossman came up with did nothing to relieve his deep anxiety. "What divides me most, and divides my response, is the sense that, in the long run, and perhaps even in the short, I have little more reason to trust my government with these arms than to trust any other. These words are bitter for me to say. Their hurt endures." Moreover, the Psi race is not a phenomenon in and of itself, he asserts, but is part and parcel of the arms race that has plagued humans for decades, of conspiracy, double-dealing, and political intrigue. We will never solve the Psi race, he concludes, until we solve the arms race. "Like Cassandra, I cry *Woe! Woe!*"

Reaching for perspective, I must remind myself that there is a whole list of other human mechanisms capable of blowing us off the map: explosives, pollution, runaway population, atomic fission among them. Psi is apparently the latest of a series to get on that threatening list. We may be so foolish as to destroy ourselves with Psi, but doomsayers remind us of yet another list, of natural catastrophes that can also do it: earth shifts, earthquakes, a new ice age, pole shifts, and more.

Each of us decides, consciously or unconsciously, how to manage the pressure of such towering contingency, in order to continue to exist: Shall I bet on humanity, or not? It's not a matter of knowledge, at last, but of faith.

I choose to bet on humanity, and take heart from an observation once made by researcher Charles Tart: "Our unconscious Psi relationship with the universe is very effective. We tend to get what we want."

Birth Pangs and Paradigms

In 1971, Alvin Toffler unveiled his jolting *Future Shock:* the specter of a technology changing so enormously and so rapidly that we cannot react to it, much less absorb it. However, much of the chaos, pain, and confusion we now experience as individuals and as a society is not technological; it arises from another sort of transition, a change in *paradigm.*

"Paradigm"—an "in" word these days—is the general cultural consensus of a people: their social outlook and perspective, their values and overall world view. Borrowed from science, it refers to "what everybody knows" about how things are and how things work.

The old paradigm is so familiar and so taken for granted, it is hard to put into words. In a nutshell, it holds that the universe, including all of nature, is a vast machine of clock-like perfection, with dependable laws and a dependable order. What this order is can be discovered by science, which is the best method not only for learning such facts, but also for controlling them. "Man"—in this old paradigm—it's always "man"—is a mechanism, blessed with the power of reason, which enables him to plumb the workings of nature and to control them. The more he learns and the more he controls, the more he progresses. "Progress," defined as ever more information and gadgets and goods, is inseparable from science, and inevitable.

The trouble is that Progress has gone sour. The old paradigm is springing leaks. It no longer "holds" the truth. There are too many exceptions.

Human beings, we now find, are more than machines, with more ways of knowing than reason, sense, and cognition. The universe also, it turns out, is not pure mechanism either. Nobel Laureate Eugene Wigner confesses that his own field of physics has made a hideous mistake to treat the universe as simply matter. We have left out its nonmaterial components, the whole realm of consciousness, which is as much a part of the "physical" world as it is of humanity.

Much of the discomfort we now feel is the wrench of leaving the old, familiar paradigm and taking on a strange new one. The tension is not simply the contradiction of technologies, as in *Future Shock,* but the conflict of patterns of consciousness; an obvious insistent example is exchanging the concept of humanity as Exploiter, for that of Partner and Conserver of nature and fellow humans.

Psi and the New Paradigm

So what does all this have to do with Psi? Quite simply, *Psi is helping to shape the new paradigm.* Its contributions, moreover, are directly in line with input from myriad sources: fresh findings from science, *e.g.,* the right-brain left-brain teamwork of intuition and cognition; from medicine—holistic medicine included; from the "human potential" experience; from Eastern insights and disciplines. One wonders how much of the "new knowledge" is, in fact, a rediscovery and retrieval of ancient wisdom.

Psi presents us with nothing less than a *new view of human nature.* A new kind of reality opens up: consciousness that moves in and of itself, heavily conditioned by body and brain, but independent of them (just how independent is not yet clear).

Psi shows us also powers of "knowing" more profound than any we have envisioned, abilities that break through the boundaries of current knowledge. They transcend the limitations of time, thus revealing the arbitrariness of the old-paradigm construct of past-present-future. They hurdle the barriers of space—one can "know" what is happening anywhere. We have discovered no geographic limits.

This unfolding kind of consciousness is a new dimension "within us" and "out there"—the two somehow profoundly related—which has never been fully tapped.

The depth and breadth of these human potentials we have only hints of: mind-over-matter capacities, for example, which also work at great distances; the incomparable powers of healing—we can heal all living things, one another; we can even heal ourselves.

The inner unity of human nature, as revealed in Psi operation, is the same "wholeness of body, mind, and spirit" that the holistic health movement celebrates.

To summarize, this more-than-physical, autonomous, unified, self-healing, and potentially powerful human nature is quite a switch from the fading paradigm of the past, which diminished us into man-the-machine, manipulated, controlled, and fragmented into "economic man," "political man," man the consumer, man the passive patient, and so on.

To discover these neglected depths of our non-physical nature is to restore our full and essential humanness. One might even say—whisper it softly—it restores the Soul.

But beyond all this, Psi presents us with *insights into the nature of the universe.* Hints of some sort of universal unity keep coming through. Individual consciousness, it would appear, is far more than individual. It's part of a consciousness we all share. Each of us is not only tied to, but part of, everyone and everything in the universe.

"Pool of consciousness?" "Clairvoyant Reality?" "Collective un-conscious?" "Super consciousness?" "Transpersonal conscious-ness?" "The Over-Soul?" Whatever it is, all great psychics know and are attuned to it. When you enter that all-enveloping state of being, as a renowned British sensitive once described it, "There is a falling of barriers—a de-localization of the soul. . . . In my deepest awareness," she explains, "I'm everything and everything is me!" Lawrence LeShan adds: "In the Clairvoyant Reality, you and I are really one. We are part of the total One that makes up the entire cosmos."

The paradox is that the deeper the Psi scientist probes, the closer he comes to the perennial mystic vision. The Unity, the One, is the central concept and experience of all mysticism, Hindu, Moslem, Buddhist, Christian, or Jewish, East or West.

Mystic poet Francis Thompson said it: "Thou canst not stir a flower without troubling of a star."

The even greater paradox is that the more the physicist, the traditional defender of materialist science, dissects physical reality, the closer he edges toward that self-same view. Quantum physicist Max Planck discovered that it is impossible to obtain an adequate version of the laws we are seeking, unless the physical system is regarded as a whole: "Each individual particle, in a certain sense, at any one time, exists simultaneously in every part of the space."

No one should be astounded at these similarities, Viennese physicist Fritjof Capra declares. "The term physics is derived from the Greek word which meant, originally, 'seeing the essential nature of all things.' This is, after all, the central aim of all mystics."

In a 1979 overview of physics for the layman, Gary Zukav notes that "Classical physics starts with the assumption of separate parts, which together constitute physical reality. Since its inception, it has concerned itself with how these parts are related. . . . Quantum mechanics is based on the opposite assumption." Physicist David Bohm at the University of London proposes that quantum physics is, in fact, based upon the perception of a new order. According to Bohm, "Instead of starting with parts and showing how they work together . . . we start with the whole." He believes that the apparently "separate parts" of the universe could be connected at a deep and fundamental level. He also asserts that the most fundamental level is an *unbroken wholeness,* in his words "that which is." "All things, including space, time and matter, are forms of that-which-is. There is an order which is enfolded into the very process of the universe."

People everywhere are now discovering the mind-blowing similarities between the new science and mysticism. Psychologist Lawrence LeShan may have been the first to spell this out, in his *The Medium, The Mystic and the Physicist.* Here he tells of a small experiment he performed.

I took sixty-two statements of how-the-world-works. Half of them were written by physicists, half by mystics. Then I mixed them up, took out the authors' names, and gave them to people to see if they could tell what persuasion the author of each statement followed. I gave this list to people trained in physics, to people trained in mystic disciplines, and others. None of these groups has done well on it. . . . It is literally impossible to distinguish the statements accurately, so consistent are the conclusions of both groups.

If Bohm's physics should become the main thrust of the future, Zukav concludes, "the dances of East and West could blend in exquisite harmony. Do not be surprised if physics curricula of the twenty-first century include classes in meditation."

No wonder we have trouble keeping the experimenter out of the experiment. *He and the experiment are one!* Observed and observer are interrelated in a real and fundamental sense.

As science reporter Zukav explains:

> With the awesome authority that we have given it, science is telling us that our faith has been misplaced. It appears that we have attempted the impossible—to disown our part in the universe. We have tried to do this by relinquishing our authority to the scientists. To the Scientists we gave the responsibility of probing the mysteries of creation, change and death. To us we gave the everyday routine of mindless living.
>
> The Scientists readily assumed their task. We readily assumed ours, which was to play a role of impotence before the ever-increasing complexity of "modern science" and the ever-spreading specialization of modern technology.
>
> Now, after three centuries, the Scientists have returned with their discoveries . . . "We are not sure," they tell us, "but we have accumulated evidence which indicates that the key to understanding the universe is *you.*"

View from the Moon

It was this Oneness that crashed in on astronaut Edgar Mitchell on his trip to the moon, "merging the boundaries of the self with the cosmos."

That tiny jewel of earth, afloat in the velvet blackness, so fragile, so helpless, so vulnerable to the destructive power of the very technology that had lofted him! Its resources ebbing, its life-system threatened, the planet cried out for a global ethic.

What if our psychic powers could be harnessed, he asked, to

transform our consciousness from narrow egotism to cosmic altruism?

Psi was, even now, bringing science and religion together, a necessary condition if we are to survive the world's problems. Then and there, Mitchell pledged his life and career to psychic exploration, at the intersect of inner and outer space. On his return, he founded the Institute of Noetic (consciousness) Sciences, which has taken up his perspective and dream.

"We can't all go to the moon," he admits, "but perhaps the deeper awareness of Psi consciousness can provide the same perspective." In this context, "the universe becomes precious to us, because it *is* us."

People were aghast when Copernicus proclaimed that the earth circles around the sun. The idea clashed head-on with the prevailing paradigm. But the facts were insistent. The new view won out.

We are at another such turning-point today. In the words of Willis Harman, President of the Institute of Noetic Sciences, "Psychic research in the next few decades may be destined to have an impact comparable to the impact a few centuries ago of the astronomical investigations of Galileo and Copernicus. I call it the Second Copernican Revolution."

Notes

CASES

Since the aim of the cases cited here is to suggest how broad is the range of psychic phenomena, the places, and kinds of people experiencing them, sources of the cases are varied also. A number are known to me personally; *e.g.,* the lost hikers in New Hampshire, the Vilayat Khan lecture, the Staten Island murder. Some are spontaneous and anecdotal, and reported in the media; *e.g.,* the Abbé Mermet's 6,000-mile water-finding feat, checked and reported in Robert Ripley's syndicated *Believe It or Not.* Others, like the dream telepathy and healing experiments, are laboratory controlled and have been reported in professional journals. Laboratory cases are usually more dependable than the average spontaneous happening, because they can be monitored and controlled.

Though some of the cases cited here have been described in several places, the following are sample sources:*

GRAD'S HEALING EXPERIMENT   "Some Biological Effects of the 'Laying on of Hands': A Review of Experiments with Animals and Plants," *Journal of the American Society for Psychical Research,* 59, 95–126.

MEXICAN EXCAVATION   Stephan Schwartz, *The Secret Vaults of Time,* pp. 222*ff.*

* For full listing of all sources other than journals, see Bibliography.

MAIMONIDES LAB EXPERIMENT	Krippner and Ullman, "Telepathy and Dreams: A Controlled Experiment with Electroencephalogram–Electro-oculogram Monitoring," *Journal of Nervous and Mental Diseases*, 1970, 151, 394–403.
ABERFAN PREDICTIONS	Herbert B. Greenhouse, *Premonitions: A Leap into the Future*, pp. 11*ff.*
BIRMINGHAM APPARITION	G. N. M. Tyrrell, *Apparitions*, Case 8.
ARIGÓ'S PSYCHIC SURGERY	John G. Fuller, *Arigó, Surgeon of the Rusty Knife*.
SEDAN CRASH INTO WINDOW	Louisa Rhine, *Psi, What Is It?*, Perennial Library edition, p. 141.
EARTHQUAKE PREDICTION	Jeffrey Goodman, *We Are the Earthquake Generation*, pp. 14, 15.
TOKYO EXPERIMENT	Hiroshi Motoyama, "The Mechanism Through Which Paranormal Phenomena Take Place," *Religion and Parapsychology*, 1975, 2, pp. 6, 7.
NEW JERSEY PSYCHIC	Scott Jacobson, *Dorothy Allison: A Psychic Story*.

THE AMITYVILLE HORROR: A TRUE STORY

Journalists Rick Moran, of New York, and Peter Jordan, of New Jersey, released exposés of *The Amityville Horror* in 1978, *e.g., Fate*, May 1978. There have been some genuine paranormal events, they say, but these were "relatively infrequent and unremarkable"—which is what the Lutzes (the house owners) reported to the press in February 1976. Author Jay Anson, they say,

> details such an incredible variety of spectacular phenomena that we immediately became suspicious. In all of our combined years of investigating such occurrences, and studying the literature of the paranormal, we had never before heard of so much psychic activity concentrated in one area, in such a short time. Indeed, the book reads like a primer of paranormal occurrences, with every conceivable type of experience reported. Either this book was the most incredible haunting case on record, we thought, or Anson's book was something less than *A True Story*. . . . When we go back to the article

in the *Long Island Press,* January 17, 1976, in which George Lutz describes his experiences while living in the house, he remarks that the only physical effect associated with the haunting involved the boy's bedroom window, which was always being found open when no one remembered having opened it.

"An eerie tale, indeed," they conclude. "Only trouble is, it isn't true."

On further investigation the two journalists repeated their claims in *Fate,* September 1979. Here they add that the book's author, a screenwriter best known for his work on *The Exorcist,* told them he didn't believe the tale himself.

In the meantime the book sells like crazy, a movie is made, and on August 1, 1979, TV host Merv Griffin devoted a full ninety-minute program to plugging it.

EXPERIMENTER FRAUD

It is important to note that, where there has been fraud in the Psi lab, it has been caught, not by outsiders, but by parapsychologists themselves, who zealously guard the integrity of their field. For the disavowal of W. J. Levy's work, see J. B. Rhine, "A New Case of Experimenter Unreliability," *Journal of Parapsychology,* 1974, 38:218–25, and his "Second Report on a Case of Experimenter Fraud," *ibid,* 1975, 39:306–25.

NOTES FOR CHAPTER 2

PSYCHIC BUSINESS ADVISERS

Sources of information for the following:

Beverly Jaegers—taped interviews from two extended visits and a training session at her place in St. Louis, clipping file, her own pamphlet materials.

Ron Warmoth—personal and taped telephone interview, demonstration session in Los Angeles, clippings, visit with his client Maria Rolfe in New York.

Sylvia Smallwood—telephone interview.

Alex Tanous—interviews with him in Montreal, St. Louis, and New York; phone conversations; observing an experiment conducted by Karlis Osis in which Tanous was the subject, American Society for Psychical Research, New York City; his lectures and writing, including his autobiography, *Beyond Coincidence;* telephone interview of his Wall Street client.

DOUGH IN THEM THAR HILLS

Paul Clement Brown—taped personal interview; additional information in Christopher Bird, *The Divining Hand.*

Earl Pyle—information in his *How to Make a Million Dowsing and Drilling for Oil.*

Background information on "doodlebugging for oil" in Walker D. Wyman, *Witching: For Water, Oil, Pipes and Precious Minerals;* interviews with oil dowsers at American Society of Dowsers, Danville, Vermont; extended interviews in Breckenridge, Texas, with Lestor B. Wood; and oil tycoons, in Mihalasky and Dean, *Executive ESP.*

PSYCHIC EXECUTIVES

Mihalasky's ESP studies have been publicized in the business press; *e.g.,* "Hunches Can Still Put Computers to Shame," *Sales Management,* February 1, 1970; "Tomorrow's New Products, Today, by the Hunch Bunch," *Iron Age,* May 16, 1972; "ESP: Can it Play a Role in Idea Generation?" *Mechanical Engineering,* December 1972; J. Mihalasky, "Hidden Career Quotient," *Financial Post Magazine,* Toronto, Canada, May 1971; J. Mihalasky, "ESP in Decision Making," *Management Review,* April 1975; "ESP, Not Science, Rules Decisions, Professor Says," *New York Times, Business and Finance,* August 31, 1969.

For reports of technical associations, see, for example: "Commercial Application of ESP," in *Proceedings of the Seventh Triennial Symposium,* Engineering Economy Divisions, American Society for Engineering Education, American Institute of Industrial Engineers, 1975.

For parapsychological reports, see, for example: J. Mihalasky, "Computer Scored Precognition Experiments," Report to Parapsychological Association, Freiburg, Germany, 1978; Report to Parapsychological Association, New York City, 1970.

Major researches of the subject are reported in *Executive ESP.* Other sources are personal interviews of both the investigators, Dean and Mihalasky, and a member of their interview team; unpublished follow-up research by John Mihalasky.

Co-investigator of *Executive ESP,* Douglas Dean, an electrochemist from Liverpool University, was a pioneer in the use of the plethysmograph for measuring ESP. This is an instrument that ascertains the amount of blood in the extremities, by measuring the contraction or dilation of tiny blood vessels under the skin. A special cup is attached to a finger, for example, and whenever there is brain activity, conscious or unconscious, including the reception of ESP messages, blood rushes away from the finger to the head. The device is connected to an electrical writing instrument, which records changes in blood volume.

Earlier findings, on which Dean and Mihalasky drew, include Gertrude Schmeidler, "An Experiment on Precognitive Clairvoyance," *Journal of Parapsychology,* 1964, 28, 93–107. See her several related articles in same volume. Using a time-metaphor test, she separated research participants into three categories: those who see time as a dashing waterfall, or a fast-moving shuttle, were called "dynamic/hasty" types; those who experienced time as a vast expanse of sky, or a motionless sea, were termed "naturalistic/passive"; and those who see time as an old man with a staff or string of beads were "humanistics." Schmeidler found that the so-called "dynamics" tend to have a sense of the future. "Naturalistics," however, tend to score low in prediction.

Dean and Mihalasky ran similar tests with their subjects. Their reasoning: Making a lot of precognitive "hits" is like being right on snap judgments or hunches in business affairs. In their test of 107 top executives, they confirmed Schmeidler's findings. Tests of more than 5,000 people in management, engineering, science, and women's groups confirmed that ESP operates in big business.

For sample interviews of ESP-oriented executives, see "ESP in Business" issue of *Psychic* (now *New Realities*), December 1974: James Grayson Bolen, "Interview: Al Pollard," and D. Dean and J. Mihalasky, "Testing for Executive ESP."

For Stanford Research Institute report on psychic coal executive Patrick Price, see Russell Targ and Harold Puthoff, *Mind Reach, passim.*

My interviews of Al Pollard were conducted at his think-tank headquarters in Little Rock, Arkansas.

Other sources: ESP Research Associates Foundation "Power of Visualization" meeting in St. Louis, July 28–30, 1978, featuring researchers, psychics, and ESP-oriented business men; *e.g.,* lecture by John Robinson of the Harper Group; interview of Bob Gannaway; and in-depth taped interview of "Ben Burton."

NOTES FOR CHAPTER 3

DOWSING: GENERAL SOURCES

Dowsing literature is voluminous. Comprehensive recent sources include Francis Hitching, *Dowsing: The Psi Connection,* and Christopher Bird, *The Divining Hand.* The former is from a British perspective, and the latter is a handsome art book; both are excellent overviews of the field. The two are notable in their treatment of the relation of dowsing to Psi. Most of the standard treatments do not mention the psychic dimension. Both Hitching and Bird review the historic background and explanatory theories (they do have their differences; *e.g.,* Hitching pushes the practice of dowsing farther back through the mists of time than does Bird, who doubts that the 6000 B.C. depictions of dowsing in cave paintings in the Algerian desert are actually dowsing) See Bibliography for other sources.

PRIMARY WATER

The developer of the Primary Water theory that experienced dowsers understand is non-dowser Stephen Riess, a Bavarian-born mining engineer. He brought the neglected geologic theory about the origin of water, posed by Swedish professor Adolph Nordenskiöld, to the United States to test. The theory and its rationale are comprehensively explained in Bird's *The Divining Hand* and his "The Drought: Rising to the Occasion—The Dowsers" in *New Age,* July 1977. See also *The American Dowser,* August 1977 and May 1978.

After years of correspondence, Raymond Willey, secretary of the American Society of Dowsers and editor of the Society's quarterly, got the U.S. Geological Survey to retract its brochure "Water Witching." The issue, as he explains it in "The Drought":

> Very simply, the almost gut reaction that surfaces among many of these professionals, is not against dowsing per se, but because the use of dowsing raises serious questions about a well-known tenet of hydrology: all water comes from precipitation. Students of dowsing do not deny the hydrologic cycle. What they do say is, that throughout the earth's crust, both on land and under the sea, there are on the order of hundreds of thousands of primary water systems. . . .

LEGENDARY DOWSERS

The definitive works on Henry Gross are the books by Kenneth Roberts: *Henry Gross and His Divining Rod, The Seventh Sense,* and *Water, Unlimited.* Evelyn Penrose's autobiography, *Adventure Unlimited—A Diviner Travels the World,* is an informative document on the successes, problems, and paradoxes of dowsing. Mermet's work is discussed in Hitching, *Dowsing,* and many other treatments. His own book of instructions on dowsing is respected, but considered too exacting by most dowsing authorities today: Abbé Mermet, *Principles and Practice of Radiesthesia.*

COAT-HANGER DOWSING AND THE MARINES

The most comprehensive treatment of Louis J. Matacia's dowsing demonstrations for the military is in Bird's *The Divining Hand.*

DOWSING EXPERIMENTS

Dowsing practitioners and their clients have all the evidence they need: their own experience. The phenomenon is direct and practical, and has, from all we can tell, been used for millennia by people who live close to the land. Despite, or because of, its widespread application, there have been few dowsing tests or formal experiments. For many of those that have been conducted, however, the results have been unsatisfactory; *e.g.,* in 1970, on behalf of the Ministry of Defense, a British engineer, R. A. Foulkes, attempted to discover whether dowsers could detect unexploded bombs from World War II. The results, no better than chance, were published in the British journal *Nature,* and have been cited ever since as "proof" that dowsing doesn't work.

There have been successful tests, however. The University of Paris conferred the degree Doctor of Veterinary Medicine on Abel Martin, for his use of the pendulum to diagnose animal maladies. In one test, it was determined by the usual methods that, in a herd of forty cows, thirty-eight were infected with TB, another was possibly infected, and the remaining one was healthy. With his pendulum, Martin quickly and effectively reached the identical diagnosis.

The problem with dowsing experiments may reflect the same difficulties found with Psi experiments in the lab, suggests Hitching:

> I think at least part of the answer must lie in the difficulty of switching into that relaxed and detached state of mind which every dowser finds necessary for success. The urge to prove oneself in front of skeptics does not mix happily with it, and Zaboj Harvalik has found, for instance, that in his experiments it is often novices who initially do better than professional dowsers, who "seem to feel they must be on their mettle and compete with the newcomers, with the inevitable result that a block sets in and they do a lot worse."
>
> The artificiality of an experiment may be another limiting factor. In the past, the conditions under which the tests took place were often grotesque, with dowsers being blindfolded, strapped up, manhandled, wired to electric meters, asked to perform at precisely regular intervals, and so on. Nowadays experimenters are much more careful to create a sympathetic environment, but, even so, it can never be completely natural. . . .
>
> I was involved in some tests with Bill Lewis (a retired electrical engineer in South Wales, universally recognized by his fellows as among the half dozen best dowsers in the United Kingdom), in which he was asked to identify whether an electromagnetic beam was switched off or on. There is enough evidence in his files . . . for any open-minded person to be convinced that he is normally a highly successful dowser, but on this occasion the results were absolutely at chance level.
>
> All of us were mystified. The dowsing reaction was strong, but also wrong. Bill Lewis could only offer as an explanation that there was "some confusion" in what he was picking up. I tried a couple of runs myself (also with chance results) and understood what he meant. It was extraordinarily difficult to keep one's mind concentrated on the simple question "Is the beam on now?" when the sound of a coin being tossed could be heard. The mental image of someone putting a screen over the beam kept occurring,

and the presence of somebody taking notes could be felt, almost as a force of its own.

Dowsers in particular seem to have difficulty with artificial situations and requirements. What turns them on, many of them report, is live contexts and real needs. Whatever the internal mechanism may be that performs the mysterious and miraculous result, it is not fooled, apparently, by lab attempts to create or imitate real situations.

BIOPHYSICAL EFFECT (BPE)

Unlike Western scientists, their Russian counterparts have no hangups about proving that dowsing is a reality. In *Psychic Discoveries Behind the Iron Curtain,* Ostrander and Schroeder note:

> Without a proper scientific birth certificate to explain where it came from, dowsing has existed in the West as a foundling, outside the realm of science. In the Soviet Union, scientists have taken in this orphan. Dowsing in the U.S.S.R. is a legitimate scientific field of study. Major geology institutes in Moscow and Leningrad have large groups of geologists, geophysicists and physiologists all researching dowsing.

Several years ago, A. J. Ogilvy, chairman of the Geology Department, Moscow State University, announced that "the Soviets stand on the eve of a new birth in the ancient field of prospecting—the discovery of the scientific basis of dowsing. Dowsing will be used to solve problems, and may supplant many contemporary geophysical methods. . . . There is nothing mystical in the ability of man's body to react to underground mines or water."

Hitching notes that "what the Soviets apparently like about the dowsing reaction is that it is physiological—a Pavlovian response: a dowser gets a body reaction with his rod in the same place every time, and since this can be seen to happen, it ought therefore to be shown (according to Marxist theory) to have a materialist explanation." Note that the term "biophysical effect," or BPE, conceals its mysterious magical origins and possibly nonmaterial nature.

A water geologist, G. Bogomolov, found to his surprise that the "wizard rod," as Soviets call it, could determine the depth of underground streams and cables, and even the diameter of water pipes. With two other engineers, he tested this and published his findings in *The Journal of Electricity,* January 1944. Since then, BPE research in the U.S.S.R. has been pushed. On October 31, 1966, the All-Union Astro-Geodesic Society of Moscow held a special seminar on dowsing. In April 1968, an important two-day scientific conference was held in Moscow, devoted exclusively to the BPE method.

IRRITATION ZONES AND NOXIOUS VEINS

For information on dowsing for noxious veins, see Z. V. Harvalik, "Cancer Caused by Influences from the Ground," in *The American Dowser*, August 1976, and Bob Ater, "Dowsing Accident-Prone Highway Locations," *ibid.* Gordon MacLean's approach is found in *A Field Guide to Dowsing*. See also *Effects of Harmful Radiations and Noxious Rays*, a compilation of papers put out by the American Society of Dowsers, Danville, VT 05828.

RADIESTHESIA

There are many European sources on dowsing that use the radiation label and approach. One of these is Pierre Beasse's *A New and Rational Treatise of Dowsing According to the Methods of Physical Radiesthésie*, which first appeared in French in 1938.

HARVALIK'S RESEARCH

Zaboj V. Harvalik, writing alone or with Wilhelm de Boer, published a number of articles having to do with the mechanisms of magnetometer-type sensing by humans, from November 1970 to August 1976 in *The American Dowser*. See also Hitching on Harvalik, in *Dowsing*, and Bird, *The Divining Hand*.

MAP DOWSING

The real stumper in dowsing is map dowsing. Electronics specialist Arthur Bailey, scientific adviser to the British Society of Dowsers until he became its president, declares that no scientific explanation begins to touch the problem. Map dowsing, he declares, contradicts the Second Law of Physics, the inverse square law, which explains how radiation energy steadily decreases in proportion to the square of the distance from the source.

Map dowsing also defies the laws of space/time. In Francis Hitching's words:

> The length of time it takes to get an answer from a pendulum is unaffected by distance. You can ask a question about life on Mars, and the pendulum will react as quickly as if you were asking about life in a local supermarket. Moreover, there is . . . remanence. You may be dowsing for something— hidden treasure, a missing person, a well—and you have a strong pendulum reaction. Yet, when you check out the site, you find nothing. But some time ago, even centuries ago, exactly what you are looking for was indeed there. . . .

NON-HUMAN DOWSING

Material on the dowsing woodpecker taken from Earl Pyle, *How to Make a Million.*

DOWSING HOW-TO'S

There are a great many books on the how-to's of dowsing, among them MacLean's *Field Guide;* Harvey Howells' *Dowsing for Everyone: Adventures and Instruction in the Art of Modern Dowsing;* and J. Scott Elliot's *One Man's Way.* There are also specialized instruction books on the use of the pendulum, the rod, and so on, though most general guides include these also.

The best bet for a would-be dowser to learn the techniques is to join the American Society of Dowsers (Danville, VT 05828), or one of its local chapters. Local societies often have their own manuals and instructions. The national society's quarterly is *The American Dowser;* its editor, Raymond C. Willey, wrote the handbook *Modern Dowsing.* The Society also conducts seminars and workshops at its annual meetings in September.

PERSONAL SOURCES

Personal contacts and taped interviews of knowledgeable dowsers include the following: from American Society of Dowsers meetings in Danville, Vt., Jack Livingston, Gordon MacLean, Bob Ater, Jim Perkins, LeRoy Osborne, Christopher Bird, T. Edward Ross (president), Edward P. Jastram, R. J. Alden, Theodora Penrose (chapter adviser), and others; from Southern California Society of Dowsers, Legory O'Loughlin, Ralph Harris, Bill Cox, Floyd Bekins, Erwin Stark, and others; from British Society of Dowsers, Enid Smithett, John Trigger, J. Scott Elliot; and from elsewhere, Thomas Sherman, Mt. View, Arkansas, Carroll and Virginia Baker (Orange Co., Ca. chapter), Karl von Mueller, Segundo, Colo., and Lestor B. Wood. Breckenridge, Tx.

NOTES FOR CHAPTER 4

HEALING AND HOLISM

So voluminous is the literature on healers and healing that no attempt has been made to include in the Notes or Bibliography more than the barest sampling of references. Much the same can be said for the recent but rapidly developing literature in holism. For a bird's-eye view of several aspects of healing, see Stanley Krippner and Alberto Villoldo, *The Realms of Healing,* which looks at healers and healing in different societies, healing in the laboratory, and explanatory theories. For an overall view of the holistic approach—history, principles and goals—see Hastings, A. C., James Fadiman, and James S. Gordon, eds., *Health for the Whole Person, A Complete Guide to Holistic Medicine*, and Leonard Pellettiri, ed., *The Journal of Holistic Health*, 1977. See also Leslie J. Kaslof, *Wholistic Dimensions in Healing: A Resource Guide*. A holistic how-to resource (with a Transcendental-Meditation emphasis) is Harold H. Bloomfield and Robert B. Kory, *The Holistic Way to Health and Happiness.*

HEALING EXPERIMENTS

The strongest evidence for psychic healing comes from the body of research where the effects of suggestion have been eliminated, or at least minimized. The key research was instigated by Bernard Grad. Detailed accounts of these experiments can be found in *International Journal of Parapsychology*, 1961, 63, 64; *Journal of the American Society for Psychical Research*, 1965, 1967; *Corrective Psychiatry and The Journal of Social Therapy*, 1966; *Pastoral Psychology*, 1970; *Journal of Pastoral Counseling*, 1972; and Gertrude Schmeidler, ed., *Parapsychology: Its Relation to Physics, Biology, Psychology and Psychiatry*. For summaries of Grad's experimental work, see Bernard Grad, "Some Biological Effects of 'Laying on of Hands' " (see notes for Chapter 1) and Laile E. Bartlett, "Bernard Grad and Energy," *Human Behavior*, June 1978.

For other studies in this area, see M. Justa Smith, "Paranormal Effects on Enzyme Activity Through Laying on of Hands," *Human Dimensions*, Spring 1972, 15–19; a series of experiments in Dolores Krieger, "Therapeutic Touch, the Imprimatur of Nursing," *Journal of Nursing*, May 1979, 784–7; Graham and Anita Watkins, "Possible PK Influence on the Resuscitation of Anesthetized Mice," *The Journal of Parapsychology*, 1971, 35, 257–72; Graham and Anita Watkins, and Roger Wells, "Further Studies on the Resuscitation of Anesthetized Mice," in Roll, Morris, and Morris, eds., *Research in Parapsychology, 1972;* and Roger Wells and Judith Klein, "A Replication of a 'Psychic Healing' Paradigm," *Journal of Parapsychology*, 1972, 36, 144–9.

TESTING HEALERS

Oskar Estabany, the subject of Grad's initial research, figured prominently in the subsequent experiments of Grad, Smith, and Krieger. Grad tested a number of others, among them Olga Worrall and Etel DeLoach. In all of Grad's experiments involving healers, the results were positive.

Formal laboratory reports of experiments with Worrall are less available than researchers would like. Hiroshi Motoyama has an electro-encephalographic device in his Tokyo laboratory by which he purportedly measures acupuncture "meridians" and yogic "chakras." His report involving Worrall reads:

One characteristic belonging to the psychic person is standard deviation of skin current of the w8 meridian (seiketsu) points which is very high compared with the ordinary person. For instance, in the average person the value is from 0.1 to 0.26, but Mrs. Worrall showed 1.0, a much higher value. . . . Then after comparison between readings before and during faith healing through her hands and fingers, meridians of the left hand fingers showed a highly significant difference. . . .

Consequently, we can infer that her psi ability is more easily projected from the left as compared to the right hand.

This and other laboratory accounts, including those of Robert Miller in Atlanta (*e.g.* the cloud chamber experiments) are in Worrall's files, and appear in Edwina Cerutti's biography of her, *Mystic with the Healing Hands.*

Experiments involving Worrall are reported in D. Dean and E. Brame, "Physical Changes in Water by Laying on of Hands," in *Proceedings, Second International Congress on Psychotronic Research,* Paris; in Robert Miller, Philip Reinhart, and Anita Kern, "Scientists Register Thought Energy," in W. Kinnear, ed., *Thought as Energy;* the experiment at U.C.L.A. Radiation Field Photography Laboratory," in Thelma Moss, *The Probability of the Impossible;* and in Stanley Krippner and Alberto Villoldo (who also report on Rolling Thunder, Pachita, and other healers) in *The Realms of Healing.* Among the many testimonials re Worrall, based not on experiments but on experience is John Carlova, "Even M.D.s Have Faith in this Faith Healer," in *Medical Economics,* September 17, 1973.

Profiles of a cross-section of healers, including Charles Cassidy and Etel DeLoach, appear in David St. Clair, *Psychic Healers.*

My own interviews of healers include several taped interviews of Worrall and DeLoach, and one each of Lawrence LeShan and Claire Balian. I have taped interviews also of psychics who are healers as well: *e.g.,* Alex Tanous, Harold Sherman, and Bob Ater.

TESTING HEALEES

For animal healees, see Grad's and the Watkins' research; for human healees, see Smith and Krieger (see "Healing Experiments" Notes, above, for all of these). Investigative reporter Allen Spraggett followed up some of those healed by Kathryn Kuhlman. See Spraggett, *The Woman Who Believes in Miracles.* Mark Jonathan Harris reported on doctor/healer/researchers Hans Engel and Valerie Hunt, in *New West,* Feb. 13, 1978.

THE HEALING PROCESS

For an overview of perspectives on healing, see James L. Fosshage and Paul Olson, eds., *Healing Implications for Psychotherapy;* and Jerome

D. Frank, *Persuasion and Healing, A Comparative Study of Psychotherapy.* For an overview of healing practices that lie outside the scientifically based medicine of Western society, Krippner and Villoldo also review paranormal healing, and suggest how these processes might be incorporated into the scientific framework, in *The Realms of Healing.* Re native healing, see also Doug Boyd, *Rolling Thunder.* Lawrence LeShan's suggestive healing experiments are reported in *The Medium, The Mystic and the Physicist, A Revolutionary Approach to Psychic Healing.* Other source: personal interview. Mary Coddington's personal quest for the mysterious unknown energy is presented in her *In Search of the Healing Energy.*

Re psychic surgery, see Krippner and Villoldo, *The Realms of Healing;* John G. Fuller, *Arigó, Surgeon of the Rusty Knife;* Hiroshi Motoyama, "Tony Agpaoa's Psychic Surgery and its Mechanism," and "Psychic Surgery in the Philippines," Institute for Religious Psychology Reports; George W. Meek, ed., *Healers and the Healing Process.*

SELF-HEALING AND HOLISM: THE PK REVOLUTION

The literature is enormous and rapidly burgeoning: e.g. Hastings, et al, *Health for the Whole Person;* Harold H. Bloomfield and Robert B. Kory, *The Holistic Way to Health and Happiness;* for the effect of mind, including the unconscious, on the body and its well-being, see Thomas Hanna, *The Body of Life.* Other sources for this chapter: the first Congress of Nurse Healers, San Francisco, June 1977, with Dolores Krieger's Workshop on healing; Body/Mind/Spirit ESP Workshop, St. Louis, 1978, speakers: Olga Worrall, Rose Gladden, and Dr. C. Norman Shealy (Director of the Pain and Health Rehabilitation Center, LaCrosse, Wisconsin); lectures by and about Jack Schwarz (whom I interviewed), subject and practitioner, who has his own center for practicing voluntary control of involuntary functions (the Aletheia Psycho-Physical Foundation, Grants Pass, Oregon).

Re self-healing, see Norman Cousins, *Anatomy of an Illness.* For a simple how-to book on self-healing, see Amy Wallace and Bill Hankin, *The Psychic Healing Book.* For an overview of self-healing in the United States today, see the special self-healing issue of *New Age,* May 1979. For the effect of attitudes and social situation on physical condition (PK?), see James J. Lynch, *The Broken Heart—The Medical Consequences of Loneliness.* Re stress and illness, see Kenneth Pelletier, *Mind as Healer, Mind as Slayer,* and Barbara Brown, *New Mind/New Body* and *Stress and the Art of Biofeedback* (both of whose lectures I have attended); also Hans Selye (whom I interviewed), *Stress Without Distress.*

Re holistic practitioners, see O. C. Simonton and S. S. Simonton, "Belief Systems and Management of the Emotional Aspects of Malignancy," *Journal of Transpersonal Psychology,* 1975, 29–47, and critique of their work,

Maggie Scarf, "Images that Heal," in *Psychology Today,* Sept. 1980; Norman Shealy, *Ninety Days to Self-Health;* Irving Oyle, *The Healing Mind,* and Alan Vaughan, "Interview: Irving Oyle" in *Psychic,* November/December 1976. Re self-help for the layman, see *Dr. Heimlich's Home Guide to Emergency Medical Situations,* a controversial holistic primer in household emergency medicine.

For broader implications, experiments, and theories, see *Beyond Biofeedback* by Elmer and Alyce Green of the Menninger Foundation, who have studied Swami Rama, Rolling Thunder, and Jack Schwarz. The Psi Search symposium, Jan./Feb. 1977, a five-week series of sessions sponsored by John F. Kennedy University, included resource people Pelletier, Schwarz, and Worrall. For books by Jack Schwarz, see Bibliography.

Jack Schwarz, who has been studied by E. and A. Green at the Menninger Clinic, conducts seminars, lectures, and runs his own Aletheia Psychophysical Foundation at Grant's Pass, Oregon.

NOTES FOR CHAPTER 5

PSYCHIC DETECTIVES: DUTCH

For books on the three Dutch sensitives, see M. B. Dykshoorn with Russell H. Felton, *My Passport Says Clairvoyant;* Norma Lee Browning, *The Psychic World of Peter Hurkos;* Jack Harrison Pollack, *Croiset the Clairvoyant.*

I have interviewed Dykshoorn and Hurkos in the United States. The former assured me that "the book Felton put together about me is fine. It *is* me, and the way I still feel." Hurkos, on the other hand, complained about the Browning biography: "There's too much Browning in it and not enough Hurkos. I'm writing my own account now."

PSYCHIC DETECTIVES: JAMAICAN

An account of Ernesto Montgomery, World War II spy for the British, Jamaican clergyman, and former member of the constabulary, can be found in Clifford Linedecker's *Psychic Spy.*

The Jamaican-born Mountie turned store detective, Reg McHugh, was one of those included in the Canadian documentary film on international parapsychology research, *Invisible Influences* (Mediavision, Toronto). Most of my information on McHugh, however, comes from personal contacts and interviews, of him and almost forty witnesses in Toronto, Montreal, and the Maritime Provinces. See Laile E. Bartlett, "The Case of the Psychic Detective," Canadian *Reader's Digest,* June 1978.

PSYCHIC DETECTIVES: AMERICAN

Though American psychics specializing in crime are reported increasingly in TV and the press, most of the material in this chapter comes from first-hand sources: personal interviews of Dorothy Allison—and people who have worked with her in New York—with follow-ups by phone; repeated and in-depth interviews of Beverly Jaegers in her home in Missouri, and discussions with her Crime Squad trainees, Phyllis DeChrysto, Jane Mock, Marilyn Kypta, Albert Petschonek, and others, as well as observer participation in one of her training courses; personal interviews of other psychic detectives, Ron Carpenter in New Brunswick, Canada, Irmgard Schmidt in Toronto, and Del St. Clair, St. Louis.

For published material on Allison, see Scott Jacobson, *Dorothy Allison: A Psychic Story;* Robert V. Cox and Kenneth L. Peiffer, Jr., *Missing Person, A Case with No Clues;* and Joseph P. Blank, "The Woman Who Sees Through Psychic Eyes," *Reader's Digest,* December 1978. Jaegers, who has had extensive TV and newspaper coverage (*e.g.,* Paul Weingarten, "Psychic Gumshoes: Solving Crime Is No Mere Hunch—It's a Case for ESP," *Chicago Tribune,* March 10, 1980), has her own line of training materials (Aries Productions, Inc., P. O. Box 24571, Creve Coeur, MO 63141.)

NOTES FOR CHAPTER 6

FORECASTING DISASTERS

For more on Louisa Rhine's collection of spontaneous cases, see her "Frequency of Types of Experience in Spontaneous Precognition," *Journal of Parapsychology,* 1954, 18, 93–123, and *Hidden Channels of the Mind.* For an overview of premonition and its uses, see Herbert B. Greenhouse, *Premonitions: A Leap into the Future.*

Re Cox's railroad research, see W. E. Cox, "Precognition: An Analysis, II," *Journal of the American Society for Psychical Research,* 1956, 50, 99–109. The study is also reported in Greenhouse, *Premonitions.*

THE REGISTRY ROUTE

For a full account of the founding of the premonition registries in Britain and the United States, see Greenhouse, *Premonitions.* In London, in April 1979, I interviewed two Britishers who have hopes of reviving the British Premonitions Bureau, R. Tempest-Woods of Penzance and Gerald Fletcher of London. From time to time I have discussed the work of the Central Premonitions Registry in New York with its director, Robert Nelson.

It is Greenhouse's contention that every human being is a potential seismograph, whose premonitions, when pooled in sufficient numbers, can begin to shape a working knowledge of the future and how to deal with it. Statistically, he asserts, the larger the number of predictions, the larger the number of hits that can serve as guides. It would seem that the time has come to give major scientific attention to the registry idea, and to the testing of "human seismographs" who are in the business of releasing prophecies.

ANIMAL PREDICTIONS

There is evidence that animals can anticipate events, *e.g.*, impending danger for the animal itself or its master, or anticipation of a positive event such as the master's return. A rigorous survey of spontaneous events of this type can be found in J. B. Rhine and S. R. Fletcher, "The Study of Cases of 'Psi-Trailing' in Animals," *Journal of Parapsychology,* 1962, 26:1–22. See also Robert L. Morris, "The Psycho-Biology of Psi," in Edgar Mitchell, and others, edited by John White, *Psychic Exploration: a Challenge for Science.*

PROTECTIVE DOWSING

Most of the dowsing literature has been focused on locating hidden resources: water, or more recently, oil and other objects. Very little has been developed by way of preventive or protective techniques. For more on this subject, see recent issues of *The American Dowser* and the *Journal of the British Society of Dowsers.*

I have spent some time talking with people in this innovative sphere: the late Gordon MacLean, Jim Perkins, Bob Ater, John Trigger, and Enid Smithett. See also articles in the dowsing journals on ley lines and the universal grid.

THE CATASTROPHISM THESIS

One of the great theoretical controversies among scientists, geologists in particular, is "Uniformitarianism" *vs.* "Catastrophism." The former, more conventional position, is that the past history of the earth is best interpreted in terms of what is known about the present. In his *Essentials of Earth History,* William Stokes explains that "Uniformitarianism would explain the past by appealing to known laws and principles, acting in a *gradual,* uniform way through the past ages." The processes we see today are thus the same processes that produced the Everests, beaches, glaciers, and so on. Catastrophism, on the other hand, explains these geological formations as the result of brief, irregular, and explosive upheavals.

Geologist A. T. Wilson, at Victoria University, New Zealand, theorizes that the Ice Ages may have been brought on by catastrophic surges of the Antarctic ice sheet. One of the most forceful and imaginative of the cataclysmic theorists, the late Immanuel Velikovsky, explained much of the present earth character in terms of cataclysmic events. In *Worlds in Collision*, for example, he argued that the earth has gone through a number of encounters with planets and comets, suffering abrupt pole shifts and wild tumbling of the earth on its axis as a result. In the most recent catastrophe, at about 1500 B.C., he contended that a comet from the planet Jupiter collided with Mars, forming the planet Venus and shifting the orbit of the earth, displacing the oceans and reversing the earth's poles.

The science fiction flavor of Velikovsky's writings—*Ages in Chaos, Earth in Upheaval, Worlds in Collision*—has made him particularly controversial: a favorite with the occult bookstore crowd, a target of the scientific community. Despite the attacks on his far-fetched conclusions, many of them have, in fact, been proved correct; for example, the existence of geomagnetic planetary fields, the negative electrical charge of the sun, the high temperature of Venus, the emission of radio sounds from Jupiter, and so on.

Jeffrey Goodman reviews catastrophism literature, comparing scientific theories and findings with psychics' insights and predictions, in *We Are the Earthquake Generation: Where and When the Catastrophes Will Strike*.

One of the most thought-provoking theories, considered also by Goodman, is the possibility that earth-events, including catastrophes, are the product of psychic energies: our thoughts! A survey of the evidence for this "fifth force" in nature is also presented in White and Krippner's *Future Science*. As Goodman observes in his "psychic-scientific" treatment: *You* are the quake!

NOTES FOR CHAPTER 7

PSYCHIC ARCHAEOLOGY

Two full-scale reports on psychic archaeology are Jeffrey Goodman's *Psychic Archaeology: Time-Machine to the Past,* and Stephan Schwartz' *The Secret Vaults of Time: Psychic Archaeology and the Quest for Man's Beginnings.*

These books began as a collaborative endeavor, then branched apart to produce two quite different reports. At the heart of Goodman's account is his own experience with a Psi-directed archaeological dig near Flagstaff, Arizona. An archaeologist with a geological background and degrees in engineering and business, his treatment is a testimonial to the uses of psychic input in the scientific field. Schwartz, a former special assistant for research to the Chief of Naval Operations, and Project Director of Deep Quest, the first experiment in deep ocean psychic archaeology, presents detailed cases of psychic archaeology in Britain, Poland, Canada, and other parts of the world, and a consideration of the implications of Psi for science generally.

Both Goodman and Schwartz draw heavily on "The Glastonbury Scripts," for which see Frederick Bligh Bond, *The Gate of Remembrance.*

Dowsing, or the "biophysical effect" as the Russians call it, has been used for some time in mineral exploration in the Soviet Union. Reports now indicate its application in archaeological projects as well. Goodman and Schwartz both cite the importance of the dowsing investigations of Aleksandr Pluzhnikov, which resolve uncertainties and conflicts about important Russian historical sites. See A. Pluzhnikov, "Possibilities for and Results of the Use of the Biophysical Method in Researching and Restoring Historical and Architectural Monuments," *The American Dowser,* August 1974.

Applying the psychic methods practiced by American Indians, a contemporary searcher for artifacts, Tennesseean Kenneth Pennington, voices a chant before he digs: "O Ancient Peoples, now slumbering . . . guide my shovel to the truth and beauties in the old fields, that I might bear witness to your life, and be your voice from the past." Pennington then follows the urge that tells him where he should dig. Among his finds are ornaments, weapons, tobacco pipes, bones, shells, and stone tools. Once, within minutes of singing, he uncovered eight beautiful pottery vessels.

The most unusual thing about Pennington's success, notes Goodman, who checked him out personally, is the number of rare Indian artifacts he finds, objects that no orthodox archaeologists have ever seen before. One psychically located skull dated back several thousand years, and had peculiar diamond-shaped markings on the brow. No one has been able to explain the meaning of these baffling marks.

I have spent a weekend at Jeffrey Goodman's base in Tucson, Arizona, going over photos, accounts, and specimens from his dig. I have also visited with him and taped interviews of the sensitive who advised him, Aron Abrahamsen, and his wife, Doris, in Everett, Washington. One of the psychics who helped with Stephan Schwartz' 1979 expedition to Egypt, Hella Hammid, spoke at a California "uses of Psi" workshop, which I attended in August of that year. Hammid is a subject whose abilities were discovered by Stanford Research Institute (see Puthoff and Targ, *Mind Search*).

PSI AND SCI

For instances of the movement of physics and physicists in the Psi direction, not only at symposiums and conferences but in the literature, see Lawrence LeShan, *The Medium, the Mystic and the Physicist;* John White and Stanley Krippner, eds., "Life Energies and the Physics of Paranormal Phenomena" in *Future Science;* Harold Puthoff and Russell Targ, "Psychic Research and Modern Physics," in Mitchell, et al, *Psychic Exploration, A Challenge for Science;* Gary Zukav, *The Dancing Wu Li Masters: An Overview of the New Physics;* J. H. M. Whiteman, "Parapsychology and Physics" in Benjamin B. Wolman, ed., *Handbook of Parapsychology;* Fritjof Capra, *The Tao of Physics.*

Physics experiments and theoretical papers in the psychic field are also being included in professional journals and reports; for example, physicist Helmut Schmidt's "PK Tests with a High Speed Random Number Generator," *Journal of Parapsychology,* 1973, 37, 105–118; E. H. Walker, "Application of the Quantum Theory of Consciousness to the Problem of Psi Phenomena" in *Proceedings of the Parapsychology Association,* 1972, 9. J. B. Hasted, "An Experimental Study of the Validity of Metal-Bending Phenomena" in *The Journal of the Society for Psychical Research,* 1976, 48, 365–383. Re the "new force" in nature, see Rex Daniels in Krippner and White's *Future Science.*

It was at the International Society for Psychical Research meetings in Edinburgh, April 1979, that I met with Psi-oriented physicist John B. Hasted, University of London. Other European parapsychologists who gave me input there were: Erlendur Haraldsson, University of Iceland; George Zorab of Zoestermeer, Holland; Martin Johnson, in charge of the parapsychology center, which I later visited in Holland; Richard Broughton of Utrecht—who "tested" me on his equipment when I got to Utrecht; Elmer Gruber of Freiburg, Germany; Renée Haynes of London, who introduced me in London to the British Society for Psychical Research.

THOUGHTOGRAPHY

For Eisenbud's thought pictures and photo effects, see the series of articles by Jule Eisenbud in the *Journal of the American Society for Psychical Research,* e.g., "Some Unusual Data from a Session with Ted Serios," *Journal of the American Society for Psychical Research,* 1967, 61, 241–253; "Psychic Photography and Thoughtography" in Edgar Mitchell, et al, *Psychic Exploration;* Eisenbud's "Paranormal Photography" in Benjamin B. Wolman, ed., *Handbook of Parapsychology;* and his *The World of Ted Serios.*

For information on the replicative tests, see Ian Stevenson and J. G. Pratt, "Exploratory Investigations of the Psychic Photography of Ted Serios," *Journal of the American Society for Psychical Research,* 1968, 62, 103–129, and their "Further Investigations of the Psychic Photography of Ted Serios," *ibid.,* 1969, 63, 352–364.

Eisenbud updated the subject in a presentation of photographs at the Parapsychological Association meetings in August 1979.

The Fukurai experiments were reported in *Clairvoyance and Thought-ography.*

Among the handful tested for this ability is the renowned Nina Kula-gina of the Soviet Union, who is reported to be able to fog films or imprint a simple symbol like a plus sign, by concentration. Though most of the subjects tested have imprinted the film intentionally, there are reports of others who, in periods of intense stress, have unintentionally produced thought-images on film.

The invention of Polaroid film with its instant development process has been a boon in such experiments, minimizing chances for tampering with the process and making monitoring easier to handle.

PSI IN SPACE

The Soviets are apparently more concerned with Psi in space than are Americans. When Russian cosmonaut Uri Gagarin became the first man to orbit the earth, flags flew from Red Square, and singing and shouting people ran into the streets with placards that announced HURRAH! THE COSMOS IS OURS!—a reflection, obviously, of official policy. A Psi training project was incorporated into the cosmonauts' training program.

Other reported Soviet researches concerned the "missing planet," Phae-ton (their theory: that a human-designed thermonuclear explosion blew it apart; pieces from it, "tektites," have been found in Australia, the Philip-pines, Czechoslovakia, and Russia—some even theorize that space visitors from the planet visited earth); the Tungusky meteorite crater in Siberia (their theory: it was deliberately set off to detonate just above the surface of the earth to attract our attention; it was a nuclear armed probe—"un-questionably nuclear"—a huge mushroom cloud reported): UFO's—fol-lowing an abrupt switch in Soviet policy, which cut off public discussion, forcing scientists underground (250 "scientifically documented reports" of UFO sightings reported. Yuri Fomin, Moscow Technical Institute, willing to confide: "I have not given up collecting evidence, because I have obtained the necessary proof that UFOs truly exist, and that their flights over the Soviet Union are taking place").

As for our U.S. psychic space travelers, I am glad to report that I have become acquainted with them both. I have had several discussions with Ingo Swann, by phone in New York and in person in California, where I've seen the display of his paintings, and accompanied him to a record company where he was cutting a musical album he had designed on the psychic universe, *Star Children.* I taped a number of long, leisurely conversations with Harold Sherman, his wife, Martha, and his dowser brother, Thomas, at his quiet and remote hideaway near Mountain View, Arkansas.

See Swann's autobiography, *To Kiss the Earth Goodbye,* and his novel, *Star Fire.* See Sherman's books, a few of which are *Thoughts Through Space* (with Sir Hubert Wilkins), *How to Make ESP Work for You, Your Mysterious Powers of ESP,* and *How to Picture What You Want.*

For an account of the Swann/Sherman space probe, monitored by Janet Mitchell at the American Society for Psychical Research in New York City, see J. Mitchell, "A Psychic Probe of the Planet Mercury," *Psychic,* June 1975; J. Mitchell, "Psychic Space Exploration," *Fate,* October 1979; and for the physical correlates of out-of-body travel (*i.e.,* electroencephalograph and so on), K. Osis and J. Mitchell, "Physiological Correlates of Reported Out-of-Body Experiences," *Journal of the American Society for Psychical Research,* 1977, 49.

NOTES FOR CHAPTER 8

DUKE OF PADUCAH

I visited the Hoys for a weekend in their home in Paducah, Kentucky, taped many interviews with David and Shirley, visited the Hoy Organization's office, and met their staff. For additional information on the Hoys, see John Godwin, *Super-Psychic, The Incredible Dr. Hoy,* and Hoy's monthly newsletter, *ESP—According to Hoy.*

SAGE OF MOUNTAIN VIEW

For information on Harold Sherman, see Notes for Chapter 7. I interviewed his staff, associates, and colleagues—pyschic and other—at his July 1978 workshop, sponsored by ESP Research Associates Foundation, in St. Louis.

LET ME COUNT THE WAYS

EDUCATION: Lozanov's educational work is cited in Jeffrey Mishlove's *The Roots of Consciousness.*

PSI IN BUSINESS: See Notes for Chapter 2. For Al Pollard's think-tank business seminars, see James Grayson Bolen, "Al Pollard in Interview: A Successful Business Leader Reveals His Belief and Practice of ESP," in *Psychic,* December 1974.

A major theme in Harold Sherman's writing is "What you visualize is what you get" (see, for example, his *How to Picture What You Want, How to Make ESP Work for You).*

CREATIVITY: For cited research on creativity, see Charles Honorton,

"Creativity and Precognition Scoring Level," *Journal of Parapsychology,* 1967, 31, 29–42. For Thelma Moss's work, see her "ESP Effects in 'Artists' contrasted with 'Non-Artists'," *Journal of Parapsychology,* 1969, 3, 57–69. For her research findings, see Shafica Karagulla, *Breakthrough to Creativity.*

SPORTS: For cited research on Psi and sports, see Michael Murphy and Rhea White, *The Psychic Side of Sports.* See also Rhea White, "Sports and ESP," in *Psychic,* December, 1974.

DOWSING: On the use of the pendulum for sundry purposes, see Greg Nielson and Joseph Polansky, *Pendulum Power;* Hanna Kroeger, *The Pendulum, the Bible, and Your Survival* (privately published); Harvey Howells, *Dowsing for Everyone;* J. Scott Elliot, *One Man's Way;* Karl George, *Dowsing.*

NOTES FOR CHAPTER 9

FOREBEARS AND MEDIUMSHIP

For the forebears of contemporary parapsychology, see R. Laurence Moore, *In Search of White Crows—Spiritualism, Parapsychology and American Culture;* Martin Ebon, "A History of Parapsychology," in E. Mitchell, et al, *Psychic Exploration.* For information on renowned mediums and their controls, see Alan Vaughan, "Famous Western Sensitives," in Mitchell, *ibid.* For exposés of fraudulent mediumship, see M. Lamar Keene, *The Psychic Mafia.*

CAUTIONS

Information about misuse and potential dangers of Psi comes from personal conversation with Lafayette, California, clinical psychologist Allan Cohen; psychotherapist Howard Eisenberg in Toronto, Canada; and Orinda, California, psychiatrist Ernest Pecci, all of whom engage in psychic salvage work.

Are automatic writing, the Ouija board, the planchette, and such devices harmful? The American Society for Psychical Research responds to queries such as this with words from Louisa Rhine (*Exploring ESP and PK,* selections from ASPR Newsletter and other material, 1976):

> The answer is, that, taken in moderation, they probably are not. However, since the response does depend on dissociation, excessive use should not be encouraged. Also, occasionally an individual of extreme suggestibility may be involved, and if he is also quite naive about the implications, the results can be upsetting. The general verdict is that these automatic responses

may be intriguing to the uninformed, but may possibly have unhealthy effects on naive, suggestible persons.

Dangers of over-involvement with the occult are presented in Martin Ebon, *The Satan Trap.* On the hazards of automatic writing, see Ian Stevenson, "Some Comments on Automatic Writing," *Journal of the American Society for Psychical Research,* October 1978.

PSI: EDUCATION

In keeping with its principles and program of education in the psychic field, J. F. Kennedy University of Orinda, California, under the direction of its dean of general studies, Pascal Kaplan, has mounted some high-quality programs in the field. In March 1976, a symposium it sponsored at the University of California in Berkeley, "Perspectives on Death, Dying and . . . Beyond," brought together nurses, doctors, administrators, professionals in the health field, and others, to share insights and information related to dying. Dr. Elisabeth Kübler-Ross, parapsychologist Charles Tart, clinical psychologist Allan Cohen, psychiatrist Ernest Pecci, and psychologist Gina Cerminara were among those who contributed valuable input.

In January and February 1977, in a five-week program of lectures and seminars, in various locations in the San Francisco area, "Psi Search," J.F.K. University assembled psychics, healers, counselors, parapsychologists, educators, and scientists. It was here that I met and was able to interview, for the first time, many leaders in the Psi field. One series featured researcher/psychic teams, who discussed their joint projects and modus operandi: Kenneth Pelletier and Jack Schwarz, Ed May and Ingo Swann, Stanley Krippner and William Erwin, Thelma Moss and Olga Worrall, Mary Jane Ledyard and Ann Armstrong.

Two notable features marked this series of events. J. B. and Louisa Rhine came from Durham, North Carolina, as speakers, to be honored on the fiftieth anniversary of their pioneering entry into the field. The *Psi Search Exhibit,* a visual presentation of where Psi is today, directed and produced by Fran Hynds and Norma Bowles and circulated by the Smithsonian Institution Traveling Exhibit Services, was presented in the San Francisco Bay Area simultaneously.

SKEPTICISM, INCORPORATED

For the voice of the Committee for the Scientific Investigation of Claims of the Paranormal, see writings by its spokesmen, Paul Kurtz and "The Amazing Randi," in *The Humanist,* and in *The Skeptical Inquirer,* edited by Kendrick Frazier, formerly *The Zetetic.* See also the splinter journal, edited by former Committee co-chairman Marcello Truzzi, *The Zetetic*

Scholar. For a sample of the articulate skeptical barrage, see James Randi, *The Magic of Uri Geller.* Another magician, David Hoy, has also blasted Geller's "psychic" performances.

For a view of organized skepticism from Committee defector Truzzi, see Jerome Clark and J. Gordon Felton, "Crusade Against the Paranormal," Parts I and II, in *Fate,* September and October 1979. For the other side of the debate, see Theodore Rockwell, "Irrational Rationalists: A Critique of *The Humanist's* Crusade Against Parapsychology," *Journal of the American Society for Psychical Research,* 1978, 72, 23–34.

For an analytical view of the debate, see Paul D. Allison, *Social Aspects of Scientific Innovation: The Case of Parapsychology,* M.S. Sociology thesis at the University of Wisconsin, 1973, and P. D. Allison, "Experimental Parapsychology as a Rejected Science," *Sociological Review Monograph No. 27,* March 1979. See also the analysis of the controversy by two British sociologists: H. M. Collins and T. J. Pinch, *The Construction of the Paranormal.* The article that involved me with the Committee was Laile E. Bartlett, "What Do We Really Know About Psychic Phenomena?" in *Reader's Digest,* August 1977.

THE CLEVE BACKSTER CONTROVERSY

Backster is not the first to have posed the theory that all living things are sentient. Aristotle held that plants have souls; the Jain sect refuses to eat growing vegetables on the same grounds. Indian scientist Sir Jagadis Chandra Bose, in a lifetime study of plant response to stimuli, concluded that plants show many bio-electrical and physiological responses parallel to animals and humans. He published a series of books in London in the early 1900s describing his findings, *e.g.,* J. C. Bose, *The Nervous Mechanism of Plants, Life Movements in Plants* (6 vol.).

A parapsychologist I consulted who liked the early Backster research explained that the non-replication reports were better formulated than were the reports of those who claimed to have replicated them.

THE URI GELLER CONTROVERSY

For a summary of the play-by-play testimony, pro and con, see Roy Stemman and David Harvey, "The Rise and Fall of Uri Geller," in British science journal *Alpha,* March–April, 1980.

THE HARRIS/MATACIA CONTROVERSIES

The account of dowsing for General Patton in Africa, cited here, is from what Ralph Harris told me. A similar version appears in Christopher Bird, *The Divining Hand* and in numerous press accounts.

The Louis Matacia controversy is much the same. There are many more references to Matacia's feats than to Harris', including accounts in the Vietnam press (see Chapter 3). For details of Matacia's dowsing activities see Bird's *The Divining Hand.*

EVIDENCE OF PSI

SCIENTIFIC: For a generally available overview of the state of the art, see Edgar D. Mitchell, et al, *Psychic Exploration.* Specialists in each segment of the field—*i.e.,* clairvoyance, psychokinesis, and so on—present up-to-date information on the area. NOTE: The collection of articles is uneven; the more speculative chapters are considered by knowledgeable reviewers to be less dependable than the others. Readers are referred for guidance to reviews, *e.g.,* J. G. Pratt, *Journal of Parapsychology,* March 1975, and John Beloff, *Journal of the American Society for Psychical Research,* October 1975.

STATISTICAL: For the most hard-nosed and dependable report on Psi evidence to date, *i.e.,* statistical evidence, see Benjamin B. Wolman, *Handbook of Parapsychology.* Hard going, almost impossible for the layman, this is the most definitive statement we have.

PRAGMATIC: I know of no fuller treatment of the applications of Psi than Part I of this book. Most Psi books and discussions tack a few afterthought pages or a chapter of "possible uses" on at the end.

SPONTANEOUS: The many collections of spontaneous cases are major, continuing evidence of Psi; among them the 1884 *Census of Hallucinations;* E. Gurney, F. W. H. Myers, and F. Podmore's *Phantasms of the Living* (1886); G. N. M. Tyrrell, *Apparitions;* Louisa E. Rhine's collection of spontaneous cases; Ian Stevenson's census of cases suggestive of reincarnation. For me, one of the most convincing collections is the mail I have received from all over the world—accounts of personal experiences, requests for information and help. See Laile E. Bartlett, "The Ground Swell of Psychic Interest," *Human Behavior,* March 1978.

The ESP survey referred to was reported by John Palmer, "A Community Mail Survey of Psychic Experiences," *Journal of the American Society for Psychical Research,* 1979, 73, 221–251.

NOTES FOR CHAPTER 10

FREUD AND PSI

The controversial remark re Freud's interest in Psi appears in a letter from Freud to the English psychic researcher Hereward Carrington. It is reproduced in Ernest Jones, *The Life and Work of Sigmund Freud,* vol. 3. Freud later denied that he had written it, but research convinced the biographer that it was authentic; hence its inclusion. Hungarian psychoanalyst and psychic researcher Nandor Fodor produced a photographed copy of the original from his files.

The statement is controversial because of Freud's ambivalence about the psychic sphere. In his early years he was violently anti-Psi. It was the reason, in fact, for his break with Jung, as described in Jung's autobiography, *Memories, Dreams, Reflections.* That same autobiography notes, however, "It was some years before he [Freud] recognized the seriousness of parapsychology and recognized the actuality of 'occult' phenomena."

Freud not only joined both the British and American Societies for Psychical Research, but contributed material for psychic periodicals, *viz.* "A Note on the Unconscious in Psychoanalysis," in the British *Proceedings of the Society for Psychical Research,* 1912, 26, Part 66, 312–18. Freud's writing in the Psi field include "Dreams and Telepathy," *Imago,* 1922, 8, 1–22; "The Occult Significance of Dreams," *Imago,* 1925, 9, 234–8; "Psychoanalysis and Telepathy" in *Gesammelte Werke,* 1941, Vol. XVII, 25–40; "Dreams and the Occult" in *New Lectures on Psychoanalysis.* Despite his early hostility toward the subject, by 1921 Freud had privately admitted that there might be something to telepathy, and he even conducted a Psi experiment, with Hungarian analyst Sandor Ferenczi, which he did not wish to be made public.

THE FIRST FIFTY YEARS

For accounts of the emergence of parapsychology as a science, see Part I ("History of Parapsychology") of Wolman's *Handbook of Parapsychology,* which includes J. B. Rhine's "History of Experimental Studies at Duke University." See also P. D. Allison, *Social Aspects of Scientific Innovation: The Case of Parapsychology;* M. Ebon, "A History of Parapsychology," in Mitchell, et al, *Psychic Exploration.* For a readable inside view of the sequence and rationale of the Parapsychology Laboratory at Duke, see Louisa Rhine, *Psi: What Is It?* For Jephson research, see I. Jephson, "Evidence for Clairvoyance in Card-Guessing," *Proceedings of the American Society for Psychical Research,* 1928, 38, 223–71.

One source of information is the Rhines themselves—I, furnishing transportation for them when they were in California; they, returning the favor when I visited them in North Carolina (the last time I saw J. B. was when he drove me from their study to my motel in Durham).

THE FIELD: BIRD'S-EYE VIEW

The shift in the field, from attention to the "Big Four"—telepathy, clairvoyance, precognition and psychokinesis—to two categories, ESP and PK, is reflected in recent treatments; *e.g.,* Carroll B. Nash, *Science of Psi: ESP and PK.* See also the current information booklet, a collation distributed by the American Society for Psychical Research: "Exploring ESP and PK." Not long hence, there may no longer be a separation of Psi into categories; it may be considered a single phenomenon.

As for the unsatisfactory label "parapsychology," Norma Bowles and Fran Hynds note in *Psi Search:* "It is ironic that a branch of science dedicated to the investigation of an unknown means of communication, should be given a particularly uncommunicative name. Some people even think that the term refers to a psychologist's assistant, in the same way that the term 'paralegal' often refers to a lawyer's assistant."

WHAT WE KNOW

The definitive presentation of what we know about Psi is the collection of materials by working parapsychologists themselves: Benjamin B. Wolman, *Handbook of Parapsychology.* See, in Wolman especially, Rhea White, "Suggested Readings in Parapsychology." For a broad but less technical presentation, see Mitchell, et al, *Psychic Exploration.* (See Qualifications, however, in Notes for Chapter 9.) A concise, illustrated treatment of Psi for the layperson is Norma Bowles and Fran Hynds, *Psi Search.* In consultation with researchers, these reporters carefully separated the findings of systematic laboratory investigation from speculation, one part of the book dealing with what is now known about Psi, another with speculation and search. For information on the place of spontaneous cases, see Louisa E. Rhine, "Research Methods with Spontaneous Cases" in the Wolman *Handbook.*

TELEPATHY. For the plethysmograph experiments, see E. D. Dean and C. B. Nash, "Coincident, Plethysmograph Results Under Controlled Conditions" in *Journal of the Society for Psychical Research,* 1967, 44, 1–13. See also E. D. Dean, "The Plethysmograph as an Indicator of ESP," *ibid.,* 1962, 41, 351–352.

For Maimonides experiments, see M. Ullman and S. Krippner, "Dream Studies and Telepathy: An Experimental Approach," *Parapsychological Monographs,* 12, 1970; S. Krippner and M. Ullman, "Telepathy and Dreams: A Controlled Experiment with Electroencephalogram-Electro-oculogram monitoring," *Journal of Nervous and Mental Diseases,* 1970, 151, 394–403. For a summary of Maimonides dream research, see S. Krippner, "Perchance to Dream Telepathically," in his *Song of the Siren,* and Ullman, Krippner, and Vaughan, *Dream Telepathy.*

For psychiatric and therapists' input, see C. G. Jung, *Memories, Dreams, Reflections;* B. E. Schwarz, "Possible Telesomatic Reactions" in *Journal of the Medical Society of New Jersey,* 1967, 64; and B. Schwarz, *Parent-Child Telepathy.* Ullman's remarks cited in this chapter are from M. Ullman, "Psychiatry and Psi," *Newsletter of the American Society for Psychical Research,* 1974, 21.

CLAIRVOYANCE. For the Pearce-Pratt series, see Wolman, *Handbook;* Mitchell, et al, *Psychic Exploration;* Bowles and Hynds, *Psi Search,* and so on. For the Colorado experiments, see Mitchell's book.

For the Puthoff/Targ "remote viewing" experiment with coordinates, see R. Targ and H. Puthoff, *Mind Reach: Scientists Look at Psychic Ability.* For Ingo Swann's accounts of the experiments, see Swann, *To Kiss Earth Goodbye.* For Puthoff and Targ's report of remote viewing experiments with several subjects, see H. E. Puthoff and R. Targ, "A Perceptual Channel for Information Transfer Over Kilometer Distances: Historical Perspective and Recent Research," in *Proceedings of the I.E.E.E.* (Institute of Electrical and Electronic Engineers), March 1976, 3, 329–54.

For Stanford Research Institute experiments with Patrick Price, see Targ and Puthoff, *Mind Reach.*

PRECOGNITION. For Helmut Schmidt's precognition experiments, see Wolman, *Handbook,* and Mitchell, et al, *Psychic Exploration.* For Erlendur Haraldsson's replications, see "Subject Selection in a Machine Precognition Test," *Journal of Parapsychology,* 1970, 34, 3.

For Bessent experiments, see above references on dream telepathy by Ullman and Krippner, and H. B. Greenhouse, *Premonitions: A Leap into the Future.*

PSYCHOKINESIS. For Swann thermistor experiments, see G. R. Schmeidler, "PK Effects upon Continuously Recorded Temperature," *Journal of the American Society for Psychical Research,* 1973, 67, 324–40; Bowles and Hynds, *Psi Search.* For Swann's view of the experiment, see Swann, *To Kiss Earth Goodbye.*

On the "Geller Effect," see Hans Bender, "The Geller Effects," *Zeitschrift für Parapsychologie und Grenzegebiete der Psychologie,* series 1974–1976.

Hasted's latest work on metal-bending was presented at the 1979 Edinburgh meetings of the British Society for Psychical Research: "Physical Features of Paranormal Metal-Bending."

For Forwald's PK work, see Haakon Forwald, *Mind, Matter and Gravitation,* Parapsychological Monographs, no. 11, Parapsychology Foundation, 1969; Wolman, *Handbook;* Mitchell, et al, *Psychic Exploration.*

For all PK experiments associated with healing, see Notes for Chapter 4.

For the PK phenomenon of thoughtography, see Notes for Chapter 7.

HOW WE KNOW

For Psi measurement and controls, see C. B. Nash, "Techniques of Measuring Psi," in his *Science of Psi;* comments on "large numbers theory" by Arthur Koestler, "The ABC's of ESP" in his *The Roots of Coincidence;* Donald S. Burdick and Edward F. Kelly, "Statistical Methods in Parapsychological Research" and its bibliography, in Wolman, *Handbook*. For parapsychological methods, see Gertrude R. Schmeidler, "Methods for Controlled Research on ESP and PK" and its bibliography, in the Wolman *Handbook*.

BEYOND PROOF

For an account of the Sherman/Wilkins telepathy experiment, see H. Sherman and H. Wilkins, *Thoughts Through Space*. For cloud-chamber experiments, see E. Cerutti, *Mystic with the Healing Hands*. For Swann's psychokinetic influence on shielded instruments, see Puthoff and Targ, "Psychic Research in Modern Physics" in Mitchell, et al, *Psychic Exploration*. For Swann's description of the experiment, see *To Kiss Earth Goodbye*.

The "decline effect" is discussed in all surveys of the field—*e.g.*, Wolman and Mitchell—as is Schmeidler's "sheep/goat effect."

For children and ESP, see Berthold Schwarz, *Parent-Child Telepathy;* Samuel H. Young, *Psychic Children;* A. Tanous and K. F. Donnelly, *Is Your Child Psychic?;* D. T. Burlingham, "Child Analysis and the Mother," *Psychoanalytic Quarterly,* 1935, 4, 69–92; H. Deutsch, "Occult Processes Occurring During Psychoanalysis" in *Imago,* 1926, 12, 12, 418–33.

For Psi in animals, see Robert L. Morris, "Parapsychology, Biology and Anpsi," in Wolman, *Handbook;* and L. Rhine, "ESP and PK in Animals" in *Psi: What Is It?*. For animal predictions, see Goodman, *We Are the Earthquake Generation*.

For Psi and altered states of consciousness, see Charles Tart, ed., *Altered States of Consciousness;* Theodore X. Barber, ed., *Advances in Altered States of Consciousness and Human Potentialities;* Tart, "Altered States of Consciousness and Psi" in *Psi: Scientific Studies of the Psychic Realm*. For the Ganzfeld technique, see Wolman, *Handbook;* Bowles and Hynds, *Psi Search*.

All major source books discuss negative Psi or "Psi missing," *e.g.:* Wolman's *Handbook*.

WHAT WE DON'T KNOW

For theories and explanations of psychic phenomena, see Part IX of Wolman, *Handbook:* "Parapsychological Models and Theories." For information on Gurvitch, see S. Ostrander and L. Schroeder, *Psychic Discoveries Behind the Iron Curtain*. For an elaboration of physicist Fritjof Capra's theory, see his *The Tao of Physics*. For Lawrence LeShan's theory, see his *The Medium, The Mystic and the Physicist*. For more on William A. Tiller's perspective, see "New Fields, New Laws" in J. White and S. Krippner, *Future Science*.

Re the problem of replication, see John Palmer's explanation of why replication does not work with parapsychology ("a probabilistic science") as it does with traditional fields of inquiry ("non-probabilistic science"), in his presidential address, Parapsychology Association, Moraga, Ca., August 1979. Based on statistical principles, probabilistic models explain the capriciousness of Psi phenomena.

Most Psi source books touch on problems of the "experimenter effect"; e.g., Rhea A. White, "The Influence of Experimenter Motivation, Attitudes, and Methods of Handling Subjects of Psi Test Results" in Wolman, *Handbook*.

For information on experiments with "random number generators" or "random event generators," see Rex G. Stanford, "Experimental Psychokinesis" in Wolman, *Handbook;* Bowles and Hynds, *Psi Search.* For Helmut Schmidt's own work, see his "Tests with a High Speed Random Number Generator," *Journal of Parapsychology*, 1973, 37, 105, 118, and "Comparison of PK Action on Two Different Random Number Generators," *Journal of Parapsychology*, 1974, 38, 47–55. See also H. Schmidt "Psychokinesis" in Mitchell, et al, *Psychic Exploration.*

NOTES FOR CHAPTER 11

In addition to references cited in the chapter, see D. Scott Rogo, "Apparitions, Hauntings and Poltergeists" in Mitchell, et al, *Psychic Exploration*. For Schmeidler's research, see G. Schmeidler, "Quantitative Investigation of a Haunted House," *Journal of the American Society for Psychical Research*, 1966, 60, 137–149. For the Watkins experiments, see R. L. Morris, "An Experimental Approach to the Survival Problem," *Theta*, 33 and 34, 1971 and 1972. Bozzano's research appeared as Ernesto Bozzano, *Les Phénomènes de Hantise*. The work of Hornell Hart appeared as Hornell Hart and Associates, "Six Theories about Apparitions," *Proceedings of the Society for Psychical Research*, 1956, 50, 153–239, and H. Hart, "Scientific Survival Research" in *International Journal of Parapsychology*, 1967, 9. Raymond Bayless' thinking appears in his *Animal Ghosts*.

W. G. Roll's theory is published as "The Psi Field," *Proceedings of the Parapsychological Association*, 1957–1964, 1; the case of the Florida mystery, in his *The Poltergeist*. The full story of the "Poltergeist Prodigy" is told by Matthew Manning himself and the British parapsychologists Peter Bander and A. R. G. Owen, who investigated him, in *The Link*. See also: A. R. G. Owen, *Can We Explain the Poltergeist?* and L. E. Rhine, *Mind Over Matter, Psychokinesis*.

AURAS AND HUMAN ENERGY

Popular literature is full of discussion of auras and aural energy and their meanings. For information on one aura-measuring device, see M.

Layne, ed., *The Cameron Aurameter.* For Hiroshi Motoyama's experiments, see his series of reports released by his Institute of Religious Psychology, 4–11–1 Inokashira, Mitaka-shi, Tokyo, Japan 181. I visited him, his machines, and his staff in his Tokyo laboratory in the spring of 1978. See Ann Nietzke, "Portrait of an Aura Reader," *Human Behavior,* February 1979, re Rosalyn Lee Bruyere.

Information on Kirlian photography is in all Psi source books. See Thelma Moss, "Psychic Research in the Soviet Union" in Mitchell, et al, *Psychic Exploration.* See also Thelma Moss, *The Probability of the Impossible.* For leading practitioners, see Ostrander and Schroeder, *Psychic Discoveries Behind the Iron Curtain,* and Gris and Dick, *The New Soviet Psychic Discoveries.*

ASTROLOGY AND PSI

David Womack set out to disprove the evil practice of astrology. His researches and findings are recounted in *Twelve Signs, Twelve Sons.* Parapsychologist Stanley Krippner's investigation into astrology—his own and that of others—is summarized in "By the Light of the Moon" in his *Song of the Siren.* See also S. Krippner, A. Becker, M. Cavallo, and B. Washburn in "Electrophysiological Studies of ESP in Dreams: Lunar Cycle Differences in Eighty Telepathy Sessions," *Human Dimensions,* Fall 1972; S. Krippner and R. Nell, "Clairvoyance and the Lunar Cycle," *International Journal of Paraphysics,* 1973, 7, 180–86.

Re planetary alignments, see J. Gribbin and S. H. Plagemann, *The Jupiter Effect.*

For the Gauquelin work, see M. Gauquelin, "Terrestrial Modulations of the Daily Cycle of Birth," *Journal of Interdisciplinary Cycle Research,* 1971, 2, 211–17, and "Possible Planetary Effects at the Time of Birth of 'Successful' Professionals: An Experimental Control," *ibid.,* 1972, 3, 381–9.

DIVINING

The Psi/I Ching research cited here is L. Rubin and C. Honorton, "Separating the Yins from the Yangs," *Proceedings of the Parapsychological Association,* 1971, 8, 6–7. Information on Tarot card reading is from D. Hoy, *The Meaning of Tarot.*

MISCELLANY

The main impetus to interest in pyramids came from Ostrander and Schroeder, "Pyramid Power and the Riddle of the Razor Blades" in their *Psychic Discoveries Behind the Iron Curtain.*

The Bermuda Triangle Mystery is described in Dykshoorn, *My Pass port.* I have discussed the Triangle phenomenon with psychics Dykshoorn and Bob Ater, both of whom attribute the effects to natural causes.

For a detailed report on the First International Congress of Unidentified Flying Objects, at Acapulco in 1977, see Marcia Seligson, "We Are Not Alone," *New West,* November 7, 1977. The most authoritative information of UFOs is probably that of J. Allen Hynek, *The UFO Experience, A Scientific Inquiry.* The topic is not mentioned in most parapsychology source books.

As for possession, all references in Wolman's *Handbook of Parapsychology* are made in the context of old-time beliefs, or primitive anthropological frameworks.

NOTES FOR CHAPTER 12

Sources for this chapter are the following:

1. Personal contact and interviews, sometimes in the subjects' own homes, over two or three days; sometimes at work places and laboratories.
2. Contact with relatives and close associates of the psychics.
3. Autobiographies, biographies, and other published material.
4. Combinations of the above.

Among those I have talked with personally—a number of them many times, often with taped interviews, telephone and correspondence follow-up, are the following:

Aron and Doris Abrahamsen	Reg and Kit McHugh
Dorothy Allison	Del St. Clair
Bob Ater	Hilgard Schmidt
Etel DeLoach	Jack Schwarz
M. B. Dykshoorn	Harold and Martha Sherman
Gen. J. Scott Elliot (dowser)	Thomas Sherman (dowser)
Uri Geller	Enid Smithett (dowser)
David and Shirley Hoy	Ingo Swann
Peter Hurkos	Alex Tanous
Beverly Jaegers	Alan Vaughan
Jack Livingston (dowser)	Ron Warmoth
Gordon MacLean (dowser)	Olga Worrall

Of the many others I have read about, but not met, Edgar Cayce is the most important. Information about him I obtained from his biographer, Gina Cerminara, associates and relatives, particularly his business successor-son, Hugh Lynn Cayce, and his grandson, Thomas Charles Cayce, now president of the Association for Research and Enlightenment, at Virginia Beach, Virginia—Cayce headquarters. Two basic sources for Cayce are the biography by Thomas Sugrue, *The Story of Edgar Cayce* (in some editions, *There is a River*), and the analysis of Cayce's ties with reincarnation, G. Cerminara, *Many Mansions: The Edgar Cayce Story of Reincarnation*. (Any of the voluminous materials concerning Cayce may be obtained from the Association for Research and Enlightenment, Atlantic Avenue and 67th St., Virginia Beach, Virginia 23451.)

Reference to psychics and their abilities, in professional journals, other parapsychological literature, and the popular press, is too voluminous to cite. Major biographical references, including autobiographies and "as told to's," for Dorothy Allison, David Bubar, Gerard Croiset, Jeane Dixon, M. B. Dykshoorn, Arthur Ford, Eileen Garrett, Rosalind Heywood, Olaf Jonsson, Peter Hurkos, Gladys Osborne Leonard, Ernesto Montgomery, Ena Twigg, and others, are listed in the Bibliography. See also G. Schmeidler, "The Psychic Personality," in E. Mitchell, et al, *Psychic Exploration*. For biographical information re leading sensitives of the past, see: L. Shepard, ed., *Encyclopedia of Occultism and Parapsychology*.

NOTES FOR CHAPTER 13

SURVIVAL RESEARCH

The old interest in the study of human survival is with us once again—now as a burgeoning subdivision of parapsychological endeavor. Along with the old familiar approaches, such as the study of mediums, controls, and their messages, are some new ones. Major lines of current inquiry are the following:

- *out-of-body research* (OOB studies)
  spontaneous; induced (chemical, electrical); at clinical death; in normal states; in the lab.

- *death-bed research*
  observations at the moment of death; cross-cultural studies

- *spirit communication*
  auditory: unexplained human sounds and voices; recorded taped voices; "telephone calls from the dead"
  visual: apparitions; spirit photos; automatic writing
  tactile: e.g., something brushing past, a cold wave
  other effects: e.g., stopped clocks, animal reactions

- *reincarnation research*
   hypnotic regression; multi-cultural cases; other-life memories, especially children's.

CASES

Prakash/Nirmal is from Ian Stevenson, *Twenty Cases Suggestive of Reincarnation.*

The woman in the operating room is from Raymond Moody, *Life After Life.*

ON BREAKING THE DEATH TABOO

See Elisabeth Kübler-Ross, *On Death and Dying,* and the subsequent flood of survival features and articles in the popular press, *e.g.,* Charles Panati, "Is There Life After Death?," *Family Circle,* November 1976; Kenneth L. Woodward, "There Is Life After Death," *McCall's,* August 1976; Daniel Goleman, "We Are Breaking the Silence About Death," *Psychology Today,* September 1976; and special issue on death and dying: "Death, the Last Taboo: Dying in America," *New Age,* November 1977.

OUT-OF-BODY RESEARCH

See Sylvan Muldoon and Hereward Carrington's books on the projection of the astral body. For a later version of personal out-of-body study, see Robert Monroe, *Journeys Out of the Body.* See also Charles T. Tart, "A Psychophysiological Study of Out-of-the-Body Experiences in a Selected Subject," *Journal of the American Society for Psychical Research,* 1968, 62, 3–27; and C. Tart, "Out-of-the-Body Experiences" in Mitchell, et al, *Psychic Exploration,* for Tart's experiment with Miss Z.

The out-of-body experiences with Ingo Swann are described in Tart, "Out-of-the-Body Experiences," in Mitchell book, *ibid.* See also Karlis Osis and J. Mitchell, "Physiological Correlates of Reported Out-of-the-Body Experiences," *Journal of the American Society for Psychical Research,* 1977, 49. A full discussion of Swann's OOB experiences, laboratory and spontaneous, is included in his autobiography, *To Kiss Earth Goodbye.* Alex Tanous relates his OOB experiences at length in his autobiography, *Beyond Coincidence.* Karlis Osis' innovative experiment with Tanous, which I witnessed at ASPR, was presented in his paper at the 1979 Parapsychology Association meetings: "Kinetic Effects at the Ostensible Location of an O.B. Projection During Perceptual Testing."

THE ROUND TRIP

See Raymond Moody, *Life After Life,* and *Reflections on Life After Life.*

AT THE MOMENT OF DEATH

See Karlis Osis and Erlendur Haraldsson, *At the Hour of Death;* and K. Osis, *Deathbed Observations by Physicians and Nurses.*

SPIRIT COMMUNICATION

The research on telephone messages from the dead is presented in D. Scott Rogo and Raymond Bayless, *Phone Calls from the Dead.* A detailed account of the remarkable Patience Worth phenomenon is reported in Naomi Hintze and J. Gaither Pratt, *The Psychic Realm—What Can You Believe?*

Re "ghosty pictures" see Jule Eisenbud, "Psychic Photography and Thoughtography" in Mitchell, et al, *Psychic Exploration.*

REINCARNATION

Comment on the endless wheel of existence is from John B. Noss, *Man's Religions,* fifth edition. See Ian Stevenson, "Reincarnation: Field Studies and Theoretical Issues," in Wolman, *Handbook,* and Stevenson's *Twenty Cases Suggestive of Reincarnation.*

LIFE AFTER LIFE?

For treatments of survival research and problems related thereto, see Allen Gauld, "Discarnate Survival" in Wolman, *Handbook,* and William Roll, "Survival Research: Problems and Possibilities," in Mitchell, et al, *Psychic Exploration.* For the relationship between parapsychological research and survival, see Nils Jacobson, *Life Without Death?*

See also the quarterly, *Theta,* A Journal for Research on the Question of Survival After Death.

NOTES FOR CHAPTER 14

CURRENT PARAPSYCHOLOGICAL RESOURCES

For an overview of parapsychology institutions and organizations, educational opportunities, informational facilities, and Psi publications, see Rhea A. White, "Parapsychology Today" in Edgar Mitchell, et al, *Psychic Exploration.*

COINCIDENCE AND ANOMALIES

For one holographic explanation, see Karl Pribram in Globus, Gordon, et al, *Consciousness and the Brain.*

On synchronicity, see C. G. Jung, *Synchronicity: An Acausal Connecting*

Principle; Arthur Koestler, *The Roots of Coincidence;* Alan Vaughan, *Patterns of Prophecy,* and *Incredible Coincidence.*

As for my elephant: A skeptic might suggest that I could have seen a poster for the circus and subliminally recorded it, to draw on later. Had I been asked at the time, I believe I would have denied it. But this is the crux of the problems we face: too many possible factors and too little knowledge of the tricky workings of the mind—the reason, of course, that we turn to the less contaminated events of the laboratory.

See J. Palmer's explanation for Psi phenomena in Notes for Chapter 10.

ON THE FUTURE OF PSI

Re Russian Psi research activity, see Ostrander and Schroeder, *Psychic Discoveries Behind the Iron Curtain;* Gris and Dick, *The New Soviet Psychic Discoveries;* R. A. McConnell, "Parapsychology in the U.S.S.R.," *Journal of Parapsychology,* 1975, 39, 129–134. Stanley Krippner, "Mission to Moscow" in his *Song of the Siren;* Thelma Moss, "Psychic Research in the Soviet Union," in Mitchell, *Psychic Exploration;* J. G. Pratt, "Soviet Research in Parapsychology" in Wolman, *Handbook.*

For Michael Rossman's analysis, see "On Some Matters of Concern in Psychic Research," in his *New Age Blues: On the Politics of Consciousness.*

THE NEW PARADIGM

For background on paradigm shifts, see the seminal treatment of the subject: Thomas Kuhn, *The Structure of Scientific Revolutions.* For Psi and transitions to the new paradigm, see Edgar Mitchell, "Introduction" and "Conclusion" to his *Psychic Exploration.* On new/old view of the universe, see F. Capra, *The Tao of Physics;* G. Zukav, *The Dancing Wu Li Masters;* L. LeShan, *The Medium, The Mystic and the Physicist;* P. Kaplan, Ph.D. thesis, Harvard University, *Toward a Theology of Consciousness: A Study in the Logic and Structure of Esotericism.*

For perspectives on the new paradigm, see Center for the Study of Social Policy, Stanford Research Institute, *Changing Images of Man;* Willis Harman, "The Social Implications of Psychic Research," in Mitchell, et al, *Psychic Exploration;* Willis Harman, *An Incomplete Guide to The Future.*

Bibliography

NOTE: For an excellent review of books in the field, see "Suggested Readings in Parapsychology" compiled by Rhea A. White, in Benjamin B. Wolman, *Handbook of Parapsychology,* New York: Van Nostrand Reinhold, 1977. Listings are annotated, and categorized as to subject matter; *e.g.,* General, Historical, Experimental Parapsychology, Spontaneous Psi, and so on.

Though space precludes journal references in the following listing, selected bibliographies of introductory materials, selections for young people, and so on, can be obtained from the American Society for Psychical Research, 5 West 73 St., New York, New York 10023. For a small charge a bibliography for instructors and students can be obtained, compiled by Marian L. Nester and Arthur S. T. O'Keefe. It reviews the following journals from January 1970 through July 1979:

Journal of the American Society for Psychical Research
Journal of the [British] *Society for Psychical Research*
Journal of Parapsychology
Parapsychology Review
Research in Parapsychology (Abstracts and papers from annual conventions of the Parapsychological Association, 1973 through 1978)

Allison, Paul D., *Experimental Parapsychology as a Rejected Science, Sociological Review Monograph,* No. 27, March 1979.
———, *Social Aspects of Scientific Innovation: The Case of Parapsychology,* M.S. thesis, University of Wisconsin, 1973.
Anson, Jay, *The Amityville Horror: A True Story,* New York: Prentice-Hall, 1977.
Barber, Theodore X., ed., *Advances in Altered States of Consciousness and Human Potentialities,* vol. I, New York: Psychological Dimensions, 1976.
Bayless, Raymond, *Animal Ghosts,* New Hyde Park, NY: University Books, 1970.
Beasse, Pierre, *A New and Rational Treatise of Dowsing According to the Methods of Physical Radiesthesie* (translated from the French, 1938), Mokelumne Hill, CA: Heath Research, 1975.
Bird, Christopher, *The Divining Hand—The 500-Year-Old Mystery of Dowsing,* New York: Dutton, 1979.
Bloomfield, Harold H., and Robert B. Kory, *The Holistic Way to Health and Happiness* (A New Approach to Complete Lifetime Wellness), New York: Simon and Schuster, 1978.
Bond, Frederick Bligh, *The Gate of Remembrance,* Oxford, Eng.: B. H. Blackwell, 1918.

Bose, Jagadis Chandra, *Life Movement in Plants*, 6 vols., London: Longmans, vol. I–V, 1918; vol. VI, 1931.

————, *The Nervous Mechanism of Plants*, London: Longman's, 1918.

Bowles, Norma, and Fran Hynds, *Psi Search, The New Investigation of Psychic Phenomena That Separates Fact from Speculation*, San Francisco: Harper and Row, 1978.

Boyd, Doug, *Rolling Thunder*, New York: Random House, 1974.

Bozzano, Ernesto, *Les Phénomènes de Hantise*, Paris: Alcan, 1920.

Brown, Barbara B., *New Mind/New Body*, New York: Harper and Row, 1974.

————, *Stress and the Art of Biofeedback*, New York: Harper and Row, 1977.

Brown, Michael H., *PK: A Report on the Power of Psychokinesis*, New York: Blauvelt, Steiner Books, 1976.

Browning, Norma Lee, *The Psychic World of Peter Hurkos*, Garden City, NY: Doubleday, 1970.

Capra, Fritjof, *The Tao of Physics: An Exploration of the Parallels Between Modern Physics and Eastern Mysticism*, New York: Bantam Books (1975), 1977.

Cayce, Edgar Evans, and Hugh Lynn Cayce, *The Outer Limits of Edgar Cayce's Power*, New York: Bell Publishing Company, 1971.

Center for the Study of Social Policy, Stanford Research Institute, *Changing Images of Man*, Policy Research Report 4, Menlo Park, CA, 1974.

Cerminara, Gina, *Many Mansions: The Edgar Cayce Story of Reincarnation*, New York: Signet (1950), 1967.

Cerutti, Edwina, *Mystic with the Healing Hands* (The Life Story of Olga Worrall), New York: Harper and Row, 1977.

Cocciardi, Carol, Cocciardi, Mary and Karen and Linda Erickson, eds., *The Psychic Yellow Pages*, Saratoga, CA: Out of the Sky, 1977.

Coddington, Mary, *In Search of the Healing Energy*, New York: Warner Destiny Books, 1978.

Collins, H. M., and T. J. Pinch, *The Construction of the Paranormal*, Social Studies Centre, University of Bath, Somerset, Eng., BA2 7AY, 1976.

Cousins, Norman, *Anatomy of an Illness*, New York: Norton, 1979.

Cox, Robert V., and Kenneth L. Peiffer, Jr., *Missing Person*, Harrisburg, PA: Stackpole Books, 1978.

Dean, Douglas, John Mihalasky, Sheila Ostrander, and Lynn Schroeder, *Executive ESP*, Englewood Cliffs, NJ: Prentice-Hall, 1974.

DeFrance, Henry, *The Elements of Dowsing*, London: G. Bell and Sons, Ltd., 1967.

Dixon, Jeane, *My Life and Prophecies*, New York: Morrow, 1969.

Dykshoorn, M. B., and Russell H. Felton, *My Passport Says Clairvoyant*, New York: Hawthorn Books, 1974.

Ebon, Martin, *The Satan Trap*, Garden City, NY: Doubleday, 1976.

Eisenbud, Jule, *The World of Ted Serios*, New York: Morrow, 1967.

Elliot, J. Scott, *Dowsing: One Man's Way*, Jersey, Channel Islands: Neville Spearman, 1977.

Finch, W. J., *The Pendulum and Possession*, Sedona, AZ: Esoteric Publishers, 1971.

Forwald, Haakon, *Mind, Matter and Gravitation*, New York: Parapsychological Monographs, no. 11, Parapsychology Foundation, 1969.

Fosshage, James L., and Paul Olson, eds., *Healing Implications for Psychotherapy*, New York: Human Sciences Press, 1978.

Frank, Jerome D., *Persuasion and Healing, A Comparative Study of Psychotherapy* (Revised Edition), Baltimore: Johns Hopkins University Press, 1973.

Fukurai, Tomokichi, *Clairvoyance and Thoughtography*, London: Rider, 1931.
Fuller, Elizabeth, *My Search for the Ghost of Flight 401*, New York: Berkley Medallion Books, 1978.
Fuller, John G., *The Airmen Who Would Not Die*, New York: G. P. Putnam's Sons, 1979.
_____, *Arigó: Surgeon of the Rusty Knife*, New York: Thomas Y. Crowell Company, 1974.
_____, *The Ghost of Flight 401*, New York: Berkley (Putnam), 1976.
Garrett, Eileen J., *Many Voices: The Autobiography of a Medium*, New York: G. P. Putnam's Sons, 1968.
Geller, Uri, *My Story*, New York: Praeger, 1975.
Godwin, John, *Super-Psychic: The Incredible Dr. Hoy*, New York: Pocket Books, 1974.
Goodman, Jeffrey, *Psychic Archaeology*, New York: Berkley (Putnam), 1977.
_____, *We Are the Earthquake Generation—Where and When the Catastrophes Will Strike*, New York: Seaview Books, 1978.
Globus, Gordon, *et al.*, *Consciousness and the Brain*, New York: Plenum Publishing, 1976.
Green, Elmer and Alyce, *Beyond Biofeedback*, New York: Delta Books, 1977.
Greenhouse, Herbert B., *Premonitions: A Leap into the Future*, New York: Bernard Geis Associates, 1971.
Gribbin, J., and S. H. Plagemann, *The Jupiter Effect*, New York: Walker, 1974.
Gris, Henry, and William Dick, *The New Soviet Psychic Discoveries*, Englewood Cliffs, NJ: Prentice-Hall, 1978.
Gurney, E., F. W. H. Myers, and F. Podmore, *Phantasms of the Living* (1886), Gainesville, FL: Scholars Facsimiles and Reprints, 1970.
Hanna, Thomas, *The Body of Life*, New York: Knopf, 1980.
Harman, Willis W., *An Incomplete Guide to the Future*, San Francisco: San Francisco Book Company, 1976.
Hastings, Arthur C., James Fadiman, James S. Gordon, eds., *Health for the Whole Person*, the Complete Guide to Holistic Medicine, Westview Press, Boulder, CO, 1980.
Haynes, Renée, *The Hidden Springs—An Enquiry into Extra-Sensory Perception*, Boston: Little, Brown and Company (1961), 1972.
_____, *The Seeing Eye, The Seeing I*, London: Hutchinson, 1976.
Herrigel, Eugene, *Zen and the Art of Archery*, New York: McGraw-Hill, 1964.
Heywood, Rosalind, *ESP: A Personal Memoir*, New York: Dutton, 1964.
Hintze, Naomi, and J. G. Pratt, *The Psychic Realm—What Can You Believe?* New York: Random House, 1975.
Hitching, Francis, *Dowsing: The Psi Connection*, Garden City, NY: Doubleday, 1978.
Holroyd, Stuart, *Psi and the Consciousness Explosion*, New York: Taplinger, 1977.
Hoy, David, *The Meaning of Tarot*, Nashville: Aurora Publications, 1971.
Howells, Harvey, *Dowsing for Everyone, Adventures and Instruction in the Art of Modern Dowsing*, Brattleboro, VT: Stephen Green Press, 1979.
Hynek, J. Allen, *The UFO Experience: A Scientific Inquiry*, New York: Ballantine Books, 1972.
Jacobson, Scott, *Dorothy Allison: A Psychic Story*, New York: Harcourt Brace Jovanovich, 1980.
Jones, Ernest, *The Life and Work of Sigmund Freud*, 3 vols, New York: Basic Books, 1957.
Jung, Carl Gustav, *Memories, Dreams, Reflections*, New York: Pantheon, 1963.

————, *Synchronicity: An Acausal Connecting Principle,* Princeton, NJ: Princeton University Press, 1973.

Kaplan, Pascal, *Toward a Theology of Consciousness: A Study in the Logic and Structure of Esotericism,* Ph.D. thesis, Harvard University, Cambridge, MA, April 1976.

Karagulla, Shafica, *Breakthrough to Creativity, Your Higher Sense Perception,* Marina del Rey, CA: DeVorss and Company (1967), 1978.

Kaslof, Leslie J., *Wholistic Dimensions in Healing: A Resource Guide,* Garden City, NY: Doubleday, 1978.

Keene, M. Lamar, as told to Allen Spraggett, *The Psychic Mafia,* New York: Dell, 1976.

Kingston, Kenny, as told to Brenda Marshall, *Sweet Spirits,* Chicago: Contemporary Books, 1978.

Kinnear, W., ed., *Thought as Energy,* Los Angeles: Science of Mind, 1975.

Koestler, Arthur, *The Roots of Consciousness: An Excursion into Parapsychology,* New York: Random House, 1972.

Krippner, Stanley, *Song of the Siren: A Parapsychological Odyssey,* New York: Harper and Row, 1975.

Krippner, Stanley, and Alberto Villoldo, *The Realms of Healing,* Millbrae, CA: Celestial Arts, 1976.

Kroeger, Hanna, *The Pendulum, The Bible, and Your Survival,* privately published, 1973.

Kübler-Ross, Elisabeth, *Death, the Final Stage of Growth,* Englewood Cliffs, NJ: Prentice-Hall, 1975.

————, *On Death and Dying,* New York: Macmillan, 1969.

————, *To Live Until We Say Goodbye,* Englewood Cliffs, NJ: Prentice-Hall, 1978.

Kuhn, Thomas S., *The Structure of Scientific Revolutions,* Chicago: University of Chicago Press (1962), 1970.

Layne, Meade, ed., *The Cameron Aurameter,* Vista, CA: Borderland Sciences Research Foundation (1952), 1974.

LeShan, Lawrence, *How to Meditate,* New York: Bantam, 1974.

————, *The Medium, The Mystic, and The Physicist: Toward a General Theory of the Paranormal,* New York: Ballantine (1966), 1976.

Linedecker, Clifford, *Psychic Spy,* Garden City, NY: Doubleday, 1976.

Lord, Walter, *A Night To Remember,* New York: Henry Holt, 1955.

Lynch, James J., *The Broken Heart: The Medical Consequences of Loneliness,* New York: Basic Books, 1977.

MacLean, Gordon, *A Field Guide to Dowsing: How to Practice the Ancient Art Today,* Danville, VT: American Society of Dowsers, 1971.

Manning, Matthew, *The Link—Matthew Manning's Own Story of His Extraordinary Gifts,* New York: Holt, Rinehart and Winston, 1974.

Meek, George W., *Healers and the Healing Process,* Wheaton, IL: Theosophical Publishing House, 1977.

Mermet, Abbé, *Principles and Practice of Radiesthesia,* London: Stuart and Watkins, 1959.

Mishlove, Jeffrey, *The Roots of Consciousness—Psychic Liberation Through History, Science and Experience,* New York: Random House, 1975.

Mitchell, Edgar D., and others, John White, ed., *Psychic Exploration: A Challenge for Science,* New York: Putnam 1974.

Monroe, Robert, *Journeys Out of the Body,* Garden City, NY: Doubleday, 1971.

Montgomery, Ruth, *A Gift of Prophecy: The Phenomenal Jeane Dixon,* New York: Bantam Books, 1965.

Moody, Raymond, *Life After Life*, Harrisburg, PA: Stackpole Books, 1976.
———, *Reflections on Life After Life*, New York: Bantam/Mockingbird, 1977.
Moore, R. Lawrence, *In Search of White Crows: Spiritualism, Parapsychology and American Culture*, New York: Oxford University Press, 1977.
Moss, Thelma, *The Probability of the Impossible: Scientific Discoveries and Explorations in the Psychic World*, Los Angeles: J. P. Tarcher, Inc., 1974.
Muldoon, Sylvan, and Hereward Carrington, *The Phenomenon of Astral Projection*, London: Rider, 1951.
———, *The Projection of the Astral Body*, London: Rider, 1956.
Murphy, Gardner, *The Challenge of Psychical Research: A Primer of Parapsychology*, New York: Harper Colophon Books (1961), 1970.
———, *William James on Psychical Research*, New York: Viking, 1960.
Murphy, Michael, and Rhea White, *The Psychic Side of Sports*, Reading, MA: Addison-Wesley, 1978.
Myers, Frederick W. H., *Human Personality and Its Survival of Bodily Death*, 2 vols., London: Longmans, Green, 1903.
Nash, Carroll B., *Science of Psi: ESP and PK*, Springfield, IL: Charles C. Thomas, 1978.
Neilson, Greg, and Joseph Polansky, *Pendulum Power*, New York: Destiny Books, 1977.
Netherton, Morris, *Past Lives Therapy*, New York: Morrow, 1978.
Noorbergen, Rene, *The Incredible Story of David N. Bubar*, New York: Morrow, 1971.
Noss, John B., *Man's Religions*, fifth edition, New York: Macmillan, 1974.
Osis, Karlis, *Deathbed Observations by Physicians and Nurses*, New York: Parapsychological Monographs, Parapsychology Foundation, 1961.
Osis, Karlis and Haraldsson, Erlendur, *At the Hour of Death*, New York: Avon, 1977.
Ostrander, Sheila, and Lynn Schroeder, *Handbook of Psychic Discoveries* (How to Discover Your Own Psychic Powers in Hundreds of Experiments You Can Do at Home), New York: Berkley, 1974.
———, *Psychic Discoveries Behind the Iron Curtain*, New York: Bantam Books, 1970.
Owen, A. R. G., *Can We Explain the Poltergeist?* New York: Garrett/Helix, 1964.
Oyle, Irving, *The Healing Mind*, Millbrae, CA: Celestial Arts, 1975.
Panati, Charles, *The Geller Papers*, Boston: Houghton Mifflin, 1976.
Pelletier, Kenneth R., *Mind as Healer, Mind as Slayer* (A Holistic Approach to Preventing Stress Disorders), New York: Dell, 1977.
Pellettiri, Leonard, ed., *The Journal of Holistic Health*, Association for Holistic Health (Box 23231, San Diego, CA, 92123), 1977.
Penrose, Evelyn, *Adventure Unlimited: A Diviner Travels the World*, London: Neville Spearman, 1958.
Pollack, Jack Harrison, *Croiset, The Clairvoyant*, Garden City, NY: Doubleday, 1964.
Psychic Magazine editors, *Psychics*, New York: Harper and Row, 1972.
Pyle, Earl, *How to Make a Million Dowsing and Drilling for Oil*, Hicksville, NY: Exposition Press, 1977.
Randi, James, *The Magic of Uri Geller*, New York: Ballantine, 1975.
Rao, K. R., *Experimental Parapsychology: A Review and Interpretation*, Springfield, IL: Charles C. Thomas, 1966.
Raudive, Konstantin, *Breakthrough: An Amazing Experience in Electronic Communication with the Dead*, New York: Taplinger, 1971.

Regush, June and Nicholas, *Psi: The Other World Catalogue, The Comprehensive Guide to the Dimensions of Psychic Phenomena*, New York: G. P. Putnam's Sons, 1974.

Rhine, J. B., *Extra-Sensory Perception*, Boston: Branden (1934), 1964.

_____, *The Reach of the Mind*, New York: Sloan, 1947.

Rhine, J. B., and J. G. Pratt, *Parapsychology: Frontier Science of the Mind*, Springfield, IL: Charles Thomas (1957), 1962.

Rhine, J. B., J. G. Pratt, B. M. Smith, and C. E. Stuart, *Extra-Sensory Perception After Sixty Years: A Critical Appraisal of the Research in Extrasensory Perception*, Boston, MA: Branden (1940), 1966.

Rhine, Louisa E., *Hidden Channels of the Mind*, New York: William Sloane Associates, 1961.

_____, *Mind Over Matter, Psychokinesis*, New York: Macmillan, 1970.

_____, *Psi: What Is It?* (The Story of ESP and PK), New York: Perennial Library, Harper and Row, 1975.

Roberts, Kenneth, *Henry Gross and His Dowsing Rod*, Garden City, NY: Doubleday, 1951.

_____, *The Seventh Sense*, Garden City, NY: Doubleday, 1953.

_____, *Water Unlimited*, Garden City, NY: Doubleday, 1957.

Robertson, Morgan, *The Wreck of the Titan*, autograph edition, New York: McClure's Magazine (1898), 1912.

Rogo, D. Scott, *The Haunted Universe*, New York: Signet, 1977.

_____, *Mind Beyond the Body—The Mystery of ESP Projection*, New York: Penguin Books, 1978.

Rogo, D. Scott, and Raymond Bayless, *Phone Calls from the Dead*, Englewood Cliffs, NJ: Prentice-Hall, 1979.

Roll, William G., *The Poltergeist*, Garden City, NY: Doubleday, 1972.

Rossman, Michael, *New Age Blues: On the Politics of Consciousness*, New York: E. P. Dutton, 1979.

St. Clair, David, *Psychic Healers*, Garden City, NY: Doubleday, 1974.

Schmeidler, Gertrude, ed., *Parapsychology: Its Relation to Physics, Biology, Psychology and Psychiatry*, Metuchen, NJ: The Scarecrow Press, 1976.

Schwartz, Stephan A., *The Secret Vaults of Time*, New York: Grosset and Dunlap, 1978.

Schwarz, Berthold, *Parent-Child Telepathy*, New York: Garrett, 1971.

Schwarz, Jack, *Human Energy Systems*, New York: Dutton, 1980.

_____, *The Path of Action*, New York: Dutton, 1977.

_____, *Voluntary Exercises for Creative Meditation and Activating the Potential of the Chakras*, New York: Dutton, 1978.

Selye, Hans, *Stress Without Distress*, Philadelphia: J. B. Lippincott, 1974.

Shealy, C. Norman, *90 Ways to Self Health*, New York: Bantam (1977), 1978.

Shepard, Leslie A., *Encyclopedia of Occultism and Parapsychology*, 2 vols., Detroit, Gale Research Co., 1978.

Sherman, Harold, *How to Make ESP Work for You*, Greenwich, CT: Fawcett, 1964.

_____, *How to Picture What You Want*, New York: Fawcett Gold Medal Books, 1978.

_____, *Your Mysterious Powers of ESP*, New York: Signet, 1969.

Sherman, Harold, and Sir Hubert Wilkins, *Thoughts Through Space*, New York: Fawcett (1951), 1973.

Smith, Susy, *The Mediumship of Mrs. Leonard*, New York: University Books, 1964.

Spraggett, Allen, *Arthur Ford—The Man Who Talked with the Dead,* New York: New American Library, 1973.

———, *Kathryn Kuhlman: The Woman Who Believes in Miracles,* New York: World Publishing Company, 1970.

Steiger, Brad, *The Psychic Feats of Olof Jonsson,* Englewood Cliffs, NJ: Prentice-Hall, 1971.

Stern, Jess, *The Miracle Workers—America's Psychic Consultants,* Garden City, NY: Doubleday, 1972.

Stevenson, Ian, *Twenty Cases Suggestive of Reincarnation,* Charlottesville, VA: University of Virginia Press, 1974.

Stokes, W. L., *Essentials of Earth History—An Introduction to Historical Geology,* Englewood Cliffs, NJ: Prentice-Hall, 1960.

Sugrue, Thomas, *The Story of Edgar Cayce (There Is a River),* New York: Dell (1942), 1945.

Swann, Ingo, *Star Fire,* New York: Dell, Eleanor Friede, 1978.

———, *To Kiss Earth Goodbye,* New York: Hawthorn Books, 1975.

Tanous, Alex, with Harvey Ardman, *Beyond Coincidence: One Man's Experiences With Psychic Phenomena,* Garden City, NY: Doubleday, 1976.

Tanous, Alex, and K. F. Donnelly, *Is Your Child Psychic? A Guide for Creative Parents and Teachers,* New York: Macmillan, 1979.

Targ, Russell, and Harold E. Puthoff, *Mind-Reach: Scientists Look at Psychic Ability,* New York: Delacorte Press, Eleanor Friede, 1977.

Tart, Charles, *Psi: Scientific Studies of the Psychic Realm,* New York: E. P. Dutton, 1977.

———, *Altered States of Consciousness,* Garden City, NY: Doubleday, 1969.

Trefethen, Joseph M., *Geology for Engineers,* New York: Van Nostrand, 1949.

Trinder, W. H., *Dowsing,* London: G. Bell and Sons, Ltd., 1939.

Twigg, Eva, with Ruth Hagy Brod, *Eva Twigg: Medium,* New York: Hawthorn, 1972.

Tyrrell, G. N. M., *Apparitions,* New York: Macmillan (1942), 1962.

Ullman, M., S. Krippner, and A. Vaughan, *Dream Telepathy,* Baltimore: Penguin, 1974.

Vaughan, Alan, *Incredible Coincidence: The Baffling World of Synchronicity,* Philadelphia: Lippincott, 1979.

———, *Patterns of Prophecy,* New York: Hawthorn, 1973.

Velikovsky, Immanuel, *Worlds in Collision,* Garden City, NY: Doubleday, 1950.

Von Daniken, Erich, *Chariot of the Gods?* New York: Putnam, 1970.

Wallace, Amy, and Bill Hankin, *The Psychic Healing Book,* New York: Delacorte Press, 1978.

Wambach, Helen, *Life Before Life,* New York: Bantam, 1979.

———, *Reliving Past Lives,* New York: Harper and Row, 1978.

White, John, and Stanley Krippner, eds., *Future Science: Life Energies and the Physics of Paranormal Phenomena,* Garden City, NY: Doubleday, 1977.

Willey, Raymond C., *Modern Dowsing, The Dowser's Handbook,* Sedona, AZ: Esoteric Publishers, 1976.

Wolman, Benjamin B., ed., *Handbook of Parapsychology,* New York: Van Nostrand Reinhold Company, 1977.

Womack, David, *Twelve Signs, Twelve Sons: Astrology in the Bible,* San Francisco: Harper and Row, 1978.

Worrall, Ambrose, with Olga Worrall, *The Gift of Healing,* New York: Harper and Row, 1976.

Worrall, Ambrose and Olga, *Explore Your Psychic World,* New York: Harper
   and Row, 1970.
_____, *Miracle Healers,* New York: American Library, 1965.
Wyman, Walker D., *Witching: For Water, Oil, Pipes and Precious Minerals,* Madi-
   son, WI: University of Wisconsin Press, 1977.
Young, Samuel, *Psychic Children,* New York: Pocket Books (1977), 1978.
Zukav, Gary, *The Dancing Wu Li Masters: An Overview of the New Physics,* New
   York: Morrow, 1979.

Index